RORY LAND

THE UP-AND-DOWN WORLD OF GOLF'S GLOBAL ICON

TIMOTHY M. GAY

A REGALO PRESS BOOK
ISBN: 979-8-88845-129-8
ISBN (eBook): 979-8-88845-130-4

Rory Land:
The Up-and-Down World of Golf's Global Icon
© 2025 by Timothy M. Gay
All Rights Reserved

Images in photo insert (pages 1–7) from Alamy Stock Photos.
Images in photo insert (pages 8–16) by Matthew Harris.

Publishing Team:
Founder and Publisher – Gretchen Young
Editorial Assistant – Caitlyn Limbaugh
Managing Editor – Madeline Sturgeon
Production Manager – Kate Harris
Production Editor – Rachel Paul

As part of the mission of Regalo Press, a donation is being made to Save the Children's work in Northern Ireland, as chosen by the author.

This book, as well as any other Regalo Press publications, may be purchased in bulk quantities at a special discounted rate. Contact orders@regalopress.com for more information.

No part of this book may be reproduced, stored in a retrieval system, or transmitted by any means without the written permission of the author and publisher.

Regalo Press
New York • Nashville
regalopress.com

Published in the United States of America
1 2 3 4 5 6 7 8 9 10

*To the memory of
Herbert Warren Wind (1916–2005),
golf sage and writer,
who would have loved describing Rory's swing.*

So hope for a great sea-change
On the far side of revenge.
Believe that a further shore
Is reachable from here.
Believe in miracles
And cures and healing wells.

The Cure at Troy

Seamus Heaney (1939–2013), Northern Irishman and Nobel Laureate

Table of Contents

McIlroy Family Tree 10
McDonald Family Tree 12
Introduction: "The Right Side of History" 13
Chapter 1: Demons and Apparitions at LACC and Pinehurst 31
Chapter 2: "Because He's Nice!" 47
Chapter 3: The Murals of Belfast 73
Chapter 4: The Devil's Tail 80
Chapter 5: A Lost Life 89
Chapter 6: Holywood's Maypole 96
Chapter 7: "Watch My Swing, Uncle Michael!" 114
Chapter 8: "Ultimate Amateur" 127
Chapter 9: Pandemonium at Portrush 143
Chapter 10: Carnoustie and County Down 150
Chapter 11: Play for Pay 161
Chapter 12: Breaking Through 172
Chapter 13: Collapse and Coronation 199
Chapter 14: Wozzilroy 229
Chapter 15: Becoming Number One 241
Chapter 16: Medinah's Wild Ride 263
Chapter 17: The Swoosh and the Slump 276
Chapter 18: Hoylake and New Beginnings 296
Chapter 19: Valhalla and Gleneagles 313
Chapter 20: Courtrooms and Courting 332
Chapter 21: Erica and Ashford Castle 342
Chapter 22: Frustrations Deepen 362
Chapter 23: Humiliation and Redemption 372
Chapter 24: The Mental and Money Game 381
Chapter 25: Beyond the Pandemic 395
Finale: "The Further Shore" 418

Sources 429
Acknowledgments 443

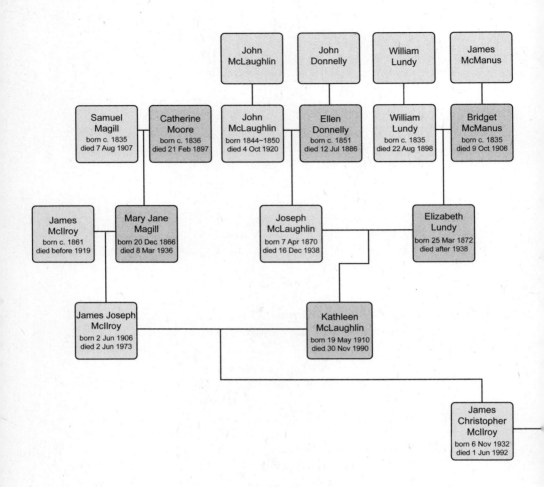

McIlroy Family Tree
Compiled by Jennifer Martin, PhD

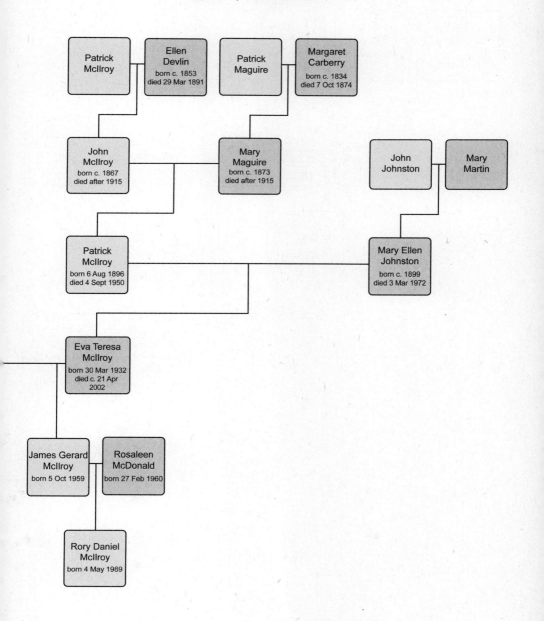

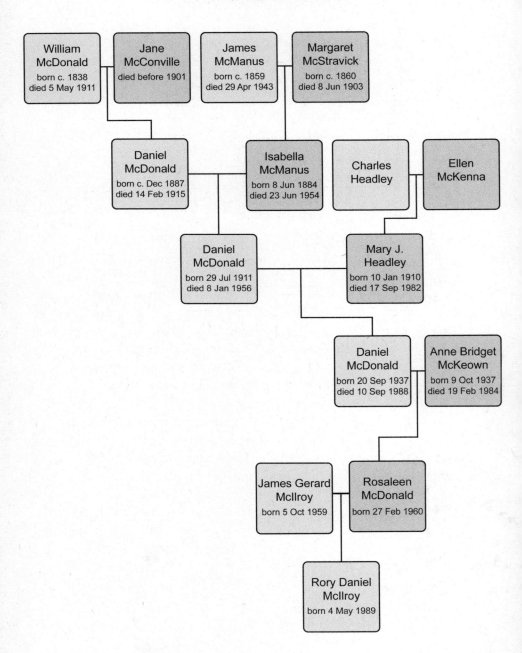

Introduction

"THE RIGHT SIDE OF HISTORY"

Okay, let's get a few things straight from the "throw-in," as the Gaelic football-crazed Irish are wont to say.

First, this ain't no hagiography. But it's not a hatchet job, either. If you're looking for a book that hero-worships its subject, or kicks a fella when—let's face it—he's down, look elsewhere.

Second, there ain't much dope within these pages on the upheaval in the subject's personal life. If you were hoping to pick up a bunch of juicy gossip or gnarly innuendo, you might want to spend your thirty bucks on the latest Kardashian exposé.

Finally, regarding our protagonist, one Rory Daniel McIlroy MBE[1]: four-time major champion, six-time winner of the Race to Dubai, three-time conqueror of the FedEx Cup, golf's ageless Opie Taylor, Every Mom's Favorite, the Perpetual Lost Boy of Augusta National (and now, sadly, Pinehurst No. 2), Ryder Cup wrangler, onetime tabloid Romeo, media darling, lightning rod, kick-ass corporate pitchman and entrepreneur, the besieged hero of Netflix's *Full Swing*, Formula One freak, wannabe Journey frontman, outspoken devotee of sports shrink Bob Rotella, compulsive sharer of self-help titles, the fella with "RORS" embossed on his TaylorMade TP5x's, Patrick Reed's BFF (*Psych!*), the player whose wrenching quest for a fifth major crown has taken on the pallor of Shakespearean tragedy, the "Rory: We-Hardly-Knew-Ye" voice

---

1 For those not enamored of BritBox or PBS's *Masterpiece Theater*, MBE stands for Member of the Order of the British Empire.... Yeah, it's a little cringy, isn't it?

of conscience of the PGA and DP World tours, the overexposed, overextended, *way* overanalyzed, profoundly human, immensely likeable superstar who supposedly spat on a billion Saudi bucks, and by his own admission, the "sacrificial lamb" of the tours' LIV Golf fiasco…you know, *that guy*!

Yeah, well, *that guy* may be likeable, but he ain't exactly an angel, as the world learned—repeatedly—in late 2023 and 2024. In rapid succession, McIlroy had a when-in-Rome carpark blowup with innocent bystander (and US Ryder Cup caddie and NBC Golf domo) Jim "Bones" Mackay; disparaged as a "dick" his then-fellow PGA Tour advisory board member Patrick Cantlay; badmouthed the leadership chops of deposed European Ryder Cup captain (and LIV defector) Henrik Stenson; f-bombed his way through season two of *Full Swing*; and having spent two years as the Tour's intrepid (and often bare-knuckled) defender in the LIV brawl, abruptly quit his board post and vowed to distance himself from "the fray" over a potential coupling with the Saudi Public Investment Fund.

Then, as his views on partnering with PIF "evolved," he spent the next few months insinuating himself back into the squabble, at one point engaging his board successor Jordan Spieth in a public pissing match. By mid-spring '24, Rory had flipped again, telling the world that he would readily rejoin the advisory panel to expedite a deal with the Saudis. His offer was rejected by board members, a couple of whom (*gee, here's a surprise*) may have taken exception to being branded ill-informed or a "dick." In yet another twist, PGA Tour pooh-bahs (read: Tiger Woods and Commissioner Jay Monahan) then put McIlroy on a special "transaction subcommittee," which appeared to be working at cross-purposes to the advisory board's agenda.

Yeesh! Got a headache yet?

Late spring '24 brought more tumult. McIlroy's marital difficulties were played out against the backdrop of two majors, the PGA Championship at one end and the US Open at the other. The initial bombshell ("*Rory Divorcing!*") came on Tuesday of PGA week, less than forty-eight hours *after* McIlroy had bushwhacked Xander

Schauffele at Quail Hollow with two eagles in the span of five holes while grabbing his fourth Wells Fargo championship. The other blast ("*Rory Reconciling!*") came less than forty-eight hours *before* McIlroy was scheduled to tee off at Pinehurst in the US Open.

McIlroy ended up losing at Pinehurst when, down the stretch, he missed two tiny putts, the first shorter than the waistband, the second barely longer than the trouser seam, of winner Bryson DeChambeau, a—*Grrrr!*—LIV defector. Rory drew flak from social media scolds and the likes of ESPN's Scott Van Pelt by vacating the Carolina sandhills without congratulating DeChambeau or confronting the media—"un-Rory"-like conduct, as the *Washington Post*'s John Feinstein put it. Rory is normally magnanimous—some would say *overly* magnanimous—in defeat, and responsive—*overly* responsive?—to the press.

A month later, at the Open Championship in Scotland, McIlroy un-Rory'd his way around Royal Troon, making a triple-bogey and two doubles to miss the cut by five "soul-crushing" strokes, in the words of Golf Channel anchor Rich Lerner.

Ouch! All that intrigue, all those gyrations and inexplicable shots, threw peers, reporters, broadcast analysts, fans, and a certain biographer for a loop. As *Golfweek* senior writer Adam Schupak described it in a 2024 email, "I still see Rory as the moral compass of the Tour but lately it seems to be spinning out of whack."

Men's professional golf in the early-to-mid 2020s became an out-of-whack battleground in a much-larger economic and political struggle. Rory McIlroy waded into a seismic fight that he and the established tours had little chance of winning.

The LIV melee gutted McIlroy, gashing his compass needle even as he rebuffed the rival circuit's overtures. At the beginning, he was like the Marquis de Lafayette, a dashing foreigner come to save an imperiled American institution. In the middle, betrayed and all but deserted, he had somehow, sadly, been reduced to Lord

Cornwallis, waving a white flag while muttering, "How in blazes could this have happened?" Later, Rory was viewed in certain quarters (especially those occupied by Patrick Cantlay and Jordan Spieth) as something of a Benedict Arnold, a disheartened patriot suddenly pushing the other side's endgame.

McIlroy's erratic play and conflicted behavior, his palpable unease amid what he came to call golf's "shitshow," all those ups and downs from a guy who earns his living getting up and down, make him an irresistible subject. The life stories of the easy and the unconflicted[2] tend to be kind of dull.

To be sure, there's much to admire about McIlroy's immaculate golf swing and a personal affability that—most of the time, anyway—registers high on the Ted Lasso Scale of Kindness. But the last time any of us looked, there was a Swoosh on the front of Rory's cap, not a halo floating above it. He makes serious coin to rock that Swoosh, one of the many perquisites of being adept, as his old Twitter bio blurb put it, at hitting "a little white ball around a field sometimes."

McIlroy's mastery at bashing that sphere has afforded him an A-list lifestyle that will never be confused with St. Francis of the Assisi's. (*What? You mean Stevie Wonder and Ed Sheeran didn't entertain at your wedding reception inside an 800-year-old Irish castle once owned by the Guinness family?*)

No, despite his commendable (if ultimately futile) efforts to safeguard professional golf's integrity, and the other hosannahs that have been shouted his way, McIlroy is much too mortal—not to mention too agnostic—to ever have his cherubic features etched

---

2 American golfer Talor Gooch comes to mind here. In his first two years on the profligate LIV Tour, where money gets spent as if drunken sailors were in charge, the obscure Gooch "earned" more than four times the combined *career* PGA Tour winnings of Jack Nicklaus and Arnold Palmer.... *"Ken: I'll take 'Obscenity' for 200."*

into the stained-glass windows of St. Colmcille's Catholic Church[3] in Holywood, County Down, Northern Ireland, his charming hometown perched along the southern shore of Belfast Lough. Less than seven miles northeast of center-city Belfast, Holywood may be pronounced like its Sodom-and-Gomorrah counterpart in southern California, but it couldn't be further removed culturally.

St. Colmcille's is where the blue-collar heroes of our story, Rosie McDonald and Gerry McIlroy—the mum and dad who worked around the clock to give their only child a chance to chase his dream—walked down the aisle. It was also the place of worship for Eva and Jimmy McIlroy, Gerry's parents and Rory's grandparents, who scrimped and saved to pull the family out of a hellhole Belfast ghetto. Like so many Northern Irish in the twentieth century, Eva and Jimmy and Rosie and Gerry were forced to endure too much heartache and tragedy.

It's the parish where Rory's dad, two uncles, an aunt, a pile of cousins, and Rory himself made their First Holy Communions. The photograph of little Rory receiving the Eucharist—eyes dewy, face freckled, hands clasped in prayer, Opie Taylor reincarnate—still hangs in his parents' home.

Holywood's Redburn Cemetery, which sits on a leafy hillside overlooking the lough, is where a host of family members are buried—among them Rory's great uncle Joseph, Jimmy's little brother, who was murdered for having the gall to be Catholic, industrious, and upwardly mobile.

Rory may look like a choirboy—even with his hair going gray he comes across as the Adorable Kid Brother from Central Casting—but acquaintances and Tour followers tell an, umm, *saltier* story. The teenaged McIlroy was a "good lad but cocky as fuck," recalls Andrew "Chubby" Chandler, the shrewd British agent who

---

3 An ancient Celtic tableau commemorating St. Colmcille's sixth-century success in converting Éire's "pagans" to Christianity gives the church's stained-glass windows an eerie and primitive feel. They're worth a look if you're ever in Holywood. Stcolmcillesholywood.org.

made the youngster a multimillionaire the instant he turned pro at age eighteen.

The "real" McIlroy loves the raunchy humor of Dave Chappelle; revels in Irish Ultimate Fighter Conor McGregor and the gruesome spectacle known as mixed martial arts; adores haughty Manchester United, the New York Yankees of the English Premier Football League; came within a whisker of committing one of the most egregious gaffes in sports history; once stormed off a course in mid-round, earning a "Turkey of the Year" award from *Sports Illustrated*; coldly dumped the veteran caddie who helped him win four majors and a ton of money; cashiered, one after the other, two firms that had landed him mega-quid endorsement deals; inked, in the middle of a raucous holiday party (*without* a barrister[4] present!), a binding contract he later claimed in court proceedings he didn't understand; is more than a bit pretentious about his knowledge of fine wine; broke off the engagement to his world-famous fiancée, tennis star Caroline Wozniacki, *after* their wedding invitations had gone out; and, in his spirited bachelor days following the breakup, titillated the tabloids by juggling rendezvous with *three* fashion models. In that same stretch, he also found time to pursue a transatlantic flirtation with American actress Meghan Markle, then the star of the USA Network series *Suits*, now—*ahem*—the paparazzi-baiting Duchess of Sussex.

In other words, Rory McIlroy did what almost every single guy in his twenties would have done, given similar circumstances…no more an angel and no more a devil than the rest of us.

Many of us aging American baby boomers were dragged through a short story in junior high called "The Man Without a Country." In some key ways, that describes McIlroy. Unlike the story's character, Rory hasn't been exiled to forever roam the seas, but he doesn't really have a nationality to call his own. He's not quite Irish, not

---

[4] "Barrister" is BritBox for lawyer.

quite British, and even though he's lived in Florida for the last dozen years and married an upstate New Yorker, he's not really American, either.

If you sort-of belong to three countries, do you really belong to any?

McIlroy grew up a "Nordie" in a fractured homeland where nationalism and religion too often have been used as bloody cudgels. It explains why he agonized over which country (Ireland or Great Britain; he ended up choosing the former) to represent in the Olympic Games and—even more telling—why he admitted in 2017 that he has qualms about the concept of "patriotism." His ambivalence is understandable: for the entirety of Northern Ireland's existence, patriotism run amok has triggered unspeakable hatred and civil chaos.

Even on the cusp of his thirty-fifth birthday, McIlroy was nervous about being seen embracing the Irish Republic's Tricolor flag. In April '24, he and pal Shane Lowry were celebrating their come-from-behind win earlier that afternoon in the Zurich Classic's two-man team competition at TPC-New Orleans. Sporting Mardi Gras bead necklaces and swigging Michelob Ultras, they stood atop a stage facing a loud and well-lubricated crowd.

Everyone in the joint was jumping, helping Rory butcher the old Journey chestnut "Don't Stop Believin'!" when someone threw the green, white, and orange banner onto the stage. The flag was handed to Lowry, a proud citizen of the Republic who would love to have hoisted it high—and have the crowd go even wilder. After all, to most Americans, the Irish flag is synonymous with one thing: "Let's party hearty!"

But before Shane did anything, he cast a knowing glance toward Rory. While rasping about a smokey room and cheap perfume, McIlroy gave Lowry a subtle shake of the head. Shane understood: he tossed the flag back into the mosh pit.

For Lowry, the Tricolor embodies something to rejoice: hard-won national independence, wrested from Britain only a century ago after nearly a millennium of bloody oppression. For many

Ulster Protestants, however, the Tricolor represents something to fear: a threat to their political and economic dominion.

Rory may have been raised Catholic, and his management company may be headquartered in Dublin, but his heart still beats up North. Even in a moment of supreme silliness, Rory McIlroy, loyal Ulsterman, could not let down his guard.

McIlroy is the child and grandchild of nightmarish conflict. None of us should be surprised that he's gone through life—and golf—conflicted.

Examine the lives of Rory's forebears back into the eighteenth century, as I have, and you'll see, in miniature, Ireland's scarred past, what poet William Butler Yeats called its "terrible beauty": the story of a destitute but dogged people struggling to survive in one of the loveliest but most depraved places on earth.

Ireland's polarity is reflected in the eyes of Rory's parents. Gerry's, bright and luminous, never seem to stop twinkling. They belong to a lifelong bartender eager to share a laugh while pouring his mates another pint. Rosie's are darker, more world-weary. As a child, she saw too much brutality perpetrated in the name of Christ; as an adult, she spent too many nights toiling on an assembly line's graveyard shift.

When put against the disheveled history of homeland and family, McIlroy's Ryder Cup fixation begins to make sense. Maybe the Cup means so much to him because in his youth, McIlroy never truly pledged allegiance to a flag or bellowed a national anthem—at least not in a full-throated way. Rory once admitted that he didn't know the lyrics to either Great Britain's "God Save the King" or to the Republic of Ireland's national hymn, "The Soldier's Song."

You know that sweet tune from the FX series *Welcome to Wrexham*, the one that urges folks not to forget to sing when they win? The Ryder Cup, at least when it goes the Euros' way, gives Rory McIlroy a chance to sing loud and proud.

A team competition McIlroy once derided as a mere "exhibition," the Ryder Cup has become his Fourth of July, Guy Fawkes Night, and St. Patrick's Day, all rolled into one.

RORY LAND

The "stubborn and headstrong" McIlroy, as Chandler has long tagged him, has been for years the ruler of his own country, a fiefdom I've dubbed "Rory Land." Rory Land doesn't belong to Ireland or Eng-land or USA-land. It's a little world unto itself.

McIlroy's reign over Rory Land became official in 2015, when at the tender age of twenty-five, he paid a whopping $20-plus million to settle an ugly legal fight and jettison his second agent's firm. For a decade now, his schedule and business affairs have been managed by the Dublin-based Rory McIlroy Management Services LTD (known in the trade as "Rory, Inc."), whose board is comprised of Rory, his dad, and a few close pals and business associates.

Maybe too close. McIlroy and his lieutenants (since their teen years, they've called themselves the "Mac Pack") endeavor to exercise complete control over Rory Land, a bubble-wrapped universe where McIlroy's brand, privacy, and idiosyncrasies are zealously guarded.

Rory Land is a wondrous but sometimes mystifying place. Like most cultures, its ways are muddled: farsighted and compassionate on the one hand; myopic, tin-eared, and insular on the other. It's a realm that empowers its leader—an only child whom Chubby Chandler, *Golf News Net*'s Ryan Ballangee, and other commentators call "impulsive and impetuous"—to do pretty much whatever he wants to do, on or off the course.

It's a land whose machinations give observers—even sympathetic ones like me—a case of whiplash. One Sunday afternoon, its ruler thrills the golfing world by going eight-under in an eight-hole stretch to win big at Quail Hollow, one of the toughest tracks on Tour. The next day, he astounds the entire world by filing for divorce from his wife of seven years.

Within hours, his supposed liaison with CBS Golf broadcaster Amanda Balionis jumped from online gossip chatter to the mainstream media, where it rattled around—unchallenged—for weeks.

After what seemed like an eternity, the rumor was finally discredited by *US Weekly*, which had helped foment the original innuendo. A few days later, Rory fanned tabloid flames all over again by choosing to hug Balionis after she finished interviewing him next to the 18th green at the RBC Canadian Open. The moment went viral when (*gee, here's another surprise*) spectators snapped cellphone pictures.

Most of the time, McIlroy exudes warmth; he's the consummate gentleman and golfing diplomat. But sometimes, he comes across short-sighted, too eager to see "Rory McIlroy" in headlines that have little to do with his profession.

"A smart fella once told me that a fine golfer only has one fine thing—and that's his fine golf. And that if he forgets that, he's a fool," the great Byron Nelson once said in appraising Tom Watson, his protégé.

It's a shame that Lord Byron can't be exhumed to have a heart-to-heart with Rory.

In Rory Land, it's easier to smash a 350-yard drive over trees and ponds than it is to make a clutch four-foot putt. It's a place where wedges and putters are fungible commodities, never allowed to linger in the bag too long if they displease their sovereign.

It's a land where Rory and his foundation (since disbanded) save the Irish Open from going belly up by taking over for four years as the tournament's host, tripling its purse and strengthening its field. But if McIlroy skips playing it now and again because it doesn't fit his schedule, he's pilloried down South. After all, he's a Nordie.

In April 2019, the fallout over McIlroy's decision to pull out of that summer's Irish Open grew so toxic that two senior Rory, Inc., executives took it upon themselves to confront then-79-year-old *Irish Sunday Independent* columnist Dermot Gilleece, who had written an article criticizing McIlroy's choice. The Rory Landers' "verbal laceration," as the now-retired Gilleece described it, "was totally unprovoked and seriously unsettling."

The incident occurred, of all places, on the grounds of Augusta National. It stopped short of becoming a public spectacle. But the fact that it happened at all is a piss-poor reflection on Rory Land's public relations judgment.[5]

Rory Land is a place where, in '22 and '23, when cameras were rolling and LIV Golf was the topic, centuries of repressed McIlroy and McDonald combativeness came boiling to the surface. Rory trash-talked LIV's leading exponents, Greg Norman and Phil Mickelson, like a Blood skewering a pair of Crips.

"[McIlroy] simply happens to be a very nice man, by any standards," Gilleece wrote following the Augusta episode. "But a stubborn streak rendering him resistant to advice has led to confusion and disappointment." Dermot's observation was delivered years before Rory's backtrack on LIV and the seesawing in his personal life.

Sometimes, Rory can't win for losing—especially with cheap-seat critics like me. On the first green of the final round of the 2023 US Open, McIlroy looked up and saw his old (but now, thanks to LIV, estranged) friend Sergio Garcia finishing his round on the adjoining 18th hole. Rory caught Sergio's eye and extended his thumb and pinkie finger up to his ear in the universal "I'll-call-you, let's-let-bygones-be-bygones" gesture. It was a classy move that led to a tender (if short-lived) reconciliation reported the world over.

But did Rory have to do it in the final round of the US Freakin' Open?! One that he ended up losing by a single measly stroke?!

Back in the day, a feuding Sam Snead and Ben Hogan might have exchanged a hand gesture, but it would have involved only one digit each.

Rory Land is a place where, in late winter 2023, McIlroy wowed listeners of the *TrapDraw* podcast with his command of every backstabbing twist and turn of *Succession*, HBO's satirical takedown of corporate America. Yet, at that very moment, he was being played in the LIV fracas by Wall Street sharpies almost as devious as the characters portrayed in the series.

---

5   The Rory Land shout-down of an eminent Irish journalist is almost as distasteful as LIV's Norman hiring two beefy security grunts to throw a credentialed Alan Shipnuck out of a Mickelson press availability. See *LIV and Let Die*.

But…Rory Land is also a place where a seven-year-old Irish boy, gravely ill with brain cancer, makes a wish for Rory, his hero, to record a video greeting. Rory Land and the Make-a-Wish Foundation do the lad one better. Rory invites the youngster to "caddie" in a practice round at the K-Club outside Dublin during the 2023 Irish Open.

Crouching down, Rory introduced himself, shook the boy's hand, asked him in a tender-hearted yet still casual way how he was doing, helped him get settled in a golf cart, drove him slowly up the fairway while keeping a steady flow of chatter going, showed him how to use a range finder, asked his advice on what club to hit from 143 yards, gave him (for keeps) a shorter version of his own TaylorMade Spider putter, and, once the moment ended, hugged him and wished him all the best.

A few days later, following a Saturday 66 that got Rory back into contention at the K-Club, he was asked about the young man. Rory not only remembered the boy's name but his parents' names. His voice trembled as he talked about how fortunate he and Erica were to have a healthy child, and how much he admired the young man and his family.

It's the sort of thing that Rory has quietly done many times, but this one happened to be recorded on camera. It's that gentle heart that led *Golf Digest* to name him the winner of its 2024 Arnie Award for community service—the second time Rory has been accorded the honor.

Many of us raise our kids to live the values championed by Rory and his parents. But those ideals are sometimes at odds with the demonic tunnel vision required to win major championships—or to end up on top in a world where "money has no conscience," as Irish journalist Brian Keogh has mused.

A big part of the adult Rory McIlroy—son, husband, father, provider—aspires to be a "normal" guy leading a "normal" life.

He talks about it all the time, and has since he was thrust into the spotlight as a kid.

But therein lies the rub. As Golf Channel savant Jaime Diaz told me at the 2023 PGA Championship in Rochester: "It's hard to be normal—and great."

It's also hard to lead a regular existence when you've spent a huge chunk of your life with TV cameras dogging your every step. Despite his protestations, McIlroy may relish being "abnormal" more than he cares to admit.

Yes, a big part of him loathes his fishbowl existence. But another part of him loves it—and may be addicted to it. In many ways, it's all he's ever known.

Notwithstanding his internal conflicts and occasional missteps, the now grown-up ruler of Rory Land has become *fear maith*—Gaelic for "good man," or, if you let your imagination wander a little, "mensch," as John Feinstein called the young Rory. Since not many of you are likely to hail from the Gaeltacht, those remote slivers of Ireland that still stubbornly claim Gaelic as their first language, allow me to further embellish *fear maith*'s definition.

In my construct, *fear maith* means "stand-up guy," someone capable of admitting mistakes and representing something larger than himself. To completely bend its meaning, let's toss in "Devoted Dad" and "Renaissance Man," too.

Rory McIlroy is that rare professional athlete whose introspection and intellectual curiosity impel him to pursue a range of passions. Golf historian Brad Klein notes that McIlroy is "not afraid to go out on a limb. He's remarkably well-spoken and worldly." Amid the early *Sturm und Drang* over LIV, PGA Tour standout Will Zalatoris said that if Rory had been born in the United States, he'd vote for him for president.

Sometimes Rory's eclectic appetites take him to places where it's not in his best interests to go, as Golf Channel anchor Damon

Hack pointed out to me. But Rory goes there anyway, because his remarkable parents implanted within their only kid a social conscience and a sense of moral responsibility—attributes, chuckled Hack and Klein in separate interviews, not normally associated with professional golfers.

"Unlike a majority of narcissistic pro golfers, McIlroy is generally able to think big picture and far beyond his self-interests," golf guru Geoff Shackelford wrote in 2023. "[McIlroy is] also able to set his pocketbook aside when declaring a position. It's why so many people respect him."

Sports Illustrated writer Bob Harig told me that McIlroy has a "down-to-earth, everyman quality" that allows him to see the game from a fan's perspective—highly unusual for a superstar.

"What comes to mind when I think of Rory is generosity of spirit," *New York Post* columnist Ian O'Connor told me. "[Rory] has a generosity of spirit the way Arnold Palmer had it—and it's a very endearing trait."

Eight-time major champion Tom Watson also evoked Palmer in discussing with me McIlroy's place in the game. "People loved Arnie because he played with such passion and joy. He loved the game. Fans loved him. Rory has that same passion. He loves the game and treats everyone in it with respect. In turn, they respect him." Watson's sentiment is echoed by former United States Golf Association CEO Mike Davis, who ranks Rory in the same rarefied Arnie air as a gentleman, an ambassador, and a "momentum player" nonpareil.

Golf historian, novelist, and screenwriter Mark Frost[6] marvels at McIlroy's ability to juggle competing demands. "What we see is a thoroughly decent human being," Frost told me. "Rory is willing to stand up for what is right and willing to speak out."

McIlroy looks for those same qualities in others. In the run-up to the 2023 Ryder Cup, he was asked about European captain Luke Donald. Rory didn't cite Donald's motivational skills or his grasp

---

6   Mark was instrumental in creating two of the coolest television shows *ever*, *Hill Street Blues* (1981-1987) and *Twin Peaks* (1990-1991).

of golf analytics. Instead, McIlroy said, "We live near each other in Florida, and I see [Luke] with his daughters. He is loving and lovely with them. It's nice to see."

Yet a few weeks later, that same soft-hearted guy chose to smack-talk Cantlay, Stenson, and Spieth, and two breaths later, rebuke anyone who disagreed with his view on the need to limit the distance traveled by modern golf balls.

McIlroy was being particularly prickly on the rollback issue since, just a year earlier, he had reversed his longstanding position. What Gilleece tartly calls Rory's tendency to "*volte-face*," has, in Dermot's words, "become an unfortunately familiar part of McIlroy."

Rory McIlroy is, like many of us, a conflicted soul grappling with a convoluted world. The difference between Rory and the rest of us, though, is that *his* goof-ups and mortal moments get debated ad nauseum by TV analysts, podcasters, columnists, and fans.

No one should shed crocodile tears, but it's not easy being Rory McIlroy—and never has been. On the surface, his life appears glamorous, full of lavish homes and parties, private planes that jet off to exotic locales, and *cha-ching* commercial shoots where his corporate partners tell him how wonderful he is.

But dig deeper. People content with celebrity and material riches don't wrestle with big issues. They don't look for new challenges or ways to stimulate their literary and emotional growth. They don't publicly thank their lucky stars—as Rory continually does—that their parents were willing to sacrifice so much to make it all possible.

"[McIlroy] is the most self-aware superstar in sports," *The Athletic*'s Brody Miller has written. "He thinks about things. He thinks about how he thinks about them. He acknowledges his weaknesses and his anxieties and all the scar tissue he's trying to shed."

Rory's self-awareness is, simultaneously, his superpower and his Kryptonite. It propels his ups and compresses his downs.

Correspondents covering the 2021 WGC-Mexican Championship asked McIlroy if he would consider jumping to the then-nascent, Greg Norman-led Premier Tour, LIV Golf's forerunner. Citing the legacy of Arnold Palmer, Rory issued an emphatic "no." Then he uttered something that ought to be taken to heart by anyone who contemplates a life in the public eye: "I would like to be on the right side of history."

Sure, his remark has been overwhelmed by all the LIV folderol that followed, but when was the last time you heard an athlete of any stripe volunteer anything remotely close to *that*?

A lot of us aspire to be something approaching *fear maith* (or its even loftier feminine counterpart, *ban-naomh*, Gaelic for "sainted woman"). We want to lead Ted Lasso Lives: meaningful, curious, caring. We don't all get there, but Rory Daniel McIlroy, despite the blemishes mixed in with those freckles, has gotten closer than most.

McIlroy has two other gifts that most of us are not likely to acquire: a swing bequeathed by the gods and a sublime golfing style that, at full expression, evokes a child at play. Golf vagabond and author Tom Coyne told me that Rory's swing is "violent yet effortless, blistering yet contained."

Rory "bounces down the fairways as if he has springs in the soles of his golf shoes," observes John Hopkins, the dean of British golf journalism. His American counterpart, Michael Bamberger, once marveled at the "boyish bounce in [McIlroy's] step, the rounded, slightly rocking shoulders that hint of swagger." What Rory projects, Bamberger concluded, is "golfing charisma," a place that was for years Palmer's exclusive domain.

"With McIlroy it is easy to tell whether he is delighted with a shot or disgusted," Karen Crouse, then of the *New York Times*, wrote a decade ago. "His heart is permanently affixed to his sleeve, advertising his emotion and his vulnerability."

After interviewing Rory on the first anniversary of his epic 2011 collapse at the Masters, Crouse was moved to paraphrase theologian Reinhold Niebuhr: "McIlroy has the serenity to accept that not everything in golf can be controlled, the drive to control what he can, and the humor to know the difference."

Amen.

Rory's gifts come from the same ethereal place that gave Ken Griffey Jr. his home run swat, Evonne Goolagong-Cawley and Roger Federer their balletic tennis footwork, Steph Curry his other-worldly jumper, and Gaelic football attacker Brendan "Benny" Coulter, County Down's own, his genius in front of the goal.

To be sure, McIlroy works hard at his craft. So does Curry and so did Griffey, Goolagong-Cawley, Federer, and Coulter.[7] Still, they all started from an aerie few peers ever get to glimpse. It's a shame their athletic artistry can never be captured in stained glass.

---

[7] Trust me: Benny is beloved in McIlroy's home county. In 2010, the year Rory turned twenty-one, Coulter led County Down's "Mourne Men" to the All-Ireland Gaelic football championship game against County Cork. Alas, "The Rebels" from Cork won.

Chapter 1

DEMONS AND APPARITIONS AT LACC AND PINEHURST

The monarch of Rory Land, ignobly taut and tight-lipped, stood on the 17th tee of the Los Angeles Country Club's North Course, peering into the abyss. Well, it was more a metaphorical abyss, although the rocky gorge guarding the green and the far-right side of the fairway sure looked like one.

It was getting late in the day; yet another major championship was slipping away from the onetime *wunderkind* who used to win them, in golf writer Bill Fields's marvelous phrase, "with the ease of someone looking to find a Guinness in Belfast."

Spectators were pleading for Rory to rally. Even with American Wyndham Clark leading the tournament, "Hollywood wanted Holywood," as wag Geoff Shackelford put it. So, surely, did the Hollywood and Manhattan magnates at NBC Sports and their Isleworth, London, counterparts at Sky Sports, the two major networks televising the event.

Seconds before, McIlroy had arrived on the tee box of the penultimate hole of the 2023 United States Open Championship, the most exacting test in golf. Then the world's third-ranked player, McIlroy had spent the entire tournament flitting around—but not quite scaling—the top of the leaderboard. A balky putter and erratic wedge play, the same demons that haunted his final round eleven months earlier at the 2022 Open Championship in St. Andrews, Scotland, were again spooking his Sunday game.

Eleven months before, despite his bitter disappointment, he had held his emotions in check while talking to the press after finishing at the Old Course. But a few minutes later, as he slipped off the grounds in a golf cart, the pain proved too much. He buried his head into his wife's shoulder and began sobbing.

With Erica, McIlroy says he tries to avoid talking shop. But he was so overwrought at St. Andrews he couldn't help himself. In painstaking detail, he recapped his final-round frustrations: the putting misfires; the failure to get up and down for birdie from just off the green at the short par-four sixth; the squirrelly second shot he'd hit at the par-five 14th; and so on.

"You know, all the shit Erica just doesn't want to hear," Rory told columnist Paul Kimmage of the *Irish Independent* four months later. "But I give her credit for sitting there and listening to it."

The last thing McIlroy wanted was a repeat of *that* heartbreak, yet it happened—not only in Beverly Hills, but again twelve months later, in a scenario only Shakespeare at his most malicious could have conceived, in the sandhills of North Carolina.

Combine the distance of the two Sunday putts (two feet six inches, and three feet nine inches) that cost McIlroy the 2024 US Open at Pinehurst No. 2—Donald Ross's diabolical masterpiece—and it would barely cover Rory's miniscule frame. He pulled the two-footer on the 70th green and pushed the (almost) four-footer on the 72nd.

His misses from short-range snuffed what had been a gutsy and disciplined display of golf. Even a shot that backfired—McIlroy's 235-yard four-iron second at the par-five fifth—was spectacular. It was a lovely tight draw, struck on a perfect line; it looked for all the world as it climbed onto the green that it would crest the slope and trickle toward the flagstick.

But as Ross historian Brad Klein has pointed out, the difference between a perfect and a putrid shot at Pinehurst No. 2 is razor-thin. Rory's ball at number 5 ended up on the wrong side of the razor. A few more inches in the air and it would have made it onto the plateau, setting up an eagle opportunity and what should have been an easy two-putt birdie.

Rory's ball, cruelly, took forever to make up its mind. Eventually, it meandered left, picked up steam, and plummeted off the putting surface, diving into the worst lie McIlroy drew all week in one of Ross's old sandpits. All he could do with his third shot was scrape it into the greenside bunker dead ahead; all he could do with his fourth was blast out to twenty-five feet and two-putt. His birdie had become a bogey. That two-stroke swing would cost him dearly two-and-a-half hours later.

McIlroy's putter, frigid on major Sundays for much of the last decade, was smoking hot at Pinehurst—until, of course, he needed it most. Rory had drained lengthy putts for birdie at 1, 9, 10, and 12, and converted a devilish five-footer for yet another birdie at the short par-four 13th.

Suddenly, unexpectedly, McIlroy had a two-shot lead in the 124th US Open when Bryson DeChambeau, who had begun the day ahead of McIlroy by three strokes, rimmed out a four-footer at 14. To be sure, Rory was drawing plenty of applause that Sunday afternoon. But for one of the few times in his career (excepting, of course, Ryder Cups played in the United States), McIlroy wasn't the crowd favorite. The *"Rorree! Rorree!"* chants were drowned out by the *"USA! USA!"* cries that DeChambeau, his arms windmilling, kept fanning from hole to hole. It was a cheeky move by DeChambeau, an odd duck who, after all, had abandoned the US tour for LIV.

Perhaps too amped up, too aware of DeChambeau, McIlroy powered his seven-iron at the par-three 15th over the green. Given the slope curling away from him, he had little choice but to pitch well past the pin. Bogey—but not a disastrous one. He still had some cushion.

Rory played number 16, a daunting par-four, like he owned it. He hit a huge drive down the center of the fairway, followed by a crisply struck iron that came out of the clouds and settled inside twenty-five feet. His birdie putt skimmed the top side of the cup before settling that fateful two feet six inches past.

His playing partner Patrick Cantlay's par putt, from the same side of the green, broke sharply to the right as it approached the cup, missing badly on the low side. Cantlay's slicer may have induced McIlroy to aim inside-left instead of straightaway. Regardless, he pulled the putt.

It careered out on the high side. Bogey—this time, a bad one.

Given the decade's-worth of scar tissue embedded in McIlroy's psyche, it signaled trouble ahead, as sports psychologist Dr. Gio Valiante shared with me the following week.

The par-three 17th had given the field fits all week. On Sunday, McIlroy pulled his tee ball hole-high into the left-side bunker. His blast-out left him a ticklish four-footer, which he converted. Par—and a good one.

He was again tied for the lead with DeChambeau at six-under, terrific scores for a course as unrelenting as Pinehurst No. 2.

The last hole, at least by Ross-ian standards, is probably No. 2's quirkiest: a peculiarly shaped, dogleg-right par-four with sand and wild fescue blighting its left side. McIlroy had hit less than driver all week there and gone birdie-par-par, no mean feat. But on Sunday, he grabbed his driver, perhaps believing—incorrectly—that he would need a birdie to force a playoff with DeChambeau, who was a hole behind.

McIlroy pulled his drive—not badly, but enough to buy a bumpy lie behind a fescue plant. He played his approach through the leaves, but it petered out in front of the green. His chip was well struck, but it ran that pesky three feet, nine inches past the cup.

It turned out that to get into a playoff with DeChambeau, Rory had to make a downhill, sidehill snake that had to be aimed a cup and a half—maybe more—outside left edge. McIlroy didn't borrow nearly enough. It missed. Badly.

Some fans boorishly chanted "*USA! USA!*" when McIlroy's putt stayed aboveground. It was another disastrous bogey—his third in four holes.

After signing his scorecard, he watched the NBC coverage of DeChambeau salvaging his par at number 18 with one of the most dramatic 72nd-hole shots in US Open history: a fifty-five-yard bunker blast to four feet underneath the cup. Bryson's par save won him the championship.

Rory, grim-visaged, smoke coming out of his ears, declined all interview requests and chose not to walk a few yards to extend his hand to DeChambeau. By the time the trophy presentation had gotten underway, the Rory Land gang was halfway to the airfield.

SportsCenter's Van Pelt, a trend-setting commentator long in McIlroy's corner, called Rory's move "classless." He wasn't wrong.

The next day, Rory began what was surely a difficult reconciliation process with Erica and tried to duck the brickbats being heaved his direction. Six-time major champion Nick Faldo, never reticent about sharing a barbed opinion, predicted that it would take "years" for McIlroy to recover. Four weeks later, after Rory's Troon Swoon, it looked like Sir Nick knew what he was talking about.

Every other person with an Instagram account, it seemed, was urging Rory to fire his caddie. Exactly how they were blaming Harry Diamond for his boss's short-putting woes was unclear, but Harry was being held to account over the tee-box clubbing decisions on the 69th and 72nd holes.

Forty-five minutes before arriving at LACC's 17th tee on Sunday, June 18, 2023, McIlroy had been frantically searching for his golf ball in the face of a deep bunker fronting the 14th green, the one just down from Hugh Hefner's old Playboy Mansion. His third-shot gap wedge from 125 yards had ballooned after hitting a little zephyr; it gouged into the trap's far wall. Former USGA head Mike Davis told me that wiry grasses had been planted around many of

LACC's bunkers, giving their edges a fearsome look but making them susceptible to plugging.

"As I was walking up to it [his third shot, from the middle of the 14th fairway], it felt like it was a perfect full sand wedge," McIlroy said later in the press center.

"Hit it hard, get some spin on it," Rory recounted. "Then while we were getting prepared for the shot, the wind started to freshen a little bit. Full sand wedge wasn't getting there, so I said to Harry, three-quarter gap-wedge would be perfect. I feel like I didn't time the shot perfectly. I hit it when the wind was at its strongest and the ball just got hit a lot by the wind, and obviously it came up short. If I had it back, I think I had the right club and the right shot. I might have just had to wait an extra fifteen or twenty seconds to let that little gust settle."

Lord knows Ben Hogan or Jack Nicklaus or Tiger Woods would have waited out the wind.

Those McIlroy major championship bugaboos—impatience and impetuosity—had again reared their heads. Fortunately, his playing partner, Scottie Scheffler, the world's number-one player, found McIlroy's embedded ball before the three-minute time limit expired.

Given a favorable—and what turned out to be a technically incorrect[1]—ruling by a USGA official, Rory was still unable to get his ball up and down for par. A chip across an ultra-slick surface led to a ten-foot putt, which wandered by on the high side.

Hard-earned pars followed on the short, par-three 15th and the long par-four 16th. Coloradan Wyndham Clark, who had led McIlroy by three shots just moments before, bogeyed both 15 and 16.

Now down by a single shot with two holes to play, McIlroy could not have left himself a thornier task. Even by the sado-masochistic standards of the US Open, the two final holes were brutes:

---

1   The USGA admitted later that its official was mistaken; McIlroy should have dropped some eighteen inches farther away from the flagstick. Would a correct drop have helped or hurt McIlroy—or made no difference? We'll never know.

the longest closing par-fours in the championship's history—respectively, 520 yards and an uphill 502 yards. Dan Hicks, NBC's lead golf anchor, called them "beastly."

Despite finishing in the top ten eighteen times since last capturing a major, McIlroy had not won one of golf's four big-ticket tournaments for nine interminable years, something the merciless media corps never failed to beat like a drum. McIlroy's long drought in the majors "has provoked rain forests' worth of column inches and terabytes worth of data," *Irish Times* columnist Michael Foley has written.

LACC marked the fifth consecutive US Open that McIlroy had entered the final round in seventh place or better; Pinehurst a year later would mark the sixth. Yet, there was no USGA hardware topped by a figurine of the mythical Goddess of Victory added to his trophy case. Yes, McIlroy owned a US Open crown, but he'd won it as a sprite of (barely) twenty-two at Congressional Country Club outside Washington DC. It was one of the four majors he'd won before turning twenty-six—a feat back then that had been matched only by Jack Nicklaus and Tiger Woods.

Over the years, as his frustrations in the majors deepened, McIlroy had become a Rorschach test—and something of a punching bag—for commentators, columnists, and retired Tour players turned critics. Some looked at Rory and saw an enormously gifted golfer with buzzard's luck. Others perceived weakness in his genial nature, contending that he lacked the dead-on focus and killer instinct (see: "Woods, Eldrick 'Tiger'") needed to win the big ones.

McIlroy is too nice a guy, too easily distracted, too wrapped up in golf's politics and ephemera, too stubborn to change his wedge mechanics or his putting technique or his allegedly provincial caddie and coach, their arguments went.

No less an authority than Nicklaus—a neighbor, mentor, and unabashed fan—said in early 2023 on Faldo's podcast, *Sir Nick's Roundtable*, that Rory lacked the "smart playing" and "total focus" needed to win the big ones.

Rory's performance in the 2023 majors had given his detractors plenty of fodder. In April at Augusta National, a place that has inflicted nasty scars on his psyche over the years, he had gone all-in on preparation, supposedly playing eighty-one practice holes, ostentatiously flying in sports psychologist Bob Rotella to salve his mental wounds, and assuring the press that he was—*Once and for all, and dammit, this time I mean it!*—over his Masters hang-up.

It all flopped—spectacularly. He played slaphappy golf Thursday and Friday, shooting a combined five-over, missing the cut, and leaving the Georgia pines with his tail between his legs. In a dicey moment during Thursday's round, he allowed the CBS crew to interview him *live*—a head-scratching decision.

Future LIV jumper Jon Rahm, McIlroy's Ryder Cup mate and rival for world number one, ended up winning the 87th Masters. Rory was smarting so badly that he pulled himself out of the next week's tournament, the RBC Heritage at Hilton Head, South Carolina, citing mental and emotional fatigue. McIlroy was forced to incur a $3 million penalty for skipping a "designated" (and cash-heavy) event—a new rule that he had loudly championed as part of the Tour's response to LIV.

McIlroy's post-'23 Masters deportment was, as political pundits would say, "a bad optic."

At the May 2023 PGA Championship at Donald Ross's august Oak Hill in Rochester, New York—Erica's hometown—Rory again got off to a sluggish start, hamstrung by a crooked driver. But on Friday, he bounced back to make the cut.

Still, he never quite climbed into contention at Oak Hill, a place that had made him an honorary member; almost every time he got some momentum rolling with a birdie, he'd follow it with a sketchy shot that presaged bogey.

Episode one in season two of *Full Swing* showed him in Oak Hill's locker room spitting mad after the final round, railing to two Rory Land cronies that his iron play stunk, especially toward pins tucked back left.

He finished tied for seventh at Oak Hill, seven strokes behind winner Brooks Koepka. The Florida State alum was a LIV renegade, the bad-hombre bandito to Rory's white-hatted sheriff in the Netflix series that, at times, took on the moral patina of *High Noon*. That weekend in Rochester, Koepka's "vengeful outlaw" bagged his fifth major, pulling him one ahead of Rory's "incorruptible lawman" in the career sweepstakes.

On-course broadcast analysts[2] like to harp on McIlroy's supposed weaknesses. Now, down the stretch at the '23 US Open at LACC with the world watching, McIlroy had a chance to prove his hecklers wrong.

He would have to do it at a venerable place whose members, as native Angelino Shackelford[3] had been pointing out all spring, were defiantly proud to be "old Los Angeles." Which is a polite way

---

[2] If you took all the career Tour wins of the leading male walk-the-course analysts for NBC Golf/Golf Channel, ABC/ESPN, and CBS Golf, and put them together…let's see…they would add up to less than one-tenth of Rory's worldwide victory total. On the flip side, the estimable on-course analyst Dottie Pepper of CBS, she of the seventeen career LPGA wins, the two major championships, and the dad who played first base in the Detroit Tiger organization? *Dottie: you can do no wrong!*

[3] An author and course designer, native southern Californian Geoff Shackelford writes an online newsletter devoted to the four majors and other big golf events called *The Quadrilateral*. He served as a deputy consultant in LACC's restoration. But the coolest thing about Geoff is that he's the son of Lynn Shackelford, the sharpshooting southpaw on the Lew Alcindor UCLA teams that won three straight NCAA titles in the late 1960s. Lynn's patented shot was a rainbow jumper from the baseline. Today, most of Lynn's old daggers would be worth three points!

of saying that LACC has been around since before those ghastly "entertainment people" had taken over.

Movie and TV types have never really been welcomed at the posh club at Sunset and Wilshire. Indeed, when the *Playboy* founder and his entourage moved into their modest bungalow in 1971, club members went to great lengths to distance themselves from Hef and his hedonistic ways.

In contrast to his performances at Augusta National and Oak Hill, Rory had played almost mistake-free golf at LACC. He started each of the four rounds by hitting mammoth tee balls—360 yards or longer—down the right-center of the par-five first fairway. As the week went on, many of the world's best players got tangled up in the nasty Bermuda or the sand down number 1's left side.

But not Rory: he kept pounding his patented draw onto the short grass. NBC's on-course reporter Notah Begay ran out of superlatives in describing the length and beauty of McIlroy's opening tee shots. Rory made four relatively easy two-putt birdies on a hole where other leaders struggled to make par.

On Thursday, with West L.A. blanketed by a cloud layer that stifled the breeze, he shot a five-under 65, bettered only by Rickie Fowler's and Xander Schauffele's matching 62s—record-breaking scores in a US Open. Rory followed with a second-round 67 and a third-round 69. John Hopkins pointed out in *Global Golf Post* that only once in the first two days did McIlroy have to hit a club longer than wedge on any of LACC's mammoth par-fours.

Rory trailed by one shot going into the final round, but only because Clark had made an improbable birdie on the 54th hole after dropping a shot on the 53rd.

Late on Sunday, as McIlroy surveyed his options—none of them good—from LACC's elevated tee box on number 17, he not only had to cope with emotional roadblocks, but a serpentine fairway that slithered left to right, then snaked back again. Left of the fairway were palm and eucalyptus trees, wicked sand, and ankle-high Bermuda rough; to the right and dead ahead loomed that stony canyon.

His choices were almost as gnarled as professional golf at that moment.

Rory had spent much of the previous two years trying to do what he saw as the right thing, serving as the PGA Tour's (very) public advocate in its efforts to combat the Saudi-bankrolled LIV Tour. LIV in 2022 and 2023 had purloined more than a dozen big names and scores of lesser ones from the PGA and DP World tours, actions that were threatening to destroy the fabric of professional golf.

On June 6, 2023—the seventy-ninth anniversary of D-Day[4] and nine days before the start of the LACC US Open—PGA Tour Commissioner Jay Monahan had stunned the sporting and business worlds (not to mention McIlroy and his peers) by announcing a framework agreement with LIV's "bank," the Saudi Public Investment Fund: the financial arm of Crown Prince Mohammed bin Salman and the Saudi royal family.[5] Monahan's bolt-out-of-the-blue abruptly ended (at least in theory) the established tours' public feud with LIV and expunged the crippling lawsuits they had filed against one another.

The reaction from the golf commentariat was searing. "It turns out that the moral high ground was a pile of money," one observer told *The Albatross*'s Bill Fields. The Tour's commissioner, Fields himself wrote a few days later, had shifted course "faster than a ship captain with an iceberg dead ahead." Kurt Streeter pointed out that week in the *New York Times* that the Tour had long presented itself "as the guy who calls a penalty on himself if he accidentally moves his ball a quarter-inch. Turns out it was the guy who makes a double-bogey and marks it down as a par."

---

[4] The fact that the Tour's acquiescence took place on the Allies' sacred day nearly did in this WWII author.
[5] If you need a primer on Saudi human rights outrages, read chapter five of Alan Shipnuck's *LIV and Let Die*.

There was no getting around it: the reversal was hypocritical on Monahan's part and a bitter betrayal of McIlroy. For months, the commissioner and his team had sent Rory out before the klieg lights to denounce LIV, its benefactors, its competitive offering, and—in terms that got uncomfortably belligerent—his former colleagues, the guys who took the PIF money and bolted.

Monahan's surrender left Rory "bereft," wrote Brian Keogh, the Irish golf correspondent who has covered McIlroy since the star's teen years. A McIlroy acolyte in Ireland that week told me that Rory was "angry and embittered." Golf seer Alan Shipnuck wrote in *LIV and Let Die* that McIlroy had his "heart ripped out" by three people he trusted. That unholy trinity consisted of Monagan and his two Wall Street *consiglieres*: PGA Tour board members Ed Herlihy of the merger-and-acquisition mega law firm Wachtel Lipton, and Jimmy Dunne of the well-connected investment banking group Piper Sandler.

Dunne's double-dealing must have been especially difficult for Rory. Jimmy had long served as a family friend and Rory, Inc., business advisor. When the McIlroys moved to Florida, Dunne pulled levers to get Rory's dad into the ultra-elite Seminole Golf Club, an old Donald Ross gem just down the road from Rory's estate in Palm Beach Gardens and not far from Rosie and Gerry's digs.

It's a sure bet that Gerry McIlroy is the only one-time custodian/barkeep who belongs to Seminole. Seminole members, like Augusta National's (in a number of cases, including Dunne's, they're one in the same), are corporate titans who fancy themselves golf's ultimate arbiters and power brokers.

It wasn't lost on McIlroy's followers in the Auld Sod that Monahan, Herlihy, and Dunne all happen to be of Irish descent. Had they lied to Rory and exploited his stature with fans and the media to cut a sweetheart deal with the Tour's sworn enemy?

On the eve of the 2023 US Open, it sure looked that way. The whole thing stunk to high heaven.

RORY LAND

The 17th at LACC faces east, away from the Pacific Ocean and the setting sun. Fewer than a fourth of the field on Sunday had hit its green in regulation. Like every other player, McIlroy's yardage books had huge "X's" scrawled through the right edge of the fairway. The ravine was to be avoided like the plague—or a subpoena from Patrick Reed.[6]

That meant plumbing the left side, which would bring the sand, the trees, and that nasty Bermuda into play. The best club in McIlroy's bag since he learned the game as a youngster has been his driver. It's his go-to, the weapon that gives him the best chance to gain an advantage.

McIlroy is a natural right-to-left drawer of the ball; his "miss" tends to be a pull left. Fortuitously for him, beyond the ugly stuff left at number 17 was the short grass of the second fairway.

In practice rounds, Rory and his caddie determined that, in a pinch, they could use the second fairway as a default zone. The angle into the 17th green from the second fairway wasn't all that penal, especially for a guy like McIlroy who can hit mid-irons into the stratosphere. Bryson DeChambeau and a couple of other big hitters had used that same route earlier in the week, as had past players at LACC.

Out came Rory's driver and *bang!!*—out went a power hook soaring up and over the palm and eucalyptus. It landed in the rough separating the two holes, pitched onto the short grass, and bounded down number 2's fairway, which tilted left-to-right, angling toward

---

[6] Reed, McIlroy's LIV foil, had his attorney, right-wing provocateur Larry Klayman, serve Rory with a subpoena on Christmas Eve 2022 while McIlroy was at home having dinner with his family. Nothing says "'Tis the Season" quite like a court order! The guy who was thrown off the University of Georgia golf team for cheating on and off the course and has been caught multiple times thrashing the rules as a pro, claimed that Rory and others had defamed him after he defected to the Saudi league. Reed's suit not only has been dismissed; it has been ruled so meritless that Reed and Klayman may have to compensate their targets.

number 17's green. His drive had gone the usual Rory-ian distance, something on the order of 340 yards—into the wind!

It left him a 210-yard six-iron, bucking a gentle breeze, that had to be struck *just so*. To get anywhere close to the flagstick, it needed to navigate a batch of trees some forty yards short of the putting surface. The pin itself was positioned on the third of the green closest to McIlroy.

Rory, as always, wasted no time. He hit a towering fade over the trees and well left of the gully. While the ball was still in the air, course reporter John Wood, a Tour caddie turned broadcaster, said it was "on a fantastic line."

Like so many of Rory's shots, it took forever to come down—so long, in fact, that the gallery seemed startled when it finally struck the green. It landed softly, just beyond hole-high, took a gentle hop, and trickled to the back edge—a sensational shot, NBC's Brad Faxon noted right away, because like all US Open putting surfaces, the green was "hard as concrete."

In his career, McIlroy has finessed a lot of brilliant mid- and long-irons—it's one of the strengths of his game, as he proved the following month on the 72nd hole in winning the Scottish Open with a spectacular two-iron. But rarely has Rory feathered an iron sweeter than the one he hit on the 71st hole of the '23 US Open.

"Nobody in golf can do what McIlroy just did!" gushed Paul Azinger, then NBC's lead analyst. "Nobody else today can hoist a ball that high and far" and get it to land so nimbly. It was reminiscent of Tiger in his prime, Azinger enthused.

McIlroy had some thirty feet for birdie, probably closer than he could have gotten had he taken a more conventional route. Southern California's dank marine layer had begun to envelop the course. It was getting so dark that McIlroy later admitted he had trouble seeing the breaks in the green.

His putt was firmly struck but stayed, just barely, on the high side, settling inches past the cup. A tap-in par on an into-the-wind, 520-yard par-four is a hell of a score—but it fell short of what McIlroy needed.

So did a similar par on the 502-yard finisher, where Rory's power fade down the right-center of the fairway was followed by a slightly tugged seven-iron that ended up almost exactly hole-high, but some forty feet left of the pin. McIlroy's approach looked like a bit of a double-cross—a soft draw when he intended to hit a soft fade. It wasn't a bad miss. But given the circumstances, McIlroy needed a perfect strike.

His final bid to tie for the lead never scared the cup. McIlroy ended up losing by a single shot. He was done in by a temperamental flat stick and the thirty-four putts it produced on Sunday, plus that upwind wedge that nosedived into the trap at number 14.

His score of 271, nine-under, would have won all but a handful of the 122 US Opens in history. But it wasn't enough to win the 123rd.

Buzzard's luck, again?

The tortured scenario that McIlroy dreaded had come to pass: St. Andrews, redux. But this time his near-miss was even closer than it had been at the Old Course.

In the media center afterward, McIlroy set his jaw, narrowed his eyes, and swore that, "I would go through a hundred Sundays like this to get my hands on another major. When I finally win this next major, it's going to be really, really sweet. I'll keep coming back until I get another one."

At LACC, his embrace with Erica was less public and less tearful than it was at St. Andrews. But it still had to hurt.

Full Swing's crew caught McIlroy in the LACC locker room, angrily chucking something against the lockers as he f-bombed a lament to Rory Landers about once again coming up short.

During his June 6 joint CNBC appearance with Saudi PIF Governor Yasir Al-Rumayyan, Jay Monahan nervously grinned and predicted that the press and public would label him a hypocrite. He was right. The commissioner's personal struggles were so pronounced that soon thereafter he took a six-week medical leave, admitting to fatigue and depression.

For months as the two sides had clashed, Rory, as chair of the Tour's player advisory committee, had devoted huge chunks of time to studying the Tour's multilayered financial structure. A prominent American journalist told me that McIlroy requested in December of 2022 a series of detailed briefings from Monahan's top business and legal advisors. Two ten-hour days at McIlroy's Florida home ensued, full of charts, graphs, and in-the-weeds presentations.

The tax implications and commercial restrictions governing a 501(c)(6) entity like the Tour are not easy for laymen to "get." But Rory got them. He may be the only big-name player who could pass a test on the nuances of the modern Tour's business model, its top revenue streams, its legal constraints, and its myriad tax considerations.

Armed with what he believed was truthful data and a compelling business strategy, McIlroy, in 2022 and the first two quarters of 2023, expended reams of personal credibility in persuading colleagues to turn down big Saudi bucks. With a bunch of now pissed-off colleagues asking WTF their sacrifice had been about, Rory was left red-faced, hung out to dry.

As Golf Channel anchor Anna Jackson, a Brit, shared with me in her Berkshire tones, "The rug had been yanked out from underneath Rory."

Rory confirmed Anna's view when he snapped on camera in *Full Swing*: "Why did I waste twelve months of my life to fight for something that was always going to come back together again?"

McIlroy admitted two days after the big announcement that the Tour's duplicity had rendered him a "sacrificial lamb." But somehow his metaphor didn't come close to capturing the venality of the PGA boss and his enablers.

Chapter 2

"BECAUSE HE'S NICE!"

Let's shove aside the nastiness over LIV for a moment. Like most fans, I find the whole rigmarole distasteful.

Instead, let's explore this question: What is it that makes Rory McIlroy *Rory McIlroy*—you know, *that guy* that a huge chunk of golf fandom, including me, pulls for week to week, despite the heartburn he causes us?

It's definitely not because of the f-bombs he tosses around with an alacrity that would turn Michelle, the foul-mouthed spitfire of the Irish sitcom *Derry Girls*, green with envy. After a wayward shot, Rory's go-to expletive, usually muttered under bated breath, is the active-tense f-verb punctuated by the personal pronoun "me." After narrowly missed putts, he'll occasionally pair the f-verb with the preposition "off."

In certain dicey situations, he'll detonate an audible f-adjective. During the final round of the 2022 Dubai Desert Classic, Rory's three-wood off the tee found some heavy undergrowth short and left of the green on number 17, a drivable par-four.

"Watch out! This could go fuckin' anyplace!" McIlroy hissed in urging gallery members to give him a wide berth. Just for good measure, he repeated the warning a few seconds later, with a TV mic picking up every syllable.

"Was that Rory swearing?" my wife (see *Favorite, Every Mom*'s) asked as she looked up from the Sunday *Washington Post*, the disillusion clear in her voice.

Uh, yeah, Sweetie. And Rory does more than just fire off quiet f-bombs in the heat of battle. True to his working-class roots,

McIlroy can "shit" and "shite"[1] like a hard-bitten boilermaker on the Belfast docks, the unforgiving place where, for decades, his grandfather Jimmy risked life and limb.

"Shite," explains County Limerick's Ivan Morris, one of several Irish golf-and-culture devotees consulted for this book, is synonymous with its cruder sibling. But the long-"eye" version, Ivan maintains, is used in more polite settings—like church, for instance, or in the presence of impressionable children.

And no, Rory isn't *Rory* because he's (almost always) as gracious in defeat as he is in victory, something that a horde of parents have pointed out to their kids on Sunday afternoons for the past sixteen years.

And nope, it's not those McIlroy drives that shriek as they leave his clubface, rocketing a fifth of a mile or more. The length he hits the ball is even more remarkable because McIlroy is a man of, well, modest size. Even straining on his tiptoes, he still comes up a couple inches shy of six feet.

Moreover, as observed by Hopkins, the British journalist who has covered golf for a half century, Rory barely tips the scale at "eleven-and-a-half stone." (*For those raised outside the shadow of Nelson's Column in Trafalgar Square, that's slightly north of 160 pounds.*) Despite his diminutive stature, McIlroy's drives go distances about which Ben Hogan and Sam Snead, postwar golf's two most admired ball strikers, could only dream.

And nuh-uh, it's not the mechanics of Rory's swing that five-time Open champion Tom Watson compares to Snead's (it's Rory's Snead-ian *shoulder turn* that gives it such zip, maintains Tom), and that two-time US Open champion Andy North likens to Hogan's

---

[1] Profanity in Anglo-Irish culture, as I learned during a two-week visit in July 2023, is less, uhh, *profane* than it is in the States. Over there, four-letter epithets are more ingrained in everyday conversation. Plus, there's the surrogate "feckin'," which really isn't swearing, avers Dermot Gilleece, a wonderful man now enjoying retirement as the *eminence grise* of Irish golf journalists. Dermot was kind enough to drive me to Portmarnock, the great links course outside Dublin, for a quick look at the clubhouse and the first tee. En route, a driver cut us off. "What a feckin' idiot!" he growled in his gorgeous lilt, then quickly confirmed that feckin' was not a curse word.

(it's Rory's Hogan-esque *hip turn* that makes it so powerful, contends Andy).

Early in McIlroy's career, when he was still playing Titleist clubs, he paid a visit to the Titleist Performance Institute in Carlsbad, California. Engineers put Rory's driver swing up on a computer model that distilled his body into a stick-figure. It demonstrated that the Watson-Snead/North-Hogan analysis was correct: Rory did indeed make a massive shoulder turn *and* an equally massive counterclockwise move with his left hip to initiate the downswing. But the technicians also discovered something they'd never seen: a moment before Rory's driver made impact, his left hip suddenly changed direction, moving almost imperceptibly clockwise. Michael Bamberger of *Sports Illustrated* was at the Titleist center that day and described Rory's driver swing as a "mad fusion golf experiment."

Over the years, many have tried to replicate Rory's action. The young Filipino-Japanese player Yuka Saso, who has won the US Women's Open twice, has perhaps come the closest to absorbing McIlroy's method. It's also eye-opening that Tiger Woods has for years been teaching his now-teenaged son to mimic Rory's swing.

So, if you combine Rory's upper- and lower-body rotations, plus all the "kinetic sequencing" claptrap that's beyond the grasp of most laymen, they add up to a *whoosh!* that gives swing geeks the vapors.

They use language like "hypnotic" (instructor Michael Breed), "mesmerizing" (journalist Lorne Rubenstein), "beautiful, elegant, powerful" (Golf Channel *cognoscente* Brandel Chamblee), "freakish" (Golf Channel correspondent Rex Hoggard), "so relaxed it makes Fred Couples' swing look uptight" (historian Brad Klein), "scary-ass good" (my 27-handicap brother), and my personal favorite, crafted by writer and Celtic links maven Tom Coyne: a "swing Michelangelo could have carved."

F-verb me! Now *that's* some good shite!

But still, Rory's swing isn't what makes him *Rory*.

Nor is it that McIlroy has evolved into someone unafraid to assert leadership, confront tough issues, put the good of the game ahead of his own bank account, or share his wide-ranging and—forgive the pretension, but there's no getting around it—*existential* thoughts with the press and public. Those riffs now include Rory's commitment to strengthening children's mental health services, plus his own frank admission that, on occasion, he suffers from self-doubt. Not many superstars are that forthright about the fragility of their nervous systems.

Nor is it all those commercials that spotlight his boyish charm. Flip on a TV most weekend afternoons and you'll bump into Brand Ambassador McIlroy shilling Omega watches, TaylorMade golf equipment, Optum health technology and services, Workday business consulting, and the NBC Sports/Rory Land, everything-from-video-swing-lessons-to-discounted-tee-times-squeezed-into-one-platform known as GolfPass.[2]

But ignore the show-biz stuff. Those ads embody cold-blooded corporate calculations. McIlroy is in those commercials because consumer research validates his popularity. Commanding that level of respect and affection from US audiences is unusual, to say the least, for a non-American. Rory has ingratiated himself so much into American culture that—at least pre-DeChambeau and Pinehurst—many Americans viewed him as practically a Yank. Even his brogue has gotten less pronounced, which no doubt aggravates folks in North County Down.

And no, it's not the endearing way McIlroy has of answering questions from the media. No matter how provocative the query, his MO is to listen to what's asked, gently nod, preface his

---

[2] In any previous era, a television network entering into a commercial partnership with a public figure it covered on a regular basis would have been roundly censured—and likely stopped. It's also disconcerting that the PGA Tour is McIlroy's business partner in a number of lucrative ventures, including the tech-infused Tomorrow Golf League (TGL) and various video productions and promotions. Business ethics have become so slipshod and the media so inert that practically no one batted an eye when Rory became the poster boy of NBC's GolfPass and the matinee idol of PGA Tour Productions and other Tour offerings.

remarks with an affirmative "Yeah," or "Hmm-hmm," then give a response that's usually thoughtful, literate, and peppered with self-effacing humor.

The golf press, starved for news, quotes, and color, loves him for it.

McIlroy would probably be better off talking in clichés, avoiding awkward topics, and relying on robotic soundbites, a la Crash Davis's[3] pupil in the movie *Bull Durham*, the bumptious Nuke LaLoosh. That was certainly true for the middle third of the LIV debate. But as Fields puts it, such restraint "is just not in Rory's DNA."

Still, we're not quite at the quality that makes Rory *Rory*, the closest thing that the PGA and DP World tours have to a rock star (*Forgive us, Billy Idol, for we have sinned!*). But moments like the ones below bring *Rory McIlroy* into sharper relief.

It's a few minutes before four o'clock on a hazy June 2023 Wednesday afternoon in Cromwell, Connecticut, the home of the PGA Tour's Travelers Championship. A bunch of kids, their parents, and over-caffeinated autograph hounds with big plans to bombard eBay are hovering around the practice facilities at TPC River Highlands.

The Travelers' umbrella logo, a ubiquitous blood-red presence at River Highlands, has been etched into the distant grass of the driving range. Subtlety be damned: the corporate symbol is gargantuan, its scarlet tint standing in stark contrast to the blue-green hills of the Connecticut River Valley.

---

[3] Crash's (Kevin Costner's) advice to Nuke (Tim Robbins)? "Learn your clichés. Study them. They're your friends. Write this down. '*We got to play 'em one day at a time. I'm just happy to be here. Hope I can help the ballclub. I just want to give it my best shot—and* (mischievously smiling) *the Good Lord willing, things will work out.*'"

The fans around the practice area are waiting for one player: Rory McIlroy. Just three days after his stinging defeat at the LACC US Open, Rory has still not made an appearance to warm up for his nine-hole stint in that day's pro-am.

Since it happens to be June 19, almost literally the summer solstice, there's plenty of daylight available. McIlroy is scheduled to tee off on the 10th hole around 4:40 with an amateur threesome that won a lottery to play with him.

Standing there, a history nerd, I can't help but wonder what the original Puritan settlers of the Connecticut Valley would make of such secular ostentation. Then again, the Puritans were Calvinists, and Calvinist Scots (by most accounts) invented *gowfe* way back when to inflict greater punishment on their already doomed souls (plus kill a little time while they tended to their sheep), so what the hell do I know?

Well, I know this much: Enfield, Connecticut, one of the hamlets where fire-and-brimstone preacher Jonathan Edwards delivered his "Sinners in the Hands of an Angry God" sermon that scared the bejesus out of colonial New Englanders (and would later come to *bore* the bejesus out of American tenth graders), is just upriver from Cromwell.

Rory McIlroy, raised Catholic—and now, it seems, like so many of us, unobservant—is no Calvinist. But with all the weird and wicked things that have befallen him in major championships over the past decade, part of him has to wonder if a pissed-off deity is exacting revenge for some sin he doesn't even know he's committed.

It had not been an easy week: The McIlroy Whammy had struck with a vengeance. Sixty-eight hours earlier, his hopes had been crushed again. His score of nine-under should have won—but didn't.

"You don't find US Opens—they find you," Jack Nicklaus has famously preached for more than half a century. Play conservatively, the Golden Bear counsels. Channel your inner Hogan. Shoot for the middle of greens. Grind out two-putt pars. Don't take undue risks. Let the other guy(s) wilt under pressure.

RORY LAND

Rory, a protégé and neighbor of Nicklaus at the Bears Club in Palm Beach Gardens, Florida, has been taken to the woodshed more than once by Big Jack for his sometimes-unfocused play. Their most recent tête-à-tête had occurred just two weeks before LACC, when Rory had shot a fourth-round 75 to fall out of contention at Jack's tournament in Ohio.

In L.A., Rory had clearly taken his mentor's rebuke to heart. He rarely put his ball in jeopardy, churning out rugged pars. After the wind picked up on the weekend and the course started playing firmer, Rory hung tough while others fell off the leaderboard.

McIlroy's discipline should have spelled US Open victory. But it didn't.

Shite, but life can be cruel! Jonathan Edwards told us that 280 years ago.

While we're waiting for Rory to arrive, I pull out my tape recorder and begin interviewing kids and their parents, many of whom have been hanging around for hours. The Connecticut sun isn't broiling, but it isn't cool, either. These folks are showing some gumption; there isn't a whole lot of shade around.

Two dark-haired sisters, dressed in nearly identical pink frocks, are standing near the plaques that commemorate past (and now, sadly, *passed*) champions from the Travelers, and from the old days, the Greater Hartford Open. (*I'll be damned*, I thought as I strolled by the tablets. *I didn't know Arnie won the GHO in '56. Very cool.*)

Gracie, age eight, tells me she has just finished third grade and will be starting fourth in the fall. Cammie, five, has to be coaxed by her dad Rubén to speak into the recorder. Eventually she overcomes her shyness to confirm that, yes, she is excited about going to kindergarten in two months.

"So, girls, who are you waiting to see?" I ask, putting the recorder between two beaming faces.

"Rory!" they yell together.

"Why do you like Rory?"

"Because he's nice!" shouts Gracie.

"Yeah, he's nice!" choruses Cammie.

Rubén, a gentleman of Latino descent with broad shoulders, a square jaw, and a well-groomed mustache, chuckles at his excitable daughters. Gracie explains that their mother had gotten the tickets through her job. Mom is at the office that afternoon.

"Somebody has to support the family while I go watch golf," Rubén says with a sly grin, his brown eyes twinkling.

"Are you guys coming back to the tournament this week?" I ask.

"Yes!" Gracie answers. "We're going as a family on Saturday. Then my dad is coming back on Sunday with 'the boys'!"

As she snaps off "the boys," she does what must be a dead-on impersonation of her mother, rolling her eyes and shaking her head in mock disgust. It's hilarious.

Rubén chortles at his impish eight-year-old. I ask if Rory is *his* favorite, too.

"Yeah, he's up there," Rubén replies. "I love his swing. Love the way he plays. And he seems to be a good guy."

"Were you pulling for him in L.A. last week?" I ask.

"Yeah, I was. Painful. I wanted him to win and end that [winless-in-majors] streak of his."

I move down the line to a family of three, a mom and dad and their freckled nine-year-old son Joshua, whose mop of strawberry-blond hair is stuffed under a bucket cap. His skin is freshly lacquered in sunscreen.

Joshua started playing golf a year ago; he's shown some promise, his dad Edward says. Edward is slight and soft-spoken, at least with a tape recorder running. He's originally from Seattle and sports a Mariners cap.

"Wearing a Mariners lid in Connecticut the week they're playing the Yanks at the Stadium? Man, that takes guts!" I kid him.

He smiles a bit quizzically when I ask if he thinks that Rory plays golf the way Ken Griffey Jr. used to play baseball for the

Mariners. Trying not to sound too sappy, I say, "You know, kind of with style."

Yeah, he nods. He's got two favorite golfers, Rory and Tony Finau.

"Do you know they've been friends since they were a little older than Joshua?" I say, again trying not to come across too dorky.

"No, I didn't know that," he responds, pleased to learn something kind of cool that he could share with his golf buddies.

His wife Holly pipes up. You can tell where Joshua gets his reddish hair.

"Well, Rory is *my* favorite, hands down," she says. (Again, see *Favorite, Every Mom's*.)

"How come?"

"Because he's a good person and I like the way he treats people."

"Did you see him last weekend at the US Open?"

"A little. I'm too busy to sit down and watch. But I was rooting for him."

I thank them and move a few feet away to chat with another family. Tony is an eight-year-old of Italian descent, a second grader who is preternaturally savvy, not only about golf (he's one of the better junior players at their Glastonbury club, his parents tell me) but about the yin and yang of interviews. He delivers several polished and enthusiastic soundbites, a la Nuke LaLoosh. The last one ends with, "I just like watching Rory play!"

"I do, too," I tell him.

His dad Dustin ("No relation to Dustin Johnson," he confirms, grinning) volunteers that he's encouraging his son to follow Rory. McIlroy, he says, "is a good role model for kids Tony's age. I love the way he stood up for the Tour and the players against LIV."

"Do you worry that the Tour's brass left him hanging on LIV?" I ask.

"Yeah, that bothers me. A lot," he replies.

"Me, too," I tell him.

A few moments later, Gracie, Cammie, Joshua, Tony, and about three dozen other kids get their wish. Rory McIlroy suddenly surfaces, shuffling toward the range. He's wearing a navy-blue Nike cap and a faintly flowered light-blue, Swoosh-adorned shirt with dark slacks.

The screeching begins. "Rory! Rory! Over here, Rory! I love you! Sign for me!"

It's another Rory McIlroy Public Interaction Moment in a lifetime full of RMPIMs. It's been this way since he was a prodigy playing—and often winning—amateur events all over Ireland, the UK, the Continent, and the United States. Sure, the adulation feeds his ego and has helped make him an extremely wealthy man; but after you observe RMPIMs for a while, you realize two things: Rory is brilliant at them; and they're not an easy way to go through life.

In researching the book, I'd been studying how McIlroy reacts with fans, especially younger ones, and the way they, in turn, react to him: in 2022 at TPC-Potomac in Maryland; in 2023 at TPC-Sawgrass in Florida, at the PGA Championship at Oak Hill in Rochester, at TPC-River Highlands, and at the Open Championship at Royal Liverpool; and in 2024 at PGA National in Palm Beach Gardens, at Bay Hill in Orlando, and at Hamilton Golf and Country Club in Ancaster, Ontario.

There's an electricity between McIlroy and his legion of young followers that—all kidding aside about Billy Idol—is not far removed from the bond that exists between rock stars and worshipful fans. No, it's not the mania that greets Taylor Swift these days. But RMPIMs are the closest thing the Tour has to it. If Tour executives could, they'd bottle Rory's charisma and sprinkle it over his peers. A nine-year-old boy at Oak Hill held up a homemade sign that read: *"Rory: I Want To Be Just Like You!!!"* The youngster had used different colored markers to make the three exclamation points.

Has a kid ever held up a sign to Dustin Johnson that read: *"DJ: I Want To Be Just Like You!!!"*? Maybe, but I'd bet against it.

Rosie and Gerry gave their son the perfect moniker for a professional golfer, a euphonic two syllables that fans love to, well, roar. *Rorr-ee!!* has become the new *Ar-nee!!* or *Ti-ger!!* No surname is required.

McIlroy relishes the attention and has since he was a kid. Palmer famously made eye contact with fans. Rory does, too; he almost never stops smiling and nodding in their direction. McIlroy's slump during the COVID pandemic probably had more to do with the lack of fan interaction than it did with any swing issues or putting woes.

It's symbiotic. He needs us and we need him—or at least *our projection* of him. We want Rory to be a hero around whom our kids can rally. He not only accepts the responsibility, he savors it; his words and actions encourage it.

Above all, as Anna Jackson points out, McIlroy appears to have the same welcoming persona, on and off camera. As an undergraduate at Brookes University in the UK, Anna studied the telegenic traits that translate into effective personas in our hyper-media age.

"Rory invites us into his world," she told me in the summer of 2023. "He's fun and charming and we want to spend time with him."

McIlroy possesses many of the qualities that drew—and sixty-odd years later, still draw—people to Paul McCartney. The same oval Irish mug.[4] The same twinkle in the eyes. The same infectious laugh. "C'mon, folks," McCartney and McIlroy both seem to wink in their public appearances. "Let's go on this crazy journey together!"

Rory's freckles give him a definite leg up in the Q-Score competition for public affection. American audiences have always loved freckle-faced characters, especially youngsters with puckish grins and playful eyes—from Mickey Rooney to Ron Howard.

---

4   McCartney grew up in Liverpool, England, of course, but claims Irish ancestry on both sides. His maternal grandfather was an Ulsterman from County Monaghan's Tullynamalrow, a village less than an hour's drive from Holywood.

Teenaged Rory had that same appeal. It hasn't waned much over the years.

RMPIMs happen every time Rory steps onto a course and, increasingly, almost every time he visits a shopping mall or a grocery store. Tiger-mania, of course, was more intense. But in his prime, Woods almost always kept the public at arm's length, often refusing to sign autographs and carefully planning every movement to keep his public exposure to an absolute minimum.

Sure, Xander and Scottie and J.T. and all the rest draw attention from fans. But not the way Rory does. My wife, new to the peculiar world of golf, watched Rory swing on the range at Oak Hill, then casually kibitz with young fans.

She turned and said, "Now I see what you mean. I get it. I see how he's different."

McIlroy smiles a studied smile at River Highlands, friendly without being exuberant, and does a little wave toward a metal fence that separates the spectators' zone from the players-only area. *I'll sign for you over there…just let me warm up for a few minutes,* Rory's gesture seemed to say.

Walking with him are two other Irishmen and longtime Rory Landers. The shorter guy is Rory's caddie, Harry Diamond, an original Mac Packer and Holywood Golf Club alum who competed against Rory on the Irish amateur circuit. Four years older than McIlroy, Diamond has the name and cleft-in-the-chin good looks of a film-noir antihero, the kind of tough-talking mook that Richard Widmark played in movies like *Pickup on South Street* and *Kiss of Death.*

Diamond, unlike Rory, grew up in a Northern Irish family with discretionary income: the Diamonds owned a string of successful

Belfast hotels and nightclubs and still do. Harry was the best man at Rory's wedding; Rory returned the favor at Harry's nuptials.

For a bagman who has maintained an exceptionally low public profile since taking over as Rory's guy in 2017, Diamond comes in for more than his share of grief. Commentators often blame Harry for not pushing back hard enough when Rory the Swashbuckler unsheathes his sword, which still happens with alarming frequency, including, perhaps, the 69th and 72nd tees at Pinehurst No. 2. At the '24 Players Championship, NBC's Gary Koch, one of golf's most respected voices, aired his view that Harry is too passive and deferential. Koch is not alone. It's a constant lament among golf's intelligentsia.

The taller fellow is McIlroy's business manager, Dubliner Sean O'Flaherty, the captain of Rory's commercial and public relations enterprises. O'Flaherty, like Diamond a superb golfer, studied computer science at Trinity College. After graduation, he caddied for a time on the European Tour, then joined Horizon Sports Management in Dublin. Soon after, he helped engineer Rory's abrupt (and costly) split from Horizon and the ultimate creation of Rory, Inc.

As any TV viewer can tell you, the business side of Rory Land is going gangbusters. Each year, it seems, Rory deepens his global brand presence. His personal wealth has become stratospheric, inexorably pushing toward a billion bucks.

The PR side? Not so much.

For a couple of years beginning in 2021, Rory's public positioning on LIV was clear-cut and forceful. Once summer 2023 turned to fall and fall into winter, his messaging became jumbled and ambiguous, at times downright contradictory.

As the post-June 6 debate over the Tour's future became more polarizing, Rory needed strategic communications counsel—and either wasn't getting it or wasn't listening to it. By then, like it or not, McIlroy had become a supercharged public advocate, the rough equivalent of a political or corporate leader ensnared in a crisis. He needed a clear objective to steer his strategy and credible messages to share with a wide swath of audiences: from Tour officials and fellow players to corporate partners, business stakeholders, media figures, and—above all—fans. He also needed colleagues and respected third parties (retired players and journalists, business leaders, officeholders, et al.) to buttress his views.

None of those things happen by accident. I know, because I spent four decades in the public affairs world.

A Dublin-based firm, The Communications Clinic, has been a Rory Land fixture for a dozen years. If its principals weren't urging McIlroy to pull back and be more consistent and less combative in his public pronouncements, they should turn in their PR badges.

Instead, Rory managed his role in the middle and latter stages of the LIV donnybrook the way, too often, he manages tough par-fours at Augusta National: by chucking the game plan and letting his emotion of the moment dictate his next move. As one seasoned journalist wrote me, "McIlroy's impulsiveness is often a detriment. He tends to overreact in an anxiety-inducing, stressful moment. He's not good at talking himself down off, or out of, a reaction—and giving himself time to make a composed choice."

Are Rory Land insiders too intimately connected, too invested in McIlroy to give him the no-nonsense advice he needs at crucial moments? For the past couple of years, it's hard to conclude otherwise.

I'm fifty yards or so removed from Rory and company as they approach McIlroy's range bay at TPC-River Highlands. Three days after their US Open heartbreak, they aren't moving with much *oomph*. If there are smiles or light banter, I don't see any.

Harry grabs a wooden folding chair, moves it over to Rory's spot, and plops himself in it—unusual behavior for a conscientious caddie. Rory doesn't seem to mind. He picks a wedge out of his bag, stretches with it some, and begins hitting it with that languid rhythm.

Big chunks of time separate each swing. There is no coach standing around to critique him, no device set up to measure the speed or accuracy of his swings. This is strictly a casual warm-up.

Why was Rory at such a (*forgive me, Travelers and the fine people of the Connecticut Valley, I mean no disrespect*) humdrum event the week after a major? Well, he had basically been hoisted by his own petard.

In 2023, the Travelers at TPC River Highlands was a "designated" tourney, one of the must-dos for the Tour's elite players. Thanks to the new regimen that Rory helped champion, the Travelers that year had a much bigger purse and a more prestigious field.

After a few minutes, Kira Dixon, a Golf Channel correspondent and the 2015 Miss America, walks up, sans crew, and greets Rory with what looks like a long-distance air hug. I am out of earshot, of course, but her friendly gesture seems to say, *I'm sorry about what happened in L.A.*

It looks like Rory gives her a wry smile and a shrug of the shoulders. *What are you gonna do? I shot nine-under.*

If Dixon asked for an interview, she didn't get one.

Rory resumes his warm-up. Now he's hitting what looks to be his five-wood off the deck, but only swinging sporadically. Harry stays planted. It is clear that neither of them is thrilled about being here. But they had a professional obligation to show up at the pro-am, smiles adorning their faces.

A couple of minutes later, a catharsis arrives in the form of Brad Faxon, the NBC/Golf Channel anchor-analyst. In one of those seeming conflicts of interest that ought to cause heartburn in the golf (and tennis) commentariat but doesn't, Faxon serves as McIlroy's putting coach and, I suspect, something of a surrogate older brother.

A genial Rhode Islander with a sardonic wit, "Fax" spent nearly three decades on the PGA Tour, winning eight times. As a player, he was the polar opposite of McIlroy, a guy with an unreliable swing but a wedge and putting game to die for. He's been trying for upwards of six years to transmit his putting magic to McIlroy, with mixed results.

Since Faxon started working with Rory in 2018, McIlroy's stroke *looks* better and appears more consistent, but the ball still doesn't drop in the cup as often as it needs to, especially on Sunday afternoons with big trophies on the line.

Six weeks after the Travelers, in early August 2023, Faxon got fed up with all the barbs directed at Rory's putting game, which had fallen from sixteenth on the Tour in 2022 (strokes gained on the green) to the middle of the pack. Brad issued a prickly broadside against McIlroy's naysayers.

"It bugs me to no end," Faxon said in an impassioned video that had to have been okayed by the Rory Land brain trust, "because when other instructors want to criticize Rory's stroke or Rory or potentially me, when they don't know anything about how a player thinks and what motivates them, what drives them. It's beyond reproach."

Beyond reproach? Man, that's feisty language. All those missed ten- and fifteen-footers on Saturday and Sunday at LACC (and later in the first three rounds at Royal Liverpool) must have touched a raw nerve.

Faxon's rant may have been well intentioned, but it didn't quiet any critics. All it did was spark renewed debate over McIlroy's fragile putting stroke and make his coaching team appear thin-skinned. It was another example of dubious public relations coming from the summit of Rory Land.

Fax, sporting a Red Sox cap, clearly had not seen the McIlroy gang since Rory had left LACC's property on Sunday night.

There are hugs all around. Diamond gets up from his chair to greet Faxon with a playful push. Whatever the New Englander says achieves the desired effect: peals of laughter start coming from the range. I still can't hear them, but Fax has them snickering. By then, O'Flaherty and his omnipresent cellphone are gone.

Rory's hitting session ends a few minutes later.

Diamond and Faxon stroll past the throng to the practice putting green, with Harry lugging the bag and Brad carrying a backpack. Rory stays behind for his first RMPIM of the day—or at least the first one that I witnessed.

Brandishing his own Sharpie, Rory begins at the far end of the fence line; he signs for every person—even the sketchier adults—who thrust paper or pennants or hats his way.

He isn't just scribbling illegible scrawl. Like his hero Arnold Palmer, who signed every autograph with care and precision, Rory tries to give each person a nice memento.

McIlroy's signature is composed of a myriad of big loops: the top half of the big "R," the bottom halves of the two "y's," and a bonus loop in the middle that could either be a "D" for "Daniel" (his middle name) or the distinctive way he denotes the unusual capital "eye"/small "l" combination in "McIlroy." As a student at St. Patrick's Primary and Sullivan Upper School, Rory had shown promise as an artist; he takes great pride in how he presents his autograph.

Handwriting experts contend that big loops indicate a person's willingness to listen to other people's ideas. Loops also mean that the writer is imaginative and emotional, someone not afraid to confront their own feelings.

Hmm. The listening-to-others stuff? That's a work in progress. But the emotion-and-feeling stuff? That's on the button.

Every second or third person along the fence line asks to take a selfie. Rory makes eye contact with all of them, smiling and making small talk as he patiently waits for the cellphone camera to get properly angled. He scrunches down to be at eye level with the kids. *Smile! Click!* He's on to the next person or gaggle.

With their pink dresses, it's easy to spot Gracie and Cammie. They're about two-thirds of the way down the line, huddled in front of their dad. When Rory reaches them, Rubén handles the autograph exchange, then asks Rory to take a picture with his girls. McIlroy ducks down and smiles, gently touching Cammie's shoulder with his right hand. *Click!*

The two girls break away from the line as if on pogo sticks. They jump up and down, squealing in delight.

"We met Rory! We met Rory!" Gracie yells in my direction. I clap my hands and yell back, "Yay!"

Cammie is probably too young to remember the moment, I suspect. But Gracie's heart just might tuck it away forever.

His full swing may be universally admired, but in mid-career, McIlroy's short game remains an enigma. He grew up learning to play on a quirky hillside track atop one of the windiest spots on the Emerald Isle. To get the ball close on Holywood Golf Club's sloping greens demands all manner of what Faldo calls "fiddly" shots: precise lobs and tight pitches into tiny windows, and crisp bump-and-runs that hug the turf and behave like putts.

How do you square that with the adult golfer who, every April, seems to squander one splendid drive after another at Augusta National's third hole, a short but treacherous par-four that requires a delicate second shot? In the final round of the windy 2024 Masters, McIlroy bashed a drive to within twenty yards of the third green. He chose a low bumper for his second shot, which was so poorly struck that it barreled past the pin, trundled through the green, and ended up five or six yards off its back edge. Rory had to make a tough left-to-right seven-footer to save par.

Sometimes, Rory pitches and chips at an elite level. But too often, his short game short-circuits, especially in the white-hot glare of a major. The great Lee Trevino once told Jaime Diaz that the key to winning the big ones is avoiding "soft" bogeys. When you miss a green, you've got to find a way to knock the next one close.

Diaz's theory as to why McIlroy has come up short in the majors since '14—and it's as compelling a take as any—is that Rory had so much success early in his career that he didn't see his short game as a relative weakness that needed to be tightened up. The quick hip and shoulder turn that makes his full swing so spectacular contributes toward a sometimes-wobbly wedge game.

The Gay Codicil to the Diaz Theorem is that by the time Rory recognized his wedge-and-putter shortfalls, certain bad habits, mainly mental but some mechanical, had crept into his game. He and a string of instructors that now includes the peerless Butch Harmon have had a hell of a time trying to fix them.

It takes Rory fifteen minutes or so to sign for everyone at the fence line, then he joins Harry and Brad on the practice green. Harry has inserted tees in a left-to-right semicircle around a downhill/sidehill cup, stepping off a four-footer, then a five-footer, and so on, around to eight feet.

It took Rory so long to get to the green that out of boredom Fax grabbed McIlroy's putter and gave the four-footer a go. One of the finest putters of his generation missed on the low side and winced as the ball scuttled away. Rather than risk a three-putt with fans watching (well, at least *one fan* watching, with his notepad and cellphone camera poised), Faxon picked up the ball and replaced it.

"Golf is half-fun," the late *Golf Digest* contributing editor Peter Dobereiner once quipped, "and half-putting." Ain't that the truth?

When Rory arrives, Fax immediately pulls a cellphone out of his pocket and shows Rory and Harry an amusing video. All three crack up.

Rory then begins the semicircle drill. The four-footer drops, but the five-footer spins out.

He has to start over again—that's the way this drill is set up. Rory has to make them all in succession. This time Rory buries the first two, but misses the six-footer on the high side.

I'm only a dozen yards or so away, but I can't quite hear what Faxon says to Rory after miss number two—whatever, it makes

McIlroy chuckle. The third time proves the charm. All five putts find the bottom. Rory hits a few long lags, then the gang departs for the 10th tee, some two hundred yards up a hill, past a couple of corporate pavilions and a big food tent.

A roped-off passageway allows the players to access the 10th tee from the practice area. There are two or three dozen people on each side of the walkway, braying for Rory to sign. So begins the second RMPIM of the afternoon.

Out comes the Sharpie and the looped signature and the posing and the smiling. This time it takes about ten minutes for Rory to work his way through the autograph-seekers.

The crowd around the tee box begins buzzing. It's amazing for a late-afternoon pro-am round, but the place is packed.

Rory pops onto the tee box and waves. The applause starts as a trickle, then everyone spots him; soon it becomes a flood. Many fans shout "*Rorr-ee!*" and rise out of their seats. They're giving McIlroy a big attaboy for coming so close at LACC. It's a sweet gesture; you can tell Rory is touched. In addition to the folks in the stands, about five hundred fans are lined up on each side of the fairway.

On the tee box are several officials, a couple of videographers and still photographers, plus the three amateurs who lucked out in the lottery. Most of the time, the pro-am folks who play with a superstar like McIlroy are celebs or heavy corporate hitters who fork over big bucks to the tournament's designated charity.

Not so for Bill Dahlin, Brad Silver, and Justin Pfeiffer. When they showed up on the eve of the tournament to register for the pro-am partner lottery, they were amazed to see Rory's name still available on the big board.

"Watch," Silver told his buddies. "We're going to win this thing and get to play with Rory!" Sure enough: they did.

All three are doing great professionally but they're not exactly seven-figure-a-year types who traveled to the tournament via corporate jet.

Bill is a vice president with energy efficiency provider Eemax, a manufacturer of sustainable water heaters. He works remotely in Saratoga Springs, New York, about a two-and-a-half-hour drive from Cromwell.

He brought along two of his chief customers, both of whom happen to be Texans: wholesale distributor Brad Silver from San Antonio and middle-man facilitator Justin Pfeiffer from Houston.

The threesome had played the first nine holes that afternoon with Chez Reavie, a former Arizona State Sun Devil who claimed the 2019 Travelers as one of his three career Tour victories. Reavie is a good guy and popular on Tour, but doesn't command a big following.

Virtually no one tagged along with them for the first nine, recalled Silver when we spoke the next week. So, imagine the spike in their combined blood pressures when Reavie left them on a deserted ninth green and they were ushered over to number 10 tee, with fans jammed everywhere.

"Yeah, we were plenty nervous," Silver conceded. It didn't help that they were waiting on the tee box, hyperventilating over their first swings, the whole time Rory was signing for the folks on the walkway.

Introductions are made, hands are shaken, and a couple of photographs and videos taken. Rory joins the efficient water-heating men in grinning ear-to-ear.

Then Rory grabs a fairway wood—a three-metal, I think—and pierces the ground with a tee, the ball resting a quarter-inch or so above the turf.

The 10th hole at TPC River Highlands is a medium-length, dogleg-left par-four, with pine, oak, and maple trees guarding the left side and bunkers and rough protecting the right. There is no need for Rory to launch one of his patented driver missiles. Something less will suffice.

The crowd goes quiet as Rory eyes his shot. At least a thousand people must have had something approximating this thought:

"Damn! I've got a ringside seat to watch one of the coolest things in sports—Rory McIlroy whacking a wood off a tee!"

Rory stands behind the ball, takes a half-swing to brush the grass, forces some air into his lungs, lets his shoulders relax, and moves forward to address the ball. As he always does just before beginning that incandescent swing, he waggles the clubhead slightly. Then his hands, his left knee, and the clubhead move back in unison, as they've done since he was a youngster. The club reaches parallel, his left hip and left shoulder fire, his hands drop to the inside as he begins his descending blow and.... *Thhhwwwaaack!!*

Wooooooo!! a thousand of us exhale.

Rory's shot soars down the right center of the fairway, draws slightly, and comes to rest a few steps shy of the last fairway bunker. Not bad for a pooped guy with a heavy heart.

Brad Silver must have drawn the short straw. He's the first of the three amateurs to tee up his ball. Their tee box is a good forty yards in front of where Rory has just swung. For a self-confessed 14-handicap whose knees must have been shaking, Silver handles the moment with aplomb. At least on the outside.

Standing off the right edge of the tee, I murmur a brief prayer: *Please, gods of golf, allow this man to get his ball airborne!*

Silver lunges a little but makes solid contact, sending the ball outside the left rough line with a bit of fade. Suddenly, my prayer needs updating.

Please, gods of golf, allow this man's tee ball to miss the trees! The gods, alas, remember their Calvinist roots, the bastards! About 150 yards away, the ghost of Jonathan Edwards makes Brad's ball bash into a branch. I hear someone yell "Shit!" then realize it's me.

Silver's ball plummets straight down into some thick grass. *Ooohhhh!* we all moan.

Now a little sheepish, Brad picks up his tee and glances back at Rory, fully expecting him to be looking away or chatting with Diamond or the VIPs. Instead, McIlroy looks Brad in the eye, smiles a sympathetic smile, holds his thumb and index finder an inch apart, and mouths, "You were *that* close to being perfect!"

In truth, Brad wasn't *that* close to being perfect. But Rory's encouragement lifted Silver's spirits and made him laugh a little, he said later.

Justin, a big-shouldered Houstonian with tree trunks for legs, goes next. He shows off a full backswing, with smooth hand action that Texan Jimmy Demeret, a three-time Masters champion, would have appreciated. His swing is punctuated by a macho-man follow-through. He crushes a draw to within shouting distance of Rory's ball, out around 250 yards or so. It is damned impressive.

He'll be reliving that shot as he drifts off to sleep every night for the rest of his life, I think. We give Justin a nice ovation.

Bill, batting cleanup, puts a soft cut 225 yards or so down the right-center of the fairway. For a guy who says he only plays "customer golf" a half-dozen times a year, he has sweet rhythm. He amazed himself, he told me afterward, by hitting that fairway-finder the whole backside.

Rory strolls into the middle of the threesome, joins them in stride, chuckles, and says, "Okay, guys, here we go!"

Off they went shoulder-to-shoulder down the fairway, with Brad admitting that he did everything but pinch himself to store the moment in his memory bank.

"Geez, these people must think we're big corporate hotshots to be playing with the likes of Rory," he was thinking. "If they only knew we're just water heater salesmen!"

Brad shared those thoughts with me a week later, his soft Texas drawl dissolving in laughter.

Truth be told, Rory didn't play all that well that evening. As the round wore on, moreover, the three energy-efficiency guys ran out of energy and were less than efficient with their short games.

But they hung in there, shooting three-under as a team after going six-under with Reavie on the front side. It was tough to get the club back and through with hundreds of people staring at them, Silver conceded.

At number 18, an uphill, straightaway par-four, Rory finally had a chance to haul out his driver. Brad, Bill, and Justin elbowed each other as McIlroy pulled off his dog-head cover and brushed a couple of practice swings.

Brad compared what happened next to the sound of a howitzer being fired.

Craaackkkkkkkk!! Out some 330 yards went a perfect draw that settled in the middle of the fairway. Rory proceeded to hit a lovely approach that struck—and stuck—hole-high, six feet right. He brought Harry in to help him read the slight right-to-lefter. In keeping with the theme of the week, he ended up missing; it grazed the cup on the high side and stayed out.

After the three of them finished on number 18, they shook hands with Rory and Harry and climbed the hill toward the clubhouse. I heard a Texas accent issue a one-word command: "Bourbon!"

They'd earned it. Sure, they finished well back in the pro-am, but nobody at TPC-River Highlands had more fun or picked up better stories.

"Rory could not have been a better guy," Silver told me. Brad and his buddies had not expected much interaction with the star but "he blew us away" with his friendly banter.

While walking down the fairway of number 14, an uphill par-four, three boys aged ten or so politely asked "Mister McIlroy" for his autograph.

"I'll sign up there," Rory told them, gesturing toward the green. The three youngsters, legs churning, all with sweatshirts wrapped around their waists, sprinted as fast as they could up the cart path. The scene caused everyone to chortle, Rory and his pro-am partners included.

I watched the three boys and their bouncing sweatshirts the whole way. With the sun going down, it made me feel young and old at the same time. The boys didn't stop racing until they reached the walkway between 14 green and 15 tee.

Sure enough, right after he holed out, Rory signed for them and several others. I couldn't quite make it out, but he said something funny to the three sprinters. The boys were ecstatic. Rory had made their summers.

McIlroy was thoroughly engaged the whole time, Brad said. He asked about their businesses, their families, and their hometowns. He also helped them read their putts.

At one point, Bill mentioned that he and his family had just gotten back from a vacation to Copenhagen and how crazy it was that in late spring it stayed light there until all hours. They compared notes on restaurants in the Danish capital, then Rory told stories about the fun times he'd had there as a young player, without mentioning a certain ex who happened to hail from Denmark.

The guys knew that asking questions about Rory's dejection at the US Open was out-of-bounds. So, the only time a reference to LACC came up, Silver recalled, is when Rory made a longish putt at number 11 and said, in a sarcastic *sotto voce*, "Well, I wish I would have putted like that last Sunday."

The truth is that McIlroy's Spider putter continued to sputter at River Highlands, at least early in Thursday's first round, when he missed a couple of birdie looks. But on the 214-yard, par-three eighth, he didn't need a putter. He did something he'd never done before on the US Tour: he made a hole-in-one!

His five-iron drew a couple of yards in the air, hit softly ten feet or so short of the flag, and rolled with unerring pace into the middle of the cup, barely touching the stick before falling. It matched the hole-in-one Rory made at the 2015 Abu Dhabi HSBC Golf Championship on the old European Tour.

His ace surely buoyed his morale. It also helped turn around his tournament. He ended up shooting 18-under, tied for seventh, five shots back of winner Keegan Bradley, New England's own.

All in all, after a gut-wrenching couple of weeks, it was pretty good stuff. His performance gave Gracie, Cammie, Tony, Joshua, Holly, Brad, Bill, Justin, and all the other new friends that Rory made in Connecticut something to cheer about.

Okay. So, are you saying that what makes Rory McIlroy Rory McIlroy is the kindness and forbearance he showed others at what was a rough moment for him?

Sure, that's part of it. But that still doesn't quite explain Rory and the Rory Land phenomenon in full. What makes his persona so fascinating, so unique, is that it was forged in a culture that, just a few years earlier, had been as bigoted and dystopian as any society on earth.

Golf's ageless Opie Taylor, his wondrous parents, and their ancestors—McIlroys, McDonalds, McLaughlins, McManuses, McKeowns, Maguires, Keegans, Lundys, Donnellys, the whole lot of them—come from a homeland as far removed from Mayberry as a place can be.

Chapter 3

THE MURALS OF BELFAST

Tucked in the bowels of South Belfast, just beyond the western bank of the River Lagan, sits a scruffy neighborhood long called "The Holylands." The name is hardly a testament to the piety of its denizens. This *is* Ireland, after all, so there are a lot more pubs in The Holylands than places of worship.

Instead, the name reflects the biblical motif that Holylands founder and financier Sir Robert McConnell, First Baronet[1]—a late nineteenth-, early twentieth-century Anglican church elder and business mogul—gave to his creation. McConnell labeled his streets after sacred places—Jerusalem, Palestine, Damascus—in the *real* Holy Lands, then slapped atop them hundreds of all-but-identical rowhouses.

Besides being a real estate developer and strident member of the Church of Ireland (the Church of England's poor relation), McConnell served a term as Belfast's appointed Lord Mayor at the bidding of his London benefactors.

He was an unrepentant Unionist: a loyal subject of Queen Victoria and her successors, Kings Edward VII and George V, and a staunch advocate of strengthening ties between Mother England and the Protestant ruling class in the North of Ireland.

Like most Belfast potentates back then, McConnell looked down his nose at the Papists who lived (mainly) in ghettos north

---

[1] If you Google "First Baronet," you'll learn that it ranks above all British knighthoods, except for the Order of the Garter and the Order of the Thistle. You'll also be reminded why America, Ireland, and a bunch of other countries fought revolutions to rid themselves of the British caste and peerage systems.

and west of The Holylands. He died in 1927, so he didn't live to see his brick offspring flip from middle-class Protestant to working-class Catholic after World War II.

As the decades rolled by, McConnell's rowhouses got more decrepit. The dormitories at nearby Queen's University Belfast (QUB), meanwhile, got more crowded. The inevitable happened: a lot of families moved out and a lot of students moved in.

Today, most Holylands residents are QUB undergrads, although there are a few immigrant families. The summer evening I visited, a three-generation Middle Eastern family was grilling on a sidewalk hibachi, listening to Arabic music. The kids were kicking around a small soccer ball.

Many of their QUB neighbors do what college kids have always done: blare music and throw parties. The students' rowdy conduct causes no small amount of friction with landlords, shopkeepers, and the local constabulary.

Sir Robert, First Baronet, is spinning in his grave.

The busiest east-west thoroughfare in The Holylands honors England's fifteenth-century victory over the French in a dustup near the Pas-de-Calais that hastened the end of the Hundred Years' War. Like much of Belfast, Agincourt Avenue and its neighboring streets are dotted with colorful drawings painted on the sides of Old Man McConnell's dwellings.

Outdoor murals are a big part of Northern Irish culture; Ulster residents have always taken great pride in street art. When the comedy *Derry Girls* (2019–2022) became a global television hit, the city of Derry gave creator Lisa McGee and her cast members the ultimate tribute: in the heart of town, it painted a mural of the five young actors, each wearing a goofy expression.

There are some two thousand open-air paintings throughout Northern Ireland, a third of which are located in Belfast, by far its biggest city. Some murals commemorate historic milestones or famed Ulster artists; others celebrate nature. Most are, more or less, areligious and apolitical.

But in Northwest Belfast, on either side of Falls Road and Shankill Road—the traditional boundaries between the Catholic and Protestant neighborhoods that too often have been at each other's throats—the murals are so sectarian, so political, their imagery and sloganeering so lurid and violent, that they leave visitors aghast.

Defiant screeds vowing vengeance scream at you. Hateful eyes glare at you through hideous masks. Rifle barrels take dead aim at your heart.

On the Protestant side, there are stark tributes to the guerillas of the Ulster Volunteer Force, the Ulster Defence Association, and other paramilitary groups that were (prayerfully, not "are") hell-bent on denying equality and power to minority Catholics.

On the Catholic side, there are memorials to the martyrs who fought (prayerfully, not "fight") for the militant provisional wing of the Irish Republican Army. The visage of Bobby Sands—the imprisoned Catholic hunger striker who sacrificed his life in 1981 to protest oppression and squalid prison conditions—gapes at you, his wan smile frozen in time.

"Our revenge will be the laughter of our children," Sands pledged just before he died, in a letter smuggled out of Long Kesh, the notorious lockup that held hundreds of alleged IRA fighters. Sands' elegy is splashed across his mural.

"There is a dark and venomous side to Northern Irish life," the late journalist and historian Donald S. Connery wrote in his book, *The Irish*. "[There are] few places in Christendom where the teachings of Christ have become so perverted."

The Irish Republic has its share of fanatics, Connery observed. But they pale in comparison to the "diseased minds" in what he called the "Neurotic North."

To be sure, much of the animosity between Catholics and Protestants has ebbed in the quarter century since the Good Friday Agreement brokered by American special envoy George Mitchell and the Clinton administration was approved by both sides. Still, threats and occasional violence flare up.

As you walk through Belfast's barricaded neighborhoods, it's hard, as writer Tom Coyne puts it, not to "feel sorry for the place, a bustling college town smeared by decades of bad press."

If only a little "good press" could make the hate go away. With their ugly "Peace Walls" made of brick, concrete, and iron, the Falls and Shankill corridors evoke, to this day, the desolation of 1960s East Berlin. On one of his first trips to Belfast, Coyne recalls seeing a sign in Shankhill warning passersby: "Anyone caught defacing Loyalist murals will be severely dealt with."

This anecdote illustrates the depth of distrust in the Northern Ireland of Rory McIlroy's childhood. On Senator Mitchell's first day as mediator, representatives from the British and Irish governments and ten different political parties were crammed into a large conference room.

"A loud voice shouted across the room to me," Mitchell remembered in remarks delivered at QUB to commemorate the Good Friday Agreement's twenty-fifth anniversary. "'Senator, if you are to be of any use to us there is one thing you must understand.'

"'What is that?' I asked.

"The speaker replied, with a smile on his face: 'We in Northern Ireland will drive one hundred miles out of our way to receive an insult.'

"I laughed, thinking it a joke, but as I looked around the room nobody else was laughing. Rather, they were nodding in agreement."

The fellow was trying to tell Mitchell that the whole place suffered from a persecution complex—and had for centuries. Studies suggest that a higher percentage of people suffer from post-traumatic stress in Northern Ireland than anyplace in the world that keeps track of societal disorders.

Senator Mitchell, now in his nineties, told me that he was never much of a golf fan until his son Andrew got him hooked. Now the two of them enjoy watching TV golf on weekend afternoons.

The Mitchells' favorite player, bar none, is Rory McIlroy. "Rory is a fine young man," the senator told me in June of 2023. "He is a symbol of hope and progress—of what Northern Ireland can be. I'm proud of him."

The Holylands are some two miles southeast of the Peace Walls. At the corner of Rugby and Damascus, a block removed from Agincourt, is a different kind of mural honoring a different kind of native son. Two stories tall and more than thirty feet wide, it depicts the young McIlroy at the "apogee" of his "full-flourish swing," as writer Charles Seibert put it in a 2015 *New York Times Magazine* profile.

In the mural, McIlroy's body is relaxed and on-balance—the key, the late swing maestro George Knudson always maintained, to consistent ball-striking. Rory's hands grasp a club that hangs around and behind his left side. His chin appears to rest on his right shoulder. His elbows have reconnected after taking a brief sojourn apart. His eyes, the bill of his cap, his right knee, and his oversized belt buckle (*What is with professional golfers and their big belt buckles?*) are all facing the target, in sublime harmony.

The painting serves as an unwitting testimonial to Ben Hogan and Herbert Warren Wind's *Five Lessons: The Modern Fundamentals of Golf*, which remains among the best instructional books ever written, seven decades after it first appeared.

Hogan was Knudson's idol. Knudson, in turn, was his fellow Canadian Lorne Rubenstein's golfing hero. Rubenstein admired Wind and wrote a book with Tiger Woods, Rory McIlroy's favorite. Together, they represent the game's unbroken chain, one of golf's most endearing qualities.

Commissioned by the city of Belfast, the McIlroy artwork went up in the spring of 2012. Rory had won the previous year's US Open at the tender age of twenty-two, the youngest US Open champion since Bobby Jones nine decades earlier.

The McIlroy mural reflects the profound change that Belfast has undergone in recent years. Much of the city's outdoor art went up amid the undeclared civil war between (largely Protestant) British Loyalists and (largely Catholic) Irish Republicans.

A Belfast artist and former IRA Provo named Danny Devenny painted the Sands mural in 1998. Fourteen years later, he did the Rory canvas. Since the Good Friday ceasefire, Devenny's art has conveyed a different tone. His confrontational themes have been replaced by conciliation; his threats of reprisals supplanted by prayers for peace.

In the arc of Danny Devenny's work, a visitor can see firsthand what Senator Mitchell calls "The Possible"—the North of Ireland's bumpy but beautiful quest to put The Troubles behind it.

Devenny's mural at Rugby and Damascus captures vintage Rory, the boy wonder with whom the golfing world fell in love.

His freckles have freckles. An unruly mop of brown hair spills out from under a ballcap bearing the name of a Persian Gulf resort that most Americans have never heard of. His cheeks and torso betray a bit of baby fat; at any instant, his polo threatens to come untucked. His too-big-by-a-bunch pant legs flap in the breeze.

He is, in sum, the antithesis of the svelte, buffed, nattily attired, super-conditioned athlete that he would become over the next few years.

Raw Belfast winters have not been kind to the McIlroy mural; it's become so tattered that it's barely recognizable anymore. Still, it's a reminder of how much Rory McIlroy has meant and continues to mean. McIlroy is "our wee golfer," the superhero who has managed to surmount labels, geographic and religious constraints, and—not to put too fine a point on it—bigotry.

Much of what he says and does still gets tossed into the cauldron of post-Troubles Ireland. It's that still-simmering pot that denied Shane Lowry the chance to hoist the Tricolor in New Orleans. It's why McIlroy has spent most of his career evading nettlesome questions about his religious and national identity.

Cruel and indiscriminate, that cauldron has seared his family's history.

Chapter 4

THE DEVIL'S TAIL

Rory McIlroy's paternal and maternal forebears—the McIlroys and McDonalds of the nineteenth and early twentieth centuries—were like most Catholic families in Ulster back then. They were "pulling the devil by the tail," Irish slang for barely scraping by.

Rory's ancestors tilled rocky soil; milked emaciated cows; sold wares in wooden carts that they hauled, sometimes by horse, sometimes by hand, down dirt roads and dirtier alleyways; weaved linen goods and woolen fabrics at home and in crude workhouses and factories; wound dangerous textile machines; stitched, scrubbed, polished, painted—anything to put food on their tables, which too often in Irish history was asking too much of life.

The potato famines that wracked mid-nineteenth-century Ireland, killing a million people and forcing two million more to flee, were less horrific up North than on the rest of the island, historians agree. Still, three counties in Ulster had fatality rates of 30 percent or higher during the famines.

Even the more prosperous northeastern villages suffered gruesome death tolls, notably Lurgan in County Armagh, the home of Rory's mum's family, the McDonalds. In 1847, the nadir of the first famine, Lurgan's workhouse for the poor absorbed one of the deadliest rates in all Ireland. Lurgan gravediggers were so overwhelmed that scores of corpses were interred in a single hole dug just beyond the workhouse well.

Were there McDonalds or McManuses or McKeowns or Headleys, the Armagh families that married into the McDonald clan, dumped into that mass grave? Almost certainly.

Many who survived the famines never fully recovered from the deadly effects of malnutrition. A photograph taken late in life of my maternal great-great grandfather Thomas Harrington, born in the 1830s in southwest Ireland's County Cork, shows a gaunt, gnarled man, bones protruding through sallow skin. The image was recorded some three decades *after* the second famine.

Seven-generations-deep research into the McIlroy and McDonald families conducted by Dr. Jennifer Martin, an Ulster University-trained genealogist, reveals a disquieting pattern of disease and early death—typical, she says, of the Northern Irish of that period.

Church birth certificates, marriage licenses, bereavement records, and sporadic census data tell tales of crowded and hungry households, of children dying young, of adults almost never leaving their ancestral neighborhoods, of families, year after year, trying to keep their heads above water—and not always succeeding.

Like so many families up North, the McDonalds and the McIlroys can trace their roots to Scotland. Exactly when they emigrated or why they chose to settle where they did is almost impossible to ascertain.

"McIlroy" in Gaelic, the ancient tongue (in various forms) of both Ireland and Scotland, is roughly translated as "the son of the red-haired youth." Originally "Ruadh" in Gaelic, "Rory" evokes the same color; it means "red king."

The red-headed clan hailed, genealogists believe, from Ballantrae in Ayrshire, along the Firth of Clyde on Scotland's western coast, the place where tens of thousands of US troops disembarked during World War II.

Did Rory's ancestors uproot themselves during the Norman invasions of the eleventh and twelfth centuries? Possibly—a lot of Scottish families did—but the more likely scenario is that Oliver Cromwell's scorched-earth rampage a half-millennium later forced the McIlroys and many other Catholic families to find passage across the Irish Sea. Sadly, there was no escaping the Puritan madman. Eventually, Cromwell's troops invaded Éire, destroying almost everything in their path.

"McIlroy" first surfaced in Ulster's County Fermanagh, where a hamlet called Ballymackilroy came into being on the east side of Lough Erne, most likely named in honor of a local strongman. Soon enough, there were villages in County Tyrone and County Antrim that bore similar names, which suggests that the McIlroys, the Mackilroys, the MacElroys, the McElroys, and other branches of the clan were moving throughout the North.

For their part, the McDonalds descended from one of Scotland's most feared and fearsome tribes. In the fourteenth century, the McDonalds' military alliance with the great Scottish monarch Robert the Bruce paid dividends: they got a big royal land grant, which produced enough lucre to underwrite explorations of the mysterious and lightly inhabited island to their south and west.

They were fierce warriors in their adopted homeland, too. For generations, the McDonalds were in great demand as mercenary fighters to resolve tribal and land disputes. Indeed, for many years the province's most powerful tribe, the O'Neill clan, deployed the McDonalds as something of a private militia.

At some point, Rosie's branch of the family settled in the Lurgan-Portadown area. Most likely, their move coincided with the mid-eighteenth-century boom in the wool and linen industry.

By 1740, English merchants had begun requesting products made of Irish wool; there was a pell-mell rush to meet the demand. Suddenly, a nascent industry took root all over the island, but especially in villages, like Lurgan, that were close to established shipping ports. As the appetite for Irish goods escalated, primitive mills, factories, and workhouses sprung up all over the North.

The pay was miserable and working conditions abominable, but thousands of families like the McDonalds became as dependent on textiles as Ireland's diet was on the potato crop. When both began to fail, it triggered a catastrophe from which the island is still recovering.

Anyone attempting to understand Northern Ireland in all its sorrow and beauty would do well to study the life of James Christopher McIlroy, Rory's paternal grandfather. Jimmy was a gritty little man who somehow managed to surmount the hurdles that life threw at him. Sadly, he didn't live long enough to see his grandson excel at the game he loved.

Jimmy was born a decade after the Protestant majority in his native Ulster rejected the prospect of joining the Irish Free State (now known as the Republic) following Ireland's war of independence from Great Britain and the internecine power struggle that followed.

Record-keeping was so slapdash that it's not easy to pin down Jimmy's birthdate; one document says 1931, others point to either October or (more likely) November of 1932. Whenever the actual birth, his childhood coincided with the worst of the Great Depression, which hit the North of Ireland as hard as it hit anyplace in the world.

He was the first child of James Joseph McIlroy, who was born in West Belfast in 1906. James toiled as a "Laborer" some years and as a "Motor Driver" in others. James' wife, Kathleen McLaughlin McIlroy, was born in 1910. Like so many in greater Belfast, Kathleen listed her occupation as a "Stitcher" in the linen industry.

They lived on New Bond Street in West Belfast, near the Market District, then a Catholic redoubt. The McLaughlin home where Kathleen grew up was just six doors removed from the crowded rowhouse where she ended up raising her own children.

Google "New Bond Street, Belfast" and what pops is a picture of a fraying wall mural with "Up the [IRA] Provos" splashed across the top. In recent decades, the Market District has been gentrified and, to a significant degree, integrated.

In the nineteenth and early twentieth centuries, however, it was a place where livestock roamed willy-nilly and dead animal carcasses were tossed into an open pit—not only creating a hideous stench, notes Belfast historian Francis Higgins, but posing a health menace. The River Lagan, which forms the eastern boundary of the Market District, also had all manner of industrial, human, and animal waste dumped into it.

Pre-WWII Belfast had no shortage of rough Catholic neighborhoods, but the one in which young Jimmy grew up was among the roughest. He was nine or ten when Nazi Germany bombed a virtually defenseless Belfast in four separate raids during the spring of 1941. By late April, about half of Belfast's population had sought refuge in villages outside the city, including Holywood and other towns along the lough.

James, Kathleen, Jimmy, and a boy named Joseph, born in 1940 or 1942 (again, records differ), survived WWII, although it must have wreaked havoc with Jimmy's schooling. Was the family forced to evacuate? We don't know: that sort of document-keeping was hit or miss in Belfast's war years. Gerry McIlroy and his siblings, moreover, have chosen to stay mum about their family's volatile past.

At some point after the war, Jimmy beat the odds stacked against Catholics and got a job with the Belfast Harbour Commission, painting and repairing the shipyard cranes that dominated North Belfast's skyline. Even today, with a skeletal labor force and only a fraction of the structures still standing, the cranes give off an eerie vibe: they look like sci-fi creatures on the lam. Irish sportswriter Brian Keogh has likened them to gargantuan "sentinels" guarding the city. No matter the metaphor, they're relics from an era that will never return.

In Jimmy McIlroy's day, however, there were a lot more cranes and thousands of workers buzzing around them. Two generations earlier, the shipyards were even more crowded as men labored on the RMS *Titanic* and its two White Star Line sister ships, the RMS *Olympic* and the RMS *Britannic*.

It is Belfast's lot in life, BBC-Northern Ireland producer Chris Thornton told me with a wry smile, to be forever defined by a disaster.[1] Founded in 1861, *Titanic*-class builder Harland & Wolff had an outsized presence at the yards; for many decades, it was far and away Belfast's biggest employer. It also had a long-standing aversion to hiring Catholics. At a time when Catholics represented nearly half of Belfast's population, they made up only a tiny portion of H&W's post-WWI workforce.

The shipyards, by the early 1920s, had become a microcosm of the hostilities happening across Ireland, argues Kevin Johnston, the author of *In the Shadow of Giants: A Social History of the Belfast Shipyards*. Amid the South's struggle to break away from England, many Protestant dock workers suddenly "identified with a Protestant state for a Protestant people," Johnston writes.

As the years went by, sectarian violence continued to mar Belfast's waterfront. Catholic workers came to believe, with good reason, that militant Loyalists were working in concert with the management of H&W to keep them away from the docks. Even amid the Allies' frenetic buildup in the early days of WWII, when the company produced hundreds of ships for the Royal Navy, H&W refused to hire Catholics.

When Jimmy got his post-WWII job with the Harbour Commission, the share of Catholics working at the yards had gotten somewhat higher but was still meager. Jimmy was told in no uncertain terms to keep his head down and his mouth shut, says historian Higgins.

"Painting" sounds innocuous enough, but in truth it was precarious work—and it's not like HBC was forced to comply with exacting health and safety inspections. Jimmy was transported to the top of the cranes via a gangway platform or a crude open-air lift whose flimsy "walls" barely reached his knees; he and his coworkers were almost never strapped into safety restraints. They went up in

---

1   In our interview, Chris also shared this piquant saying, which, more than a century after the infamous iceberg, is still popular in Belfast: "It took a thousand Irishmen to get the *Titanic* afloat and one Englishman to sink her."

all kinds of weather, juggling paint cans, chippers, and brushes of various shapes and sizes while being heaved upwards.

Back then, Higgins notes, the paint Jimmy and his mates were scraping and applying was heavily lead-based, highly toxic to the cardiovascular system. If a shipyard painter was fortunate to survive being hauled up and down over the years, there was still a scary chance that he would contract a deadly lung or heart disease.

Many Catholic shipyard workers lived in fear of being attacked on the job; Protestant assailants were rarely prosecuted.

What would Jimmy McIlroy's experience at the yards have been like in the 1950s, '60s, '70s, and '80s? "All Catholics working on Queen's Island [the spit of land on which the Belfast shipyards were located] would have had it tough," avers Higgins, who wrote a memoir called *Tall Tales & Short Stories: The Men of the Belfast Shipyard*.

"Catholics would have been the butt of jokes and snide remarks," Higgins told me. "They would also have observed the annual unofficial Orange Order parade around the east side of the Island which was still going in the 1980s."

The procession was part of the Ulster Protestant community's yearly—and, too often, incendiary—July 12 celebration of King William of Orange's victory over Catholic forces. It "was to let 'Taigs'[2] or 'Fenians' know that the Island belonged to the Protestants. Catholics were only permitted to work there if they kept their heads down and said nothing," Higgins wrote.

How many times did Jimmy witness members of the Orange Order and other Loyalist groups marching around the yard in garish outfits, banging drums, screeching flutes, blathering about their beloved "King Billy," and vowing death to the Pope and Irish

---

2   "Taig" is one of the many derogatory slurs used by Loyalist Protestants against Catholics. It's derived from the Gaelic term for the male name Tadhg. "Fenians" in early Ireland fiercely defended the island against invaders. The term has come to be associated with Irish Republicanism and Irish Catholic causes.

Republicanism? We don't know, but it probably numbers north of three dozen.

The harassment against Catholics on the docks was reignited by The Troubles in the late 1960s. In his *A Labour History of Ireland, 1824–2007*, Professor Emmet O'Connor of Ulster University Derry writes that the "official" H&W stance during The Troubles was that sectarianism stopped at their entrance gate.

"Reality was more chequered," O'Connor asserts. "Groups of Catholics were evicted from the shipyard on four occasions between 1970–1972, reducing their numbers from 400 to 100 in the 10,000-strong workforce."

It's hard to imagine that the Harbour Commission labor force in that era was impervious to the bloodletting going on next door at H&W. In at least one instance, perhaps others, armed Loyalist thugs forced Catholic workers to swim for their lives. At roughly the same time, Catholic laborers were also run out of Belfast textile factories, O'Connor reveals.

If Jimmy McIlroy didn't personally experience these pogroms, he witnessed them from an uncomfortably close distance, no doubt sharing some of the details with his wife. In his mid-twenties, he had married Eva McIlroy, née McIlroy, of Carryduff, a County Down village a few miles south of Belfast. Eva's father was Patrick McIlroy, originally of Whitehouse, County Antrim. Eva's mother was Ellen Johnstone McIlroy of Belfast.

Were Patrick and James related, which meant that Eva was a cousin of Jimmy's? We don't know, but it's a distinct possibility, says genealogist Martin. Was the marriage arranged, as many were back then? Again, that's certainly plausible. Eva was twenty-seven when she gave birth for the first time—practically an old maid by Irish standards back then.

Five children came along in rapid succession, beginning with James Gerard (Gerry) in 1959, followed by Brian, Colm, and Rosaleen. Sadly, another child of Eva and Jimmy's did not survive infancy.

By the time little Gerry was born, the McIlroys had somehow saved enough to move from New Bond Street out to Holywood. It was only a few miles northeast, but it was as if Eva and Jimmy had transplanted themselves to another planet. Gone were the awful stench and the hemmed-in claustrophobia of a rowhouse ghetto.

They were now living in a comfortable home in a wooded area within walking distance of a village. For the first time in their lives, they had a decent kitchen, room to stretch, a front- and backyard, and—most remarkable of all—Protestant neighbors. It was an integrated area in a Protestant-majority community; religious tension was more muted in Holywood and would stay that way a decade later when The Troubles intensified.

To be sure, the town was, at its core, Unionist and Loyalist. But by the early '60s, most of its residents had adopted a live-and-let-live attitude.

Less than a quarter mile up the hill, away from town, was another integrated place that would come to fascinate Jimmy McIlroy: the terraced fairways of Holywood Golf Club. HGC's membership was back then and is today a mix of wealthy and middle-class folks. Jimmy, by all accounts, developed a kick-ass short game.

In the main, HGC golfers will proudly tell you, they check their religion in the parking lot. Spiritual convictions still matter, of course, but they can be set aside, especially if certain golfers help them beat those effete snobs from the Royal Belfast Club.

Holywood and its welcoming golf course were anomalies. For much of Northern Ireland, the sectarian fires that were reignited in the late 1960s blazed out of control.

Chapter 5

A LOST LIFE

It was bitter that early Tuesday morning in Belfast, so cold that with each jangled breath, the two assassins must have spewed mist through the mouth holes of their *balaclavas*. Tiny slits allowed them to squint through the dank November light. They were cloaked in black from head to toe, including rubber-soled shoes that helped deaden the sound of their movements.

The hitmen needed disguises; without them, their identities might have been blown as they skulked toward the getaway car. Both were highly trained Protestant paramilitary guerillas; police and intelligence accounts vary, but they were either members of the Ulster Volunteer Force's East Belfast Battery or the Ulster Defence Association's notorious Baker-McCreery Gang. The UVF's rallying cry was: "For God and Ulster." UDA's motto was *Quis Separabit?*—Latin for "Who will separate us?" Although united in their hatred of Catholics, the groups were rivals; each claimed responsibility for a chilling number of murders and robberies.

The two triggermen were crouched in a backyard garden along Sandhill Drive, fingering their weapons as they peered through frosted-over windows. They were on familiar turf: East Belfast's Orangefield neighborhood had long been a Protestant stronghold, a mix of parks, playgrounds, brick rowhouses, and prim duplex cottages, like the one they were now stalking.

Orangefield and its boys' secondary school were known to rhythm-and-blues fans as the places that nurtured the great singer-songwriter Van Morrison. Van the Man's boyhood home, 125 Hyndford Street, was just a quarter mile west of Sandhill Drive.

But Hyndford's cramped rowhomes couldn't compare to the cozy dwellings that had sprung up a few blocks away.

The upscale development was only four years old at that point, a year younger than "Brown-Eyed Girl," the breakthrough hit that had made Morrison a star. Van's Protestant old man was, for many years, a carpenter on the Belfast docks—the same place that Jimmy McIlroy and thousands of other Northern Irishmen were working at the time.

Sandhill Drive's houses were a source of considerable pride in East Belfast, symbols of the shared prosperity to come if Prods would only stick together to combat the Fenian threat. The UVF and its ilk swore that affluent Protestant neighborhoods like Sandhill Drive would never be soiled by Catholics.

The song "Orangefield," from Morrison's 1989 album *Avalon Sunset*, is a tender homage to his old neighborhood. It recalls "a golden autumn day" from his childhood.

Orangefield's early morning hours of Tuesday, November 21, 1972, may have been autumnal, but they were anything but golden. That year, The Troubles degenerated into pandemonium. By early fall, some five hundred people in Northern Ireland had been killed and nearly five thousand—the bulk of them innocent civilians—had been wounded, their lives forever shattered. In the bleak assessment of Northern Irish golf commentator David Feherty, who turned fourteen that summer, "Life was not normal."

Nothing and no one in those days went unscathed. Up North, merely flying the Republic's Tricolor could get people tossed into prison. Even something as anodyne as "Orangefield" had inflammatory connotations.

Protestants believed that King William III, William of Orange, conducted a troop review on the flatlands east of the River Lagan in the year 1690 while preparing for what became the Battle of the Boyne. "King Billy" then marched his legions south to Drogheda and routed the forces of the Papist King James II, keeping the British crown Protestant—and making the color orange emblematic of Protestant rule. It still is.

There was next-to-no evidence documenting the claim that Orangefield was, in fact, hallowed territory, but that did not dissuade hard-core believers. Nor did the reality that nearly three centuries had elapsed since James' sad-sack "army" had been drubbed along the River Boyne. In Northern Ireland, tribal triumphs endure forever, while old grievances die hard. As Patrick Radden Keefe put it in his epic *Say Nothing: A True Story of Murder and Memory in Northern Ireland*: "People had a tendency to talk about bygone calamities as though they had happened just last week."

By late '72, three Protestant militia cells were ambushing Catholics in their homes and workplaces: the UVF, the UDA, and some ruffians who branded themselves the Tartan Gangs. The IRA's Provos and other Republican paramilitary groups were equally bloodthirsty. No one was safe.

It was in this apocalyptic world on a chilly November morning that the two Protestant militia commandos slipped into the Sandhill Drive backyard of a Catholic father of four named Joseph McIlroy. He was the son and namesake of sixty-six-year-old James Joseph McIlroy, the younger brother of forty-one-year-old Jimmy, and the uncle of thirteen-year-old Gerry.

Given the shared Christianity of attacker and victim, the McIlroys' New Testament names—Joseph and Mary—made the crime somehow more horrific. Joseph McIlroy's temerity in moving his family into a Protestant neighborhood put him on the assassination list. But it was, likely, his success as a self-taught, thirty-year-old computer technician for British-based International Computers Limited (ICL)—a pioneering technology hardware manufacturer—that moved him to the top.

Loyalist militiamen despised Catholics who had achieved professional rewards, believing that they had come at Protestant expense. Joseph had gotten up early that morning to work on a broken washing machine; the McIlroys' first-floor laundry room stood next to their kitchen in the back of the house. Mary had just joined him downstairs, most likely turning on more lights. Upstairs, still sleeping, were their daughters: Kathy, nine; Maria, six; Geraldine, four; and Helen, two. The gunmen no doubt saw stirrings inside the house, despite the frost on the back windows. They may have waited until Mary left the kitchen before pouncing. The Police Service of Northern Ireland (PSNI) later determined that at least five or six rounds were fired, including a near pointblank fusillade delivered through the window closest to the laundry.

Lost Lives, the massive book that details the agony on both sides during The Troubles, says that Mary began shrieking as she heard the gun blasts, then watched in horror as her husband came stumbling into the living room, profusely bleeding. She tried to break his fall as he collapsed onto a sofa. Blood gushed over her hands and face. She ran out the front door and onto the street, screaming for help.

"I'll never forget it as long as I live," a neighbor was quoted in *Lost Lives*. "Mrs. McIlroy ran out of the house and stood on the step shouting.... By this time, the gunmen had disappeared."

Joseph McIlroy was pronounced dead at the hospital. He was the seventy-fourth victim of wanton assassination in Northern Ireland that year—a staggering number in a place with fewer than two million inhabitants. His murder was never solved by Northern Ireland's police services, which conducted a half-assed investigation, as they did for most violent crimes back then when the victims were Catholic.

Gerry and his siblings were old enough to remember, in grisly detail, their uncle's murder and funeral. Fearing retribution, family members—including Gerry's first cousins, Joseph and Mary's daughters—were taught never to discuss the assassination or the shameful probe that followed. In the tortured culture of 1970s

Northern Ireland, saying nothing was preferable to saying something—and suffering the consequences.

It was an admonition Gerry surely shared with his wife and their only child.

As 1998's Good Friday peace accords were being embraced throughout the North, young Rory would come into the public eye as a nine-year-old sensation who had just won a boys' "world" championship. In the afterglow of Rory's victory, *The Kelly Show*, a popular Belfast television program hosted by broadcaster Gerry Kelly, invited the youngster to show off his golfing skills.

Rory's trick in front of an adoring studio audience was recreating something that he enjoyed doing at home to amuse his mum and dad: chipping golf balls into the open door of a front-loading washing machine. It took Rory a few whacks in the studio, but soon he was zinging balls into the washer. Kelly and the crowd, which included his parents (Gerry was skipping a big tourney of his own that day), loved it.

Young Rory had no way of knowing, but he was hitting balls into the same sort of appliance his great-uncle was repairing on the morning he was murdered twenty-six years before.

Joseph McIlroy never got to see his daughters grow up. There's no telling how far he might have gone at ICL. He was in on the ground floor of a tech company poised to help revolutionize the global economy. ICL would end up as the fulcrum in several big corporate transactions in the years to come. If he'd gotten an equity stake, Joseph—not his great-nephew—might have been the first McIlroy multi-millionaire.

Four decades after Joseph was assassinated, the PSNI announced that it was reopening unsolved crimes from The Troubles' era. If

McIlroy family members learned anything new, they chose not to share it. For more than a half-century, they've maintained what can only be called a dignified silence. In May 2023, the *Irish Times* gained access to intelligence files that supposedly pointed to members of the UDA's Baker-McCreery Gang as the culprits—but the family refused to comment on the *Times*' story.

Michael Maguire, a former PSNI ombudsman who now serves as an honorary professor at the George Mitchell Institute at QUB, has spent years trying to help families cope with the harsh limitations of Northern Ireland's judicial system. He has developed a philosophical framework defined at one end by "Justice" and at the other by "Truth."

If a family is seeking "Justice"—if they're determined to see their loved one's killers arrested, tried, and convicted—they'll be devastated all over again, Maguire says. "Justice" in that sense will not happen.

But, says Maguire, if a family can settle for a semblance of the "Truth," maybe that will help them deal with their grief. "Truth" in this context doesn't necessarily mean finding out the identity of the assailants. It means understanding the circumstances surrounding the crime, accepting the fact that it was likely carried out by a certain paramilitary or military unit, and recognizing the intransigence of the British government. Whitehall does not want ex-soldiers arrested or prosecuted, no matter how reckless their actions might have been.

Nevertheless, Professor Maguire remains optimistic that bloody sectarianism is in Northern Ireland's past. "While there are those who remain committed to violence, and continue to be a threat, on the Republican and Loyalist side, they are on the margins. Neither group has the resources, skills, financial or community support required to return to a large-scale conflict," he told me.

But he also issues a warning: "Political instability may undermine [the desire for peace]. The capacity for Northern Ireland to shoot itself in both feet should not be underestimated. Longer term, a united Ireland is more likely now as a result of Brexit [deeply opposed in Ulster] and a dysfunctional Stormont [the now-largely dormant Northern Irish legislature] than it has ever been."

Chris Thornton, the American expat who along with a half-dozen other journalists spent seven long years writing *Lost Lives*, also believes that The Troubles have run their course. Reconciliation with the Republic is still years away, he argues, but there will come an economic and cultural "tipping point" that will finally bring the North and South together.

Lost Lives is 1,600 pages long, eight times the size of Irish writer James Joyce's 1916 classic, *A Portrait of the Artist as a Young Man*. "When the soul of a man is born in this country," Joyce wrote in *Portrait*, "there are nets flung at it to hold it back from flight."

Those nets are less lethal now. But they're still there. So are the Peace Walls and the murals and thousands of gravestones like the one that belongs to Joseph McIlroy.

When I visited Redburn Cemetery, I brought a bouquet to place on Joseph's grave. To my delight, a vase with flowers was already there.

Chapter 6

HOLYWOOD'S MAYPOLE

The towering white maypole that sits at High Street and Shore Road, the heart of Rory McIlroy's hometown, has been there in one form or another since the 1700s. Folklore has it that the pole was the legacy of a Dutch ship that ran aground in Belfast Lough, stranding its captain and crew for weeks while the vessel underwent repairs.

To thank villagers for housing and feeding them, crew members erected a maypole so that, each spring, the townspeople could celebrate renewed hopes for fertility, which—*wink-wink*—is what May Day was about way back when. Over the centuries, the landmark became a totemic presence along the lough's southern shore, a symbol of Holywood's prosperity.

It also became a token of civic pride. Hewing to a grand Roman-British tradition, Holywood hosts annual May Day festivities. The centerpiece of the celebration is the race around the maypole. Little girls show off their yellow summer dresses, clutching ribbons wrapped 'round the pole.

There's also a Bonny Baby competition, the crowning of the May Day Queen, and a fancy-attire contest. The 2023 fancy-dress contestants were encouraged to don outfits that commemorated the coronation of King Charles III earlier that year.

Over the centuries, the town has been forced to replace or repair the maypole any number of times, thanks to natural decay and storm damage. But the biggest threat to the pole came in October 1995. A lorry driver, blinded by autumnal sunlight, barreled into its base, smashing it to the ground.

RORY LAND

Public funds from the Ards and North Down Borough Council were used to rebuild the pole, as they were again in 2021, when wind gusts caused a chunk of it to splinter.

The latest iteration[1] now reaches some sixty feet into the air. About a third of the way up, a perpendicular bar evokes the look of a sailing mast; a series of little wooden sailboats are perched atop the bar. A Union Jack, the national flag of the United Kingdom, hangs from the top.

When combined with the other Union Jack and God Save the King[2] flags that flutter from front porches and lampposts, the plethora of Protestant churches, the prim shops and storefronts, the historic architecture that has earned conservation protection for many of its buildings, the parks and flower beds, and the well-endowed church school that sits atop a gorgeous greensward, the maypole gives Holywood the feel of a proper English village.

Therein lies the problem. Holywood isn't in England. It's in Ireland.

That vaunted maypole steeped in British folkways? It's the only permanent one on the entire isle of Éire, North or South.

That Anglican school straight out of *Goodbye, Mr. Chips*? It's Sullivan Upper, Rory McIlroy's alma mater that's run by the (very) Protestant Church of Ireland.

A dozen steps removed from Sullivan Upper's gated campus, astride a side street called Abbey Ring, sits a flower bed at the base of a combination lamppost/flagpole. A visitor can tell at a glance that great care has gone into the grooming of the little garden and the stonework that encircles it. Even in the middle of summer, the flowers looked fresh.

It's all meant to spotlight the banner at the top, a flag commemorating the fiftieth anniversary of the founding of a local Loyalist

---

1 The Maypole Bar, the pub next to the landmark, is known to locals as "Ned's." I write this with reverence: with the lone exception of the St. James Gate Brewery in Dublin, Ned's serves the finest Guinness this Irish-American has ever tasted. And trust me: I've tasted a lot of Guinness! Having a couple of pints at Ned's is a must-do if you're ever in Holywood.

2 God Save *this* King?

"brigade." Not "unit." Not "group." But "brigade," with its chilling martial connotations.

On the opposite side of Belfast Road, down a small hill toward Kerr Park, is the Holywood Rugby Club, where Gerry McIlroy worked as a custodian and bartender for much of Rory's childhood. Besides a restaurant-bar and locker facilities, the place boasts a set of bleachers around its main paddock and a couple of nicely maintained practice pitches. The day I was there, which happened to coincide with the "Twelfth," the traditional July 12 Protestant Marching Day, a Union Jack flew from a lamppost near the top of the road curving down to the club.

Are you beginning to get why Rory McIlroy has had to walk such a cultural and political tightrope? I stayed in Holywood for a week and didn't see a single Tricolor.

But I saw hundreds of Union Jacks, and God Save the King symbols, and the faux flag of Northern Ireland, the Ulster (Six Counties) Banner, a variation of England's Cross of St. George flag. The Ulster Banner has no official status but has become the graphic shorthand for identifying someone from Northern Ireland. In keeping with the province's violent past, it has a blood-red hand stuck into the cross's middle. The red hand, in Gaelic culture, honors great warriors; it's an emblem that came to be associated with the omnipotent O'Neill tribe.

Today, if you get off the Northern Ireland Railways' Green Line at the Holywood stop and begin walking up the hill toward the maypole, three sights grab your attention.

The first is in the plaza next to the rail line: the town's Great War Memorial. It depicts a Tommy infantryman in action, Enfield rifle at the ready, although it looked in the summer of 2023 as if vandals had filched the marble bayonet.

Its inscription reads, "In Grateful Memory of the Men of Holywood and District Who Gave Their Lives in The Great War,

1914–1918." The names of many of the 108 local soldiers who made the ultimate sacrifice are listed.

If Private Daniel McDonald, Rory McIlroy's maternal great-great grandfather, had grown up closer to Holywood, his name would be enshrined there, too. But his home was in Lurgan, a County Armagh community thirty miles west.

Daniel McDonald was twenty-eight years old when he was killed on Valentine's Day 1915, at what soon would become the Second Ypres battlefield in Belgium. He was a member of the Second Battalion of the Royal Irish Fusiliers.

Was he picked off by a sniper or a machine gunner? Or killed on a reconnaissance probe? Or hit by friendly fire or somehow caught in the wrong place at the wrong time?

We don't know, and it's not likely we'll ever find out. We know he didn't die from chemical contamination, because the Germans didn't begin deploying asphyxiating gas on the Western front until later that spring. Private McDonald's remains are interred at the Menin Gate Memorial at Ypres, in panel number 42.

More than fifty thousand Allied soldiers perished while attempting to break out of the Ypres salient, a patch of land just twenty-four kilometers square. The Allies didn't gain full control of the salient until the summer of 1917, thirty months after Daniel died.

Back home, Daniel had been a factory "Weaver," which meant he had run and fed textile machines, almost certainly in grimy conditions. He and his wife, the former Isabella McManus, had been married in February 1905 at Lurgan's St. Peter's Catholic Church. He was eighteen; she was twenty-one. On their marriage certificate, Isabella listed her occupation as a "Winder," which meant she wound and rewound, by hand, some of the textile machines that her husband and fellow weavers operated.

On their wedding record, Daniel was forced to make his mark in lieu of a signature; like many Ulstermen and -women of that era, he could neither read nor write. But six years later, at least as recorded in the 1911 Census of Ireland, Daniel indicated that he was now literate, which suggests that in his late teens and early twenties he'd taken laudable initiative, almost certainly with Isabella's help.

Irishmen were not subject to conscription during the Great War, so why did Daniel serve? Did he sign up out of a sense of duty? Or did the pay of a British soldier look enticing to a subsistence worker who had to care for a growing family?

Did he think the war would be over in a few months and he'd be back home? A lot of young Europeans on both sides in late 1914 bought into the shameful propaganda pushed by their governments.

Daniel wasn't the only martyr from County Armagh, of course. Nearly four hundred soldiers from Lurgan alone died in the War to End All Wars. After the November 1918 Armistice, hundreds of other Armagh men returned home maimed and broken, suffering from disabling wounds, or shell shock, or poisoned lungs, or all three. Many succumbed within months.

In many Ulster communities, Catholic WWI veterans were treated with contempt, reveals historian Higgins, now a tour guide at the Belfast shipyards. The little assistance that was available went to returning Protestant soldiers and sailors; Catholic veterans were often left begging.

Moreover, as Higgins notes, many Irish Catholics regarded their brethren who'd fought in the Great War as turncoats who had prostituted themselves for the British Empire—which, at that moment, included Ireland in its entirety.

For Isabella, the prospect of raising children alone must have been petrifying. Two years after her husband's death, she married a Lurgan man named Henry Doran and proceeded to have more children.

Ireland would not achieve its independence from Great Britain until 1921 and would not get beyond its own calamitous civil war until two years later. Six of Ulster's nine counties ended up refusing to join the new Irish Free State. The North's Protestant majority in those six counties insisted on staying directly tethered to the

United Kingdom. More than a century later, that unruly geopolitical stepchild called "Northern Ireland" still is.

It's doubtful that Daniel McDonald ever fingered a golf club or gave the gentlemen's game a second thought. For the Lurgan McDonalds of the early 1900s, there would have been no time or money for that sort of nonsense.

Ninety-nine years after Daniel died on a Belgian battlefield, his namesake would win Europe's most prestigious tournament. In doing so, Rory Daniel McIlroy would earn more money in one afternoon than his great-great grandfather ever dreamed of in his tragically short life.

Daniel left behind Isabella and sons James, Patrick, and Daniel, who was born in 1911. Young Daniel turned out to father another young Daniel.

It was Daniel number three who was the father of Rosie McDonald McIlroy, Rory's mum. The choice of a middle name for her only child was not lightly made.

Holywood is known as "The Gem of the Lough," which is what it says in big letters on the signs welcoming visitors to town. In smaller letters, the signs say: "Home of Rory McIlroy."

Townspeople are proud of Rory, of course, but not everyone is a certified member of his fan club. After a few days of talking to locals, a tourist senses their ambivalence. They've grown tired of trying to make sense of his off-kilter performances in the majors. Plus, Rory doesn't get home as often as he used to, which has stirred some resentment.

Over a Guinness, one fellow mused that Rory was not everyone's "slice of Marmite." When this American stared back, uncomprehending, the person explained that Marmite is a thick savory spread that gets slapped on bread and toast. I sampled it the next morning; it tasted even more bitter than I had imagined.

But it's the lough itself that's the second thing that focuses your eyes as you walk up Shore Road. You'll never see a prettier sea inlet. Twelve miles long and five miles across at its widest point, the lough connects the Belfast yards to the North Channel of the Irish Sea, the conduit that made the place a major shipbuilding port. Glance out to the water, and you're likely to see freighters, tankers, trawlers, and cruise ships, many of them gigantic.

Often when a cruise ship docks at Belfast, a few of its golf-nut passengers will take a taxicab pilgrimage over to Holywood Golf Club. They want to pay their respects to HGC's famous member and admire the trophies and mementos on display. As HGC member Karen Murray told me while she and her husband Trevor played the devilishly downhill par-three sixth, "We're used to cruise-ship people walking around the place."

If you're lucky and the day is clear, from the top of Shore Road you can see across the water to Carrickfergus, the County Antrim village that's home to one of the island's coolest castles. The Normans built the fortress eight centuries ago to protect their Irish land claims and warn clan chieftains to toe the line—or else.

During WWII, the relic was put to good use as an air-raid shelter; it surely saved lives during the Nazis' bombing blitz that killed nearly a thousand people.

Now you've reached High Street, the village's main thoroughfare, so turn your gaze southward and you'll spot landmark number three: the steeple of St. Colmcille's Catholic Church, which dominates the sight line in the middle part of town. St. Colmcille's has been around since 1874, when its foundation stone was hauled to Holywood from the ruins of a church in County Donegal, the place where St. Colmcille himself was born in the sixth century.

One of Ireland's three patron saints,[3] St. Colmcille helped convert thousands of natives to Christianity and established some thirty monasteries around the island. He also managed to foment—over a disputed interpretation of The Psalms, no less!—a tribal war that culminated in the Battle of *Cúl Dreimhne* out west. It ended up backfiring. Colmcille and a dozen acolytes (mainly monks) got shipped off to Iona, a remote island off the western coast of Scotland. But give the dude credit: even in exile, he couldn't stop proselytizing!

On Iona, he built yet another abbey and continued his converting ways, this time bringing Picts (Scottish clansmen) and Saxons (English clansmen) into the flock.

Like the remnants of the church beneath it, the St. Colmcille's steeple is ornate French Gothic, a unique style in Irish church architecture. The fact that it's there at all is remarkable. The church was heavily damaged in an August 1989 fire, when Rory McIlroy was four months old.

When it was rebuilt, a modern sanctuary, circular in shape, was added. When extra chairs are folded in, it's big enough at holiday time to accommodate many of the parish's two thousand families.

Also added in the rebuild were stained-glass windows, woodwork, and statuary, all reflecting ancient Celtic influences. Somewhere, St. Colmcille is smiling; like St. Patrick, Colmcille was careful to let the natives keep their "pagan" and tribal imagery and—to a certain extent—their belief systems. Ireland's patron saints weren't looking to persecute heretics; they were looking to gain converts.

Much of Ireland's indigenous spiritualism was woven into the island's early Christianity. And now, 1,500 years later, that big-tent philosophy is on display at St. Colmcille's.

---

3   Ireland's other patron saints are Saint Patrick, who in spite of the legend, did *not* banish snakes from the island (most likely, the Ice Age did), and Saint Brigid of Kildare, a sixth-century nun so beloved that she was said to possess the power to turn water into beer. Now, *there's* a myth worth believing!

For a long stretch of the village's history, roughly 1640 until 1800, Catholics were not welcomed. In the seventeenth century, English overlords imposed a plantation system that confiscated Irish-owned lands; soon thereafter, the Crown and Parliament enacted penal laws that denied Catholics in Ireland human and property rights.

A story told to Rory and other Holywood schoolkids, no doubt apocryphal, suggests that by the mid-1700s, the presence of a Catholic was so rare that when a Fenian coachman happened to drive his rig through town, villagers ran out their doors so they could say they'd actually seen a Catholic in the flesh.

In Latin, Holywood translates as *Sanctus Boscus*, literally "Holy Wood." Holly trees still dot Holywood's landscape, mixed in with pine, oak, and beech. Magpies, sparrowhawks, and common redshanks flit from tree to tree. With the lough, the green hillsides, and all the parkland, it's a gorgeous little place. Just ask the twelve thousand people who live there.

St. Patrick's Primary, the elementary school that Rory attended from ages five to eleven, sits just up the hill from St. Colmcille's, at the intersection of My Lady's Mile and Church View. Although the school is next door to the church, the two properties are separated by a patch of trees, which gives St. Pat's a secluded feel. The school is no more than a McIlroy three-wood from the family's original home a couple of blocks north on Church View, and barely a driver and a wedge from their second home off Belfast Road.

His parents could have chosen to send him to Holywood Primary, the town's nonsecular elementary school. Instead, young Rory went off to a Catholic institution that prides itself on its broad-minded curriculum and its nurturing of lifelong learning.

Principal Chris O'Neill was not around in Rory's day. But he's a good-natured Ulsterman from County Tyrone, a proud descendant of the *Ua Néill* clan. His hair may have receded a bit, but his sense of humor hasn't.

At the top of our interview, he expressed amazement that a Guinness-loving American had been in Holywood for a full day and still hadn't discovered Ned's. "Ned's pours the finest pint of Guinness in town," he said with a bemused look as he reviewed a stack of papers.

Chris has been at St. Pat's for a decade. He says he's not a huge golf or McIlroy fan, but like almost everyone else up North, he follows Rory in big tournaments. Just down the hall from his office, there's a painting of Rory, grinning ear-to-ear as he holds the Claret Jug after winning the 2014 Open Championship at Royal Liverpool.

A power-of-positive-thinking poster is pasted onto the wall underneath Rory's portrait. In bright pastels meant to mirror a rainbow, it reads:

Train Your Brain and Develop a Growth Mindset

Instead of...	*Try thinking...*
I'm not good at this.	What am I missing?
I give up.	I will use a different strategy.
It's good enough.	Is this the best I can do?

The Growth Mindset messages should be taken to heart by aspiring duffers, especially, "Is this the best I can do?" Hell, Rory's sports psychologist, Dr. Bob Rotella, may borrow the themes for his next bestseller, inevitably entitled, *Everything You Need to Know About Golf You Learned in Grade School.*

Stroll around St. Pat's with Principal O'Neill and you'll learn that fully one-third of the student body isn't Catholic; moreover, its instructors take pride in teaching subjects and values that would have gotten them banished to Iona in the old days.

As you reach the pint-sized auditorium stage, you'll hear a story about how the school held an all-student assembly in 1998 to celebrate Rory's victory in the Publix ten-and-under championship at

Doral. With beaming teachers and administrators looking on, the nine-year-old McIlroy talked about how much fun it was to fly to Miami with his dad and how proud he was to be from Holywood and St. Pat's.

Then he reprised the chipping exhibition he performed on Belfast TV. Still standing onstage, Rory pitched a ball down the center aisle and out the open double door into the hallway, to riotous applause from schoolmates, many of whom had never before witnessed a golf shot.

Sullivan Upper, Rory's other alma mater a quarter mile down Belfast Road, has a green and freshly scrubbed look. It boasts an acre or more of rugby and field hockey pitches and a circular drive that deposits visitors on the doorstep of its nicely appointed administrative offices.

St. Pat's has none of those amenities. It's a little dank and scrappy, befitting the backgrounds of the blue-collar families, like the McIlroys, fortunate enough to send their kids there.

In Rory, St. Pat's has something of a model alum, a guy devoted to a growth mindset. One of Rory's more appealing traits is that he relishes new challenges. He's forever praising the merits of books and movies. His teachers and parents, moreover, instilled in him a social conscience that has given rise to his dogged philanthropic work.

When Rosaleen McDonald, Rory's mum, came into this world at Lurgan Hospital in February 1960, her family lived in a hardscrabble rowhouse on Arthur Street, not far from the town center and the home of its (very Fenian) Glasgow Celtic Football Club fan headquarters. In Lurgan's Catholic neighborhoods, almost everyone pulled for Glasgow Celtic, especially when they played their Scottish Premiership archrivals, the Protestant-backed Glasgow Rangers. The same sectarian split that animated the Celtic-Rangers rivalry back then still persists today.

As a young man, Rosie's dad Danny listed his occupation as Weaver, which meant, like so many Nordies of that era, he'd found work in the textile industry. Danny had grown up in another Arthur Street rowhouse, across the road and twenty doors down from the place he lived two decades later.

His wife, the former Anna Bridgit ("Bridie") McKeown of Lisniskey, a hamlet in nearby Portadown, had also worked as a Weaver and Stitcher. Bridie grew up a farmer's daughter. Her parents, John and Annie McKeown, ran a small farm in western Armagh.

Life was not easy for Bridie and Danny McDonald. Married in 1957 when each was twenty, they had five children on a meager income that got even leaner when Bridie stayed home to raise the kids.

At some point, the family's financial situation must have turned dire. Danny may well have lost his textile job; many Ustermen did in that era. The McDonalds were forced to move into a cramped apartment in Taghnevan Estate, a government-subsidized Catholic housing project.

They weren't alone. Thousands of families in County Armagh and tens of thousands across the North—Catholic, Protestant, and agnostic—found themselves in desperate straits. As the 1960s morphed into the 1970s and Northern Ireland's economic and societal tensions deepened, Taghnevan and other indigent estates became breeding grounds for The Troubles.

Lurgan had always been divided along sectarian lines, acknowledges Peter Hanna, the head professional at the Lurgan Golf Club, one of the few places in town where Catholics and Protestants mingled without rancor. Still, the club was so conscious of potential friction that, each year, the captaincy of the club rotated between the two sects. It still does today.

Unlike northwest Belfast, there weren't big walls separating the Catholic section of Lurgan from the Protestant side. But the divide was so pronounced that if a car turned a certain direction at the town's central traffic circle, observers would know whether it was a

Catholic or a Protestant behind the wheel. It was dangerous business for Lurgan Catholics to stray into Protestant neighborhoods and vice versa.

Chris Thornton—the Vermonter who came to Belfast on a journalism internship four decades ago and never left—shared two common expressions about Lurgan in our interview at the headquarters of BBC-Northern Ireland, where Chris serves as a producer.

The first is, "Your face looks as long as a Lurgan spade," which means someone appears dour and depressed. The ground around Lurgan and nearby Lough Neagh tends to be so crusty that it requires an elongated shovel to pierce it. The phrase is not a flattering commentary on the emotional well-being of Lurgan residents.

The other adage is even more damning: "Keep your head lower than a Lurgan Catholic's." Rife with Jim Crow overtones, its meaning is ugly and unmistakable.

During The Troubles, Thornton revealed, Catholics in Lurgan were taught to keep their eyes fixated on the ground, lest a Protestant bully (or bullies) take offense. Catholic parents begged their kids not to make waves. Don't draw attention to yourself. Only speak when spoken to. Lurgan may not have had separate Catholic and Protestant restrooms or drinking fountains, but the town was viciously segregated.

Taghnevan Estate in Rosie McDonald's tween and teen years was a haven of defiance, a place where exterior walls and interior hallways were full of hand-scrawled messages saluting the militant wing of the Irish Republican Army and vowing death to any Protestant or Englishman who got in their way.

"[Ulster Unionist leader] David Trimble will tremble when the Provos reassemble," read one sign that young Rosie must have walked past dozens of times a week. Other Taghnevan Estate murals bragged about the cache of rifles at the Provos' disposal.

The Protestant housing projects on the other side of the traffic circle, meanwhile, were littered with signs that threatened reprisals against the IRA and Ulster's Catholic leaders.

By the early '70s, so many bombings and assassinations occurred in and around Lurgan that it earned a reputation as Northern Ireland's "Murder Town"—a terrifying epithet for a community of fewer than thirty thousand souls.

When Rosie was twelve, three British soldiers were killed by a booby-trapped bomb planted in a derelict home just blocks from Taghnevan. When she was fifteen, three Catholics were murdered at a Lurgan social club by members of the militant Protestant Action Force. Tit-for-tat killings in Lurgan did not recede until well after 1998's Good Friday Agreement.

How many scary encounters did Rosie and her siblings have while going back and forth to school, or church, or the grocery store, or playing on Taghnevan's fields, or just sitting in their flat? Surely, they saw ambulances and cop cars from the Police Service of Northern Ireland and the Royal Ulster Constabulary—the law enforcement agencies that Catholic kids learned they couldn't trust—shrieking through the neighborhood, sirens blaring.

At some point, Rosie's dad started driving an ice cream truck. It's hard to know how much revenue a mobile ice cream vendor cleared back then, but given the cost of gasoline and maintenance repairs, coupled with County Armagh's poverty and habitually bad weather, it could not have been much.

The McDonald kids—in order, Michael, Rosie, Fiona, Gregory, and Leanne—had it rough. Young Mickey's brilliance in soccer and Gaelic football must have given the McDonalds much joy and some degree of notoriety. But even after he began bringing home a little money from his athletic exploits, it could only have helped the family's situation around the margins.

Not many Northern Irish kids of that generation finished high school, Thornton noted in our interview. With more mouths to feed, many families needed extra income—and, in many instances, the extra space.

In her teens, Rosie often rode along with her dad on his truck route. She learned the value of every sixpence. Later, she would put those budgeting skills to work in figuring out how to meet the travel, equipment, and training expenses that her young offspring was incurring.

Rosie left St. Mary's High School at sixteen to work along the assembly line at UK Optical Ltd. (now Crossbows Optical) in Craigavon. She was described as a "bubbly" teen in a 2014 profile in the *Belfast Telegraph*, someone who enjoyed socializing at The Coach Inn, a hangout in nearby Bainbridge. In her early twenties, she moved with friends to Belfast. Rosie started waiting on tables and serving as a barmaid. Somewhere along the line, she met a young barkeep from Holywood four months her senior named Gerry McIlroy.

They got married on Wednesday, January 13, 1988, when Rosie was twenty-seven and Gerry twenty-eight, oldish by Irish standards back then. It's interesting that they chose to wed in the groom's hometown instead of the traditional bride's home. Between St. Comcille's and the attractions along High Street, Holywood might have presented a more appealing setting. Eva and Jimmy McIlroy, moreover, might have had a few quid to put into a small celebration.

The bride and groom continued to work in the restaurant business and rented a small duplex on Church View in the heart of Holywood. Rory came along a year and a half later, on May 4, 1989.

Sadly, Rosie's parents did not stay in good health; neither lived long enough to see their grandson. Bridie died of breast cancer two weeks before Rosie's twenty-fourth birthday; she was just forty-six.

Danny passed away four years later from throat cancer and liver disease, common maladies among the men in Rory's family on both sides. Lord knows that the McIlroys and the McDonalds aren't the only Irish families plagued by alcohol and tobacco addictions. But mortality records from generation to generation demonstrate that they've been chronic problems. When Gerry McIlroy quit smoking a while back, it was a big day in the McIlroy household.

Growing up poor in a place called Murder Town produced a resilient young woman. Surely, Rosie must have resolved never to let her own child suffer from the deprivation she'd known.

If you want to know the key to Rory's character, look at his mum. That's what Irishman Paul McGinley, a former European Ryder Cup captain and now a commentator for Sky Sports and the Golf Channel, told me at the 2023 PGA Championship. She's tough as nails, he said, suppressing a smile.

In a 2024 Mother's Day interview after he won for the fourth time at Quail Hollow, Rory allowed that his mum was the "glue" that held their family together. He also admitted that he wished he were more like her.

As a kid, Rosie McDonald faced hardships a bit more harrowing than a tee shot over water.

Gerry McIlroy is one of those agreeable Irish souls with sparkling eyes, a shock of Spencer Tracy hair, and an infectious grin. He has the bearing of a *seanchaí*, the wiseman in an ancient Irish village who was the keeper of folklore and the teller of tall tales. Gerry exudes the same avuncular charm that, in our imaginations, the late Nobel Prize-winning Irish poet Seamus Heaney had in abundance.

"Believe that a further shore is reachable from here," Heaney implored in *The Cure at Troy*, his most admired poem. It's a phrase that could describe the lives of Gerry and Rosie McIlroy. They believed that their gifted son could reach a distant shore if only they gave him a skiff, a pair of oars, and a nudge.

On that conviction, they upended their own lives. And not just in some peripheral way. Their faith in Rory's potential drove them to take on multiple jobs, work literally around the clock, forsake social lives, save every penny, get their child the best possible coaching, and travel to junior tournaments in exotic locales (Miami, San Diego, Honolulu, Milan) about which most of their blue-collar neighbors could only dream.

In January 2024, after Rory won his fourth Dubai Desert Classic, photographers asked Rosie and Gerry to join their son in kneeling behind the huge winner's trophy. "Hold up four fingers," the photographers urged each of the McIlroys. Gerry looked at the hand he was holding up, noticed a gnarled pinkie finger, and with impeccable comedic timing, blurted, "I've only got three-and-a-half [fingers] on this hand."

Gerry's remark caused Rory and Rosie to crack up. Caddie Harry Diamond was standing out of camera shot a few yards away; Rory wanted his pal to share in the levity.

"'Har,' did you hear what Dad said?" Rory yelled. "'I've only got three-and-a-half on this hand'!"

More belly laughs ensued. Rosie and Gerry were laughing so hard they had to steady themselves on the ground.

It all made for a delightful photo opp. The McIlroys, this tight-knit trio that, together, had been through so much, were letting the world in on an inside joke. Years ago, Gerry must have mangled his pinkie while scrubbing a toilet or installing a beer keg, or doing one of the thousand other things he did to make ends meet.

It was, no matter how you slice it, an enormous gamble. For every prodigy who makes it big in golf, or tennis, or music, or whatever, there are thousands of promising youngsters who don't.

Gerry had so much confidence in Rory that, when the lad was only fifteen, he put together a group of friends to wager £100 each (a total of $683 back then) at 500-1 odds that Rory would win the Open Championship before reaching age twenty-six. When Rory delivered the goods at Hoylake, in his last Open blast before turning twenty-six the following year, Gerry and his buddies cashed in big, winning the tidy sum of $342,000, divided four ways.

That sort of money would have been unimaginable to the young James Gerard McIlroy. He was the third "James" in succession, but Eva and Jimmy must have wanted their eldest child to have his own identity, so they started calling him "Gerry." It stuck.

Gerry spent most of his young life in North County Down, developing a syrupy swing while playing with his old man and younger brothers at the par-69 course up the hill.

He left high school early to help Eva and Jimmy provide for his three younger siblings. Gerry worked odd jobs in Holywood, then served as a waiter and eventually a barman down the road in Belfast.

By his mid-twenties, Gerry was flirting with scratch and the Lurgan-born waitress he'd met on the job.

Unlike Tiger's father, Earl Woods, Gerry never set out to build his son into a golfing machine. It just happened that young Rory showed preternatural skill for the game—and couldn't get enough of it. As Rory's childhood wore on, Gerry recognized his son's talents and was smart enough to reach out to his old friend Michael Bannon at the Bangor Golf Club. Then Gerry got out of Rory's way—and stayed there.

The contrast between Earl and Gerry could not have been more pronounced. Earl, a career noncom, wanted Tiger to approach the game with a military mentality. Ingest plenty of "prick juice," Earl advised his son. It worked—but at a frightful cost to Tiger's emotional equilibrium and sense of self.

Gerry had a different philosophy. Be supportive, not intrusive. Don't push—let the kid develop at his own pace. And try to keep it as light and fun as possible.

Chapter 7

"WATCH MY SWING, UNCLE MICHAEL!"

Did Wolfgang Amadeus Mozart truly climb out of his crib, sit down at his old man's harpsichord, and begin banging out a sonata? The sonata stuff sounds suspicious, but since Mozart toured Europe to rousing ovations as a six-year-old—while performing his own compositions, no less—the story may not be far off the mark.

Did Rory Daniel McIlroy really drive a golf ball forty yards as a two-year-old and sixty yards a year later? Did he truly shoot an even-par round at age eleven? How about out-driving his old man and his uncles—fine golfers, all—that same summer? Or recording multiple holes-in-one before hitting puberty?

There are so many folks at Holywood Golf Club who swear those stories actually happened that we'd be crazy to discount them all.

This much is certain: young Rory was crawling around the HGC practice putting-and-chipping green before his first birthday, trailing his dad and uncles Colm and Brian. Soon thereafter, Gerry bought the youngster a set of plastic clubs that Rory, a la "Bamm-Bamm Rubble" of *Flintstones'* fame, would bash in and around the house at all hours, driving his parents (and, no doubt, their next-door neighbors) to distraction. Every few weeks, Gerry would have to replace the plastic sticks because his youngster would wear them out.

Gerry used to put tiny Rory in a pram and wheel him over to HGC's "range," which back then consisted of a patch of flatland atop a hill overlooking the 17th fairway. Golfers walking up the hill had to keep a wary eye out for practice balls whizzing around.

Now, courtesy of its most celebrated alum, HGC has a first-rate practice facility, outside and inside—as good as any in Ireland, Paul McGinley told me. HGC's Tom McKibbin, a rising star on the DP World Tour, is the direct beneficiary of those improved facilities. Members no longer risk bodily harm as they trudge up number 17.

As a baby, Rory would sit in the stroller, mesmerized, his eyes following the arc of his father's shots. In his toddler years, Rory's great aunt Frances—the younger sister of Bridie, Rose's mum, who died five years before Rory was born—often looked after him at her home in Bainbridge, some fifteen miles south of Holywood. Her backyard become one of Rory's first practice grounds and photo-shoot venues, since Frances enjoyed taking pictures of her great nephew "flailing at the grass," as writer Josh Sens put it in a 2011 *GOLF* profile.

"He first played with his wee putter on my back lawn," Frances recalled two decades after her babysitting stints. "I remember him well in that wee Aran jumper—he could barely hold the club."

The wee lad with the wee club wearing the wee outfit (*Derry Girls*, which was set in the Northern Ireland of Rory's childhood, spoofed the culture's compulsive use of the adjective by creating a Wee Shop that sold only wee items),[1] continued to amaze HGC club members with his uncanny skills. Onetime HGC ladies' club president Pat McCoy recalled that Rory "was the most polite little lad. His father always said, 'If he gives you any cheek, you let us know.' And you know what? Rory never did."

The wee prodigy got a firsthand look at competitive golf when he accompanied his dad to amateur tournaments. Gerry was one

---

[1] My favorite encounter with "wee" during my 2023 trip came at the 236-year-old Linen Hall Library in Belfast. As I peppered a reference librarian with questions about a certain resource, she urged me to "take a wee seat," while she located it. When my questioning persisted, she reiterated her instruction, this time enunciating the words slowly and emphatically, yet never losing her smile. It was a fabulous putdown. I clammed up, walked back to my table, and took a wee seat. She arrived a couple minutes later with the resource, still smiling. Linen Hall Library is so beloved that the great Van Morrison did a fundraising concert for it a while back. His show wasn't wee.

of the better players in Northern Ireland, a guy with a fluid swing who won an HGC club championship and several HGC match play tournaments. For a time, he held the course record at a track in County Donegal. In 1998, Gerry spearheaded the HGC squad that won the Belfast and District Cup tournament, a feat Rory would replicate seven years later as a sixteen-year-old.

Young Rory soaked it all up and caddied for his dad when he got a little older. Rosie joked that her husband and son hit so many courses together that Rory "was strapped" to Gerry's bag.

When Rory was still small, his dad got him an instructional video featuring Nick Faldo. Rory became smitten, spending hours mimicking the prospective Sir Nick.

"We'd say, 'Rory, show us your Faldo!'" remembered former HGC president Wilbur Walker. "And he'd do a perfect imitation of Nick Faldo. That beautiful, flowing swing that you see today, it is incredible. It's pretty much the same one he's always had."

The youngster couldn't get enough. His mum knitted him sweaters to wear as he skipped down the fairways of HGC. His dad got him a little bag to carry his cut-down clubs. At bedtime, Rory would fall asleep holding a club whose special handle was designed to encourage the interlocking pinkie grip that his father taught him. Rory hoped that nocturnal muscle memory would somehow induce lower scores.

His family moved from its tiny stucco home ("sized for hobbits," Sens quipped), to a modest brick duplex less than a half mile southwest. Gerry installed an artificial putting and chipping green in the front yard of the home off Belfast Road, which must have prompted some eye-rolling from the neighbors, especially when Gerry erected an eight-foot-high fence to give wee Rory greater privacy. Just about everyone in town knew that Rosie and Gerry were raising a prodigy. Most cut the McIlroys some slack.

Wee Rory became a full-fledged member of HGC at age seven, when the club adjusted its rules to accommodate him. Members recall Rory filling out fictitious "scorecards" from St. Andrews, Augusta National, and other famed courses, asking folks in the pro shop to help with his arithmetic to ensure that he was concocting a winning score.

How many wee'ns *even know about St. Andrews*, let alone tell an adult to switch their make-believe score from par to birdie on the par-three eighth to make sure they "win" the Claret Jug?

As an homage to his then-hero, he would sign the scorecards, "Rory *Nick Faldo* McIlroy." The cocky kid also left autographs inscribed "Rory McIlroy, US Open Champion," and "Rory McIlroy, Open Champion."

McIlroy was not quite eight when Tiger Woods burst onto the scene by winning the 1997 Masters. Instantly, Tiger become Rory's new idol, relegating Faldo to the back bench. Woods became the object of a Rory fixation that, in many ways, persists to this day.

The kid pasted Tiger's fourth-round Augusta scorecard in '97 onto his bedroom wall and began committing to memory Woods's amateur record, with its six successive USGA titles. In time, Rory's grasp of the minutiae of Tiger's early triumphs would become something of a parlor game in and around HGC. His dad's buddies would try to stump Rory on what Tiger did on such-and-such a hole in his 1996 US Amateur triumph at Pumpkin Ridge in Oregon, or Woods's winning score in the finals of the 1992 US Junior Amateur at Wollaston Golf Club in Milton, Massachusetts.

Rory was bulletproof. In his mid-thirties, he can still spit out Tiger's pre- and postpubescent accomplishments like a fourth grader reciting multiplication tables. He knows more about Tiger's *curriculum vitae* than Tiger does. Michael Bamberger, who witnessed the nineteen-year-old Rory summoning Tiger fun facts, called it a "carnival act."

Young McIlroy got many of his athletic genes from his maternal uncle Michael, Rosie's older brother. "Mickey" McDonald was that rare athlete who managed to become a legend in two professional (well, more accurately, semi-professional) sports: soccer, where the

Lurgan native played for Glenavon and Cliftonville; and Gaelic football, where—at the same time he was playing the *other* football—he captained the County Armagh fifteen[2] and continued to play at an elite level for many years. His kick over the crossbar to seal Armagh's dramatic 1982 win against County Donegal is an iconic moment in the chronicles of Gaelic football, one that still gets bandied about decades later.

Like so many in the McIlroy and McDonald families, Michael also had made himself into a fine golfer, at one point serving as captain of the Silverwood Golf Club outside Lurgan. Whenever the family gathered for picnics and holiday fêtes, wee Rory couldn't wait to show off his golf swing to his famous uncle, Mickey told the *Irish News* in 2020.

"Watch my swing, Uncle Michael! Watch my swing!" Rory would bleat as parents, uncles, aunts, and a bevy of first, second, and third cousins would scatter to avoid being conked by a plastic club or sphere.

Sadly, Mickey died in the fall of 2022 from a brain aneurysm suffered while on a golf vacation in Turkey. He survived the initial attack and was flown back to Northern Ireland to receive treatment. He never recovered.

Rory's parents worried that all the attention would go to their kid's head. "We brought Rory up to always treat people the way you expect them to treat you," Gerry McIlroy told *GOLF* in 2012. His dad's mantra was straightforward (and 180 degrees removed from Earl Woods): "It's nice to be nice—and it doesn't cost you a penny."

Young Rory may not have given HGC adults much "cheek," but he also wasn't shy about letting people know his grand ambitions. "From the age of six or seven years old, I would tell everyone

---

[2] Yeah, I had to look up how many players are on a Gaelic football side. Geez, fifteen seems like a lot, doesn't it?

I was going to be the best golfer in the world," McIlroy recounted in 2020 to *Whoop*'s Will Ahmed.

At age eight, Rory began working with Bannon, the club pro from up the road in Bangor. Gerry knew from experience that Bannon had the gift of taking complicated swing thoughts and distilling them into their simplest forms.

Bannon is a slightly stoop-shouldered Ulsterman with the mien of an accounting professor. Since 2012, he has devoted himself more or less full time to being Rory's swing coach, although he dislikes traveling and would prefer to stay home.

The coach took a video of Rory at age eight that for many years he kept loaded on a laptop. The montage begins with Bannon querying young Rory about what he shot that day, as the youngster is stroking putts on the practice green.

A squeaky voice emits, "Eighty-six." As Rory glances into the camera, his ears and freckles dominate the frame. He's suddenly shy and cocky at the same time.

"Good man," Bannon interjects. "Okay, let's take a look at your swing, then." Rory moves beyond the edge of the putting green and begins a series of deliberate swings.

"It's there already," poet Charles Siebert rhapsodized in his 2015 *New York Times Magazine* piece. "The same sweet, full-sweeping parabola, nothing withheld, the club wrapped all the way back around its fully-torqued wielder, his own head nearly swallowed in a self-imposed half-nelson."

The half-nelson boy was having trouble finding local kids with whom to rassle. In the late 1990s, no youngster at HGC or its neighbor, the Royal Belfast Club, could keep up with Rory. Gerry knew his youngster was good, but how good? To find a decent measuring stick, Gerry and his kid would have to go abroad. But in which direction? And how could the McIlroys afford it? Imagine the Sunday night bookkeeping conversations between Gerry and Rosie around the kitchen table after Rory went to bed and they tried to figure out how they could afford this or that expense.

Despite his tender age, Rory was already a known quantity to officials at the Golfing Union of Ireland. Even at the height of The Troubles, certain sporting organizations, including the GUI and the Irish boxing federation, were cross-border. In other words, the groups provided financial assistance to promising athletes up North as well as in the Republic, regardless of religious affiliation.

In Rory's preteen and teen years, the GUI became the family's guardian angel, helping to defray the costs of travel and training. Exactly how much assistance the organization provided over the years is not known: GUI officials declined to talk. But given the number of trips and the expenses incurred, it must have been many thousands of Euros. And GUI's lead instructor, Niall Manchip, became one of Rory's coaches, helping the youngster with his short game and urging him to bulk up his core muscles.

When Rory was eight and nine, the McIlroys traveled to San Diego for the Junior World Tournament at Torrey Pines and to Hawaii for the World Junior Masters. In 1998, when Rory was nine, he and Gerry flew to Miami for the Publix ten-and-under world championship at Doral's vaunted Blue Monster. Rory, a year younger than many of the competitors, won at Doral by five shots and wowed onlookers with the length and maturity of his game.

One of the most fortuitous moments in young Rory's life occurred at Doral. Golf instructor Jim McLean, a former tour pro and *Golf Digest* instructor, happened to have a ten-year-old son playing in the tournament. It wasn't hard for McLean to spot Rory's natural gifts. "He looked pretty much like he does now—powerful and fluid," McLean told me in a 2023 interview.

"Some kids are super-talented, with incredible gifts, but you don't know if they're going to continue with golf and become great players. Rory was just better than all the other kids. He was astonishingly good."

Gerry flagged down McLean in mid-tournament. McIlroy senior asked McLean for a quick evaluation of his son's potential. McLean told him that Rory's swing was head-and-shoulders above anyone else's in the tournament—including McLean's own kid—and that Gerry's boy seemed to have an intuitive feel for the game.

Would Rory benefit from professional supervision? Gerry asked. And should he be competing in other high-level youth tournaments in Europe and the United States?

Yes, and yes, McLean replied, perhaps not realizing the far-reaching impact his words would have on the McIlroys' work schedule and bank account. Their son's success in South Florida convinced Gerry and Rosie that they needed more money to give Rory a chance to reach his full potential.

Soon, Gerry would be working three jobs during the day: as a morning custodian at the Holywood Rugby Club; as a lunchtime barman at the rugby pub; and as an evening bartender at the Holywood Golf Club. Rosie would work the post-midnight shift at the 3-M plant in Bangor, stacking rolls of scotch tape into cardboard boxes along the assembly line.

Their daily routine, repeated many hundreds of times over the next eight years, would go something this: Gerry would get Rory out of bed, feed him a quick breakfast, drive him to school, and go to work at the rugby club. In mid-afternoon, Gerry would pick Rory up from school, get him a snack, take him to HGC or Bangor for practice, bring him back home, and assume his position behind the HGC bar for the evening hours. Rosie would feed Rory dinner and help with homework. Gerry would come home after closing down the HGC bar, which would then allow Rosie to head off to Bangor for her job at the plant.

It was a grueling schedule and sacrifice above and beyond the call of parental duty.

The Doral tournament was important for the McIlroys in another respect. It was there that Rory befriended the boy who finished second: a kid from Orem, Utah, named Scott Pinckney. Since their youngsters were paired together in the final round, Gerry, in turn, got friendly with Scott's father, Doug.

Rory and Scott became email buddies, staying in touch as the months and years went by. Doug persuaded Gerry that Rory would benefit from spending a summer in Utah playing the well-organized Utah Junior Golf Association circuit.

Gerry and Rosie were raising their only child to be independent, so off Rory went, at age eleven, to spend the summer of 2000 in the Wasatch Mountains.

"I cried for days," Rosie admitted years later.

The boys had, as Scott put it, an "awesome time" hanging out, although Rory's adventure in the Beehive State got off to a stinging start. The *Deseret News* reported in 2011 that on day one, the Pinckneys dropped Scott and Rory off at a pool, only to discover hours later that the "fair-skinned Irishman," as the *News* put it, had failed to apply sunscreen.

Rory ended up with blisters all over his chest and shoulders. He spent that night worshiping the porcelain god. The next morning, Scott's chagrined mother had to phone Rosie and Gerry, seven hours ahead given the time difference.

"My mother called his parents. It was like, 'We're taking real good care of him. He's sick. He didn't put on any sunscreen,'" the *Irish Examiner* quoted Scott Pinckney eleven years later.

Young Rory didn't quite rip up Utah's courses. He played well, but curiously, not well enough to win any of the eleven tournaments he entered. His name did appear, however, in the agate type of the *Salt Lake City Tribune's* sports section, quite possibly the first time "Rory McIlroy" ever showed up in a US newspaper.

Near the end of his trip, Rory also spent a couple of nights with a pair of Salt Lake City brothers with whom he'd gotten friendly. One of those brothers is now an instantly recognizable pillar of the PGA Tour, a guy whose story was featured in year one of *Full Swing*.

Milton Pouha "Tony" Finau's odyssey is as improbable as anyone's in professional golf. Of Samoan and Tongan descent, Tony's parents settled in Salt Lake City on the recommendation of a Mormon missionary.

At the ages of seven and six, respectively, Tony and his younger brother, Gipper, got hooked on golf when Tiger won the 1997 Masters. Tony got so good at whacking balls against an old mattress that they propped up in their garage that he won the 2006 Utah Amateur at age seventeen, which is precisely when his pal Rory was dominating amateur play in Ireland and Europe.

There's a classic photograph taken in the summer of 2000 that shows a surprisingly pudgy Tony and a surprisingly skinny Rory standing shoulder-to-shoulder. Tony is four months younger than Rory, but he's at least a head-and-a-half taller.

In 2011, Scott Pinckney, then playing for Arizona State, qualified for the US Open. He shot 79-75 to miss the cut at Congressional but had the thrill of playing a practice round with his old chum.

"[Rory] hasn't changed, he's completely down to earth. It was like nothing had changed, like we were best of friends," Scott said at the time.

When eleven-year-old Rory's plane touched down at George Best International Airport in August 2000, his parents were shocked to discover that he had peroxided his hair. His curly locks were now blond—or at least blond-ish. More worrisome, his Irish accent had all but disappeared. He was now speaking in the nasal cadence of an American preteen. Fortunately for Rosie and Gerry, both his hair and his lilt quickly recovered.

Rory may have struggled to win in Utah but he had no such issues back home. The next two summers, 2001 and 2002, playing against youngsters considerably older, he won the Ulster Boys Under-15 Championship. In 2003, still only fourteen, he won the Ulster Boys Under-18 Championship at County Down's Donaghadee Golf Club, a lovely links fifteen miles east of Holywood. The next summer, he delighted friends and family (who turned out in full force) by winning the Under-18 at HGC. In 2005, at sixteen, he defeated local legend Tony McClements to capture his only HGC club championship.

Rory became the third McIlroy to have his name embossed on the clubhouse championship board. His dad won the club championship in 1993, three years after Gerry's younger brother Colm had taken home the trophy.

David Feherty, the golfer turned comic broadcaster, grew up a few miles north of Holywood. Early in his career, before Rory came along, Feherty served as the assistant pro at HGC, where he became chummy with bartender Gerry and his better half.

The funnyman remembers spotting Rory coming up the 18th fairway during a visit to HGC in the year 2000 or thereabouts. "Someone pointed him out to me. They said, 'That's Gerry and Rosie's kid.' He was carrying his bag and he was walking as if he owned the place. Without seeing him hit a shot, I thought, 'This kid is going to be a star.' One of the few times in my life I got something right."

When young McIlroy and Feherty finally did meet, John Feinstein writes in *Feherty*, the wiseacre gave McIlroy an inside-joke nickname: "Scunger."

It's Irish slang for a shitty golfer.

The Ulster Boys champion in 2003 was an eighteen-year-old from HGC named Harry Diamond. Harry had won his trophy at County Armagh Golf Club; he was four-plus years older than Rory and probably not thrilled in '04 to be beaten by a punk kid. Nevertheless, they became fast friends.

It was at some point in '03 that Michael Bannon had an epiphany while watching Rory swing. His pupil had been traveling; it had been several weeks since Rory made the trip to Bangor to be evaluated by his coach. In the interim, Rory's swing had gotten sharper and his teenaged body stronger. All of a sudden, the ball was flying off the middle of Rory's clubfaces, soaring prodigious distances. Rory was ten or more yards longer with every club.

"How long have you been hitting it like this?" a pleased Bannon inquired. "A few weeks now," Rory replied with a big grin.

Bannon had always known that Rory had a bright future. But it wasn't until that moment that he thought Rory had a chance to become a generational talent.

Young McIlroy's stature within the Irish sports community was growing. At fifteen, he was named Ireland's Junior Sports Personality of the Year.

Also, that same year, he was appointed a member of Europe's Junior Ryder Cup team. The junior matches were held at Westfield Country Club south of Cleveland, Ohio, in mid-September—a week before the real Ryder Cup was contested in suburban Detroit. Instead of a team of twelve, the junior Ryder Cuppers had half that number: six boys, aged sixteen or under. Their head-to-head match play competition, however, mirrored the adult Ryder Cup.

Rory's teammates included Oliver Fisher of England. Fisher, a Londoner, was eight months older than Rory; he had almost as decorated an amateur career and was often cast in the British and Irish press as McIlroy's archrival.

McIlroy and his mates trounced the US squad, 8½-3. As a team, they made 65 birdies overall to the US team's 46.

Rory was the first Irishman ever to play Junior Ryder Cup or its forerunner. He enjoyed it, although his own play was mixed at Westfield: he only took half a point from two fourball matches.

The junior gang then headed to Oakland Hills, where the *actual* Ryder Cup took place the following week. It was heady stuff. They watched a European squad captained by Bernhard Langer and starring Padraig Harrington, Sergio Garcia, Darren Clarke, and Miguel-Angel Jiménez throttle an underachieving US team helmed by Hal Sutton and featuring Tiger Woods, Phil Mickelson, Davis Love III, and Jim Furyk. The Euros won by a record 18½-9½ score, the biggest thrashing an American Ryder Cup team has ever absorbed.

Rory shared with anyone who would listen that fall that he was determined to play on the world stage soon. Observed British journalist and McIlroy chronicler Frank Worrall: "The boy was hardly short of confidence or ambition."

Chapter 8

"ULTIMATE AMATEUR"

If there were a Mount Rushmore of Irish amateur golf—and thank God there isn't, because it would be an eyesore wherever they'd chisel it—the amiable mug of Eddie McCormack would be in its middle. As Eddie puts it in his charming but nearly impenetrable Midlands' brogue, for three-plus decades he's been Ireland's "ultimate amateur."

McCormack was far removed from his teen years when he first encountered an upstart McIlroy in the late spring of 2005. Contested at the rugged Westport Golf Club links in County Mayo, the Irish Amateur Close Championship back then ranked at the top of Ireland's annual amateur golf competitions—and still does. Eddie was double Rory's age in '05, which was a just-barely sixteen.

Eddie had grown up in Cavan, the seat of County Cavan (it's in the province of Ulster, one of the three northern counties back in the early 1920s that chose to join the Free State). When he was in *his* mid-teens, he was struggling to break 90. Eddie had been a good athlete as a kid. While still in high school, the thick-shouldered McCormack began playing for County Cavan's Gaelic football squad—nicknamed the *Breffni* (Gaelic for "Hill") *Blue*—and didn't stop for a long stretch. His football experience taught him how to "get inside an opponent's head," he says, a skill he later put to use in match play.

He was the son of a compositor (typesetter) at the *Anglo Celt*, a local newspaper whose masthead captured the divided nature of North Irish society back then. Eddie's Catholic old man took a dim view of golf, viewing it as a "Protestant sport," a rich man's indulgence well beyond his family's means.

Dad was flummoxed when fourteen-year-old Eddie, the last of his five children, became smitten with the game. One of Eddie's pals acquired a set of old clubs. Since the nicer athletic fields in Cavan were off-limits to Catholic youngsters in those days, Eddie and his buddy dragged the sticks to a vacant pasture and began hacking away.

Eddie gripped a golf club back then the same way he held a "hurley," the curved wooden stick used in the ancient Irish game of hurling. He grabbed the club with a split cross-handed grip, his left hand barely grazing the leather, and proceeded to "Happy Gilmore" his way around the meadow. His friend tried to show him the traditional right-hand-low grip with fingers interlocked or overlapped—but Eddie stuck with his hurley split. He was amazed when a couple of his wild whacks actually got airborne.

That summer, he and his mate continued to bang balls *au naturel*. Finally, it dawned on them that—for a couple of quid—they could try their hand at a round of real golf at Cavan Golf Club, an eighteen-hole parkland course whose discounted fees encouraged kids to take up the game.

After his split grip was mocked at CGC, Eddie gave in to peer pressure and started holding the club with his right hand low. Eddie slowly began improving, although he chuckles that his swing at that stage was "still pure shite."

Much to his dad's consternation, Eddie spent every available minute at the course, soaking up knowledge from the club's better players. By age eighteen or so, he had whittled his handicap into the single digits. By his mid-twenties, he was close to scratch.

In 1997, at age twenty-four, he decided to take the competitive plunge and entered a tournament in County Sligo. Nervous and out of his depth, he shot 88-85 in the two medal-play qualifying rounds and finished at the bottom of the heap.

But Eddie was hooked. He never got good enough to consider going pro. Instead, he became an amateur's amateur, winning a number of big competitions and getting particularly adept at match play.

Eddie and the rest of the Irish golfing world had heard the buzz about the teenaged phenom from County Down in the weeks leading up to the '05 Close.[1] Two months earlier, the "Holywood Hotshot"—as *Irish Sun* golf writer extraordinaire Brian Keogh had anointed him[2]—had grabbed headlines by winning the West of Ireland Amateur Open at County Sligo Golf Club at Rosses Point while still a fifteen-year-old.

Rory McIlroy was the "new kid on the block" that spring and summer, Eddie remembered in a 2023 telephone interview. "Everyone just knew Rory would be great," Eddie recalled with a sly chortle. "And he was."

As always at the Close, two rounds of stroke play winnowed the field to the top sixty-four players, who then competed head-to-head in match play. Eddie qualified in the middle of the pack, then worked his way to the finals, getting his wish to take on the lad from Belfast Lough.

Eddie was used to performing in front of thousands of screaming and beer'd-up partisans in Gaelic football. But on a golf course, he'd never played before more than a handful of fans, usually pub mates and blood relatives. Three or four hundred people, Eddie estimates, followed the final group at Westport back in '05—and there weren't any gallery ropes to restrain them. The crowd made Eddie uncomfortable, but he soldiered on. Rory, McCormack remembered, thrived amid all the hubbub.

---

1 "Close" means closed to professionals.
2 Keogh, an engaging guy and a colorful writer who covered Rory from his teen years on, also dubbed the young McIlroy the "Teen Sensation," the "Ulster Ace," and the "Mop-Top Marvel." There were others, but you get the idea.

Eddie overcame his nerves to play a solid match, only losing 3 and 2. McIlroy, despite struggling with a finicky contact lens, took control around the turn, winning holes 8, 9, and 10.

At the 10th, both players missed the green with their approaches. Eddie hit a "lovely little chip" to about six feet, a shot that all these years later he still savors in his mind's eye.

Rory's bump-and-run, meanwhile, slipped some twelve feet past.

"Maybe I have a little opening here," Eddie remembered thinking. His thought didn't percolate long. Rory "rammed" his putt into the back of the cup, Eddie recalls, while his own effort grazed the lip. The momentum had swung against the ultimate amateur.

Before the round started, Eddie, who had heard all the stories about McIlroy's other-worldly length, had vowed not to watch the kid swing. "I held true to my plan and did not look until it was nearly over," Eddie told Justin Doyle of the *Irish Sun* a decade ago. "But I could hear his ball striking, and I had never heard, and have still never heard to this day, anything like it.... If there were 20 players striking the ball, and you were blindfolded, you would unquestionably know the sound of Rory's strike."

Eddie finally broke down on number 14 and watched Rory hit a tee ball. It was a medium-length par-three playing into a stiff breeze, quartering left-to-right.

Rory deliberated a few seconds before pulling a five-iron. Eddie looked on as the kid thumped an "expertly shaped" draw against the wind. It hung forever in the sky before landing a few feet from the flagstick.

It was as gorgeous a golf shot as Eddie McCormack had ever seen—and it was struck by someone half his age! Now two down, Eddie had no choice but to try and muscle a four-iron. His shot ballooned into the wind and plunked down well short and right.

McCormack's chip came out stubby; his par putt also went awry. Rory never had to stroke his birdie chance. Suddenly, Eddie was three down with four holes to play. Rory cruised to the trophy presentation.

Despite the spanking, Eddie enjoyed the match and getting to know the McIlroy men. Gerry walked alongside Rory but never interfered. They were both "complete gentlemen the whole day," Eddie recalls.

Rory pulled a rare twosome in 2005, followed the next year by an even rarer foursome. He won the West and the Close in the same season two years running.

McIlroy's "grand slam" made the Holywood Hotshot even hotter. He became the vessel into which the sports-obsessed Irish began pouring their dreams. It was intoxicating stuff, to be sure. But it put enormous pressure on Rory to deliver—a psychological burden that, two decades later, he's still trying to sort through.

Eddie's star hasn't dimmed in the intervening years. Today, he works in agribusiness as a sales representative for BWG Food Service in Galway and runs a dairy farm along Galway Bay. He constantly frets about the health of his cows.

McCormack's game, despite his protestations that it's "shite," hasn't slipped. In 2023, Eddie celebrated his fiftieth birthday by winning the European Senior Men's Championship at County Cork's Douglas Golf Club.

Eddie and the McIlroys have stayed in touch over the years, swapping stories and enjoying an occasional drink or meal together. At the Honda Classic in 2012, Eddie and his wife were in South Florida visiting friends when they spotted the TV blimp hovering over PGA National and decided, on the spur of the moment, to take in a round. They caught up with Rory's group and bumped into Gerry and Rosie in the gallery.

Pleasantries were exchanged; they all ended that evening on the veranda of a nice place for dinner. The McIlroys picked up the tab and Rory ended up winning the tournament.

A decade later, at the Open Championship at St. Andrews, Eddie took a funny picture as Rory was handing his club back to Harry. Eddie had a good spot in the gallery and is sure that Rory had seen him standing there with his cellphone cocked sideways. Just as Eddie clicked, Rory gave him a sidelong look with his eyes narrowed in mock anger.

It was Rory's way of saying hi to an old friend.

For much of the spring and summer of 2006, Rory worked with GUI's Manchip on his putting and chipping. It paid immediate dividends; clutch putting helped him successfully defend his West of Ireland title.

A few weeks later, he defeated Simon Ward 3 and 2 in the finals to win his second consecutive Irish Close. He became the first Irish golfer since Joe Carr in 1965 to win successive Close championships.

The precocious McIlroy zeroed in that week on what would prove to be his biggest on-course weakness: a tendency to let his mind wander. He admitted to the press that sometimes he struggled with lapses in concentration.

"At times I play games with myself because of complacency, not boredom," a perceptive remark from a seventeen-year-old and a harbinger of a mental challenge that would continue to dog him.

Later in 2006, he became the European Amateur Champion by vanquishing the field at Biella Golf Club outside Milan, Italy. He shot three rounds in the 60s to win by three strokes. Winning the European Amateur meant that Rory had achieved a boyhood dream: qualifying for the following year's Open Championship at Carnoustie, Scotland.

The encomiums began to grow. The *Irish Times*, the *Belfast Telegraph*, and the *Irish Examiner* all named McIlroy their Irish sports star of 2006—amazing validation for a kid fresh off of failing his first driver's test.

RORY LAND

In February 2007, McIlroy, still just seventeen, became the number-one amateur in the world, according to the metrics kept by the World Amateur Golf Ranking. He was toppled from the spot a few days later but regained it by winning the Grey Goose Cup (formerly the Sherry Cup) along the Mediterranean in southern Spain.

In Sotogrande, McIlroy beat his Junior Ryder Cup teammate Marius Thorp of Norway, becoming the first Irishman to win the Sherry/Grey Goose since Padraig Harrington in 1991. In the Grey Goose team competition, McIlroy played with his longtime pal Shane Lowry, then nineteen, from County Offaly. The pair narrowly lost to two Danes.

Back then, Irish amateur golf "consisted of Rory and the fat kid," chuckles Keogh. The chunky youngster, like McCormack, grew up in Ireland's middle, a soccer and Gaelic football nut. At age nine, Lowry joined a pitch 'n putt league—a "bizarre variant of golf," as Jim Moriarty described it in *Golf World*, "demanding 30- and 40-yard flop shots to greens roughly the size of carpets sold in Middle Eastern bazaars, with an old golf ball, generally the color of a dying tooth, that bounces as high as a pink grapefruit."

Lowry is from Clara, a little town blessed with a nearby inland links course, Esker Hills. The place was designed by the great Irish player Christy O'Connor Jr.,[3] a cocksure character from County Galway dubbed "Himself." Between pitch 'n putt competitions and O'Connor's roguish greens, Lowry developed superb touch.

Shane's father Brendan was a Gaelic footballer who, five years before his son was born, helped lead tiny Offaly to the 1982 All-Ireland Championship, a feat not unlike a rural Indiana high school winning the state basketball tournament, a la *Hoosiers*. Forty years later, the people of Offaly still buzz about the lads from "The

---

3   David Feherty once joked that O'Connor's entire pre-match warm-up consisted of shrugging his shoulders once, then downing a pint of Guinness.

Faithful County," as their cherished squad is known. Ask any Irish sporting scribe about Shane and they'll start talking about Brendan.

To this day, whenever Shane goes home, he's a mainstay at O'Connor Park, Offaly's soccer stadium and the home of the GAA's Faithful County.

Shane is two years older than McIlroy; while still in their early-to-mid teens, they began competing against one another and became great buds. Rory, Shane, Simon Ward, and Seamus Power would win the gold medal in July 2007 at the European Amateur Team Championship at Western Gailes, a links up the coast from Troon, Scotland. Rory tied for low medalist that week.

Lowry succeeded Rory as the 2007 Irish Amateur Close champion. Two years later, Lowry shocked the golfing world while still a twenty-two-year-old amateur by winning the 2009 Irish Open at County Louth Golf Club. McIlroy was among Shane's buddies who dumped water, champagne, and beer over the champion's head after Lowry's par putt beat the sweet-swinging Brit, Robert Rock, on the third hole of a playoff.

Rory, then in his second full season as a pro, finished well back in the pack that week. His pal Shane accomplished something that McIlroy never had: winning a professional tournament without being able to accept the winner's check.

Fourteen years later, their big-brother/little-brother bond became further ingrained in Irish hearts when Shane stood up for Rory amid the 2023 Ryder Cup brouhaha. Their countrymen, my Irish friends say, liked how broad-shouldered Shane, an Offaly kid and the son of a Gaelic sports legend, backed up the wee Nordie from County Down.

As Irish golf and culture aficionado Seamus McEnery of County Clare put it two days after the '23 Ryder Cup, "Everyone here [in Ireland] is delighted with Rory and Shane, the fighting Irish.... The way Shane and Rory [handled themselves] went down fantastic on this island."

"This is the thing about Rory," McEnery concluded. "He can say this and that but when the squeeze is on, he is one of us to the core."

The core boy went for a three-peat at the West of Ireland championship at Rosses Point in April 2007 but came up short, losing in the semifinals.

By then, as agent Chubby Chandler remembered sixteen years later, the strategy he had worked out with the McIlroys for Rory's future was firmly in place. Rory shared with Keogh in early 2007 that the goal was to turn pro after competing in the Open Championship at Carnoustie in July and the Walker Cup at Royal County Down in September.

It was also abundantly clear that the McIlroy family would be retaining the services of Chandler's Cheshire (UK)-based International Sports Management group, which at the time represented South African Ernie Els, Irishmen Darren Clarke and Paul McGinley, and Englishmen Lee Westwood and David Howell, among many others.

Darren Clarke, a burly Ulsterman from Dungannon, County Tyrone, and a longtime ISM client, helped persuade the McIlroys to sit down with Chubby. Clarke had taken an interest in the Holywood kid, inviting him to participate in Darren's youth golf academy, eventually giving the youngster his private phone number, and urging him to track him down with any questions. As the years went by, young Rory did just that.

Like virtually everyone in Northern Ireland, Clarke had brushes with The Troubles. His "worst and first job" was tending bar at the Inn on the Park in Dungannon. One night during the 1986 holiday season, the pub got a warning from the IRA that a bomb had been planted inside. Everyone, including Clarke, evacuated just in time. Darren was still uncomfortably close when the bomb detonated.

By late 2006, Chandler recalled, Rory had received something on the order of six dozen queries from US colleges, many of which, sight unseen, were offering scholarships to a kid who was no longer enrolled in high school. Gerry and Rosie were overwhelmed at the interest in their son and unsure how best to proceed.

The cautionary tale of Englishman Justin Rose, eight years older than Rory, was hard to ignore. Rose had finished fourth at the 1998 Open Championship at Royal Birkdale as a seventeen-year-old amateur, holing a dramatic wedge from the fairway on the 72nd hole (broadcaster Mirk Tirico, now with NBC Sports, says that Rose's hole-out was the loudest roar he's ever heard on a golf course). Justin turned pro the next day.

It took Rose twenty-two starts on the European Tour before he made a cut and earned a paycheck. Rose has gone on to become a star in both Europe and the US, but it took him a while to become a consistent check casher. If Rory was going to experience similar struggles, his parents reasoned, maybe he should go to college in the States.

Chubby assuaged their fears about Rory taking too long a time to start making money. Rory at eighteen was a more complete player than Rose was at seventeen, Chubby told the McIlroys.

Going to college would not appreciably help Rory prepare for the pro tours; continuing to play amateur golf in Europe would be the best training. All the while, ISM would be exploring commercial opportunities. The youngster would get the same treatment, Chandler emphasized, as such ISM rainmakers as Westwood and Clarke. A scholarship offer that McIlroy had tentatively accepted from East Tennessee State ended up going to Irishman Seamus Power.

Team McIlroy had a plan: build the kid's reputation and marketability by playing well at Carnoustie and Royal County Down, line up some sweet endorsements and appearance fees, and turn pro in September, immediately after the Walker Cup. Chubby and ISM would take care of the details and the negotiating. To give Rory a taste of the good life to come, Chubby had already arranged for the teenager to lease a 100-series BMW through a UK car-dealer friend.

Was such professional largesse in accordance with the amateur bylaws of the Golfing Union of Ireland? We don't know: the GUI declined to answer queries. In a similar situation in the US, at least in the pre-NIL (Name/Image/Likeness) era, an amateur athlete driving a luxury automobile that was not purchased by his parents would certainly have raised eyebrows—and likely induced a visit from investigators.

Correspondent Keogh remembers bumping into the teenaged Rory driving a Beamer with UK markings idling in a crowded tournament car park. McIlroy's girlfriend Holly Sweeney was in the passenger seat. For a couple of North Down kids from modest backgrounds, they were living a sweet life.

By most accounts, they first locked eyes on the practice grounds at Holywood Golf Club when Rory was fifteen and Holly fourteen. His golfing prowess had already made him a big name around Holywood and big (figuratively speaking) man on campus at Sullivan Upper. Holly, from a Protestant family, was a year behind him at Sullivan, a popular blonde with theater and broadcast dreams. She could style her hair and makeup in ways that made her appear older, a valuable asset for an ambitious young woman.

In an article entitled "My Famous Babysitter," written for a 2008 book celebrating Sullivan Upper's history, Isobel Smith-Meharg, then a student at the school, remembered the excitement in her household when she was little and the golf hero would accompany Holly on babysitting assignments.

"My grandpa was the Captain at Helen's Bay Golf Club in 2006," her story begins. "My mum and dad had a drinks party before going round for Captain's Night dinner. The adults all had a few glasses of wine when the doorbell rang. I ran to let my two guests in.

"Everyone turned 'round to say 'Hello' to my babysitters. One of daddy's friends who had been golfing that day, said, 'Wow. You really look like Rory McIlroy!'

"I laughed and said, 'That's because he IS Rory McIlroy!'

"None of the golf-mad dads could believe that mum and dad had managed to get Rory McIlroy to babysit." Rory often went along with Holly on her babysitting gigs to the Smith-Meharg home, Isobel wrote.

"Rory is so lovely, even when dad tortures him for coaching on that perfect golf swing! I love spotting him on TV playing golf all over the world, and feel so proud to say, 'There is my babysitter!'"

Isobel and her two sitters and all the young people who attended Sullivan Upper were lucky kids. Like many American prep and English "public" schools, it could have been a stuffy or spartan place that looked down its nose at students from less affluent and non-Protestant backgrounds.

Instead, the school, not unlike St. Pat's, prided itself on its open-minded and enlightened attitudes. Its Gaelic motto, as dictated by founder Robert Sullivan, was, *lamh foisdineach an uachtar*, "The gentle hand foremost."

In that 2008 book, former principal John Stevenson wrote that Sullivan insisted the "gentle" school named in his honor would provide nonsectarian education that emphasized "enduring values of truth, honest endeavor, academic, sporting and cultural achievement and a broadly Christian and caring ethos."

No doubt the school didn't always live up to those ideals. But talk to Sullivan alums today and you'll hear mainly positive things about their experiences. One Catholic graduate now in his thirties told me that he never felt intimidated by the religious instruction at the Anglican school; it was genuinely ecumenical. The school encouraged creativity in all forms, especially writing, he remembered. A woman still in her twenties told me that, at Sullivan, girls had essentially the same opportunity to excel in academics and athletics as boys.

Future broadcast journalist Dermot Murnaghan, a class of '76 alum, wrote in the anniversary book, "As sectarian strife bubbled up to destroy communities and lives, Sullivan Upper was a steadfast bulwark against the madness." Murnaghan maintained that "Sullivan was, and is, true to its founding ethic, a sanctuary from the divisions scarring society. No heed paid to specific religion, creed or belief system, simply a nurturing supportive environment designed to foster curiosity, inclusivity, and learning."

Sure, Murnaghan's reminisce contains the sort of overwrought language that typically appears in brochures. But any Ulster institution that during The Troubles could be described as a "bulwark against the madness" is worth singling out.

Rory was so fixated on golf that by his own admission he was a middling student. From his first day, Sullivan's administrators recognized that he would need to be excused for long stretches to accommodate his busy tournament schedule. His teachers were flexible; they went to considerable lengths to bring him up to speed on assignments and provided special tutoring sessions before exams.

It's a shame that Rory never had the chance to absorb what Sullivan had to offer. He has the kind of inquisitive mind that Sullivan prizes, but was chronically behind in his schoolwork. He conceded later that he should have worked harder and tended to give short shrift to classes he didn't like.

For the first three years at Sullivan, male students had to play either field hockey or rugby; the two sports' practice pitches give the campus a gorgeous sheen. Rory chose the former; according to school chums, he got pretty decent at hacking and flicking.[4] In his fourth (and what proved to be final) year, Rory gave up field hockey because he worried that the constant wrist-whipping was bad for his golf swing.

---

4   Real honest-to-goodness field hockey terms, and yeah, I had to look them up.

Sullivan had a limited-schedule golf program. In early spring 2002, the Sullivan team won the Ulster Schools Cup, beating archrival and heavily favored RBAI (the Royal Belfast Academical Institution) in the semifinals and Bangor Grammar in the finals.

Rory, an impossibly tiny twelve-year-old, was nevertheless the number-one player for Sullivan, carrying a three-handicap that soon became zero. Sullivan and RBAI were all square in a tense morning match at the City of Derry Golf Club when Rory pushed his tee ball on a par-three into some trees short and right of the green.

As recollected by schoolmate Jonathon Warnock, a 2006 Sullivan graduate who's now a physician, McIlroy had a "bunker to cross with the narrowest of gaps in the trees to hit through. His opponent [was] sitting pretty on the other side of the green. It looked for sure that Rory would have to get up and down or defeat was inevitable. But then, 'THIS IS MCILROY,' and even at this stage we knew this guy was always going to be special. Out comes the wedge, he flops the ball perfectly through the trees, over the bunker, and lands it on a sixpence. The ball rolls in to three feet, it's hard to do justice to this shot. 'Inst.'s' number one (a talented player in his own right) is choked and fluffs a chip."

In the afternoon final, Sullivan and its Lilliputian leader steamrollered Bangor Grammar 5-0 to win the Ulster Cup, a trophy that practically belonged to RBAI back then.

In a 2008 Q&A with a Sullivan school publication, when he was in his second year as a professional golfer, Rory was asked: "While most of our pupils worry about university or future studies, you were privileged enough not to have these pressures. Do you feel that you had to greatly compromise your school life?"

He replied: "Yes, as I knew that at the end of the day, I wasn't going to end up being a doctor or a barrister. I wanted to play golf. In that respect I felt that exams didn't matter to me as much."

Exam performance may not have mattered much to McIlroy, but it meant a great deal to the Sullivan administration and faculty. As he got older and his travel commitments got more daunting, Rory fell further behind. It became increasingly difficult for his teachers to catch him up. There were apparent concerns, former schoolmates say, that McIlroy's exam scores were dragging down Sullivan's class average, hurting the school's standing among elite Ulster institutions.

Brad Faxon and other commentators often state that Rory left school at age seventeen, which suggests that his departure came a few weeks short of graduation and was not that big a deal, especially since McIlroy ended up passing his GCSE (General Certificate of Secondary Education—high school equivalency) tests.

The truth, however, is that the McIlroys and Sullivan administrators reached an agreement in late winter 2005, when Rory was still fifteen, for him to withdraw. It could not have been an easy decision. Rosie and Gerry were both high school dropouts who'd spent their lives toiling in blue-collar jobs with little prospect for career advancement. Surely, a big part of them wanted their only child to have a more robust education, particularly at a school as esteemed as Sullivan Upper.

But his parents concluded that Rory needed greater latitude to practice and play. The academic demands at Sullivan Upper were taxing. It was tough enough for "regular" kids to keep up with their studies; for one of the best amateur golfers in the world, hopping on airplanes to get from one tournament to the next, it was close to impossible.

So, the formal education for one of the nimblest minds in professional sports ended before the equivalent of his sophomore year in an American high school. The fact is, school pals remember, McIlroy had already missed big chunks of the 2003–2004 and 2004–2005 academic years.

Classmates were not shocked that he chose to leave school early, but many were surprised that it happened so quickly. The news that Rory would no longer be enrolled was made one morning via Sullivan's public address system; it floored some of his closest buddies, who thought of themselves as part of Rory's posse, wannabe Mac Packers. Certain schoolmates viewed Rory and his earnings potential as their ticket to the big-time. For a select handful, it was.

It's curious that putting coach Faxon, since 2018 a member of McIlroy's inner circle, has been permitted to perpetuate the myth that Rory left school two years later than he actually did. Quitting school at fifteen is not in keeping with Rory Land's vision of the McIlroy brand, so it has chosen not to correct the misinformation.

Far more than any professional golfer, Rory likes to share with the press his reading habits: his love of books and his passion for various intellectual pursuits. Is it because he's overcompensating? Is it because part of him wanted to finish his studies at Sullivan Upper, walk across the stage with his classmates to receive his diploma, and go on to matriculate at QUB or Ulster University or Trinity in Dublin? Or maybe emulate Englishmen Luke Donald and Matthew Fitzpatrick and study at an elite American university like Northwestern?

When Rory was first starting on the European Tour and was asked by reporters about his background and aspirations, he liked to list all the places his Sullivan friends were going to school—not just in Ireland and the UK, but abroad, too. It doesn't take an advanced psychology degree to recognize that Rory was living vicariously through those friends.

It also doesn't take a PhD to see that Rory's references to books and Big Ideas are another form of trying too hard—his way, perhaps, of showing off to his peers, almost all of whom, in one capacity or another, attended college.

It might also explain, in part, why Rory felt the need to insinuate himself in the debate over LIV. He not only served as the two tours' spokesman, but steeped himself in the PGA Tour's business practices.

Collin Morikawa, for example, is an alum of the University of California at Berkeley's Haas School of Business, one of America's most respected undergraduate business programs. Yet Morikawa and comparably educated PGA Tour colleagues—Cal's Max Homa, Wake Forest's Will Zalatoris, and UCLA's Patrick Cantlay, among many others—chose to stay all but mum on LIV. They let Rory, the high school dropout, absorb the flak.

It wasn't fair.

Chapter 9

PANDEMONIUM AT PORTRUSH

Hard by the North Channel of the Irish Sea, less than fifteen miles from Scotland, the village of Portrush is charming, but a little long in the tooth. It looks like it could have been the setting for an old *Foyle's War* episode, one where Detective Chief Superintendent Foyle—and Foyle alone—figures out how Nazi U-boat captains have been secretly signaling saboteurs.

Seagulls never stop swooping and squawking at Portrush. The whole place, *Golf Digest's* Jerry Tarde wrote years ago, smells like "sweet Guinness." Portrush may be a bit weathered and tacky, but it's the proud home of the island's most beloved amusement park and one of its most revered golf courses.

During the second round of medal-play qualifying at the July 2005 North of Ireland Championship at Royal Portrush, a huge crowd began following a certain threesome on the homeward nine. For two members of the trio, it was an unnerving experience; they had never played in front of such a boisterous throng.

Well, "in front of" isn't exactly accurate. Since there weren't any ropes or marshals restraining the gallery, it was more like "amongst."

By the time they reached hole number 13 that afternoon, there were people galloping everywhere. Rabid fans were making it close to impossible for Stephen Crowe and Aaron O'Callaghan to concentrate.

O'Callaghan and Crowe were two of the more promising Irish amateurs in the field. Crowe, known as "Stevie" to his buddies, was then in his early twenties, learning the ropes of his family's Belfast-based residential construction business while trying to hone his game. Aaron was a nineteen-year-old who in a few weeks would be heading off to the States to begin his freshman year at Southeastern Louisiana University on an athletic scholarship.

The folks tromping around designer Harry Colt's renowned Dunluce Course agitated Crowe, who was having a tough ball-striking day. Soon enough, however, it occurred to Stevie that the extra bodies could help him find shots that kept straying into the wispy rough.

The other member of the threesome needed no such assistance. Sixteen-year-old Rory McIlroy was having the greatest round of his young life. Rory's exploits at Royal Portrush that day defy belief; two decades later, they're still the stuff of legend.

When McIlroy's instructor, Michael Bannon, got a call at home that evening that his star pupil had shot a 61 on the Dunluce Course,[1] Bannon thought the caller was playing a prank. A kid barely taller than his golf bag breaking the course record by three shots at Royal Portrush, one of the world's most exacting links? It was not possible, Bannon thought.

Brian Keogh did Bannon one better. He called McIlroy's round at Portrush, which included an unearthly 28 on the backside, "almost sacrilegious."

---

[1] Also designed by the legendary Harry Colt, Portrush's other 18 is known as the Valley Course. Although widely admired, the Valley is not considered as challenging as the Dunluce. The Valley is where Graeme McDowell grew up playing.

RORY LAND

The 18-year-old McIlroy poses at Royal Portrush, the Northern Irish links where two years earlier he stunned the golfing world by shooting a record-breaking 61.

Chubby Chandler, the agent then casting covetous eyes toward McIlroy, couldn't stop talking about Rory's record round. The 2005 North of Ireland was being contested the same week as the 134th Open Championship at St. Andrews (Rory's hero, Tiger Woods, blitzed the field, winning wire-to-wire). Dermot Gilleece, then the lead golf correspondent of the *Irish Times*, told me that Chandler spent that week walking around the Old Course in a semi-daze, bragging about young McIlroy's 61 at Portrush to anyone who would listen. Chubby, who knew he had the inside track on signing him, started referring to Rory as "my pension plan."

Chubby's retirement package had shot a 71 in the first round of stroke-play qualifying at Portrush's Valley Course—a nice score for a youngster who may not have owned a razor blade, but not anything that would make the world quake. But Rory's next round caused tremors from the R&A clubhouse at St. Andrews to the USGA headquarters in Far Hills, New Jersey. In many ways, it was the beginning of the global phenomenon that became *Rory McIlroy*. Even stodgy American golf publications took note.

Eddie McCormack, Rory's opponent earlier that year in the finals of the Irish Close, had already finished his round and was having a libation in the clubhouse bar. When word hit that young McIlroy was on a heater, Eddie and friends made a dash for the door, many with pints still in hand. "People were running all over the place to catch up to Rory," Eddie chuckled in our interview.

It took Rory a while to get rolling that day, Crowe recalls: McIlroy was "just" two-under through eight holes. Almost from nowhere he got to six-under.

"Rory always had a positive demeanour about himself," Crowe wrote in a 2023 email.[2] "Not in a cocky way, [but] confident. He always bounced down the fairways and he certainly did that day."

He was not the only Crowe who had the chance to observe Rory up close. His younger brother Darren was an accomplished amateur who played on several Irish youth squads with McIlroy. The following year, 2006, Darren won the North of Ireland championship at Portrush with his older sibling on the bag.

Stephen now plays a lot of golf at Royal County Down, so he knows his classic links. He had a ringside seat to watch the County Down pup dismember Portrush. Stephen's future bride Jill was caddying for him that afternoon. Gerry McIlroy often looped for Rory back then but that day Rory's buddy Ricky McCormick, a future pro at HGC and an original Mac Packer, was toting McIlroy's bag.

---

[2] In as fortuitous a circumstance as I've ever experienced, amid a huge gallery at Royal Liverpool watching Rory exit the 18th green following the 2023 Open Championship's Wednesday practice round, I happened to choose Stephen and Jill Crowe and their two adorable young boys to interview. I had no idea until I began chatting with them, tape recorder in hand, that Stephen not only knew Rory but had played against him in their amateur days. Cue the *Twilight Zone* theme. The Crowes are lovely people. Since that day at Hoylake, we've become email friends.

"There are not many golf runs that I remember every shot, but that day I do," Rory told the *New York Times* in 2019. McIlroy narrowly missed a birdie putt on the first hole, then drove the green at the short par-four second and two-putted for birdie. He also birdied the longish par-three sixth.

Around the turn, McIlroy "caught fire" by going birdie, eagle, birdie to put him six-under after the 11th hole, Crowe remembers. A couple of holes earlier, one of the guys in the group ahead unleashed a fist pump after draining a putt. "Why would you fist pump during a qualifying round?" a clearly disapproving Rory tsk-tsked to Crowe and O'Callaghan.

After McIlroy's birdie putt disappeared into the cup at 11, Rory punctuated the moment with a big slash of his right fist. As the group approached the next tee, Crowe and O'Callaghan began teasing him. "What was that about 'no fist pump,' McIlroy?"

Rory laughed, Crowe wrote me eighteen years later, "but he must have known deep down that something special was going to happen."

McIlroy proceeded to par numbers 12 and 13, then, Crowe recalls, "got back on the birdie train on the 14th," Portrush's infamous par-three known as "Calamity Corner."[3] It's well-named: catastrophe awaits any golfer whose tee shot fails to find the green.

"I remember he hit a towering draw with a long iron into Calamity, which was an unbelievable shot on such a difficult hole," Crowe wrote, in words that echo Eddie McCormack's praise of Rory's five-iron tee ball in the Close championship a few weeks earlier. Rory's Calamity ball settled to about twenty feet, where Rory's putt again found the bottom.

By now, Portrush townspeople had gotten word that the Holywood Hotshot was torching the place. Hundreds of people

---

3   With Dunluce's redesign, Calamity Corner now plays as number 16.

began surging toward their threesome, without a steward or marshal in sight.

An amusing video produced years later by the R&A shows Rory trying to weave his way through masses of people. It looks more like a frenetic Easter egg hunt than a golf match.

McIlroy was definitely in sync with the big crowd, Crowe remembered. Caddie McCormick, meanwhile, was trying to keep people from pummeling his guy.

There was a delay on the tee of the par-five 17th, which gave Rory a chance to wander away and collect his thoughts. "I think I had probably caught myself thinking about it a little too much," he told the *Times* fourteen years later. "I wanted to go clear my head a bit and start afresh with a new golf shot."

McIlroy banged a perfect drive down the 17th fairway, then played a long iron that landed on the front right third of the green, setting up an easy two-putt for another birdie.

For his part, Crowe can't bring back too much about holes number 15 through 17, except that Rory continued to make birdies as the gallery got larger and more raucous. On number 17, Stephen had to shout and wave to get people's attention so he could play his third-shot approach.

"By the time we got to number 18, it felt like the entire population of Portrush was following us," Crowe recalls. "Rory didn't hit it that close after splitting the fairway. He was about thirty feet from the hole but he rolled the putt in again—and there was an enormous roar! It was probably a bit like what Seve Ballesteros used to do—he 'willed' that putt into the hole!"

In 2019, the year the Open came back to the seaside resort for the first time in seven decades, TaylorMade, Rory's equipment manufacturer, issued a special 61-degree wedge in his honor. Rory's 61 at Portrush is so ingrained in people's memories that almost lost in the exaltation is the fact that he didn't win the tournament. McIlroy ended up losing in the third round of match play.

Aaron O'Callaghan nicely acquitted himself at Portrush in '05, shooting a 70 at the Valley Course and another 70 on the Dunluce amid Rory's rampage. O'Callaghan ended up losing in the first round of match play.

No doubt distracted by all the wandering souls, Crowe shot 77 at Dunluce that day and missed the cut.[4] Along with his father Mark and brother Darren, Crowe today is a principal in the family's construction firm, M.E. Crowe LTD.

After graduating from Southeastern Louisiana in 2009, Aaron O'Callaghan tried to make it on the European Tour, but never got beyond the second stage of Q-School. He took a club job, played satellite tournaments in Europe and the States, then in 2014 went into coaching as an assistant at the University of Louisville. After four years at Louisville, he moved to Wake Forest University in Winston-Salem, North Carolina, the alma mater of Arnold Palmer, Curtis Strange, Webb Simpson, and a host of other great players. Assistant coach Callaghan is still working at Wake today.

McIlroy shot 33-28 that day, with only 26 (!) putts. Rory had signed autographs before, but never like he did that afternoon at Portrush. It took Ricky and Rory a long time to wade through the admirers in the car park.

Chubby Chandler, Michael Bannon, and the Mac Pack had company: a lot of people were now seeing Rory McIlroy as part of their pension plan.

---

[4] All these years later, Stephen still shakes his head and mutters while discussing his 77 that day. On behalf of high-handicappers everywhere, I've assured him that 77 in those circumstances was a hell of a score! Seventy-seven under *any* circumstance, anywhere, is a hell of a score!

Chapter 10

CARNOUSTIE AND COUNTY DOWN

Chubby Chandler, aka "Chubbs," the pugnacious former British touring pro who helped catapult McIlroy's career, has never shied away from a cocktail, a Cuban cigar, or a controversy. In his twenties and thirties, Chubbs tried to scrape out a living on the European Tour, enjoying himself but missing a lot of cuts along the way.

Chandler never ranked higher than 44th on the European Order of Merit, the circuit's old money list. In 1989, he said to hell with it after several of his tour buddies agreed to hire him to manage their business affairs. The legend is that Chubby's start-up capital for what became International Sports Management emerged from gambling-den intrigue at a Cheshire golf club. ISM took off a year later when Irish amateur Darren Clarke, who was destined to do great things and command the respect of his colleagues, asked Chandler to take over as his agent.

As the '90s rolled along, Chubby expanded his portfolio to include cricketeers, footballers, and other luminaries. Remarkably, when Clarke broke through to win the 2011 Open at Royal St. George's, ISM clients had combined to win four of the five previous major championships: Clarke; South African Louis Oosthuizen (2010 Open at St. Andrews); South African Charl Schwartzel (2011 Masters); and McIlroy (2011 US Open).

Whatever tension may have developed between McIlroy and Chandler was years away when Chubby was sitting at the McIlroys' kitchen table in 2006 and '07, excitedly plotting Rory's future.

RORY LAND

ISM not only represented athletes in its salad days but was also retained by the European Tour to plan and manage tournaments, a bit of vertical integration that nineteenth-century American robber barons would have applauded. In May '05, Chubby arranged for the barely sixteen-year-old McIlroy to play in the ISM-run British Masters at the Forest of Arden, a parkland course in the heart of the UK's Midlands.

The weather that week was brisk and blustery. During the Wednesday pro-am, Rory impressed officials with a one-over 73. Conditions got even tougher for the Thursday opening round—too tough for the rookie.

In howling winds, Rory shot a ten-over 82. McIlroy's first round in a pro tournament was marred by a triple-bogey, three double-bogeys, and five bogeys. Rory ended up missing the cut by a wide margin. Gerry confessed that his teenager spent a lot of time staring at scoreboard names and gawking at the galleries.

Chubby wired another dozen pro tournaments for the amateur McIlroy over the next couple of years. In early February 2007, Rory made his first pro cut at the Dubai Desert Classic, shooting back-to-back 69s. Three months shy of his eighteenth birthday, he ended up finishing tied for fifty-second.

As they practiced in the spring and summer of 2007, McIlroy and Bannon established a goal for his appearance in the Open Championship at Carnoustie: they wanted Rory to become the first Irish amateur since Joe Carr, forty-two years earlier at Royal Birkdale, to make the cut.

Anytime a teenager plays in a major it's a big deal, but it was especially portentous for Rory. Tiger Woods was the Open's two-time defending champion, edging American Chris DiMarco at Royal Liverpool in 2005 and lapping the field a year later at St.

Andrews. Woods was the odd-on favorite at Carnoustie, with Sergio Garcia and Padraig Harrington also near the top of bookies' lists. Had Tiger won, he would have been the first golfer since Australian Peter Thomson (1954–1956) to win three Opens in succession.

Rory, of course, wanted to mimic Justin Rose at Birkdale in '98, not only making the cut and winning the Royal & Ancient's Silver Medal as low amateur, but throwing a scare into the leaders.

After Rory, Shane, and company won at Western Gailes in early July, McIlroy went home, took a couple of days off, and tried to wrap his head around the enormity of competing in an Open.

He and his family arrived at Carnoustie the weekend before the tournament. They walked around the course and the village, soaking up the atmosphere. Unlike St. Andrews, a picturesque college town a few miles down the North Sea coast, the village of Carnoustie is a bit grimy. Early that week, Darren Clarke joined Rory on the course, pointing out places to be aggressive and places to exercise caution.

Carnoustie, known far and wide as "Car-nasty," has the reputation of being Scotland's prickliest links, which is saying a lot. McIlroy would be making his Grand Slam tournament debut at a course that is universally respected but not universally loved.

"We see Carnoustie," linksland raconteur Tom Coyne wrote in the *New York Times* in 2018, "and imagine our own dreams turning to sand in our hands and passing through our fingers. We fear the place, but we really fear what it proves to us: that this game we love doesn't love us back."

On Monday and Tuesday, Rory practiced with South African Trevor Immelman (destined the following year to win the Masters), Swede Niclas Fasth, a six-time winner on the European Tour, and Englishman Richie Ramsay, who'd won the previous year's US Amateur at Hazeltine in Minnesota. Three-time Open champion

Nick Faldo joined the group on Monday, but left after four holes once the drizzle became a downpour.

On the eve of the championship, Seve Ballesteros announced his retirement. More than one commentator wondered aloud if an all-time great was bidding farewell while another's career was just getting underway.

Tom Watson's latter-day caddie, US political strategist Neil Oxman, recalls that early in Rory's Open Championship career, Watson was hitting range balls a few yards away. Neil walked up to the kid, introduced himself, pointed to Watson, and said, "See that guy? He played in the Open Championship with Gene Sarazen. And now *you're* getting to play with *him*." Rory understood the import of the moment, grinning and nodding in appreciation.

Rory's first major championship round would be in the company of Swede Henrik Stenson and Spaniard Miguel Angel Jiménez, a Seve protégé. They teed off in weather that was dicey at times. Rory was sporting a Titleist ballcap, black slacks with an oversized Puma belt buckle, and a dark windbreaker with a faux argyle design splashed across the chest.

In their wildest dreams, his mum, dad, agent, coach, and girlfriend, plus the scores of folks who'd made the trek (via car ferry, mainly) from North County Down, could not have imagined a better scenario than the one that unfolded on Thursday, July 19, 2007. McIlroy's performance on the first day of the 136th Open Championship was exactly what Chandler had longed for: Rory unveiling himself to the world with poise and chutzpah.

Written for Irish fans desperate to revel in their favorite son's big moment, Keogh's lede invoked the specter of Rory's idol: "Redhot Rory McIlroy said 'Hello World' as he lit up the Open and outgunned Tiger Woods. The Holywood idol, 18, posted the only bogey-free round of the day as he scooted round in three-under par 68 at savage Carnoustie."

Three-time Open champion Nick Faldo, once part of the kid's "autograph," was eleven strokes in arrears. Future Open champion Darren Clarke, another one of the kid's mentors, was four shots back and also destined to miss the cut.

Keogh wasn't the only member of the press corps rendered incredulous. The ESPN/ABC highlight package shown in the States that night spotlighted Rory. For millions of Americans, including this one, it was the first time they'd seen him swing.

One guy who saw Rory swing up close that afternoon was his caddie, Gordon Faulkner. It was Clarke who recommended that McIlroy team up with the veteran Faulkner, who had once looped for Darren, among others. After round one, Faulkner told BBC Sports that Rory "probably left a couple of shots out there. But it won't bother him too much. His temperament is too good. He's about fifteen years ahead of where he should be when it comes to the mental side of golf."

The BBC also caught up with Rory's mum. "It was an incredible day," Rosie said. "Totally above all of our expectations."

When asked about the vocal support he'd received from the hometown folks who had vacated Belfast Lough for the Barry Burn, Rory said, "It was just like a chill down the back of my spine with the ovation I got [on the 18th hole]. It's fantastic!" He also saluted the GUI for their financial and technical help over the years.

What about being in the same field with Woods—would Rory be able to sleep? "Yes, I'll be able to sleep," he responded. "I'm knackered. But it's just, yeah, it's a pretty special feeling to say that you shot one better than Tiger Woods," McIlroy said with the *sangfroid* of a veteran.

Round two didn't go nearly as well for the highlight boy. In bumpy conditions, McIlroy carded a five-over 76. He made four frontside bogeys before finally birdieing 12 and 14, then stumbled toward the clubhouse with three late bogeys.

Scores soared on day two, so McIlroy's 144 made the weekend. He was eight strokes back of Garcia's lead but the only amateur to make the cut, so he was guaranteed possession of the Silver Medal.

Still, McIlroy wanted more. "I want to play in this [the Open] next year and the easiest way to do that is to finish in the top ten," he said.

Stenson, then ranked seventh in the world, acknowledged that he was impressed by the youngster who consistently outdrove him over the two days. "He has it all and I think we will hear a whole lot about him in the future," the Swede said in a sentiment echoed by British broadcasting icon Peter Alliss and others.

On the 16th green on Friday, Jiménez took Rory aside and calmed him down. McIlroy had stomped his feet on the previous two greens after missing from inside five feet. The cigar- and red-wine-loving "Mechanic," worshiped by European fans, didn't want Rory's putting frustrations to seep into his ball-striking.

"[Rory] is a great kid," Jiménez told the media. "He's been playing since he was so very small and you can see that he is keen to get out there. He's so young and fresh."

Even as the fresh kid slid down the leaderboard—his third-round 73 put him thirteen strokes behind Garcia—the Ulster kid continued to draw on-air raves from Alliss and other commentators.

On Sunday, Ireland celebrated twice over: another McIlroy mentor, Padraig Harrington, took the Claret Jug by beating Sergio by one shot in a four-hole aggregate playoff. Paddy became the first Irishman since Fred Daly at Hoylake in 1947 to win the Open. Harrington nearly threw away the Jug by double-bogeying the 72nd hole, but Sergio then bogeyed the same hole to allow Padraig to slip into a playoff.

Rory finished at Carnoustie with a one-over 72, for a five-over total of 289, tying for 42nd place. His round ended with a flourish when he birdied the 72nd hole after feathering a short-iron inside eight feet. The ovation he received was not as deafening as Rose's nine years earlier, but it earned bouquets from broadcasters. As Rory doffed his cap to the crowd, they predicted that McIlroy would be a factor in major championships for a long time.

A couple of hours later, after confidently striding across the front of Carnoustie's clubhouse to shake hands with R&A dignitaries and accept the Silver Medal, Rory said he was "overjoyed."

He also said he was looking forward to enjoying some down time in Dubai—a getaway present arranged by Chandler's team at ISM, another gift that, had it been given to an American high school kid, might have raised questions about his "amateur" status.

But first Rory thought he might do some partying with his buddies in nearby Dundee, just a couple of miles west. "I've got a few of my friends that are staying over there this week, so I might go out for a while tonight."

Ireland was agog: their way-back-when golfing heroes finally had company in the record books: Paddy had equaled the great Fred Daly, and Rors had matched Joe Carr.

The last amateur event of Rory McIlroy's career was a big one: the 2007 Walker Cup contested at Royal County Down in Newcastle, a seaside village a half-hour's drive south from Rory's hometown. Considered one of the world's most demanding courses, County Down is more adored than Carnoustie—but still has its share of detractors, none of whom were around in 1889 when Old Tom Morris was brought over from St. Andrews to lay out the course for a sum "not greater than four pounds."

Some purists contend that there are too many blind shots at County Down, too many guesswork tee balls, and too many slippery approaches to tiny targets. But no one denies its natural beauty. Nestled between Dundrum Bay and the Mourne Mountains, County Down is elegant to look at and exhilarating to play.

Walker Cup officials on both sides of the ocean knew all about County Down's oddities when they chose it for their 2007 venue. Established in 1922 by then-USGA president George Herbert Walker, the maternal grandfather of President George H.W. Bush, the biennial competition between amateurs from the United States versus their counterparts from Great Britain and Ireland had long been circled on McIlroy's calendar. It was a dream come true: a chance to end his amateur career in front of a home-county crowd. As a youngster, he'd caddied for his dad at County Down and loved the quirky place.

Since McIlroy and Chandler had not been subtle—Gilleece, Keogh, Bamberger, et al., had written extensively about McIlroy's plans to pass up college and turn pro—the golfing world knew that Royal County Down would be Rory's amateur swan song. He wanted to go out with a flourish, to help lead GB&I to a victory over an American team chock-full of future Tour stars, among them Dustin Johnson, Rickie Fowler, Webb Simpson, and a lippy Floridian named Billy Horschel.

The Americans were captained by Main Line Philadelphia luxury car magnate Buddy Marucci. Buddy was, for many years, one of America's best amateur golfers and—as Rory could have recited back then—the fella who'd hung tough against the nineteen-year-old Tiger Woods, losing in the finals of the 1995 US Amateur at Newport Country Club, the second of Tiger's three successive US Amateur triumphs.

The GB&I squad was led by Scotsman Colin Dalgleish and composed of a number of UK players that Rory had faced in various amateur competitions, including a skinny nineteen-year-old from Yorkshire named Danny Willett, who nine years later would win the Masters after Jordan Spieth splashed two balls at number 12. At least on paper, as Bamberger pointed out at the time, the GB&I guys had no business competing against the star-studded Americans.

Rory spent hours on the range honing his game—so many hours, in fact, that he tweaked his back, aggravating an injury that would bother him, on and off, for the next couple of years.

He was so tiny that the team tried to order an "extra small" adult shirt for him; none could be found, so Rory had to settle for wearing "small" GB&I tops during the competition.

The Walker Cup is a two-day match play competition, with four fourball (best ball) or foursome (alternate shot) matches in the morning and singles both days in the afternoon.

Keogh noted that Captain Dalgleish was counting on young Rory to be an "inspirational" force for his squad, getting the Ulster gallery revved up. Dalgleish's move didn't exactly pay off. Instead of roars, Rory's play on day one (Saturday) elicited mainly silence—and the occasional groan.

The day started off well: Rory was wildly cheered during that morning's opening ceremonies. He accepted GB&I's invitation to hoist the Tricolor while a band played the Republic of Ireland's anthem. Given his apprehension about being associated with the green, white, and orange, it's fascinating that young McIlroy, in the heart of Ulster, raised the Republic's colors to the top of a flagpole.

His first swing as a Walker Cupper also drew loud cheers. It was a patented McIlroy draw that split the fairway 320 yards distant on one of County Down's "easier" holes: the then-530-yard, par-five opener.

Playing foursomes with fellow Ulsterman Jonathan Caldwell of Newtownards, McIlroy watched a nervous Dustin Johnson lace a long-iron down the middle. Johnson later swore that his heart was pounding so hard that he started swinging before the public address announcer finished introducing him. D.J. was playing with Texan Colt Knost, a Southern Methodist University undergrad who had, remarkably, won the US Amateur and the US Public Links championships earlier that same summer.

In truth, Rory's play was less than stellar that morning. No one in their quartet lit it up. It seesawed back and forth, but the match ended up all square. Indeed, the entire morning session was halved, 2-2.

After lunch, as promised, Dalgleish did put Rory out number one in singles against Horschel. But the only fireworks in the match were set off by the other guy. McIlroy was outplayed that afternoon by Horschel, who irked GB&I partisans with what Irish correspondents panned as "grandstanding."

Rory, agitated and perhaps trying too hard, had less than his best stuff that day and for most of the weekend. He also admitted sixteen years later that Horschel pissed him off so much that he wanted not just to beat him but to punch him.[1] In the ensuing years, McIlroy and Horschel have become pals, but in September 2007 they were anything but. They went head-to-head in three of the four matches that weekend.

Horschel won one-up over Rory in the day one singles match, but the GB&I guys managed to win four points that afternoon, so the match was tied at six apiece as they went into the Sunday morning fourballs.

There's a reason Buddy Marucci has sold so many high-priced sedans over the years: he knows how to close a deal. After their captain's rousing day-two pep talk, the US guys went out and pummeled the GB&I squad 4-0 in the morning team matches. What had been a nailbiter was now a laugher: the US team led by four points going into the Sunday singles.

Horschel combined with Rickie Fowler that morning to beat the Ulster boys, Caldwell and McIlroy, 2 and 1. After a mid-round harangue from Marucci, the Americans crushed the Irishmen with a backside surge that overcame an early four-down deficit.

Horschel's on-course comportment had not improved: he continued to provoke the crowd. With the outcome of the match still in doubt, he hit a bunker shot that looked for a while like it would find the cup.

"I come down like a damn cheetah, yelling at the top of my lungs, running after the ball, 'Go in! Go in!,'" Horschel recalled a decade later on his Walker Cup buddy Knost's podcast, *Subpar*.

"And it lips out," Horschel said, laughing. "I guess [McIlroy] was pissed about that. I guess he was pissed about the day before when we played our singles matches."

It looked like an American runaway. But Dalgleish's vision began to crystallize in the Sunday afternoon singles. Rory went out in the first match against Horschel and gained at least a measure

---

1   Horschel conceded in 2023 that he was so obnoxious at the '07 Walker Cup that, by rights, he should have punched himself.

of revenge, winning 4 and 2, and in doing so, firing up the crowd and his teammates.

Horschel remembered Rory "nuking" his drive on the par-five first: "I mean, he hit one so far down there, he had, like, literally an eight-iron into the green," which Rory proceeded to hit fifteen feet from the flag. Billy played the hole more conventionally, putting his third-shot wedge to about ten feet.

"And he makes this eagle putt," Horschel told podcast listeners, "and he gives out the biggest yell, because he's letting me know, 'This shit ain't happenin' anymore! This is my house today!' And I was like, damn, I'm fucked."

He was. The match never got close.

The roars triggered by Rors didn't stop reverberating around County Down for a while. GB&I won 4½ points in the first five matches: after Rory polished off Horschel, Rhys Davies beat Rickie Fowler, 3 and 2; Danny Willett halved his match with Colt Knost; Lloyd Saltman dusted Trip Kuehne, 2 and 1; and Caldwell drummed Kyle Stanley, 2-up.

Suddenly things were getting "tense," Marucci remembered. The US team was in free fall.

Horschel recalls that the entire US team was gathered around the 18th green to cheer on Jonathan Moore in his match against Nigel Edwards, which was all square in the middle of the final fairway. Moore unleashed a 235-yard downwind five-iron that hit short of the green and somehow scuttled to within four feet.

It ended up winning the Walker Cup for the American side. Video shows Marucci kneeling on the green, gesturing as he helps Moore's caddie read the putt. Moore's ball snuck in the right side, setting off a riotous celebration.

"It was a very special weekend for me on home territory—it was just a pity that the result didn't match the occasion," Rory said afterward.

Rory and his tender back went 1-2-1 in the competition. It was not what the youngster had hoped. But very soon his results *would* match the occasion.

Chapter 11

PLAY FOR PAY

On Wednesday morning, September 19, 2007, it became official: Rory McIlroy signed papers making him the youngest affiliate member then playing the European Tour. Chubby Chandler had orchestrated every step of the eighteen-year-old's journey from amateur (although "junior-pro" would be more accurate) to overt professional.

Thanks to Chubby and his team at ISM, Rory was getting paid to swing Titleist clubs, wear FootJoy golf shoes, (eventually) sport Oakley sunglasses and apparel, make appearances for two Irish-based companies, Bennett Construction and an equity investment firm called FL Investors, and among other deals, lend his name—for mega Emirati dirham—to a string of Dubai-based luxury resort hotels owned by the Jumeirah Group.

Jumeirah's chief financial officer happened to hail from Holywood. He'd had his eye on Rory and his marketing potential for years. Their partnership sprung from Rory's back-to-back appearances in the Dubai Desert Classic as a sixteen- and seventeen-year-old.

It all added up to major bank for the working-class kid. Rory had said all along that, once he turned pro, he never wanted his parents to work again; soon enough, he got his wish.

Before long, his dad left his positions at the Holywood Rugby Club and the Holywood Golf Club and his mum retired from the 3-M plant. His parents worried that Rory was spending too much too quickly; he'd already put money down on a big home near Holywood.

He wanted to be close to his parents' place, he joked with the media, so his mum could do his "wash." Once the new place was renovated, his parents spent a lot of time there, with Holly Sweeney to follow within the next year. Chubby installed a putting-and-chipping facility at Rory's new place that put the old one to shame.

The teenager with a scant understanding of macro- and microeconomics had an intuitive feel for supply and demand, plus the intrinsic value of brand-building and affinity marketing. "As I hopefully grow as a professional golfer," he said at the press conference announcing his plans, "[my sponsors] will grow as brands. I think that is a perfect combination."

For a time, it may indeed have been the perfect combination—and lord knows his deals were giving the McIlroys the financial security about which they'd dreamed for years. But his early corporate sponsorships had something of a grab-bag feel: they lacked strategic definition and synergy.

It took Rory four years—and a long heart-to-heart with tennis immortal and ace brand-builder Roger Federer—to figure out that he wanted to use his corporate affiliations to project his own unique brand, not just be a walking billboard.

Rory emphasized at the press session that he had "played Titleist all my life and it was great that they wanted me as a staff player." Then, in words that would prove ironic given his club-fiddling down the road, he said, "I don't want to be changing clubs and tinkering with things."

In truth, Titleist didn't pay its staff guys much back then—and they still don't, at least not compared to TaylorMade, Callaway, or Srixon. So, when Nike came calling five years later and TaylorMade a few years after that, Rory found it impossible to resist their siren calls.

Rory would be making his professional debut in the same tournament in which, two years earlier, he had first appeared in a European Tour event. But the venue was different. The 2007 British Masters was held at the Brabazon Course at The Belfrey, a resort not far from Birmingham, the home of Tommy Shelby and his fellow *Peaky Blinders*.

At his presser that week, Rory talked about his "trust" in Darren and Chubby. "I just want to go out and enjoy myself in my first event as a pro," Rory said. "I have a number of events to try and get my card and if that doesn't happen, I have Tour School, as well."

His first round as a professional was a bogey-free 69, shot in stiff crosswinds that made it difficult to hold fairways and greens. A lighter putter helped him make some tough par putts. Plus, he chipped in for birdie on number 12, which "settled the nerves a bit," he said.

He said he was surprised at his calmness. "Always get butterflies on the first tee but not as nervous as I was at the Open or the Walker Cup.

"Mum probably was nervous," he conceded. "Dad's all right. He doesn't care—well, he cares, but it doesn't matter to him if I shoot 69 or 79. He's just happy that I'm playing golf."

Day two did not go nearly as well for the nerveless one. In windier conditions, McIlroy shot 78 and was fortunate to make the cut. His round turned ugly on number 10 when he hit into a fairway bunker, was forced to come out sideways, and made a double-bogey after hitting a sloppy third.

"Hopefully, my luck will turn a bit over the weekend and I can shoot a couple of rounds in the 60s and get myself up the leaderboard again."

His luck did indeed turn, but only slightly. He shot a 70 in round three, punctuated by a bad bogey on the last hole when he pushed his drive right and couldn't get it up and down.

"Hopefully, [the 70] will give me an extra hour in bed," the teenager wished aloud to chuckles in the press tent. The added sleep didn't do much good. He ended up shooting 73 on Sunday to finish tied for 42nd. Fellow ISM client Lee Westwood won the event going away at 15-under.

McIlroy gave himself a B-minus for the week. "There's room for improvement. There always is."

His first professional payday wasn't bad, a check for €15,128—a huge chunk of his parents' yearly earnings, a fact surely not lost on the McIlroys. Asked what he was going to do with the money, Rory caused more pressroom titters by allowing that he might take his girl to the cinema.

The Chandler-choreographed schedule called for Rory, Darren, and their respective dads to christen Castle Dargan, Clarke's new course in County Sligo, before Rory tackled his second tournament as a pro.

Sadly, it rained hard in Sligo that day, holding the gallery to just three hundred spectators. "The McIlroys took the money, and more importantly, the bragging rights," the *Irish Independent* reported the next day. Rory and Gerry beat Darren and Godfrey, 5 and 3. Gerry played off a two-handicap; Godfrey played off a seven.

The fourball match ended on the 15th green, which meant the four competitors could climb out of their rain gear and into a warm beverage at the Castle Dargan Hotel that much quicker. A photo in the *Independent* showed Gerry McIlroy drenched head to toe—a shame, Rory said, since his old man had been working hard at his game. Gerry chuckled: "It's always nice to beat the Clarkes. I didn't play great, to be honest, but it was great craic (Gaelic for 'fun')."

Clarke joked that the McIlroys had given themselves "a decided advantage by going to bed early [the night before]. You can be sure neither myself nor my dad did that."

Some "wooly hats" might be needed for his sojourn the following week to Scotland's Dunhill Links, Rory laughed.

Another golfing legend that week volunteered that he was a big admirer. Nick Faldo was asked about Rory as Faldo opened up his own resort along Lough Erne, near Enniskillen in County Fermanagh. Faldo reminded the questioner that Rory had been a participant in his Faldo Series youth program, beginning at age thirteen. What impressed Faldo most about the County Down kid was his confidence.

"He's got that self-belief and swagger," Faldo said, "which is going to be very important to him. Rory showed at the Open that every part of his golf game is there but you've got to have serious belief in yourself going out on Tour."

That swagger helped Rory breeze through the first stage of European Tour qualifying school that week. It also got him, thanks to Chubbs, a gig as one of the Lough Erne resort's traveling pros and possession of a sweet condo. Lough Erne was only a ninety-minute drive from Holywood.

Rory's self-belief was on full display the following week at the Dunhill Links, the European Tour's counterpart to the old Crosby clambake, now the PGA Tour's Pebble Beach Pro-Am. The Dunhill is contested on three classic links along the North Sea and its firths of Forth and Tay: the Old Course at St. Andrews, Carnoustie, and Kingsbarns.

The rest of the '07 Dunhill field was formidable: Lee Westwood, who'd just won at The Belfrey; 1999 Open champion Paul Lawrie, who won at Carnoustie; Lawrie's fellow Scotsman Colin Montgomerie; and a voluble twenty-five-year-old Brit named Nick Dougherty, another Faldo Series alum.

Rory started modesty enough, carding a 71 at Car-nasty. But consecutive rounds of 67 (Friday at St. Andrews; Saturday at Kingsbarns), coupled with a final round 68 at St. Andrews on Sunday got McIlroy to 15-under, one behind Justin Rose and three behind surprise winner Dougherty.

On Friday, McIlroy's round at the Old Course began with a splash. He chunked a 106-yard wedge into the Swilcan Burn that guards the first green and made a quick six.

"But [McIlroy] hit back with birdies at the third, fourth, fifth, and seventh before hitting top gear on the back nine," wrote Keogh Friday evening from St. Andrews.

Rory's "top gear" included a feathered lob wedge to four feet at the 10th, which got him to four-under for the tournament and onto the leaderboard. He then birdied the par-four 13th after another lovely approach.

But McIlroy saved his best moment for last. On the par-four 18th, his second shot spun back into golf's most notorious swale, the dreaded Valley of Sin. His birdie bid had to negotiate some forty feet up and over one of the most daunting hillocks in Christendom. Somehow, Rory's putt found the back of the cup—and dropped!

To secure his European Tour card for 2008, McIlroy needed to pocket €200,000 at the Dunhill. Journalist Bernie McGuire remembered McIlroy, having completed his final round, watching from behind the 18th green as Lawrie surveyed a five-foot putt for par.

If Lawrie made the putt, he would tie McIlroy for third, denying the youngster a few thousand Euros and forcing him to win a nice check at his next tour stop to earn his '08 card. If he missed it, Rory would—already, in just his second professional event—obtain a spot on next year's tour, an amazing feat at his age.

"McIlroy watched intently," McGuire wrote, "as Lawrie's birdie putt failed to drop in.

"'Well, that's my Tour card,'" said McIlroy. As was his MO back then, Rory was wearing his Jumeirah cap crushed down on his scalp, which forced his unruly hair to spill out in all directions.

Between the Belfry and the Dunhill Links, Rory had earned a cool €226,000. It meant he could skip the second phase of Tour qualifying school and go right to its finals, where a perfunctory score would get him his card. He became one of the youngest-ever members of the European Tour.

RORY LAND

Next up was the Open de Madrid, where Rory again finished in the top five, this time knotted for fourth. For a long time that Sunday, McIlroy had the Spanish gallery buzzing as he crept closer to becoming the youngest winner in European Tour history.

His eagle on the par-five 10th hole induced squeals as Rory pulled within a shot of the leaders. But a couple of late bogeys forced Rory to settle for a final round 70 and a tie for fourth. McIlroy expressed frustration in Madrid that more putts didn't fall, which would become a recurring lament in his career, as it is for most pros who play the infernal game.

The Madrid check meant he finished the 2007 European Tour season with €277,255, finishing in 95th place on the Order of Merit, not bad for a kid who had been a pro for less than a month.

Given McIlroy's auspicious start, ISM and the European Tour the following winter and spring were eager to showcase their teenaged phenom. But as so often happens, the phenom went into a sophomore slump.

The first two-thirds of the 2008 season proved frustrating. It began when he missed the cut at the Hong Kong Open, his first MC as a pro. That Friday night, forlorn, sans parents, agent, and girlfriend, he wandered around Hong Kong solo, ending up eating dinner at an automat. "So much for the glamour and glitz of professional golf," he thought as he wandered back to his hotel.

His game brightened a bit the following week at the Australian Mastercard Masters, where he finished tied for 15th at the Huntingdale Golf Club, a daunting sand-belt course in greater Melbourne. The €12,000 McIlroy earned Down Under was the highlight of his winter campaign.

Rory missed one cut after another as the European Tour completed its Middle Eastern, South African, and Asian swings and boomeranged back toward Europe. In mid-May 2008, just days after his nineteenth birthday, Rory was psyched to play in his first Irish Open as a professional, this one at Adare Manor in County Limerick. At Adare, he was asked about his prolonged funk.

"I think going out last year and getting my Tour card so quickly probably put a lot of expectations on my shoulders," he responded. "You just have to keep working hard because all the other guys are working hard out here to try and beat you."

The new lessons he had absorbed did indeed put him in good stead that week. After three 70s and a 72, he finished seventh, making a tidy €75,000. It was, to date, his biggest payday of the year. It could have been better, Rory said on Saturday.

"I just didn't hole enough putts again.... I gave myself a lot of opportunities but really didn't make many."

It would become McIlroy's Achilles heel: his putting never quite matched the consistency of his ball striking. After he became a pro, those ten-to-fifteen-footers started becoming harder to make; his stroke got less natural and more mechanical. After his flatstick frustrations began to build that season, Team McIlroy sought help. It wouldn't be the last time.

His top-ten showing in County Limerick proved illusory. He went back to missing cuts, failing to qualify for the 2008 Open Championship at Royal Birkdale, which for the second year in a row was won by Paddy Harrington.

McIlroy was saying all the right things—that he wasn't getting discouraged, that he was still hitting the ball well, that he just needed to hole a few putts here or there. But privately, he and his team had to be worried. Even when he made a cut, he wasn't coming close to contending.

All that changed in September when, after missing three straight weekends, he played lights-out at the European Masters at Crans-sur-Sierre, Switzerland. By then, Rory had J.P. Fitzgerald, a veteran caddie originally from Castleknock outside Dublin, on his bag. Ernie Els, who had recently dismissed J.P. as his bagman, recommended that Rory give J.P. a try.

Fitzgerald was all-business on the course. He could be owlish at times, perhaps *too* prickly about distractions coming from the gallery. Like Harry Diamond in Rory's post-2017 era, he often got criticized for not reining in the headstrong McIlroy. Still, J.P. was the steadying presence that young McIlroy needed.

Besides Els, Fitzgerald had worked for fellow Irishmen Paul McGinley and Darren Clarke. J.P. was on McGinley's bag when the Dubliner rolled in the putt that won the 2002 Ryder Cup for the Euros. Today, McGinley laughs that he had to tell the intense Fitzgerald to "shut up" as the two hovered over the putt.

When asked to comment back then about Rory's new bagman, Chubby Chandler delivered a classic Chubby-ism: "He may not be the best caddie in the world, but he's the best caddie for Rory."

The McIlroy-Fitzgerald coupling clicked; eventually, it proved extremely lucrative for both parties.

Four months after his nineteenth birthday, McIlroy in Switzerland was vying to become the third-youngest winner on the European Tour, behind only Seve Ballesteros and an obscure South African named Dale Hayes.

On Thursday, Rory shot his best-ever round as a pro to that point, a sparkling 63 that was only one shot off the course record. He said afterward that his ball striking was solid, but that for the first time all year, his putting and wedge play were stellar.

On Friday, he shot a 71, a typical score for him, he said, following an ultra-low score. His Saturday round began with a thunderbolt when he eagled the 543-yard, par-five first hole. His drive was so long and the Alpine air so thin that he only needed a nine-iron for his second shot. "That settled my nerves," Rory laughed.

Six birdies later, he ended up shooting 66; he took a four-shot lead into the final round. Rory, it appeared, was on the cusp of making history.

On Saturday night, Chubby Chandler and the ISM team arranged for a private plane to fly them from the UK to Switzerland so they could be part of the next day's celebration of McIlroy's first win as a pro.

It was not to be. Rory played mistake-prone golf and was unable to get any momentum going. His even-par round ended with a nervous bogey—a missed five-footer at the mountain course's slippery 18th hole, a par-four that looks more like a ski slope than a golf hole. His late miscue allowed Frenchman Jean-François Lucquin to force a sudden-death playoff. Lucquin won on the second playoff hole when Rory missed a putt of less than two feet, a gaffe that induced gasps from the Swiss gallery.

Still, his second-place earnings thrust him into the Top Fifty of the European Order of Merit and qualified him for the year-end Volvo Masters in Spain. His mentor Harrington sought Rory out after his Swiss mountain collapse, urging him to put missed short putts out of his head—a gesture that meant a lot to Rory.

McIlroy's prospects turned around toward the end of the '08 season. He didn't win, but he finished in the top ten in four of his six final outings. For the second year in a row, he had an impressive finish at the Dunhill, ending up in eighth place, just four off of Swede Robert Karlsson's winning score. Only a third-round 78 kept Rory out of contention.

At Valderrama, playing in what proved to be the last Volvo Masters, he finished well back but won a check for €29,500 to finish the season with more than €400,000 in earnings. He and ISM claimed that his winnings exceeded their goals for the year—which surely wasn't true. They had to be disappointed.

In late 2008, he surprised perhaps even himself by finishing second against a superb field in the Hong Kong Open—the place where he had started the year with a disconsolate MC.

Rory began the tournament with a 70 and followed it with three scorching rounds in the mid-60s. It should have been enough to win, but it was only good for a three-way playoff with Taiwanese player Lin Wen-tang and Italian Francesco Molinari. The first playoff hole eliminated Molinari, when the Italian failed to birdie the short par-four 18th.

It looked like McIlroy was going to win it outright on that first extra hole, but Wen-tang threaded a miraculous pitch through the trees on the left side of the fairway to within a few feet of the cup and matched McIlroy's birdie.

On the second extra hole it was Rory's turn to pull his drive into the left rough. His approach didn't get near the flagstick. The match ended when Wen-tang pitched to within tap-in distance for his birdie. For the second time in weeks, Rory had lost an agonizing playoff.

McIlroy also finished fourth that fall in the Barclays Singapore Open, which meant, in toto, he had surpassed Tiger Woods' rookie-year earnings, becoming the youngest player to exceed €1 million in career winnings. His performances in Hong Kong and Singapore presaged good things to come.

Chapter 12

BREAKING THROUGH

Given his run of top-five finishes on the European Tour, it's a bit surprising that it took McIlroy nearly eighteen months to win outright. He was still a teenager when it happened at the Dubai Desert Classic, in midwinter 2009.

After losing the playoff the previous November in Hong Kong, Rory finished tied for third at the 2008 South African Open, played that December at the Pearl Valley Golf Club, a Jack Nicklaus design in Val de Vie, South Africa's wine country.

Rory's South Africa finish jumped him to 39th in the world rankings. More importantly, it earned him an invitation to the 2009 Masters—the championship he'd dreamed about since he was a kid.

At Dubai five weeks later, McIlroy and the rest of the field had to withstand searing heat and a strange fog that forced a suspension of play in the first round. But Rory got his opener in before the pea soup condensed: he shot an eight-under 64 that put him a stroke ahead.

His playing partner that morning was two-time major champion Mark O'Meara. As a kid, Rory had seen O'Meara play at the World Match Play championship at Wentworth. At age nine, just days before winning the ten-and-under championship at Doral, Rory wormed his way to O'Meara and had him sign a golf ball. The ball with O'Meara's autograph was still in Rory's bedroom back home.

In Dubai, O'Meara came away impressed. "Ball striking-wise at 19, [McIlroy] is probably better than Tiger was at 19. Rory's technique, I think, is better."

On Friday, Mark's new buddy stayed at the top of the leaderboard with a 68. Henrik Stenson shot 65 to close within a stroke; Justin Rose was another stroke back after a 66.

Saturday's third round was cut off by nasty weather. Just before play was suspended, Rory had eagled the 10th hole.

On Sunday morning, he birdied the par-four 11th and the par-five 18th to finish off his third round with a 69, putting him two shots ahead of South African Louis Oosthuizen and Australian left-hander Richard Green, with Brit Justin Rose lurking another stroke back.

"We will see what happens tomorrow," Rory had said on Saturday evening. Then, in deference to his frustrating experiences in playoffs, he added: "Avoiding the playoff tomorrow, that's the plan."

The plan worked—but in consummate McIlroy fashion, it wasn't without a few hitches. His finale began with a brilliant birdie-birdie-birdie start. But on the par-four fifth, Rory's short-sided himself with his approach, barely got his chip onto the putting surface, and yanked his ten-footer for par.

He then played his bogey putt too quickly, causing the broadcast crew to scold, "No, No, No, Rory!" when his three-footer lipped out. His putt for double-bogey was longer than his bogey putt, but Rory holed it.

He'd let the field back into the tournament. It would, weirdly, happen again later in the round. But in between, the kid put on a clinic.

He reeled off five birdies on the spin, starting with a fifteen-footer on the par-four ninth. When he finished the barrage at the par-five 13th with an easy up and down, he was six clear of the field—and cruising.

The cruise hit some snags beginning on the par-three 15th, when his tee shot buried into a thick grass bunker short and left of the flagstick. Rory did well to pop the ball out to within twenty feet of the cup; his par putt didn't come close. Suddenly, his playing partner Rose had new life.

Rory's drive on number 16 was pushed "a million miles right," the TV guys said. He tried to clip it back onto the fairway but the ball ticked a palm tree and fell short. McIlroy was forced to make a six-footer to salvage a bogey.

On number 17, he pushed another tee ball into the desert, leading to a seven-foot putt for par. Rory pulled it left—his habitual miss in the clutch.

Justin was now just one back with one hole left, the par-five 18th with a massive pond guarding the green. This time Rory's tee-ball three-wood found the fairway. He chose to follow Rose in laying up.

The Brit went first, hitting a so-so wedge to twenty feet. McIlroy then hit a no-no wedge through the green; it tumbled into the back bunker, sending an anguished Rory to both knees in the fairway.

But the penitent's prayers were answered. The ball stayed on the bunker's upslope. He had plenty of room to finesse it down toward the cup. He hit it with near-perfect pace; it nestled two and a half feet south of the stick.

It was now Rose's turn to make a clutch putt. He couldn't do it. So, the door was open for Rory to win in his thirty-seventh start as a professional. His putt rolled true.

McIlroy admitted that the pressure had made it difficult, saying: "You see guys coming down the stretch with a four or five shot lead, and you think it's easy—but it's not."

"This win is definitely for my parents, who were here. They have never been pushy. They have done so much for me and it's nice to be able to repay them in some way."

Rory's win generated "Finally!" headlines throughout Ireland and the UK—a strange phenomenon for a nineteen-year-old.

Later in February, Rory made his first trip to the US as a professional, securing one of the sixty-four spots in the Accenture World Match Play Championship at Dove Mountain in Marana, Arizona.

Rory must have been chuffed, because Tiger was playing in his first tournament since undergoing knee surgery after his playoff triumph over Rocco Mediate eight months earlier at the 2008 US Open at Torrey Pines.

McIlroy did okay in his first-ever World Golf Championship event. He dispatched South African Louis Oosthuizen in the first round, 2 and 1. In the second round, he beat American Hunter Mahan, then at the top of his considerable game, 1-up. Up next was another South African, Tim Clark, whom Rory put away, 4 and 3.

In the quarterfinals, Rory ran up against Aussie Geoff Ogilvy, the 2006 US Open champion at Winged Foot and a two-time WGC-event winner. Ogilvy was at the apex of his form, making eight birdies, including three in a row on the backside, in beating McIlroy, 2 and 1. Ogilvy went on to win that year's Match Play.

Overall, Rory was pleased by his US pro debut. When the press asked if his goal was to overtake Tiger as world number one, Rory deftly sidestepped the question, asserting that all he wanted was to get into the world top ten "and see how it goes from there."

Despite Chandler's aversion to having his guys play in the States, Rory and Chubby had devised a schedule that kept McIlroy in the country for much of the late-winter, early-spring swing through Florida and Texas. Rory finished tied for 13th at the Honda Classic near his future home in Florida and tied for 19th at the Shell Houston Open.

But the centerpiece of Rory's early-'09 tour of the Lower 48 was his maiden trip to Bobby Jones's "cathedral in the pines." The soap opera that is "Rory McIlroy at the Masters"—a nearly two-decade-long melodrama full of passion, intrigue, remorse, and more than occasional self-flagellation—unfolded innocently enough.

The lords of Augusta, never known for a sense of whimsy, decided to give the media a fun storyline. They put together three

Masters rookies: McIlroy, 19, American Anthony Kim, 23, and Japanese teen sensation Ryo Ishikawa, just 17.

Counted on to shoot off fireworks, the threesome produced duds—at least in round one. Rory matched par, Ishikawa shot a two-over 74, and Kim, a cocksure Korean-American who had electrified the golfing world by zapping Sergio Garcia in the lead-off singles match at the '08 Ryder Cup, shot a dim 75.

On Friday morning, Kim managed to get crosswise with green-jacketed BSDs by bringing his cellphone onto the range and plugging in earphones so he could enjoy his playlist while warming up. Earphones or no, Kim was violating the club's strict no-cellphones policy. He was told to put the phone in his bag and keep it there.

Maybe the range dustup snapped Kim out of his funk. In just his second competitive round ever at Augusta, Kim despoiled Alistair MacKenzie's pristine grounds by making a record eleven birdies! Kim's 65 could have been lower had he managed to avoid a double-bogey and two bogeys.

Rory, for his part, also generated heat that day—but not in a good way. McIlroy stood on the 16th tee four-under for the day and the championship. Lawrence Donegan of the *Guardian* galleried McIlroy on Friday and said that the Irish youngster pulled off one "wonderful" shot after another.

Donegan's favorite was a "towering long-iron" second on the par-five 13th that settled just a few feet from the cup, leading to Rory's first-ever eagle at Augusta, which meant Rosie was getting some new crystal for the dining room hutch.[1] Suddenly, McIlroy was on the first page of the Masters leaderboard, which must have sent people into delirium at the Dirty Duck Alehouse[2] and other Holywood pubs, where it was all happening on a Friday night!

But the phantom that has always haunted McIlroy at the Masters grabbed him on the 16th tee and sent his ball into the

---

[1] The Masters traditionally awards crystal highball glasses to any player making an eagle during the course of the tournament.
[2] Rory's favorite hangout in Holywood, "The Duck" sits on the edge of the lough. It has a stunning view of the water from its upper-floor dining room.

par-three's pond. He walked off the green fuming over his double. Things got worse two holes later when a tee-ball misfire led to an approach that landed in a greenside bunker.

Rory's attempt to vacate the trap didn't come close to clearing the lip; the ball trickled back toward his feet. Thus ensued what Donegan called "a complicated affair" that took four hours to resolve and must have sent shivers down McIlroy's spine.

"Put simply," Donegan wrote, "McIlroy acted his shoe size and not his age, kicking the sand in frustration after duffing his first shot. Such conduct, if proven, carries a two-shot penalty. Significantly, [McIlroy] signed his card without reference to the possible penalty." That card included a seven, a painful triple-bogey, at the concluding hole.

After his round ended, Rory stormed past the press guys gathered around number 18 and avoided the media pavilion altogether. Unbeknownst to him, Masters competition committee chairman Fred Ridley (now Augusta's big boss) was reviewing McIlroy's behavior—and not happily.

Ridley called McIlroy and asked him to examine the video and discuss his intentions. Did his "kick" at the sand materially affect his next shot? What was McIlroy's thinking when he thrust his foot forward once his first shot failed to get out of the bunker?

McIlroy said he hadn't done anything wrong and did not feel the need to meet with Ridley—a cheeky response for a Masters rookie. As the *Florida Times-Union* put it the next day, "Not many players would think to tell one of the highest-ranking officials of the Augusta National Golf Club 'no,' when asked to have a chat."

But Rory changed his tune when Ridley called him back a half-hour later. In an ominous lawyerly tone, Ridley informed McIlroy that "it would be in your best interest to come up and see the tape."

Rory told the rules maven (and 1976 US Amateur champion) that his foot action was more a "sweep" than a "kick," that he liked to smooth out the sand with his feet after playing a bunker shot, and that it was not his intent to try and improve the lie of his next shot.

Ridley heard Rory out, let him go, then consulted with his committee members before phoning the youngster back a couple of hours later and telling him that he wouldn't be penalized or suspended.

McIlroy had dodged a bullet. His intent was certainly not to bend the rules, but allowing his adolescent anger to boil over—even for an instant—at a place like Augusta was brooking trouble.

Rory's Saturday one-under 71 didn't help him climb the leaderboard. His Sunday 70, however, put him at two-under, allowing him to tie for twentieth. It was a more-than-respectable showing for a youngster playing in his first Masters and just his second major overall.

Having been churlish with the press on Friday, McIlroy more than made up for it over the weekend. "I don't feel like a nineteen-year-old," Rory said after Saturday's round. "I feel like I've matured very quickly since coming on Tour." It may have been manufactured bravado, but he also claimed that he was not "overawed" by Augusta.

Still, the bizarre happenings in his second round set the tone for McIlroy at the Masters: flashes of brilliance followed by dubious shot-making and even more dubious decision-making.

His confidence must have taken a hit a few weeks later when he missed the cut at his first Players Championship at TPC Sawgrass in Ponte Vedra. Pete Dye's design through the wetlands of North Florida was another place that would give Rory the willies until he broke through with a win in 2019.

Now twenty, McIlroy returned to the European Tour that spring. At Wentworth, he was competing in the BMW championship for the second time as a pro. The year before, 2008, McIlroy had failed to scare the cutline.

At the century-old Harry Colt-designed gem southwest of London, often called the "Augusta National of the UK," Rory finished tied for fifth. A reporter there asked how Rory was coping with sudden stardom. McIlroy went on a riff about how his pals helped keep him grounded.

"Most of my friends are at university so [they're] either back in Belfast or there's a few in Dundee, a few in Edinburgh, a few in Newcastle.... It's like two different lives—I've got my life out here where I'm working hard and trying to win golf tournaments and my life back home where I've got my family and my friends, my girlfriend, and just trying to be a normal guy."

"Just trying to be normal" would become a continuous refrain in McIlroy's life—indicative, perhaps, of an internal struggle: Rory the Enigma, the Guy Who Never Seems Satisfied. The more famous and celebrated he got, the more he pined for a "regular" existence. The more accomplished he became on the course, the more he wanted credit for other pursuits. The more he was saluted for his interpersonal skills and charisma, the more, it seemed, he wanted to retreat into a quieter and more contemplative world.

Rory's debut in the US Open came on the toughest track imaginable, A.W. Tillinghast's starkly named Black Course at Bethpage State Park on Long Island. Bethpage Black is so difficult that it comes with its own warning sign, urging high-handicappers[3] to think twice before tackling it.

McIlroy nicely acquitted himself on a layout where shooting level par was playing lights out. Even Rory's hero, Tiger Woods, who'd won the previous US Open held at Bethpage seven years

---

3   "The Black," as Long Islanders call it, is the hardest course this high-handicapper has ever seen.

earlier, ended up shooting even-par in the '09 tourney, finishing tied for sixth.

McIlroy's more than creditable 72-70-72 put him at four-over Saturday night, eleven shots back of eventual winner Lucas Glover. On Sunday, Rory shot two-under 68 in brutal conditions, propelling him up the leaderboard. He ended up tying for tenth—a damned fine showing for a guy six weeks removed from being a teenager.

In July 2009, Rory played in his second-ever Open Championship, this time at Turnberry on Scotland's western coast. After shooting a 69 on day one, McIlroy quickly fell out of contention, finishing in a tie for forty-seventh.

Everyone at Turnberry that week—including eventual winner Stewart Cink—played second fiddle to Tom Watson, the then-fifty-nine-year-old who nearly pulled off the most remarkable coup in golf history.

Watson ended up losing a heartbreaker when his 72nd-hole eight-iron caught a downwind gust and bounced through the green, leading to a bogey and a four-hole aggregate playoff with Cink, which he lost. The Hall of Famer handled his disappointment better than media members, who had been shamelessly rooting for him. When he got to the press center and saw all the long faces, Watson urged everyone to buck up.

"Ain't nobody died!" he cracked with a wicked smile.

As the years went by, and his heartache in the majors deepened, McIlroy would come to parrot Watson's sentiment, perhaps more times than he would have liked.

The 2009 PGA Championship is where McIlroy made his first indelible mark in a major. It was held at Hazeltine National Golf

Club, a Minnesota course originally laid out by Robert Trent Jones Sr. Hazeltine has hosted numerous US Opens and PGAs—even a Ryder Cup—but rarely makes the list of anyone's favorite courses.

Only nine players broke par, and only two—Taiwanese player Y.E. Yang and Tiger Woods—got deeper than three-under. Remarkably, Tiger lost a 54-hole lead in a major—the only time that happened in his career.

Rory, for his part, never broke 70, yet still finished tied for third. His final round, a two-under 70, shot him up the leaderboard when almost everybody else was going backward in stiff crosswinds. McIlroy ended up finishing at three-under 285, tied for third with fellow Chandler client Lee Westwood.

It was a coming-of-age moment for McIlroy. In just his fourth major as a professional, Rory hung tough on a demanding course.

That fall, Rory became the youngest player since Sergio Garcia to earn a spot in the world's top ten. McIlroy finished 2009 as number nine. He ended up finishing second to Lee Westwood in the European Tour's inaugural Race to Dubai (money list) that year. All that, and he still had five months to go before he was legally able to order a beer in the States!

"McIlroy," wrote Keogh that winter, "has talent beyond belief but lacks what the old boxing aficionados call 'ring craft.'"

Two-thousand-ten would bloody Rory a bit; it helped turn him into a cagier pugilist—but not, perhaps, cagy enough.

McIlroy's 2010 began with solid showings in both Abu Dhabi and Dubai. At the Abu Dhabi Championship played at his sponsor, Jumeirah Estates, he shot four rounds in the 60s and finished third behind Germany's Martin Kaymer. At the Desert Classic, he finished sixth behind Miguel Angel Jiménez.

Between a tender back (Rory called the discomfort a "niggle") and his frustration over uneven putting, he was heading off to the States for his late winter/early spring swing with a couple of nagging questions. He approached Chubby about the prospect of hiring a "mental coach," someone who could help him work through the emotional challenges of getting to the top of the heap.

Given the state of Rory's game, the 74th Masters could not have come along at a more inopportune time. He lacked confidence in every phase of his game.

A couple of short-game mistakes led to a desultory 74 in the first round. The next day, Rory's 77 was so slipshod it triggered speculation in the media center that his sore back was worse than he was letting on.

"Sometimes I just think I need to get back to the way I was when I was a kid, just going out there and whacking it, finding it and whacking it again," McIlroy said after missing the cut. "Sometimes your head can get a bit muddled up with a lot things—I just have to enjoy it again."

Fortunately for Rory, it only took two-and-a-half weeks of de-muddling before he got back to finding and whacking.

At the 2010 Wells Fargo Championship at Quail Hollow in Charlotte, North Carolina—a tricky layout originally designed by George Cobb and later toughened by Arnold Palmer—Rory swore he was feeling better about his game. Still, it looked like he was going to miss what would have been his third successive cut.

However, late in his Friday round, he eagled the par-five seventh (his 16th hole) with a sensational long-iron second. It helped him make the cut on the number at one-over.

What transpired over the weekend had broadcasters and reporters scrambling for the record books. He shot a combined 16-under for his third and fourth rounds, which would have been a hell of a score on a municipal layout. At a track like Quail Hollow, which has hosted PGA Championships and international competitions, it was gob-smacking.

His Saturday 66, which got him on the bottom rung of the leaderboard, four shots behind third-round leader Billy Mayfair, was sparkling enough. But it didn't hold a candle to the pinwheels that Rory set off Sunday.

His choice of attire that day did not foretell greatness. He was wearing a horizontally striped, lime green and white shirt that stubbornly refused to stay tucked. His slacks were vintage early McIlroy—bright white baggy jobs that billowed in the breeze. As was almost always the case back then, he was a month overdue for a haircut. His bird's nest spilled out from under a white Jumeirah cap that was at least a size too big.

As the Irish press contingent pointed out, it was Portrush redux—but this time, McIlroy sustained the brilliance over two rounds and came away the winner. He shot a 10-under 62, breaking the Quail Hollow course record by two strokes and winning by four over the newly crowned Masters champion, Phil Mickelson.

Mickelson barely knew what hit him when Rory reeled off six consecutive threes on his scorecard—among them an eagle-three at the uphill par-five 15th—to end his round. McIlroy became the youngest winner on the US Tour since Tiger Woods captured the Walt Disney World/Oldsmobile Classic at the age of twenty years and nine months, just a few weeks younger than Rory in Charlotte.

McIlroy seemed as stunned as everyone else. "I just got in a zone and didn't realize that I was going eight-, nine-, ten-under," he said. "I just knew that I got my nose in front and I was just trying to stay there."

The "nose in front" guy scribbled "3" on his scorecard a staggering twelve times that day. Rory was tied for the lead with Argentine Angel Cabrera as they entered the stretch run. His birdie at number 14 put him at seven-under on the day and 12-under for the tournament; suddenly, he was two ahead of Cabrera and Mickelson.

After stuffing a five-iron at number 15 to set up his kick-in eagle, he proceeded to birdie the 16th, feathering his approach from the right-side fairway bunker inside five feet. On the 17th, a hairy par-three over water, he played a tee shot into the fat side of the green. His fifty-five-foot lag looked good the whole way, but trickled three feet away for par. The narrow miss caused the crowd to groan and Rory to double over.

On Quail Hollow's famous finisher, Rory's three-wood found the right side of the fairway, away from the demonic creek that runs down the left side. His second shot was hit exactly where it should have been: into the middle of the green, some forty feet short of the flag.

Rory's putt was hit a bit aggressively for the circumstances but never left the middle of the cup. As it chugged northward, Jim Nance in the CBS booth started cackling in anticipation. When it hit the geometric center of the hole and plopped in, Nance shouted: "How about making it? He does, indeed!" Nance's broadcast partner, Nick Faldo, Rory's boyhood idol, yelped, "That's ten-under today! Whoa!"

When asked how he'd done it, McIlroy shrugged his shoulders. "I was just seeing my shots and hitting it and seeing the line of putts really well and everything was going in."

Now just a couple of days removed from a legal drink in the States, McIlroy allowed that, "I am going to have a bit of a [birthday] party on Tuesday night.... If I was back home and had a win like this, I'd be having a good one tonight."

He had plenty of pals with whom to have a quick—if technically still forbidden—beer in Charlotte. Padraig Harrington, Lee Westwood, and Lee's caddie, the gregarious Brit Billy Foster, stuck around Quail Hollow long after they finished their rounds. As Rory came off the 72nd green, Harrington playfully pushed the kid around. Marveled Paddy: "That was some bit of stuff."

What was Rory going to do with the $1.17 million in prize money? He told reporters that he was in the market for trees. He wanted to plant more trees around the practice range he was building at Robinhall, his fourteen-acre estate eight miles south and inland from Holywood. A secluded range would nicely complement Robinhall's built-to-spec putting-and-chipping green, its tennis court, and its well-stocked fishing pond.

"Trees are pretty expensive," McIlroy noted, to chuckles in the press room.

Given his bravura performance in Charlotte and his tenth-place finish at Bethpage the previous year, Rory was among the favorites at the US Open at Pebble Beach in June 2010. Sure enough, an Ulsterman ended up winning at Pebble—but it wasn't McIlroy.

It was Rory's first-ever visit to the Monterey Peninsula. But he claimed to know every inch of the place since he'd played Pebble so many times in video games. After a couple of practice rounds, he conceded that it was easier to play Pebble on Play Station than it was atop the actual cliffs along Carmel Bay.

Nevertheless, Rory loved the place. He called the postage-stamp-sized seventh hole "just a little chip." He thought holes 8 through 10 hard by the beach were "spectacular." And number 14, the monster that has devoured almost every golfer that's ever ventured up its hill, was "the most difficult par-five I've ever played."

Rory was staying at the Pebble Beach Lodge, just a short walk from the course. He couldn't wait to get to his first hole (the 10th) in Thursday's round, since the USGA had mischievously put Rory and Japanese youngster Ishikawa together with sixty-year-old Tom Watson. It was the first time that Rory had played an official round with the legend who, three decades earlier, had won a US Open at Pebble.

Maybe McIlroy was *too* excited. Neither the prodigy nor the legend had rounds to remember on Thursday.

Rory parred his first four holes, then fell victim to his own prophecy on the par-five 14th. He put his third shot long and left of the green, leaving himself a tortuous downhill/sidehill chip from underneath the bough of a tree. His fourth shot whacked the tree branch and bounced backward, producing a double-bogey that could have been worse.

Watson had also put his short-iron third long and left. But the veteran knew how to play a bump into the mound guarding the left side of the green. Tom saved bogey but couldn't save Rory's round from going south.

McIlroy proceeded to bogey both numbers 16 and 17 when his tee balls drifted right. He also failed to birdie the par-five 18th.

After the turn, he hit another poor tee shot and bogeyed the shortish par-four third. Only a late-round birdie at the par-five sixth kept Rory from a round in the high 70s.

Pebble played rough that week. Graeme McDowell, by then a hardened vet, said after day one: "You come in here and recognize that par is a good score. You've got to keep your head on and find the fairways and greens."

The Portrush Plugger kept his head on. The Holywood Hotshot? Not so much.

Needing something around par to get into contention, Rory flamed out on Friday with a 77 that, like so many rounds at Pebble, got uglier as the day wore on. At 10-over, McIlroy missed the cut by two teeth-gnashing strokes.

His playing partner Watson gave Rory a lesson in how to get around a prickly layout, shooting a level-par 71. Tom ended up shooting a 70-76 on the weekend for a thoroughly respectable 11-over.

County Antrim's own, meanwhile, shocked the world by shooting even-par 284. On Sunday, Graeme overtook a stumbling Dustin Johnson and held off a late-charging Ernie Els. Turns out G-Mac was right: par at Pebble really *was* a good score.

A month later, Rory not only got a chance to live a childhood dream by playing an Open Championship at St. Andrews; he also had the opportunity to add "McIlroy" to a distinguished list of young Open champs, beginning with Young Tom Morris but including Willie Auchterlonie and the sainted Seve Ballesteros. Oddsmakers liked Rory's chances: in his last eight rounds on the Old Course, he had broken 70 each time. Rory, still the world's ninth-rated player despite his Pebble struggles, was installed as betting favorite number two, behind only Tiger. Rory preparation for his third-ever Open Championship hinged around a quick visit to Royal County Down to play some links golf with his old man.

Four hours into Thursday's first round, Gerry's kid not only had a chance to make Old Course history, he had an opportunity to make *major championship history* by becoming the first man ever to shoot 62 in a Grand Slam event.

It should have happened. On number 17, one of the stingiest par-fours in the world—the infamous Road Hole—McIlroy hit a drive over the old railroad shed and followed it with an exquisite six-iron that settled just three feet from the cup. A birdie-birdie finish would have given Rory that elusive 62.

He admitted to the press corps that the gravity of it all stuck in his brainwaves. He lipped out the putt at number 17, a miss that became even more aggravating a hole later when he buried his seven-footer for birdie.

Rory made the turn in three-under 33 and ended up coming home in 30, with three birdies in a row beginning at the 10th, as well as birdies at the par-five 14th and the par-four 15th.

"It would have been lovely to shoot 62, but I can't really complain," Rory said.

Sixty-three was still lovely—so lovely, in fact, that for twelve hours it sent the golf world into a frenzy. Then the second round started.

Thirty- and forty-mile-an-hour wind gusts came barreling through the Kingdom of Fife. At first, Rory was merely frustrated; before long he became flummoxed. On a day when the guys who got the roughest weather were at least five or six shots worse than their Thursday rounds, Rory took the booby prize. McIlroy shot 80—*seventeen shots* higher.

The weather was so nasty Friday morning that R&A officials considered postponing. Instead, they sent out the early starters, McIlroy included, then chose to suspend play for sixty-five minutes when, as Associated Press put it, "howling winds" caused balls to "wobble" on the greens. Rory started par-par-par—excellent for the conditions—and didn't want to be taken off the course.

When play was resumed, the winds actually worsened. So did Rory's game.

"I don't think they should have called us off the golf course," he said afterward. "When we got back out there, the conditions hadn't changed. The wind probably got a little bit worse."

Official missteps notwithstanding, McIlroy's greenness showed. His seven-iron approach to the par-four fourth got tangled in a zephyr, triggering a bogey. He failed to save par on three of the next four holes, making the turn in an ugly 40.

"[McIlroy's] eyes rolled," Doug Ferguson of AP wrote. "His head swayed. His shoulders slumped. Rory McIlroy looked like he was on the verge of a full-scale tantrum."

A few hours earlier, he had been the toast of golf's chattering classes, the boy wonder leading the Open Championship at the venerable Old Course. "Now," Ferguson observed, "he was just a kid not getting his way."

It had been a wild ride, but the kid was at one-under 143 for the tournament and had survived the cut. Yet he now trailed—by eleven shots—Louis Oosthuizen, who had gotten a favorable tee time on Friday afternoon, missing the brunt of the bad weather.

It is a testament to Rory's resilience that on Saturday, in circumstances that were by no means easy, he came back with a clutch 69. It could have been lower, but the Road Hole, which has a way of always getting the last laugh, bit him. After a solid drive into the breeze over the edge of the hotel, Rory's 175-yard seven-iron caught a bolt of wind, ending up well beyond the green and a few inches from the stone wall that borders out-of-bounds.

Here's Keogh's description of what Rory was up against: "Impeded in his backswing, he was unable to chip directly at the flag and could only knock his third shot across the 18th tee to the run-off area behind the green, from where he chipped to eight feet but missed the bogey putt." It was the quintessential, shit-happens, Road Hole double-drop.

To his credit, he bounced back to make a birdie on the closing hole. Breaking 70 on such a tough day shot him back up the leaderboard. There was no catching Oosthuizen, who was basking in one of the great Open performances ever, but Rory was redeeming himself.

The redemption vigil continued on Sunday. He shot an almost-mistake-free 68. He'd flirted with the Claret Jug but wasn't going to carry it away—not this time, anyway.

His Sunday round secured him third place at eight-under, eight shots behind Oosthuizen. Had he been able to keep Friday's hemorrhaging to a minimum, and maybe shot a 75 instead of that big fat 80, would he have had a shot at Louis?

Maybe. What was certain is that his third-place finish won McIlroy some nice consolation money, a check for €305,536. It also boosted him from ninth place to seventh in the world standings and equaled his best finish in a major.

The 2010 PGA Championship at Whistling Straits along Wisconsin's Lake Michigan shoreline will be forever remembered for the bunker-or-no-bunker?[4] brouhaha surrounding Dustin Johnson's second shot on the 72nd hole. The PGA of America's decision to

---

[4] For what it's worth, I've always come down on the side of the PGA of America. If D.J. wasn't sure whether he was in sand, all he had to do was ask an official.

impose a two-shot penalty—one of the most contentious punishments in golf history—caused D.J. to miss the playoff between eventual winner Martin Kaymer and Bubba Watson.

Johnson had played beautiful golf throughout the four days; after he birdied the 71st hole, it looked like he was poised to lift the Wanamaker Trophy. But the Golfing Fates, as those bastards often do, entertained other ideas. The Fates steered Johnson's tee ball at number 18 into a hilltop sandy patch well right of the fairway, in an area that had been trampled by fans. Johnson didn't realize he was in a hazard and grounded his club.

Gotcha! smirked the Fates.

Almost lost in the discord over D.J. is that Rory McIlroy played out of his mind for much of that tournament, only missing the playoff by a single stroke. In Sunday's final round, the McIlroy Malady—spotty putting down the stretch in a big one—surfaced in a big way. Otherwise, Rory might have won outright, or at least qualified for the extra holes.

Leading up to Whistling Straits, Rory had gotten plenty of advice, most of it unsolicited, from his three Irish mentors, Messrs. Clarke, Harrington, and McDowell. The latter two were major champions; the former, a soon-to-be major winner. G-Mac and Paddy kept telling reporters that Rory needed to pull in the reins and play with more restraint. Ulsterman Clarke was even more explicit.

"Be patient, you Muppet!" Clarke had snapped at McIlroy when they played together at the Irish Open in Killarney the previous month, reported Keogh.

"Hearing the famously short-fused Clarke—apparently a reformed character these days—advising people to be patient was 'a bit like the kettle calling the pot black,'" McIlroy retorted.

"Yeah, well, 'Kettle' has been there, 'Kettle' knows," Clarke rejoined.

"You guys know," Clarke told the press later. "[Rory] wants to take on every flag. He wants to go at every pin. He's one of the best players in the world. I was the same way. But patience hasn't come to me easy. I am trying to help him because I didn't heed what people were telling me."

After his Tuesday practice round at Whistling Straits, Rory conceded Clarke's point. "Everyone tells me, 'Rory: just be patient,' but sometimes it's hard to do that [when] you're trying to get somewhere so fast."

The young man in a hurry shot a one-under 71 on Thursday, and followed it with two glittering efforts: a 68 on Friday and a 67 on Saturday that had Jim Nance & Co. on CBS wagging their tongues about "the next Tiger."

McIlroy went into Sunday tied with D.J. at 10-under, three strokes back of solo leader Nick Watney, an American who'd been riding a hot hand all summer. Martin Kaymer was another shot back of D.J. and Rory at nine-under.

On Sunday, Rory was in the next-to-last group, paired with thirty-one-year-old Chinese professional Liang Wenchong. It was the first time that McIlroy had teed off that late in a major. The nerves showed. The impeccable ball striking and putting of the previous two rounds weren't there—at least not early. He missed a makeable par putt on number 4 and again at number 8, offset by a birdie at number 7. He rolled in a birdie from outside ten feet at the 10th hole, then gave himself comparable opportunities at the next three holes. None dropped.

But at the 14th, he coaxed a birdie putt into the hole and grabbed a share of the lead at 11-under. Alas, Rory gave the stroke right back at number 15, when he misread a four-footer that turned out to be dead straight, not a left-to-right breaker.

Worse, he failed to take advantage of the par-five 16th, settling for par. On both of the closing holes, he was inside twenty feet for birdie, but couldn't get either putt to cooperate. He ended up with his highest score of the week, a level-par 72.

The admonitions from the Irish triumvirate had stuck with him. "I stayed very patient and didn't let anything get to me or my head drop once, which was one of the main objectives going out today. I was very happy with the way I dealt with the start. I was shaky but I didn't let it get to me and I saved pars."

It was his second successive third-place finish in the PGA Championship. Throw in his tied-for-third at St. Andrews in the 2010 Open, and Rory had three career top-five finishes in majors. Most twenty-one-year-olds would have been over the moon.

But not the Muppet who fired at too many dicey pins.

Rory McIlroy's oft-contentious association with the Ryder Cup began with his first appearance in 2010. That early October, the Cup was held on the Twenty-Ten course at Celtic Manor, a resort in the lush Vale of the River Usk outside Newport, Wales.

"Lush" in that part of the world is synonymous with "gets a shit-ton of rain." Twice the 38th Ryder Cup was delayed by storms, necessitating its first-ever Monday finish. Even when the rain dissipated, the autumnal fog in southern Wales rolled in. Rory's first-ever Cup singles match, against American Stewart Cink, was played in nearly impenetrable mist.

Euro captain Scotsman Colin Montgomerie had a formidable team: rookies McIlroy and Peter Hanson, with veterans Lee Westwood, Martin Kaymer, Graeme McDowell, Ian Poulter, Ross Fisher, Francesco Molinari, Miguel Ángel Jiménez, and captain's picks Luke Donald, Padraig Harrington,[5] and Edoardo Molinari. It was the first time in Ryder Cup history that two brothers were on the same squad.

---

5 Donald and Harrington had spent the bulk of the 2010 campaign playing in the United States and had not earned sufficient European Tour points to qualify for the Ryder Cup. For the '12 Cup, the Euros changed their eligibility requirements to accommodate the guys playing mainly on the US tour.

The American unit was captained by Corey Pavin and consisted of Phil Mickelson, Hunter Mahan, Bubba Watson, Jim Furyk, Steve Stricker, Dustin Johnson, Jeff Overton, and Matt Kuchar, along with captain's picks Zach Johnson, Tiger Woods, and Cink.

Having never experienced the camaraderie of a Ryder Cup locker room, McIlroy's ambivalence was understandable. He felt, as his hero Tiger had earlier in his career, that despite all the hullabaloo, the Cup didn't mean a whole lot. The previous year, McIlroy had posted on social media a statement that caused hand-wringing among his European elders.

"It's not that important an event for me," he wrote. "It's an exhibition at the end of the day. Obviously, I'll try my best for the team. But I'm not going to go running around and fist-pumping."

It didn't take long for Rory to eat those words.

Apprehension about McIlroy's indifference toward the Cup, however, paled in comparison to the angst he caused Montgomerie and the Euro brass when he chose to lip off about Tiger Woods. There was one immutable rule in the Tiger Era: never, ever, piss him off by saying anything that he could construe as trash talk.

For a smart guy who could recite Tiger's record (and revenge-seeking) chapter and verse, Rory should have known better. But in the days leading up to the Ryder Cup, here's what McIlroy said to *Yahoo! News*: "I would love to face [Tiger]. Unless his game rapidly improves…I think anyone in the European team would fancy their chances against him. There are a lot of American players playing better than him at the minute but it's always an advantage to have Tiger Woods on your team."

Whoa! So, in the same breath, a twenty-one-year-old with zero Ryder Cup experience managed to be dismissive *and* condescending toward the greatest player of his generation. To be sure, this was the post-sex-scandal Tiger, not the colossus who had once dominated the golfing world. Woods's game, like his brand and dignity, had taken a hit. Still, he was *Tiger Woods*.

Rory's braggadocio wasn't cajónes. It was callow naiveté. He knew that he'd screwed up as soon as the story hit and the media—starved for Ryder Cup storylines—jumped all over it.

Captain Montgomerie did his best to downplay it, but McIlroy's loose chatter had created a PR headache for the Euros. Tiger didn't fire back for public consumption, but Woods made it known that he would be happy to give the cocky kid what he wished for—a *mano a mano* contest.

Aware that McIlroy was feeling skittish, McDowell and his caddie surprised Rory on the first tee during Tuesday's practice round. Weeks before, G-Mac and his looper had purchased as many dark wigs as they could find to spoof Rory and his shaggy hair. Jim Moriarty of *Golfweek* wondered if they'd shorn every black sheep in Wales. European team members and caddies alike showed up on the first tee with the wigs tugged underneath their Ryder Cup caps.

Sporting grins, they gathered around the tee box, stuck Rory and his real mop top in the middle, and posed for photographers. Rory couldn't help but howl. He admitted later that his teammates' needling lifted his spirits.

The smart money before the Tiger Tempest was that Monty would send out the two Northern Irishmen—Rory and Graeme—in the initial fourball (best ball) match on day one, anticipating that Pavin would counter with Woods and someone else. But given the hubbub, Lee Westwood, McIlroy's ISM stablemate, went to Monty and suggested that Westy and Kaymer lead off Friday morning. Monty agreed, but Pavin decided not to tap Woods at the outset, sending out Mickelson and D.J. instead.

Westwood and Kaymer promptly knocked off the Americans, 3 and 2. Which left Rors and G-Mac to take on the second US pairing, Stewart Cink and Matt Kuchar. Rain dogged them for the first few holes, then returned in mid-round to force a two-hour delay that pushed the completion of the matches to day two, Saturday.

Kuchar and Cink got into a good groove and stayed in it through much of the round, whereas the "Macs," perhaps nervous at the start, struggled. The Ulstermen were down two with seven holes to play when they began to rally in better weather.

McIlroy cut their deficit in half on the par-three 13th when his tee shot spun back into tap-in range for his first birdie of the competition. Four holes later, he squared the match by sinking a thirty-five-foot, left-to-right uphill snake on the 213-yard par-three. Once the putt disappeared, McIlroy punched his right hand into the air, twice bellowed "C'mon!" to the gallery, and raced over to McDowell to deliver a thunderous hand slap—precisely the sort of celebratory "running around" he claimed would be beneath him in the Ryder Cup.

Rory's adrenaline was surging as he played the par-five 18th, a 575-yarder over water and into the wind. No doubt he and G-Mac decided that Rory would give it a go in two, and McDowell would take a more judicious route to the green.

McIlroy's big drive found the right edge of the fairway and gave him a good angle to a left-center pin. But his three-wood was scruffy; it never had a chance and landed in the middle of the pond. His fourth shot also found the water, so it was up to McDowell to secure the half with a par, which he did. Had it not been for Rory's long putt, the Americans would have grabbed a 3-1 lead; instead, it was a 2½-1½ for the US team as the match turned to foursomes (alternate shot).

The Ulster pair, inevitably dubbed "G-Mac" and "Wee-Mac," was back at it that afternoon—and so were their opponents Cink and Kuchar. Another back-and-forth tussle ensued; the Americans came out on top, 1-up.

With the US squad still ahead, Captain Montgomerie gave his guys big pep talks on Saturday, begging for more "passion." It worked—at least for "G" and "Wee." In the third go-round, they played Zach Johnson and Hunter Mahan. The Ulstermen smoked the Americans, 3 and 1, in what Keogh coined a "MacAttack."

There's no doubt that by rebuffing Johnson and Mahan, the Macs had helped give Monty's guys a big momentum push. Following Sunday's rain postponement, the Euros went into the final session on Monday up three full points.

In his first-ever Ryder Cup singles match, Rory again went up against Cink, the third time he had faced the Georgia Tech alum that week. Cink was playing the kind of crafty golf that had won him the Claret Jug: keeping the ball in front of him and relying on his putting and wedge play. He was up against a young stud who was the antithesis of all that.

When they teed off Monday morning, Celtic Manor was still trying to shake off its cloud cover; they could barely see the first fairway. Cink drove into the right rough of the par-four opener, then left his long-iron approach short and right amid a batch of bunkers.

Rory banged his drive down the right-center of the fairway; his four-iron second shot knifed through the fog, perfectly on line. It settled on the green about twelve feet short of the pin—a fabulous way to start a Ryder Cup match. His putt seemed to stagger as it reached the edge of the cup—but it dropped.

McIlroy doubled his one-up lead on number 2, then Cink rallied to win the next three holes. Remarkably, there wasn't a tied hole in the match until number 6.

So it went, back and forth, with neither player able to grab command. On the par-five 11th, following a crooked tee shot, Rory's third-shot wedge spun to eight feet underneath the cup. He stroked an uphill left-to-righter that was in all the way. On number

RORY LAND

12, Rory got it back to all square with a brilliant wedge that nearly backed into the hole, stopping a foot away.

But on the 13th tee, the *other* Rory showed up. On a 185-yard par-three over water with the wind gusting sideways, Rory tried to muscle a seven-iron; it fell short and backed into the hazard.

Amid groaning from his on-air colleagues, European Tour commentator Jay Townsend—an American who, over the years, has drawn McIlroy's ire by criticizing his tendency to make unforced errors—hissed, "That is a mistake you *cannot* make when you've got the honors in a tight match!"

Indeed, if Cink had converted on two short putts down the stretch, Rory would have been toast. But the putts missed—one high, one low—and they remained all square as they walked to the par-five 18th.

Rory rocketed a big drive down the middle. Cink pulled his into the left rough and laid up just inside one hundred yards. McIlroy countered with his three-wood, the same club that two days before had sent a ball into the drink. He pushed it right, but it had just enough juice to carry the pond. It plunged into the middle of the cavernous bunker. There was nothing routine about Rory's third shot, especially after Cink's wedge spun back to twelve feet above the hole, giving the American an excellent look at birdie.

Townsend and crew quickly pointed out that Rory had little margin for error on the sand shot. McIlroy was nine feet below the putting surface. With the green tilting right-to-left and downhill, Rory would have to hit a soft lob well to the right—and hope his ball trickled down toward the cup.

Instead, Rory chose to go straight at the flagstick. His ball landed on the green, but immediately began dribbling left and backward. Sure enough: it fell back into the trap, which caused another torrent of tsk-tsking from Townsend and his colleagues, one of whom lamented that "Rory always tries to be the hero," instead of playing more conservatively.

With Cink staring at a makeable birdie putt that would have won the match, Rory had to go back to work in the bunker. This time he hit a spinner that came down softly and stuck four feet underneath the hole.

Cink's birdie effort slid by, Rory made his putt, and a wild, fog-shrouded singles match ended as it should have: in a draw. The Euros need Rory's half-point, because the Americans came roaring back that afternoon. The Ryder Cup came down to G-Mac vs. Hunter Mahan in the anchor match, a spirited battle that went down to the wire until Mahan muffed a pitch.

The Euros won the Cup, 14½-13½, with Wee-Mac leading the charge to leap all over G-Mac as the champagne began to flow. You would have thought that Rory's jumping for joy meant that he was now treating the Ryder Cup with reverence.

And you would be wrong.

Chapter 13

COLLAPSE AND CORONATION

Rory and the Holywood posse who hung out with him in Augusta during Masters week 2011—the usual Mac Pack crew: Harry Diamond, Ricky McCormick, Mitchell Tweedie, maybe one or two others—were fascinated by American football and determined to learn how to throw a forward pass without embarrassing themselves. Tossing any kind of ball overhand, especially getting a regulation-sized football to spiral, is not an easy athletic task for guys weaned on soccer and rugby. So, besides checking out the action at Augusta's watering holes, one of the first things the twenty-somethings did upon arriving the weekend before the Masters was purchase a football.

With beer flowing and hip-hop music booming, they began chucking the old pigskin around the rental house's cul-de-sac, which happened to be located in one of Augusta's tonier neighborhoods. The boys, being boys, didn't allow something as trifling as sundown get in the way of their good time; lampposts cast more than enough light.

They were so enthusiastic, in fact, that they managed to piss off the neighbors. One lady marched across the street and "told them off," as Rory put it to the press. Chastened, they turned down the music and put the ball away—at least for a while.

In the bright glare of daylight, when the neighbors got a better look at the hooligans, they were tickled to discover that the short guy was none other than golf's most promising young star—and a favorite to win that week's Masters.

The Augustans may have had to do a double-take. For his third appearance in the Masters, McIlroy had gotten a haircut. The usually unruly mop top just barely spilled outside his cap. By Sunday, he probably came to regret the decision to trim his locks: like the Biblical Samson (or the late rocker David Crosby), it may have been the source of his strength. Two months later, when Rory showed up for the US Open, his mane again flowed.

"With rosy cheeks that appear in no need of shaving…McIlroy could easily pass for a high school kid and, at times, would just as soon act like one," Larry Dorman of the *New York Times* quipped that week. His piece called Rory a "carefree spirit" with "maturity and perspective" beyond his years.

His temporary neighbors might have taken issue with that last bit—and by Sunday night, they would have been joined by a lot of people.

Team McIlroy made another big change in their approach that spring. Probably to give his son a greater sense of independence, Gerry McIlroy elected not to come to Augusta. Gerry's absence may have clouded Rory's peace of mind, especially when things started to go sour on Sunday. At Congressional Country Club two months later, Rory's old man would be inside the ropes, never far from sight.

McIlroy's dad may have been missing on Sunday from his son's cheerleading contingent, but Rory's on-again, off-again girlfriend Holly Sweeney—a real-life cheerleader—was there, but on the downlow. The Sweeney-McIlroy relationship, by Rory's own telling, had been bumpy in the months preceding 2011's first major. During the holidays, in fact, the couple had separated after Rory told her he needed to devote more time to his profession.

"I didn't have a great couple of weeks before Christmas [2010] but you've got to do what's right for yourself," Rory told James Corrigan of the (London) *Daily Telegraph*.

While they were broken up, Holly threw herself into her cheerleading duties at Ravenhill rugby matches and took up dancing. She also took a break that semester from her studies in sports technology at Ulster University. By some accounts, the couple had reconciled in late winter, with Rory groveling to get her back. By other accounts, they'd stayed in touch, but only as "friends." Whatever their exact status, the relationship was not in a particularly good place in April 2011.

Which makes agent Chubby Chandler's decision to surprise Rory by flying Holly to Georgia—unannounced—all the more curious. What was no doubt in Chandler's mind was to create a heartwarming tableau: Rory's hometown sweetheart running across the 72nd green to buss her boyfriend amid rapturous applause as he won his first major championship.

The ISM gang saw big money in packaging Holly and Rory as golf's young glamour couple. Holly, for her part, had ambitions to become a TV spokesmodel or show-business personality; she knew the video of her smooching the newly crowned Masters champ would go viral. She had in the past couple of years gone from a darker blonde wearing her hair down to a platinum blonde with a teased style worn up, making herself more "adult" and telegenic.

"It was supposed to be a fantastic celebration, a joyous snapshot to go around the world," Corrigan wrote on Monday. "Instead…it all spiraled into humiliation."

"Ireland is a sports-mad nation," journalist Justin Doyle, a McIlroy chronicler, has written. "When one of their own is involved in the business end of a major sporting event, every man, woman, and child in the country is transfixed."

A few minutes before five o'clock on April 10, 2011, Ireland's young sporting icon stood on Augusta National's 10th tee, already living one of golf's hoariest clichés: "The Masters doesn't begin until the back nine on Sunday."

How many times in Rory's boyhood did he and his dad hear some variation of that adage while, given the five-hour time difference, they wolfed down a late snack in front of the TV? Surely, those emotions were rattling in Rory's nervous system as he strode from the ninth green to the 10th tee, nursing a one-shot lead in the final round of the 75th Masters. When he'd arrived at the first tee two-plus hours earlier, he'd held a four-shot advantage and was clearly the hottest golfer inside the onetime nursery.

On Thursday, he'd shot a scintillating 65, with birdies at numbers 2, 3, 4, 9, 11, 14, and 15; remarkably, it was the first time in seven rounds that he'd broken 70 at Augusta. On Friday, he did it again, shooting a 69 with four birdies and only one bogey (at number 12, his first of the tournament), to take the outright lead over Aussie Jason Day by two strokes.

His two-under 70 in tough conditions on Saturday put him at 12-under, giving him a four-shot bulge over four players: Day, Argentine Angel Cabrera, Korean K.J. Choi, and South African Charl Schwartzel. McIlroy's Saturday round had started wobbly, but he rallied by making three birdies in his final six holes to take what writers and commentators (most of whom should have known better) called a "commanding" lead. McIlroy's friend and mentor, Graeme McDowell, texted him Saturday evening with best wishes. "It may have been the beer talking," Rory chuckled to the press, but G-Mac said he "loved" him.

Rory, despite his tender age, was a student of past Masters. He knew how quickly a four-shot lead could disappear. "I'm not getting ahead of myself," he said Saturday evening, with the practiced patter of a veteran. "I have to go out there, not take anything for granted and go out and play as hard as I've played the last three days. If I can do that, hopefully things will go my way."

He couldn't. And they didn't.

RORY LAND

Rory's final round in the 2011 Masters has been studied with Talmudic precision by golf scholars. It's often seen, correctly, as the "bad" counterweight to the "good" one that took place two months later when Rory romped at Congressional. If it's true that people learn more from failure than from success, then Rory learned a ton that late afternoon in northeast Georgia.

That Masters was the first time McIlroy had slept on a third-round lead in a major. Paired with Cabrera, Argentina's combative *El Pato* ("The Duck"),[1] a two-time major champion, Rory's nerves showed right away.

After a solid drive up the right-center of the first fairway, Rory's thinned approach banged through the green and wandered left, just off the back fringe. His lag chugged some seven feet past the cup, with Nance on the CBS telecast imploring it to slow down, to no avail. Rory's par attempt was pulled left and never scared the cup, presaging similar pulls to come.

McIlroy wasn't the first Masters leader to struggle on the opening hole; it's considered one of the toughest curtain-raisers in major championship golf. Augusta's second hole, however, is a benign par-five, traditionally one of its easier birdies; it sets up perfectly for Rory's big draw. McIlroy stood an excellent chance, posthaste, of getting that stroke back.

But McIlroy's tee ball traveled too long and too straight. It bounced into the trap on the far right of the fairway. He had a decent lie in the bottom of the bunker and decided to try and push it as far down the fairway as possible. He went for too much; his shot whacked the lip and tumbled only a few yards away.

Rory still had all of a three-wood left to the green, which he proceeded to hook into the left greenside bunker. The cup was

---

1   Cabrera's nickname comes from his ungainly style of walking, which resembles a duck waddling. His out-of-control predilection for violence isn't amusing in the least. Cabrera served nearly three years in Argentinian prisons for domestic battery. He has since joined the PGA Tour Champions.

in its usual Sunday short-right position, so McIlroy had to navigate the entire breadth of the putting surface. He clipped it out with near-perfect weight; the ball settled only a couple of feet past the cup.

CBS analyst Ian Baker-Finch said he hoped that the gritty par would calm McIlroy's nerves. It did—but only for a few minutes.

His drive on number 3, the short par-four that was one of MacKenzie's favorite holes, found the fairway. He then feathered a nice wedge that caught the inward side of the ridge that cleaves the green. It rolled to within a dozen feet. But his birdie putt slid past, this time on the high side.

At number 4, the long par-three, he made an impeccable pass at his long-iron ("The only thing that moved were his eyelids," quipped his dad's old friend David Feherty in the tower). Rory just missed his twenty-five-footer for birdie. Maybe Baker-Finch and Feherty's fond hopes were being realized: Rory's game seemed to be settling down.

But on the fifth, following a big drive, his weakly struck second came up short and right. His chip through the green's forbidding hillocks ran out of steam ten feet short of the flag. Another pulled putt missed left; suddenly, McIlroy was two-over on the day and leaking oil.

Led by the South Africa's Charl Schwartzel, all kinds of players were now jamming the leaderboard, including Rory's playing partner, *El Pato*. The patrons, sensing that the tournament was now up for grabs, were roaring as birdie putts dropped ahead of the McIlroy/Cabrera twosome.

The Argentine was one of the few players on Tour whose pace of play was quicker than McIlroy's. What Rory needed more than anything was to relax, slow down, and stop the hemorrhaging. Instead, he found himself trying to keep up with The Duck's frenetic tempo. Soon enough, McIlroy's ball-striking went from bad to worse.

At number 7—the tricky, sloping par-four that would come to give him fits in future years—he hit a booming drive, followed by a short-iron inside twenty feet of the mid-right pin placement. For the first time all day, he hit a confident putt that found the middle of the cup.

McIlroy has "righted the ship!" CBS's Peter Kostis exclaimed as Rory pulled the ball out of the hole. Except McIlroy hadn't righted anything: his boat was about to founder.

At number 8, the uphill par-five, Rory's second-shot three-wood went long and right—the one place a Sunday contender doesn't want to go, Faldo told viewers. McIlroy faced a daunting downhill chip to the back-right pin and duffed it; the ball barely stumbled onto the putting surface. Two putts later, McIlroy walked off the eighth green with a par that must have felt like another bogey.

More frustration followed on the par-four ninth. Rory's short-iron approach nestled inside twenty feet, giving him a makeable uphill look. But again, his birdie bid didn't come close. His front-side, one-over 37 let a lot of players back into the tournament, a thought surely not lost on him as he glanced at the scoreboard on his way to the 10th tee.

Wanting to make something happen, he grabbed his favorite club, his driver. Most pros favor the three-wood on Augusta's 10th tee, given the pronounced right-to-left tilt of its fairway. Better to find the downhill chute with your three-wood, their reasoning goes, than risk missing the fairway with your big stick and have the ball start bounding in the wrong direction.

Rory must have thought: "To hell with it! I'm busting one around the corner and making birdie!"—exactly the mentality that his Irish mentors had warned him about. It was not the percentage move. His big whip produced one of the most critiqued misfires in the history of the Masters. Augusta National is the Indy 500 of golf: people tune in for the crack-ups. Rory gave them one for the ages.

McIlroy's pileup happened so quickly that CBS's spotters couldn't follow it. It took a while before the crew was able to locate Rory's ball and get cameras trained on it. His tee shot had struck a tree no more than seventy yards or so down the left side of the fairway and ricocheted left and backwards. Amazingly, Rory's ball had come to rest just short of Augusta National's famous cabins, only fifty yards or thereabouts from the tee box—and still a quarter-mile from the 10th green!

As Nance, Faldo, and the rest of the gang were scrambling to find out where McIlroy's tee shot had landed, Rory can be heard asking if it had gone out-of-bounds, which only served to fuel Faldo's trademark tut-tutting. Sir Nick didn't go easy on the young man who once incorporated "Nick Faldo" into his own signature.

Journalists who'd covered the Masters for decades couldn't recall anyone close to where McIlroy's ball had come to rest. They also couldn't believe that there weren't any white out-of-bound stakes protecting the cabins' backyards. McIlroy was, miraculously, still in-bounds and had an opening through the trees to at least get his ball back in play. His ball had come to rest not far from Butler Cabin, the home of the globally televised Masters green-jacket ceremony—a gruesomely awkward ritual.[2]

Nance at that moment came up with one of his inimitable bon mots, volunteering that he knew Rory was anxious to get to Butler Cabin—but not quite that soon. "[He's] just trying to find a way to get it back on the map," Nance said a moment later as Rory eyed his options from a vantage point that Masters viewers had never before seen—and may never see again.

Rory's map-finder, a hooked iron, did its job, screeching through the opening and scooting down the right-center of the fairway. He still had 240-plus yards to go to the green, but at least he had an unobstructed shot.

It was McIlroy's next swing that snuffed his chances of winning the 75th Masters. He turned the toe of a three-wood over so badly that the ball ended up in Position Z, well left of the 10th green, stuck among thick-trunked pines. Given the treacherous downhill pitch to follow, it was the last place McIlroy wanted to be.

---

[2] Attempting to make small talk before presenting winner Seve Ballesteros with his green jacket, Augusta National chairman Hord Hardin, in his thick Southern drawl, once asked the elegant Spaniard how tall he was.

Rory's fourth shot banged a tree and rocketed left and backwards so quickly it caused his head to snap. His fifth shot, a low runner, barely found the putting surface. His thirty-foot putt to salvage double-bogey never had a chance. In the blink of an eye, he'd gone from having a one-shot lead in the Masters to trailing by two.

As he slunk toward the 11th tee, his body language—head down, shoulders slumped, eyes shunning the crowd—was the obverse of the usual upbeat Rory, the guy who liked to feed off the gallery's energy. Still, he was able to gather himself to hit a decent drive and an approach inside twenty feet. His birdie putt failed to dent the cup; inevitably, he missed the short comebacker, too.

Rory's performance was now bordering on the farcical; it was beginning to resemble the all-time Masters' collapse: Greg Norman's final-round flop against Faldo in 1996. At number 12, one of the world's most famous par-threes, McIlroy managed to put his tee ball hole-high some twenty-five feet left. Then Rory got to relive the nightmare that had ended—he thought—twenty minutes earlier. He rammed his birdie putt four or five feet past. His par effort didn't touch the cup, either. Ditto his three-footer for bogey—yet another pull.

His putting was so inept that Baker-Finch, a kind-hearted Aussie and a putting coach in his off-hours, began schooling McIlroy from the tower: "Pull the putter straight back now, Rory. Straight back."

Rory couldn't.

On number 13, the venerated dogleg left par-five, Rory again tried to muscle his driver and again hit a wild hook. This one crashed into the pines and found the bottom of Rae's Creek. Much to Chubby Chandler and ISM's chagrin, the photo of Rory leaning against his driver in despair became *the* emblematic image of the 75th Masters.

By then, any thought of having Sweeney surprise Rory on the course had been shelved. Chubby and his people kept her closeted in the clubhouse until after Rory signed his scorecard.

Tossing in the 10th hole, he'd gone six-over in Amen Corner, the most celebrated stretch of holes in the golfing world. He was living a nightmare. Cruelly, he had five holes left to play and no place to hide. In the span of a half an hour, he had become irrelevant, no longer in contention and barely shown in TV coverage. It was Cabrera who was attracting the cameras. *El Pato* stayed on the leaderboard until a late bogey at number 16 derailed his chances.

"Not his day, but he'll be heard from in majors," Feherty vowed as Rory sputtered toward the finish line. On the final hole, Nance noted that if Rory made his five-footer for birdie he could break 80. Alas, Rory's putt didn't hit the cup.

He ended up shooting a ghastly 37-43, eight-over par. He had plummeted into a tie for 16th and had to watch Schwartzel win the green jacket by two shots over a pair of Australians: Jason Day and Adam Scott. Remarkably, the South African birdied the last four holes to win—a scenario that seemed totally implausible when Charl had teed off.

It's what happened *after* he departed the 72nd green that forever endeared Rory McIlroy to fans and reporters. Rather than ducking the press center and running for cover, like most twenty-one-year-olds would have done, McIlroy sucked it up and handled every interview request—the obverse of his reaction to losing at Pinehurst thirteen years later.

In 2011, "McIlroy talked to everyone, including TV and print reporters, inside and outside the locker room," John Feinstein wrote the next week in *Golf World*. "[Rory] answered every question. He even tweeted congratulations to Schwartzel. There were no excuses and no Normanesque declarations that he'd actually hit the ball pretty well. McIlroy was clearly upset but never snappish, and he didn't take his angst out on anyone."

RORY LAND

Feherty was so concerned about his fellow Ulsterman's well-being that, once his broadcast duties were done, he called Chubby and got the street address of the home Rory and his buddies had rented.

"I didn't want to call because it wouldn't be the same, and [Rory] would say, 'I'm O.K., thanks for calling,'" Feherty recalled in a moment recounted by Feinstein in his 2023 biography, *Feherty*.

As Feherty pulled up in the cul-de-sac, he was surprised to find Rory and his mates kicking a European football around the front yard. Under the strained circumstances, the Rory Landers probably wanting to kill time doing something they were good at rather than fumbling around with something they weren't, like tossing an *American* football.

Feherty asked if he could hang out for a while and swap stories. Rory and the guys said sure. They went inside, no doubt raided the refrigerator for brew, and pulled up chairs around the dining room's big round table. Feherty launched into sidesplitting stories of inebriated caddies, berserk partying, and crazy-ass golf from the old days on the European and South African tours.

"For the next hour, maybe longer, [Feherty] did what kind of became his stand-up act," McIlroy told Feinstein. "At one point, I was laughing so hard—we all were—that I was almost crying. I remember thinking, 'This is the second time I've cried today, but this time feels a lot better.' It was just classic David. He was going to be *sure* I didn't spend the night sulking and being sad."

On his way out the door, the broadcaster-cum-comic pulled McIlroy aside for a private moment. "The kid really was O.K.," Feherty remembered. "I was amazed at how mature he was. Then he went out and proved he was O.K. two months later."

The April 25 *Sports Illustrated*, under a header that read, "Kid is All Right," reported that Rory assuaged Feherty's concerns by saying, "If that's the worst day of my life, I'm a whole lot luckier than most people."

Showing up unannounced was a brilliant gesture on Feherty's part and exactly the tonic that McIlroy needed. No matter how much beer he'd downed, it must have been tough for him to get to sleep that night as he relived his horrific trek through Amen Corner.

The morning after Feherty's visit, he admitted to choking back tears as he commiserated with his mum and dad on the phone. Most accounts of that conversation hinge on Rory comforting his mother by saying, "It's only a golf tournament. It's not the end of the world."

But other accounts, including one advanced by Dermot Gilleece, suggest that Rosie summoned her Lurgan-bred toughness and told her only child to buck up and buckle down. He had to learn from this episode and not let it happen again, Rosie said through gritted teeth.

The day after Rory's collapse, ESPN's Jeff MacGregor penned a lovely essay on the meaning of "failure." It began, "Understand first that there was no cruelty in what happened Sunday. It was as natural and dispassionate as gravity. Rory McIlroy's return to earth on the back nine at the Masters was not a calamity, it instead restored order to things. We were never meant to fly."

"Failure," MacGregor concluded, "is the default setting of everything we know. Of everything human. Sports. Politics. Science. Art. To win is the rarity."

Did Rory read MacGregor's piece and take it to heart? Probably not, but there's little doubt that the '11 Masters made him a better golfer and a more empathetic person. That spring is when Rory McIlroy, the brooding but still buoyant existentialist, came into being.

Chubby Chandler was so worried about his young charge being down in the dumps that he flew over to Belfast the day after

McIlroy got home. Chandler took Rory out to lunch and asked about his state of mind.

There's nothing to worry about, Rory assured Chubby. He was fine, feeling okay about life and looking forward to that week's Malaysian Open and June's US Open. Chandler was amazed by his client's otherworldly calm, but perhaps worried that Rory was whistling in a graveyard.

McIlroy proved his mettle the next week in Kuala Lumpur. Accompanied by Ms. Sweeney, Rory threatened the top of the leaderboard all week, shooting 14-under and finishing third, just two strokes behind Italian teen sensation Matteo Manassero.

After Kuala Lumpur, Rory took a couple of weeks to rest and recharge. In mid-May, he went to Andalusia, Spain, for the World Match Play Championship at the Finca Cortesín Golf Club alongside the Mediterranean. He beat South African Retief Goosen in the first round but lost to Belgian Nicolas Colsaerts in the second. The next week he finished a haphazard five-over at the BMW Championship at Wentworth—once again off his game.

Rory's next start was at the Memorial, Jack Nicklaus's tournament in Dublin, Ohio. His first-round 66 got everyone excited, but he came back to earth on Friday and Saturday with rounds of 72 and 71 before finishing with a flourish at 68. He ended up five shots behind winner Steve Stricker.

"I played really good this week. I just made a few too many mistakes, which really cost me," McIlroy told Sky Sports. "We'll have to try and cut those out before the US Open in two weeks' time."

Did he ever.

It's easy to use words like "redemption" or "vindication" to describe Rory's performance in the 111th US Open at Congressional Country Club in Bethesda, Maryland. Most of the previous US Opens were closely contested nail-biters where the winner was rarely more than a few strokes beneath par and often at or above it. There have been exceptions, of course, notably Tiger's blitzing of the field at Pebble Beach in 2000. And who can forget Jim Barnes's derring-do at the 1921 US Open at Bethesda's Columbia Country Club, a few mere miles from Congressional?[3] Barnes won by nine shots over a field that included the nineteen-year-old Bobby Jones.

There was little evidence that Rory would lap the field at Congressional. His play in the wake of the Augusta debacle was solid but not spectacular. He was still having trouble sustaining good play over four rounds.

After his putting went south at Augusta, on the advice of several colleagues, he sought out Dave Stockton, a four-decade veteran who won ten times on the regular Tour and fourteen times on the Champions Tour. Dave's stock-in-trade was his short game, which more than made up for a middling long game. The two first got together at Wentworth during the BMW Championship.

Stockton preached simplicity. He urged Rory to pick the apex of a putt's line, then with his eyes focused, "draw" a line back to a spot an inch or two in front of the ball. Minimize doubt in your stroke, Stockton counseled. Get the speed right while taking perpendicular practice strokes *behind* the ball. Don't take practice strokes while standing next to it—that might mess up your alignment. When you get over the ball, re-find your spot and stroke the ball directly over it. Don't agonize or stall: retrace the line with your eyes and let the putter blade go. Keep the back of your left hand steady and smooth.

Rory took Stockton's admonition and added a two-word mantra: "Spot and Process," with the latter pronounced with a long Anglo/Irish "o."

"Spot" was a mental reminder to read the putt precisely (which remains, more than a decade later, one of Rory's biggest challenges). "Process" was a reminder to repeat and ritualize every move on a green—and never deviate.

---

[3] In truth, I'd never heard of Barnes's big win in '21 until I went looking for supportive factoids.

In mid-June, "Spot and Process" helped Rory master the eighty-seven-year-old greens at architect Devereux Emmet's Congressional Blue Course.

Earlier in 2011, McIlroy had agreed to become UNICEF's Ireland Ambassador. The year before, a quake had struck the heart of Port-au-Prince, Haiti's capital, claiming many thousands of lives. A week before the US Open, McIlroy spent two days visiting the ravaged nation.

He visited a school that had been destroyed, marveling at the students' resourcefulness in protecting themselves from contracting cholera and other diseases. As he was leaving the island, he learned that bad weather that day had caused flooding and landslides that killed another twenty people.

The experience had a profound effect on the young man. He wrote on his website: "The chance that these kids are getting—to be kids and enjoy themselves—is so important for their well-being. Nothing could prepare me for meeting the children in Haiti and I am truly amazed by how happy they are."

When he met the press at Congressional, he couldn't get the children of Haiti out of his mind. "It has instilled in me a feeling that the next time I struggle on the golf course or whatever, I'll think of the people of Haiti. That will change my mindset pretty quickly."

McIlroy liked what he saw of the Blue Course in practice rounds, recognizing that many of the longer holes favored his métier, a long draw off the tee. The last time a US Open had been held at Congressional was 1997, when Ernie Els won his second American national championship and wowed spectators with his pinpoint iron play. Fourteen years later, Ernie was back in Bethesda singing McIlroy's praises.

"I think he's a future world number one, without any doubt," Ernie told the press. "He's got that kind of talent that is going win a lot of majors."

You could almost hear Rory's groan when he was told about Ernie's remarks. "It's very flattering and it's great that people are saying I'm going to win majors, but I need to do it first. Hopefully, I'll be sitting in front of the media on Sunday night saying, 'Yeah, maybe I could be a multiple major winner.'"

He got his wish.

Golf historian and journalist Brad Klein, then of *Golfweek*, was inside the Blue Course's ropes watching Rory negotiate his second round. Klein told me that he had a superb view of McIlroy's second shot on number 16, a downhill-then-uphill 580-yard par-five, with a sharp ridge that separates the first third of the green from its upper two-thirds. The flagstick that Friday was positioned a few paces beyond the top of the swale. If McIlroy wanted a makeable look for eagle, he would have to hit a softly feathered shot.

Over the decades, Klein has seen tens of thousands of shots struck by thousands of the world's most gifted golfers. But Brad says he'll never forget the swing that produced as magnificent a long-iron as a golf geek could ever hope to witness.

Rory had, in the words of NBC/ESPN commentator Andy North, "murdered" his drive down the left-center of the fairway, leaving him 222 yards uphill into a slight breeze. He had a good angle, North told viewers, to attack the mid-right flagstick that was uncomfortably close to a steep bunker. Rory pulled a four-iron from caddie J.P. Fitzgerald's bag and aligned himself to hit a high fade.

Bill Pennington of the *New York Times* was also standing nearby, watching the other members of Rory's group survey their second shots. A few seconds earlier, Phil Mickelson, in the fairway twenty-two yards behind McIlroy, "lashed" a shot that "bounced in front of the green, rolled forward, and checked up 45-feet from the cup."

Lefty was so pleased, Pennington wrote, that he shared a little hand slap with caddie Bones Mackay. Mickelson was near the end of a fine US Open round; he'd already recorded four birdies against only one bogey. Maybe his blistering shot at number 16 would finally help him gain some traction against McIlroy, who was on a heater of his own, with three birdies and an eagle to go on top of his first-round 65.

Call the moment up on YouTube. You'll see why Klein still extols Rory's swing and why Pennington chose to spotlight it. McIlroy takes the four-iron back in a lovely wide arc, gets the club perfectly parallel to the ground, points the clubface at his target, then fires those shoulders and hips down and through, reaching equipoise in his follow-through. He makes an extremely difficult shot look effortless. He strikes the ball so smoothly that it makes that *fzz-fzz-fzz* noise that Golf Channel instructors are always yakking about.

With that daunting bunker on the right, Rory had aimed some three or four yards left of the flag. He hit it so high that there's a pregnant pause in North's narration. McIlroy's ball came to earth a couple of yards above the ridge, bounced gently, then began rolling like a putt just past hole-high, bending toward the cup as it came to rest. It settled no more than eight feet away.

Klein and Pennington weren't the only ones to spot Rory's Hogan-esque mastery. In real time, the entire NBC/ESPN crew did verbal somersaults.

North emitted a groan that sounded like "Rrrummmph!," which must be Wisconsin guttural shorthand for "Man, that was sweet!" Up in the main tower, Terry Gannon sputtered, "All you can do is shake your head and laugh."

At that point, Rory was 11-under, eight shots clear of the field. He was the first US Open competitor in history to have reached double digits under par while still playing his second round. If he made his eagle putt on number 16, he would become the first US Open player *ever*, at any point, to reach 13-under.

McIlroy struck the putt with near-perfect weight. It hung just left, missing by a millimeter. Rory's tap-in birdie got him to 12-under, a mark that had been reached at that point in the US Open only by Tiger Woods at Pebble Beach in 2000 and Dr. Gil Morgan, also at Pebble, in 1992. The kid who eight weeks before had blown a four-shot lead in the Masters now had a nine-shot lead in the US Open.

And that epic four-iron at number 16? It wasn't even his best shot of the day!

No one at Congressional would come close to challenging Rory's big lead. He was playing against the same guy he played against at the Masters—himself. But this time, he wouldn't let that "other Rory" win.

He struck almost every iron with the same relaxed precision of his second-round four-iron at number 16. At that point he'd hit 86 percent of his greens in regulation—the most, noted the *New York Times'* Dorman, since the USGA began keeping records of such things.

In the hometown *Washington Post*, columnist Sally Jenkins on Saturday celebrated McIlroy's "easy, ambling brilliance…he played with a stalking rhythm, hitting a succession of high, soft irons that sent wedges of turf flying in the air."

Jenkins, the daughter of the late golf writer Dan Jenkins, the guy who in the pages of *Sports Illustrated* made golf writing cool (and who, along with Herb Wind, defined the modern professional Grand Slam), wrote that Rory's "ball striking was so pure it made other players—even great ones like Phil Mickelson—seem like coarse hackers."

RORY LAND

McIlroy's stalking rhythm began on Thursday at 1:35 p.m., EDT. No doubt heartened by overnight rains that softened the course, Rory strode onto the 10th tee to warm applause.

Analyst Paul Azinger, a reliable prophet of doom (excepting CBS, he worked for every US network that carried the sport, plus the BBC), attempted to establish an ominous storyline. He predicted that Rory would have "some real-live jitters," given what had happened at Augusta in his last major. It was a reasonable assertion. But it turned out that Azinger could not have been more wrong.

Rory's tournament began with one of the most intimidating shots on the Blue Course: a mid-iron over the pond that guards the 220-yard par-three. McIlroy smoothed a five-iron just over the flagstick, leaving himself inside fifteen feet for birdie. His putt slid by on the low side.

He made his first birdie (of eighteen more to come, plus an eagle) on the 455-yard, par-four 12th; his wedge, from 124 yards, kissed off a backstop behind the flag and rolled back inside five feet, drawing raves from broadcasters Dottie Pepper and Peter Jacobsen.

On number 17, a peculiar par-four with a huge dip two-thirds of the way down the fairway, Rory hit less than driver, leaving him 177 yards. Another unhurried swing produced a shot that caused announcer Mark Rolfing to label Rory the "laser man," since so many of McIlroy's irons were scorched at the flag. It hit hole-high and stopped ten feet past.

So far, it had been an "impressive" round for Rory, Pepper noted just before McIlroy's putt disappeared for birdie. At that point, he'd missed only one fairway and one green. He was now two-under.

On Congressional's signature hole, number 18—the one with the frightening water hazard and the dramatic vista of the clubhouse atop the hill—Rory's drive found the first cut of rough on the left side of the fairway. Johnny Miller noted that it gave McIlroy a good angle to go at the right-hand flag.

Rory's approach fluttered a bit, but it hit mid-green and pitched forward to about twenty feet from the pin. It left him an awkward uphill left-to-right putt. Rory proceeded to make one of his best strokes of the entire tournament. It danced on the left edge before falling.

McIlroy had gone out in three-under 33 and was atop the leaderboard. He never left it.

On the shortish par-four first hole (his 10th), a smart fairway wood down the right-hand side left him a punch wedge, which he put to about six feet underneath the hole. He played his putt just inside the right edge and poured it into the middle. He was now four-under.

On the par-four fourth, he again fired a short-iron and used the backstop behind the hole. As if on a string, the ball spun back down the slope to within a couple of feet. He was now five-under—and beginning to leave everyone in the June dust.

At the par-five sixth, Rory's 320-yard drive him left with 250 yards to a flagstick tucked in the back left. His long iron—"Ooh. Beautiful balance," cooed Gary Koch as Rory let it rip—hit in the middle of the green and darted forward, stopping on the back fringe only twenty feet or so from the flag.

Even as Rory's eagle bid missed a few inches left, ESPN's Curtis Strange and NBC's Koch and Pepper competed to come up with the best superlative to describe the quality of McIlroy's play, toggling between "awesome" and "flawless." He was now six-under.

At the skinny ninth, a par-five with a forbidding gulch guarding its green, Rory hit his worst shot of the day—a pulled second that found the thick rough just short of the tree line on the left.

Again, McIlroy wowed the experts. He put the ball back in his stance and punched a flier wedge that banged down just beyond the edge of the green and traveled some ten yards onto the putting surface before settling twenty feet or so underneath the hole. His birdie putt lacked pace, so his par meant he had finished with a 65.

It also meant he'd hit seventeen of eighteen greens in regulation. That's just not done in the US Open, as Koch and Jacobsen noted. The next-best score on day one was a 68 from Sergio Garcia, Charl Schwartzel, Taiwanese Y.E. Yang, Aussie Scott Hend, and Korean Kim Kyung-tae.

Rory hit all the right notes in his post-match interview with ESPN's Tom Rinaldi. "I'm going home tonight with a quiet mind," he said in a voice as measured as his iron play had been that afternoon.

It was more of the same Friday morning. Rory started par-par-par, then made his longest putt of the week, a thirty-footer for birdie on the par-four fourth. Two holes later, he chose to lay up on the par-five sixth. His towering wedge backed up to within four or five feet of the pin; his birdie putt found the middle. He was now eight-under—and the gallery had begun stampeding in his direction.

On the eighth hole, he gave fans a thrill worth the price of admission. He also gave ESPN broadcasting icon Chris Berman an excuse to wheel out "Boomer's" signature call. Rory's wedge sailed over the flagstick so dramatically that it looked for a moment like it would trickle off the far edge. But the backspin that McIlroy had imparted took effect as the ball reached the fringe. It began slowly trickling toward the flag.

As ESPN's coverage went live, Berman filled viewers in on the early morning goings-on. Rory's backed-up wedge served as the centerpiece of Boomer's highlight tease. Berman dredged up his trademark (and some would say grating[4]) homerun call by yelling, "Back...back...back!" as Rory's ball wandered down the hill. It caught the left edge of the cup and somehow, miraculously, fell in!

McIlroy was now ten under par in the US Open—and he hadn't even come close to completing his second round! Rory was the quickest ever to double digits under par in a US Open—just twenty-six holes. Koch pointed out that Rory was now eight-under

---

4   This baseball geek would be among them.

on just the Blue Course's par-fours alone—unheard-of marksmanship in a US Open.

On number 14, McIlroy hit another laser inside seven feet. He was now 11-under and still had the par-five 16th to play. The Klein-Pennington four-iron got Rory to 12-under and looking to go even lower.

On the next hole, he became the first player in the annals of the US Open to get to 13-under. A solid iron off the tee was followed by a flawless short-iron to eight feet or so. *Bang!* as Boomer was wont to say.

On Friday's closing hole, he hit his only real turbulence of the week. He pulled his drive badly into the gallery on the left. With trees interfering with his approach, he made both a mental and physical gaffe. Given his huge lead, he should have punched out of the rough, taken the water out of play, and left himself a short wedge to try and save his par. That way, the worst score he would have made was bogey.

Instead, hell-for-leather Rory took over. His iron barely found the slope in front of the green before bouncing back into the water. His adoring fan club in the TV towers suddenly turned surly. "There was absolutely no reason" for McIlroy to have brought the water into play, scolded Koch.

A decent chip still left Rory with ten feet or so to save bogey. In a replay of his putting woes at Augusta, he pulled his putt left. The double-bogey left him at 65-66, 11-under, a fabulous score for the halfway point of a US Open, but not quite what it should have been.

Naysayers seized on McIlroy's 36th hole blunder, suggesting that the weekend could be the Masters all over again. It didn't happen. But for just an instant or two Saturday morning, it looked like it might.

McIlroy's third round got off to a shaky start when he ballooned his opening tee shot to the right and was forced to pitch out from beyond the gallery ropes. But his third-shot wedge from inside eighty yards came within inches of going into the hole. He also saved par at the fourth, getting up and down from a greenside bunker, again nearly jarring his shot.

As McIlroy climbed the elevated tee box for the medium-length par-four fifth hole, NBC's Dan Hicks referenced that day's *Post* column by Jenkins. Her piece had quoted Hicks's broadcast partner Miller, who called McIlroy's swing the best in golf because he used his legs so effectively and extended through his full-swing shots with such elasticity. The acceleration in Rory's swing, Miller maintained, was rooted in "gravity," which explained why Rory's shots went so long and high—and, usually, straight.

A beautifully drawn gravitational three-wood on the fifth tee box set Rory up with a 139-yard second, which he hit hole-high left to about fifteen feet. His left-to-right putt jumped into the middle. He was now back to 12-under.

He made another birdie at the par-five ninth, when he hit another dazzling second, this time with a five-iron. As Rory twirled his club a la Tiger, his shot creased the middle of the green, ran to the far edge, then took the slope of the green some twenty-five feet back toward the flagstick. It set up a doable look at eagle. Rory's putt just slid by on the left. He had an easy birdie tap-in.

At the uphill par-four 11th, his drive found the rough on the left side of the fairway. His eight-iron from 177 yards almost hit the top of the flagstick, settling fifteen feet past. His slick left-to-right downhiller banged into the back of the cup. He was again entering uncharted US Open terrain and about to discover a new frontier.

After another three-wood down the middle, the time from the 14th tee, Rory lasered a short-iron over the flagstick and knocked in a ten-footer. After fifty holes of the US Open, he was now 14-under par.

After narrow misses for birdie at numbers 16 and 18, he finished at 14-under. Rory now held an eight-shot lead over Y.E. Yang and a nine-stroke advantage over Jason Day and Robert Garrigus, both of whom had shot 65 on Saturday.

This time, commentators were justified in calling McIlroy's lead "commanding."

That Saturday evening, Chubby Chandler, Lee Westwood, and Rory went out to dinner together for the third consecutive night. Chubby, according to Josh Huggan's account in *Golf World*, had footed the bill for Thursday's meal. Westwood had taken care of Friday's tab. So, Saturday's repast would be on Rory.

Rory's security detail got bigger—and quicker—as the week wore on. After Rory finished his media obligations Saturday evening, NBC's Hicks described on-air how McIlroy was whisked away by a couple of security guards, marched out of the Congressional clubhouse through the back door of the kitchen, then deposited in a black SUV with the motor running—precautions worthy of a presidential candidate.

Chubby, the guy who no doubt helped arrange the security shield, sized up the competition between his two charges on Saturday evening: "All Lee can do is go out and set a target for Rory. If Rory plays well, [Westwood] won't have a chance, though."

Chubby was correct: the only suspense in Sunday's round was the margin of Rory's victory. That margin got even fatter on Rory's opening hole, when his second-shot wedge plopped inside eight feet. He added another birdie at number 4 on yet another superbly judged wedge that backed up to within a putter's length of the cup.

But his signature shot of the entire week came on the par-three 10th amid the natural amphitheater set just beyond Congressional's stately clubhouse. With thousands of people chanting "*Rorr-ee! Rorr-ee!*" his soaring six-iron came down just past hole-high, stopped about ten feet due north of the flagstick, briefly came to a halt to titillate the crowd, then began inching back toward the pin as so many of his irons had done that week. As if remote-controlled, Rory's orb neatly circumnavigated playing partner Y.E. Yang's ball, which was positioned five feet or so past the cup.

To coax his ball closer, Rory tossed a couple of genuflections into his follow-through, his right knee bending as if trying to find a kneeler during a crowded Christmas mass at St. Colmcille's. Rory's ball looked for the longest time like it had enough *oomph* to reach the cup, but it finally petered out three or four inches short. He'd almost pulled off his second miracle eagle of the week.

As he tapped in to go 17-under, thousands of people in the Congressional congregation exploded into a "*Let's Go Rorr-ee!!*" chant. It didn't let up for the entire back nine. They knew they were witnessing some very cool history.

After knocking in his par putt on the 72nd hole, Rory displayed what would become his go-to major-championship victory move: a slow-motion right-handed fist pump with shoulders gently rocking and a bemused how-'bout-that smile. It reflected as much relief as jubilation.

He shook hands with Yang and Yang's caddie, hugged J.P., thanked the USGA spotters and volunteers, then yelled, "Happy Father's Day, Dad!" and shared a long embrace with Gerry, with the crowd hollering its approval.

During the trophy ceremony, Rory repeated the Father's Day wishes to his dad and in the next breath was quick to thank his mum. His parents had sacrificed so much on his behalf that he was dedicating the USGA trophy to them, he said.

When NBC's Bob Costas, conducting the live interview, listed the record-busting that Rory had done that week[5]—including lowest raw score, lowest score relative to par, and the fact that Rory had become the youngest US Open champion since the twenty-

---

5   In all, as the *Times* pointed out, Rory had broken a dozen US Open scoring records.

one-year-old Bobby Jones had triumphed in 1923 at Long Island's Inwood Country Club—you could see the pride rising in McIlroy's eyes. But when Costas quoted 2010 champion McDowell as saying that the odds of two Northern Irishmen winning back-to-back US Opens was like buying a winning lottery ticket, Rory narrowed his eyes, pursed his lips, and with nimble timing deadpanned: "I thought I had a pretty good chance." The audience howled.

By the time Rory finished with all of his media commitments and USGA press-fleshing, it was completely dark. Bushed, he and his dad went back to the Bethesda Marriott and held an impromptu celebration, sipping champagne from the trophy and even pouring in a couple of bottles of Guinness.

"It's not quite the same and doesn't travel well to the States," McIlroy joked the next day. "But no complaints."

Rory Land decided it needed a better party atmosphere than a hotel lobby, plus certain Mac Packers wanted to drink Guinness out of a tap. So, with the clock ticking and someone presumably calling ahead, they piled into a couple of SUVs to celebrate at Ireland's Four Provinces, a popular pub along Connecticut Avenue, NW, in DC's Cleveland Park neighborhood.

The Sunday night scene at the "Four P's" was pretty subdued when Rory's posse pulled up. Things got noisy in a hurry. Despite the late hour, word spread that Rory and his gang had shown up and—even better—were picking up the tab! Before long, the place was jammed. A lot of Guinness and shooters went down. The revelry went on until the wee hours, although it's not clear how long Rory hung around.

McIlroy knew how to handle a sore head. First thing the next morning, he was at the hotel having breakfast with his dad and Chubby and being applauded from every corner of the restaurant and foyer. The Marriott staff kindly produced that morning's newspapers, which included a color photo in the *Washington Post* of Gerry and Rory embracing.

Chandler and the McIlroy men had to hustle off to the private plane terminal at Reagan National to catch a flight to Cape Cod. On the ride to the airport, they placed a call to Rosie. Journalist Justin Doyle reported that Rory's end of the conversation went something like: "Listen, I'm sorry I didn't ring you last night…yes, he's here beside me…yeah, US Open champion. It's great!"

On the plane, Rory curled up in his seat and tried—apparently without success—to get some shut-eye as his dad and Chubby pored over more papers. In going to the Cape, Rory was fulfilling an obligation that Chandler had arranged months before. As a brand ambassador for luxury watchmaker Audemars Piguet, Rory was scheduled to play in an exhibition at Willowbend Country Club in Mashpee, Massachusetts, part of the company's investor appreciation day for a key financial backer, Fireman Capital Partners.

Nobody—including the folks at Audemars Piguet and Willowbend—would have blamed Rory for skipping out on the outing after his big weekend at Congressional. But he'd made a commitment to one of his corporate sponsors—and stuck to it.

"He's a wise man," Chubby told Bill Higgins, the sports editor of the *Cape Cod Times*, after they pulled into the Willowbend parking lot. Here's how Higgins described Rory's appearance: "His shirt tail was untucked; he was bleary-eyed and needed a shave. He had been up all night and hadn't slept a minute. He was hungry. And yet Rory McIlroy never felt better in his life."

Rory was rubbing the sleep out of his eyes as he chatted with Higgins. "It hasn't sunk in yet," McIlroy told him. "It's all a big blur, but I know I played very well and it's nice to get my major career up and running."

Higgins pulled Gerry aside and asked if his son's big win would go to his head. "His mother won't let it happen," Gerry said. "When he's home he still has to pick up his laundry and dishes. He'll stay grounded, believe me." Rory's life, "already a whirlwind, will now travel at warp speed," Higgins predicted.

McIlroy was one of a half-dozen pros on tap for the private event: Ian Poulter, Vijay Singh, Christie Kerr, Anthony Kim, and Rocco Mediate were also at Willowbend.

Lugging the trophy, Rory walked into the dining room just as the pre-tourney brunch was getting started. For the second time that morning, a restaurant erupted in applause. The trophy was passed from table to table, with Rory posing for pictures. Eventually, the jug became an impromptu centerpiece for the McIlroys' table.

Higgins was able to grab Rocco for a couple of minutes. "I'm not surprised one bit by what Rory did. He's been special his whole life," the forty-eight-year-old Mediate said. "His ability to swing the club and hit golf shots is there for everyone to see. He's going to improve, too."

Rory admitted to Higgins that he was pooped and couldn't wait to get on the plane at Logan Airport so he could sleep a little. McIlroy also told Higgins that, as a big tennis buff, he was hoping to make good the following week on the invitation he'd received to attend Wimbledon.

"'I'm looking forward to taking a break. I want to see my family and friends and enjoy this,'" he said, patting the trophy. "I only get to keep it for a year.'"

Chandler, wrote Higgins, was quick to interject: "'Not necessarily, Rory. Let's win it again next year, too.'"

Since the McIlroy gang needed to get from Mashpee to Logan in a hurry, the club had requested an escort from the Barnstable sheriff's office. Lieutenant Barney Murphy, a native Dubliner who'd become a member of Barnstable's canine unit, was happy to oblige. Lt. Murphy had "Jaxx," a Dutch shepherd, in the back of his cruiser.

Rory took one look at the dog and asked if he could ride in the cop car instead of the SUV with his dad and agent. Okay by me, said Murphy. Would it be alright if I petted him? Rory asked. Sure, came the reply.

As the two-car caravan cruised down Route 3, lights flashing, Barney and Rory chatted away about all kinds of stuff. "He was absolutely a normal guy," Murphy later told the *Boston Globe*. "He's so down to earth."

It occurred to Murphy that his family back in Ireland would never believe him if he didn't provide evidence of his famous passenger. He punched the Skype button on his I-Pad and dialed his sister, Joan Dodd, in Dublin.

"You'll never believe who I have with me," he told Joan.

"Jaxx?" she guessed, since the shepherd's snout was dominating her screen.

Joan, a big McIlroy fan, was flabbergasted when the countenance of Ireland's most famous athlete suddenly appeared, grinning and waving. She yelled for her son Sean to come downstairs. The boy excitedly told Rory about how much he loved playing golf with his dad.

"That's how I started as a young boy, playing with my father. Keep it up and maybe one day you'll be where I am now," Rory told him.

When they got to Logan, Rory gave Jaxx one last pet and joined Chubbs and his dad in hustling through the terminal. When they got to Heathrow, fellow passengers were amazed to see him hanging out at baggage claim and schlepping his own luggage and clubs. More spontaneous applause ensued. Pictures were snapped and autographs scribbled.

A couple hours later, Gerry and Rory were off to Belfast's George Best Airport for a joyous homecoming. It was pelting rain as they approached the McIlroy homestead. Rory embraced Rosie and presented her with the USGA trophy.

More hugs. More tears, especially after Holly Sweeney joined the party.

Rory took a picture of the trophy sitting on his kitchen table and posted it on Twitter, with this self-effacing note: "Great to be back home. Even nicer to have this on my kitchen table…and for anyone who's interested, there will be no open-top bus parade through Belfast! I'm a golfer, not a football team!"

The band went out for Chinese food. They discovered that, literally overnight, congratulatory banners hailing "Our Rory" had gone up all over North Down. One of the signs was planted just outside the Holywood Golf Club.

The next day, Rory stood on HGC's balcony, cradling the trophy. A big crowd had gathered below.

"I'm so proud to be from here," he said. "I've won this US Open trophy but I'd just like you to know that it belongs to all of you."

A little while later, Rory visited Sullivan Upper. Surrounded by students in blazers, Rory told the assembly: "I didn't think a few years ago that I would be back here and experiencing [this]—teachers coming up to me and asking for autographs!"

At some point in all the partying, his Uncle Colm pulled him aside and said, "Well, I guess all this means I can't call you the 'Wee Hacker' anymore."

"Not for a couple of weeks, anyway," Rory jabbed back.

Chapter 14

WOZZILROY

Rory McIlroy was a busy guy in the four weeks separating the 2011 US Open from the Open Championship at Royal St. George's on the English Channel. Between figuring out how to invest the $1.44 million winner's check from the USGA, catching up with Holly and other pals, showing up at all the receptions being thrown in his honor, and doing the media and commercial shoots arranged by ISM, he barely had time to squeeze in two trips to Wimbledon. He and buddy Harry Diamond, nicely turned out in blazers and ties that might have been purchased that week from a haberdashery on Saville Row, sat in an exclusive box at the All-England Lawn and Tennis Club.

Chubby Chandler revealed that four of McIlroy's corporate sponsors would be paying the golfer big bonuses for winning the US Open, per the contracts that ISM had negotiated on Rory's behalf. The agent backed, at least publicly, McIlroy's decision not to play a tournament between the Opens, which kicked up a bit of a hornet's nest in the golfing press. The Barclays Scottish Open, won by Luke Donald, was held the week before Royal St. George's at Castle Stuart Golf Links, in Inverness, Scotland. There is little question that Castle Stuart did not present the sort of golfing challenge that St. George's did; still, Rory went a long time between competitive rounds.

Barely a month past his twenty-second birthday, Rory had already salted away more than €11 million in his brief career—but that represented only a fraction of what he was capable of earning, Chubby told the media. McIlroy was as big or bigger than Seve

Ballesteros in his prime. The difference, Chubby pointed out in his inimitably direct way, was that Seve "wasn't everyone's cup of tea," whereas just about everybody loved Rory.

It all sounds pretty dizzying, but they would prove to be four of the most pivotal weeks in young Rory's existence—and probably not in a good way. In his heart of hearts, if McIlroy could somehow get a "mulligan" for one stretch of his life, it might well be late June and early July of 2011.

The tabloid sensation that Rory himself labeled "Wozzilroy"[1] began innocently enough. Or so it would appear.

In the spring of 2011, just ahead of his coronation at Congressional, Rory posted a couple of Facebook musings that expressed admiration for women's tennis. The postings caught the eye of Danish star Caroline Wozniacki, then the world's number-one-ranked player.

Over time, Caroline responded with Facebook posts of her own that conveyed her appreciation for Rory's golf game and congratulated him for winning at Congressional. As they went back and forth, Caroline began getting a bit flirtatious, letting the world—and Rory—know that she thought he was kind of cute. McIlroy responded, but more subtly. Holly, his paramour, was, at that moment, back on-again.

On June 27, five days after Rory got back to Holywood, Caroline was upset in the round of sixteen at Wimbledon, 6-1, 6-7, 5-7, by Dominika Cibulkova of Slovakia. It marked the fifth time in Caroline's career that she had failed to reach the quarterfinals at the All-England Club. Tennis scribes were beginning to question whether Wozniacki had what it took to win a Grand Slam title.

She may have been down in the dumps at that particular moment and looking for something—or someone—to lift her spirits. Some people suggest that Rory and Caroline were introduced

---

[1] "Permission to take a puke break, sir?" *"Permission granted."*

during McIlroy's visits to Wimbledon in late June—but it's not clear they spent any meaningful time together that week.

Most likely, staffers from the two camps set up a camouflaged meeting. Wozniacki's people made it known that on Saturday evening, July 2, Caroline would take in a heavyweight championship bout in Hamburg, Germany. Billed as "The Talk Ends Now!" the match pitted reigning world heavyweight (and former Olympic) champion Wladimir Klitschko of Ukraine against British boxer David "The Haye-maker" Haye.

Somehow, Rory got the message that he should fly to Hamburg and attend the fight. Somebody was smart enough not to put Caroline and Rory next to one another, which would have set tongues wagging and social media afire. Instead, they sat a row apart, so whatever interaction they may have had would look spontaneous.

They saw a hell of a fight. The bout went the distance. Klitschko won a unanimous decision, successfully defending his heavyweight titles.

The "Talk" may have ended that night between Haye and Klitschko, but it had just begun for Wozniacki and McIlroy. It's not known, of course, what kind of romantic jabs may have been tossed that evening, but they landed hard enough to spark a subsequent flurry of public tweets and private texts and calls between them.

Via Twitter, Rory kidded the still-twenty-year-old Caroline that she wasn't old enough to drink alcohol in the United States. With her twenty-first birthday looming in mid-July, she responded by coyly suggesting that Rory buy her a legal drink in the States.

On Monday, July 18—barely two weeks after his excursion to Hamburg and, not coincidentally, the day after the Open Championship ended at Royal St. George's—Rory broke the news to a heartbroken Holly.

She knew things were amiss when Rory walked into their County Down home, "dodged" her, and went to greet their dogs.

Holly later confided to *Irish Sunday Mirror* show business columnist Paul Martin that she surmised "something was up" because Rory had gone radio silent during his trip to Hamburg. McIlroy "sat me down and told me that he met with her in Germany and that he wanted to see how it would go with her.

"When he was watching the women's games he always said he fancied her but I didn't take it that seriously—little did I know.... I never thought he would do this to me."

Looking back, Martin called Rory's breakup with Holly "pretty ruthless."

McIlroy's management team confirmed the news that week. Rory and Caroline were officially a couple; Holly and Rory were officially kaput.

At Royal St. George's, Ulsterman Darren Clarke's great triumph, Rory had played like a guy whose mind was elsewhere. McIlroy only broke 70 once in finishing seven-over and tied for twenty-fifth.

In the run-up to the championship, brash young Rory managed to piss off links enthusiasts, purists in the press corps, and his future biographer by complaining about the Channel area's lousy weather. He intimated that he didn't like changing his high-ball-flight style of play for just one week of the year—heresy that might have ripped Old Tom Morris out of his grave.

Months earlier, by some accounts, Rory had begged to get Sweeney back. In late June, Holly had appeared on *Rory's Major Breakthrough*, a Belfast television feature welcoming Rory home after winning his first major; while on camera, McIlroy had praised her to high heaven. Now, less than three weeks later, he was breaking up with her—this time, it appeared, for good.

Holly rebounded in style. She lengthened her sabbatical from Ulster University to concentrate on what the *Irish Independent* called her "showbiz career." She continued to cheerlead at rugby games, did some modeling, posed for a Belfast photographer of note (at least one provocative shot was scrubbed after a brief appearance on the shutterbug's website), and, alongside gossip writer Martin, became one of the cohosts of a Dublin-based television show called *Celebrity Come Dine with Me*.

The TV3 program featured loosely defined Irish and UK "celebrities" breaking bread with Sweeney, Martin, and the show's other mainstays, all competing to put on the perfect dinner party, with small cash incentives offered to the "winners." Its mildly snarky undertone took a jagged turn in late 2012 when Sweeney came up with a dinner-party theme—"Golf Pros and Tennis Hos"—that grabbed media attention on both islands and the Continent.

The *Belfast Telegraph* reported that Rory got wind of his ex's "Pros and Hos" zinger on the day the taping was scheduled. Holly was already on the set, preparing her appetizers, when Rory sent her a "slew" of texts, supposedly crying foul and pleading with her to bag the show. According to coworkers, Holly tittered as she put her phone away and didn't miss a beat in the kitchen.

"She just laughed and carried on cooking," a show insider told the *Telegraph*.

Once the taping started, she turned up in a form-fitting tennis outfit, complete with a short skirt, a headband, and a towel wrapped around her shoulders. Although predominantly white in color, the revealing ensemble might have been frowned upon at starchy Wimbledon.

There was nothing subtle about Holly's modus operandi. At the top, the show's narrator quipped to Sweeney, tongue-in-cheek: "So, you get dumped by the then-world's-number-two golfer who is now with the world's number-one tennis player and you decide to give your dinner a golf and tennis dress code? It's a brave choice."

"My theme is a tennis and golf theme," Holly responded. "I chose it tonight because I used to go out with Rory. The tennis thing is obviously a little joke because Caroline is world number one."

Her "little joke" fell flat with one of her co-diners. Decked out in golf attire, the C-lister urged Holly to stop "harping on" about

McIlroy. Others chimed in, pro and con. It made for awkward TV—but TV3 didn't complain about the ratings.

If Holly was looking to draw blood from Caroline, she succeeded. Weeks later, within a day or two of the show's airing, the Dane issued a tweet skewering Sweeney for her failure to accept the breakup and move on. Caroline's advisors apparently went to the same shoot-yourself-in-the-foot PR school as Rory Land principals.

Led by the *Telegraph*, the media had a field day. "You may call it the work of a bitter ex-girlfriend, but I say it's genius," cracked American sportswriter and syndicated radio host Larry Brown, the founder of *Larry Brown Sports*.

Holly held her fire vis-à-vis Caroline, but couldn't resist taking another shot at her ex while he was nursing a wrist injury. She tweeted: "Rory McIlroy wrist injury fears: Well, that's what happens when ye get rid of yer girlfriend"—a wonderfully witchy put-down that must have been saluted left and right in Irish pubs.

It was never given a cutesy nickname ("Sween-roy?" "McIl-holly?"), but Holly Sweeney's relationship with Rory lasted six years, give or take. For at least two years they shared Rory's big home and a couple of dogs.

It all worked out for Ms. Sweeney. She was regularly featured in tabloid chatter in Martin's column and others while out socializing with friends in Belfast, Dublin, and Derry. Within a year or so, she started dating Jeff Mason, a Massachusetts native and former Providence College (class of '05) hockey star, then playing defenseman for the Belfast Giants of the UK's Elite Ice Hockey League (EIHL).

Once his playing days ended, Mason became an assistant coach for the Giants. In 2022–2023, he accepted the head coaching position of the EIHL's Dundee Stars in Scotland, but left that job to return to the Giants as an assistant for the 2023–2024 season.

The couple had a baby boy in 2014 and were married in a 2016 Belfast ceremony that concluded in a ballroom at the upscale Merchant Hotel. When their little guy was born, Rory sent the couple a congratulatory note and a pair of Nike baby boots.

McIlroy fell hard for Wozniacki—and it's not hard to understand why. Caroline was such a striking young woman that—after being dumped by Rory three years later—she appeared in *Sports Illustrated*'s swimsuit edition, not only showing off her physique but letting her ex know that she wasn't sitting at home, sulking.

Lithe and quick on the court, off of it she carried herself with the feline insouciance of Grace Kelly in a Hitchcock film. When she went out clubbing, men buzzed around her; she was considered one of the most alluring and marketable female athletes in history. Like her new boyfriend, she was blessed with an electric smile and an engaging personality ideally suited for media swarms.

Wozniacki's upbringing could not have been further removed from McIlroy's. She was not only raised in privilege, but in a household full of elite athletes.

Her parents moved from their native Poland when her father Piotr was offered a contract with one of Denmark's most popular football clubs, the Odense-based Boldklubben 1909, nicknamed B1909. Her mother Anna had been a member of Poland's national women's volleyball squad. Her older brother Patrik also played professional football.

Fourteen months younger than her beau, Caroline was a junior tennis phenom at exactly the same time Rory was becoming a dominant player in amateur golf. Wozniacki won the Wimbledon juniors and the prestigious Orange Bowl championship in 2006, the same year that Rory swept the West of Ireland and Irish Close tournaments for the second season running. She also made a splash in her debut on the Women's Tennis Association tour, earning the "top newcomer" accolade in 2008, which coincided with Rory's first full season on the European Tour.

At the 2009 US Open, Wozniacki reached her first Grand Slam final at the precocious age of nineteen, losing to Kim Clijsters of

Belgium, 5-7, 3-6. Caroline's forte was speedy footwork, which allowed her to hone exceptional defensive skills.

Unlike Rory, who won a major at twenty-two, she didn't win a Grand Slam tournament until the 2018 Australian Open, when at age twenty-seven she defeated Romania's Simona Halep in three sets. It would turn out to be her only victory in a Slam.

Their relationship helped spring both into an earnings stratosphere that had been unimaginable a few years earlier. As the holidays approached in 2012, Caroline accompanied Rory to a warm-weather tournament and sat in on a press conference. When asked by the moderator if she had any questions for her significant other, she coquettishly asked if Rory would hint at what she was getting for Christmas, since she'd "been such a good girl." It caused much giggling. Rory sidestepped the question, but whatever the gift may have been, it was expensive.

A decade later, Americans don't quite get the bigness of Wozzilroy. Their relationship got some notoriety in the States, but nowhere close to what it sparked in Europe. For nearly three years, Caroline and Rory were persistent tabloid fodder. It was Ben Affleck and Jennifer Lopez meets Chrissie Evert and Jimmy Connors (*Too dated a reference? How about Taylor Swift and Travis Kelce? Okay, not that big, but you get the idea.*)

On those rare occasions when their schedules would allow them to get together, either for a getaway weekend or a tournament where one played and the other spectated, they were hounded by paparazzi. Nosy fans and video cameras followed wherever they went.

The pair encouraged—even solicited—a lot of it, leaking travel plans, popping up at A-list parties, and never shy about engaging in public displays of affection. Aware that photographers were around, they smooched after intimate dinners in Manhattan, Monte Carlo, Dubai, London, and Sydney, held hands while out on shopping sprees and strolls through parks and town squares, and were seen emerging from ski chalets, weight rooms, and gymnasiums all over the world, glistening with sweat and making goo-goo eyes at one another.

As *The National* put it back then, "The young sweethearts Caroline Wozniacki and Rory McIlroy are so cute that we risk insulin shock by looking too closely."

She made a one-time junk-food junkie a fitness freak and a gym rat. When they first started going out, Caroline used to say with a cackle, Rory couldn't hack one of her forty-five-minute runs up and down the hills of Monte Carlo, where she had a condo. But after hitting the gym, the treadmill, and the exercise bike, Rory became leaner and fitter. Soon enough, he was able to match her stride for stride.

"The improvement I have seen with his fitness is unbelievable," Caroline told Karen Crouse of *The New York Times* in early spring 2013, when they'd been dating for about twenty months. "He loves [the gym] more than me, and I like going to the gym."

There's little doubt that his new-found fitness helped Rory compete on the course. His upper body went from flabby to chiseled. He got more buff as the years went on and stayed committed to the weight room.

"I want to be the best player in the world," McIlroy told reporters soon after they became an item. "She's number one in the world and I've got a major and we sort of both want what each other [has]. She's got a great work ethic and it's something I can probably learn a lot from."

The parallels between Wozniacki and McIlroy were striking. Both had been child stars interviewed on national TV before their tenth birthdays. Both had turned professional while still tender teens and enjoyed success almost right away. Both were close to their parents in ways that most prodigies aren't. And in their first full year as a couple, they'd earned loads of money, north of €15 million each, Crouse estimated. Each was continually posing for cameras and endorsing this product or headlining that press gig.

In a 2012 BBC-Northern Ireland documentary, *Rory: Being Number One*, Caroline said, "When he plays amazing, I know how he feels. And also, when he's going through a rough patch, I know how that feels and how to handle the situation."

With brutal schedules and microphones continually thrust in their faces, the two stars had a lot of situations to handle. Just setting up Skype or Facetime sessions was hard. Arranging vacations and intimate weekends was even harder. One of them was forever running to catch a plane to fly halfway around the world to steal a few moments with the other. It had to cause bruised feelings and heavy guilt and stress.

Still, it must have been intoxicating, so much so that Rory had "Wozzilroy" inscribed on a custom-built golf club that he gave to Caroline. Here they were, at the top of their respective worlds, among the most celebrated athletes on the planet…*and they were an item!*

Given his spectacular play at the US Open, Rory was one of the favorites at the 93rd PGA Championship at the Atlanta Athletic Club. On the eve of the championship, Rory admitted that he "was still getting used to" all the attention coming his way from both Congressional and Caroline.

But a day later, playing with Charl Schwartzel and Darren Clarke, Rory "was getting attention for an unanticipated reason," wrote Bill Fields in *Golf World*. "McIlroy hit his tee shot on the 475-yard third hole into trees left of the fairway. His ball settled just behind a fairly substantial tree root about two inches in diameter."

It was the definition of a dangerous lie. Clearly, the prudent play, as Fields' piece and the CBS broadcast crew pointed out, was for Rory to hit a gentle chip back into the fairway and not risk an injury colliding with the root—especially since it was only the third hole on day one. There would be plenty of time for McIlroy to make up for the stroke he might lose by playing conservatively.

But "prudent" and "conservative" were often inimical to the young McIlroy. Broadcasters began sounding the alarm as McIlroy, with caddie J.P. looking on, started rehearsing abrupt up-and-down swings. It looked like Rory was going to try and lift a seven-iron over the trees in front of him while seeking to avoid the big root.

Predictably, it backfired. McIlroy was lucky that he didn't fracture his wrist or damage tendons. "It was dangerous," Rory conceded later. "I thought [if] I could make contact with the ball and just let the club go, I might get away with it."

He didn't. His seven-iron caught the root, jarring Rory's right wrist. He yelped as his wrist began to swell and the pain spread to his forearm.

"Hindsight is a great thing," a rueful McIlroy said later in the press tent. "It was a mistake in judgment." Asked if J.P. had urged him to take a more judicious approach, McIlroy rejoined, curiously, "He's my caddie, not my father."

An athletic trainer was summoned. He applied an ice pack to Rory's arm; most analysts figured he would withdraw from the tournament, not willing to risk further injury. The analysts were wrong. Bullheaded McIlroy bulled ahead.

David Feherty, never one to miss a fat pitch, quipped in the broadcast booth: "He's twenty-two. His wrist muscles should be the strongest in his body."

It was the sort of comment that should have brought down a world of hurt on the acerbic Ulsterman. Strangely, it didn't happen. Maybe it was said so deftly that the suits at CBS missed it.

At any rate, McIlroy gutted out an even-par round of 70 on Thursday, despite the throbbing wrist. It turned out to be the best score he shot all week. He finished in a tie for sixty-fourth, which had to be a big disappointment eight weeks after his bravura performance at Congressional.

The *Belfast Telegraph* noted, however, that Rory was smiling ear-to-ear as he finished up on the 72nd green. He explained to reporters that he was rushing to see Caroline at the Western and Southern Open in Cincinnati—typical of the manic schedule he was keeping those days.

Caroline, still ranked number one and seeded number one at Cincinnati, ended up losing in the second round, an early sign of the Wozzilroy Slump that was to hobble her game for much of the next two-plus seasons.

Thirteen months later, Crouse filed an amusing piece about the bedlam Caroline caused at the Deutsche Bank tournament in Norton, Massachusetts. Nursing a sore knee, Wozniacki had lost 2-6, 2-6, to 96th-ranked Irina-Camelia Begu of Romania in the first round at the US Open in New York. Suddenly, the Danish ingenue had some time on her hands; she decided to join her guy at TPC-Boston.

Word spread like wildfire that Caroline was walking the course; given the warm weather, she was sporting a one-piece outfit that in a less correct era would have been described as "fetching." Half the male population of New England, it seemed, hurried toward Rory's group, jostling one another to get the best possible view—not of the golfer, but of his girlfriend. Rory went on to win the tournament, brilliantly holding off Tiger and Louis Oosthuizen.

For a long stretch, Caroline and Rory stood, together, bestride the world. Rory, especially, had a big second half in 2012 that included three other global wins besides Boston—the PGA Championship at Kiawah Island, the BMW leg of the FedEx Cup at Crooked Stick in Indiana, and the European Tour's season-ender at Dubai.

It was all going swimmingly—at least on the surface. But turbulence was beginning to roil the water below.

Chapter 15

BECOMING NUMBER ONE

On Sunday, March 4, 2012, Rory McIlroy achieved a dream he surely fantasized about as he signed those make-believe scorecards as a youngster. That afternoon, four-and-a-half years after turning professional, he officially became the world's number-one player. McIlroy could not have chosen a better venue or a more worthy opponent for the occasion.

The venue was the Honda Classic at Jack Nicklaus' fearsome Bear Trap: the 15th, 16th, and 17th holes at the Champion Course at the PGA National Resort & Spa in Palm Beach Gardens, Florida, the village that would soon become Rory's American home. The opponent was Tiger Woods, another transplanted Floridian.

Tiger came from out of nowhere to shoot a final-round 62, threaten McIlroy's lead, and assume the role of one of the most menacing "clubhouse leaders" in Tour history. Remarkably, the 62 was the lowest final-round score in Tiger's career. For more than an hour, Rory had to stare at Tiger's finishing score of 270 on scoreboards as he negotiated some of the toughest holes on Tour.

Rory Land had given BBC Sport-Northern Ireland permission that season to follow their guy around the US, Europe, and the Middle East with a documentary crew. BBC-NI ultimately produced the January 2013 feature: *Rory—Being Number One*. Between his five wins on two continents, the appealing presence of Wozniacki, and a McIlroy Ryder Cup performance that provided, umm, unanticipated drama, the crew was provided plenty of A- and B-roll.

Rory's "people," however, had undergone a huge change: Chubby Chandler and ISM were no longer representing the Ulsterman. McIlroy stunned the sports world in October 2011, three months into Wozzilroy, by firing Chandler and his firm. At the suggestion of Graeme McDowell, his Ryder Cup compadre, McIlroy was moving his business to Dublin-based Horizon Sports Management. McDowell, a one-time ISM client, had transferred his business to Horizon in 2007 and apparently persuaded McIlroy that his new shop provided more bespoke service.

Chubby had a crowded stable in 2011: major champions Ernie Els, Darren Clarke, and Charl Schwartzel, plus Lee Westwood and a bunch of other notables. Chandler wasn't subtle back then about his Eurocentricity. He wanted his guys plying their trade mainly in the Old World, where ISM managed a number of events for the European Tour and had other pecuniary ties. Chubby wanted his clients to play sparingly in the States—and on Chubby's terms, not the PGA Tour's. To gain full membership on the PGA Tour, a player had to commit to playing fifteen tournaments a season, a rule Chandler viewed as prohibitive.

Horizon was a leaner operation than ISM. McIlroy no doubt wanted to be a bigger fish in a smaller pond—and have his portfolio handled by the firm's top principals. Despite McIlroy's assurances—one of which came in the summer of 2011—that the European Tour would remain his top priority, by late that season, he realized that the greater prestige and the bigger bucks lay in the US.

His new love interest was doubtless instrumental in making Rory recognize that the US market was where he needed to be. At a late-season banquet honoring the year's leading tennis players, Caroline introduced Rory to one of his idols, Roger Federer, then the winner of sixteen of what became his twenty career Grand Slam titles. Federer and McIlroy apparently talked for nearly an hour. Much of the conversation revolved around the need for great athletes to establish a strategic brand platform—and build off of it.

Perhaps more than any athlete of that era, Federer had forged—and monetized—a unique persona. Roger's brand mirrored his play on the court: sleek, smooth, urbane, cosmopolitan. He had a cachet that cut across geographic, socioeconomic, and gender boundaries, precisely the appeal that Rory was seeking to cultivate.

Federer had a ton of other commercial endorsements, but it helped his brand back then, he told Rory, that the Nike Swoosh was the only corporate logo visible as he throttled opponents and piled up Grand Slam wins. The Swoosh gave Federer a "cool" look in the Marshal McLuhanesque sense, enhancing his athleticism and making him appear more polished and less like a corporate tool.

A loyal Phil Knight acolyte back then, Federer may have also put in a plug for Nike, pointing out that he, and, not incidentally, Rory's idol Tiger Woods, had done pretty well by the Oregon-based athletic apparel and equipment company.

In Rory, Federer had an apt audience. Maybe Caroline and others had told McIlroy that the "NASCAR driver" look of competing logos on his hat, shirt collar, shirt chest, bag, et al., was cluttering his image. By then, Rory was in full, Caroline-inspired workout mode, with a body suddenly getting yoked. He saw himself as an athlete in the Federer mold and wanted to project a similar persona.

For whatever reason, McIlroy came to the conclusion that ISM couldn't or wouldn't deliver that new image. And perhaps he felt that Chubby's firm wouldn't approach Nike the way he wanted it approached.

McIlroy broke the news to Chandler in an airport lounge after they'd taken a long plane ride together. Rory had clearly been thinking about the move for a while. He told Chandler how grateful he was for Chubby's help and direction. A different agent, eager to cash in, might have burned out the young McIlroy—and Rory knew it. Chandler went to great lengths to ensure that McIlroy was protected, not only against greedy forces, but from McIlroy himself.

ISM's firing came as a bolt out of the blue, "a massive shock," Chubby confirmed to me a dozen years later. Sports journalist Neil Cameron, then with *The National*, was one of many in the industry dumbfounded by McIlroy's action. "The move astonished

Chandler, an Englishman who has tried to be polite but has let it be known he [has] been badly hurt," Cameron wrote.

Jason Sobel of the Golf Channel deduced that Rory was "put off" by Chandler's Europe-first philosophy. Dermot Gilleece pointed out that the then-current issue of *Golf Digest Ireland* carried a cover story on Chandler, tabbing him "Golf's New Kingmaker." The publicity that Chubby was getting for himself may have irked Rory and Gerry, Gilleece speculated. Rory earlier that year had called Chandler a "celebrity manager," which in turned may have rubbed Chubby the wrong way.

Others conjectured that Wozniacki felt that ISM wasn't being aggressive enough on her boyfriend's behalf. Worse, she may not have been personally enamored of Chandler, who could be a little rough around the edges.

SI's Alan Shipnuck revealed weeks later that the Horizon team won Rory's business by laying out a twenty-year strategic branding plan. The four-hour session was conducted around McIlroy's kitchen table. Several pots of coffee later, they had a deal.

It took a number of weeks for the two firms to make the transition. "Everyone acted in good faith," Chubby told me. An accommodation apparently satisfactory to all parties was reached before the holidays.

Horizon head Conor Ridge purportedly doubled the size of his staff, virtually overnight, to handle all the work that the McIlroy account would generate. Rory ended up signing the new deal at Horizon's December Christmas party, which must have been especially festive given McIlroy's presence and what it meant for the *cha-ching!* in the firm's cash register. The spiked punch and eggnog must have been flowing freely. Well-connected Dublin business sources suggest that it was not McIlroy's first reception of the day; he'd been out on the holiday circuit for several hours before stopping by the Horizon offices.

The contract-signing scene that ensued sounds like a bad parody of *Kramer vs. Kramer* meets *Jerry McGuire*. Whatever happened, happened too quickly—and without adequate thought or supervision. Rory later claimed that he signed the Horizon document without a lawyer present and without fully understanding its ramifications. In little more than a year, he came to believe that the deal gave Horizon undue compensation and unwanted control over his business affairs.

It was an uncomfortable start to what would soon become an untenable relationship.

Rory chose to abandon the gruff, ex-duffer charm of Chubby Chandler for an Irishman who was a slick marketeer, a guy who had enjoyed a meteoric rise through the ranks of Dublin's corporate public relations community. Twelve years older than Rory, Conor Ridge was raised out west in Galway and educated in Dublin at prestigious St. Mary's College. In 1998, he earned a bachelor's degree in Business Communications from University College Dublin.

Ridge was of medium build; he no doubt looked better in a business suit than his predecessor. His oval face and tousled dark hair gave him something of a Mark Ruffalo look.

He had started his career on one of the bottom rungs of Drury Communications, at the time Ireland's biggest public relations agency. But he quickly moved up, honing an expertise in sports management that enabled him to hit the ground running with Horizon a few years later. His practice took off when he signed McDowell away from Chubby and ISM in 2007. Three years later, when G-Mac won the US Open, Ridge and Horizon had huge paydays.

Ridge spelled out a strategy for approaching Nike that Rory must have liked. Whatever his pitch, it worked. In 2013, Horizon wired for McIlroy a five-year deal with Nike to wear its apparel, including golf shoes, and to use its clubs, which at the time were a relatively new (and controversial) offering for the mega sports retailer.

The size of Rory's initial deal with Nike has never been pinned down. Estimates range from $100 million to $250 million, but Rory has always pooh-poohed big numbers. Sources close to the negotiations (read: Horizon executives leaking information flattering to them) threw around some huge claims that got snapped up by the press.

Whatever the actual number, it set Rory up for life and accomplished his goal of presenting a sleeker image. But like most professional golfers making an equipment change, it took a long time for Rory to get used to his new ball and sticks.

Hiring a new agent wasn't the only change in Rory's life in late 2011 and early '12. That winter he announced plans to move his base of operation from the North of Ireland (with frequent visits to the place he'd bought in Dubai) to Florida. A year later, he bought for $12-plus million a waterfront property on the Intercoastal Waterway in Palm Beach Gardens. Five years after that, he sold the waterfront home, at a substantial loss, and bought from Ernie Els a spread at the Bear's Club, a mile inland. Ernie's humble estate[1] included a private pool and tennis court. The Bear's Club boasted a Jack Nicklaus-designed golf course and what was then a state-of-the-art practice facility, with maximum privacy for touring pros.

But all that was in the future as Rory began his 2012 campaign. It got off to an encouraging start when Rory finished fifth at the Dubai Desert Classic and made it all the way to the finals of the

---

1 Ernie and his wife Liezl were kind enough to host young Rory and his parents at the Els's Bear's Club home on one of the McIlroys' early trips to Florida. It was the family's first visit to the place that Rory would eventually acquire. During dinner, Rosie looked out the window and asked who lived in the home beyond the courtyard. "We do," Liezl answered, sheepishly. It was a separate wing of the same huge manse. Rory loves telling that story.

Accenture World Match Play in Arizona before losing to match-play maestro Hunter Mahan.

Then came the Honda Classic, where Rory not only ascended to number one in the world in winning the tournament but had the pleasure of socializing with Mr. and Mrs. Eddie McCormack of Galway Bay. Caroline flew to Florida that week and walked the course with Gerry, creating a buzz wherever she and her designer sunglasses alighted.

If Rory wanted to forget that the world's number-one perch was on the line, the Irish media wouldn't let him. No Irishman had ever achieved the ranking; the golf-mad country was agog that their twenty-two-year-old star was on the cusp of doing it. He did it in such style that Dan Hicks, Johnny Miller, Jimmy Roberts, Roger Maltbie, and the rest of the NBC crew had to recycle the same praise they lavished on him eight months earlier at Congressional.

On both Saturday and Sunday, the medium-length, par-five 18th played downwind, blowing slightly from the right. Each day, Rory nuked his drive, turning it over right-to-left, and making a challenging hole look easy.

His four rounds—66-67-66-69—were low enough to hold off both Tiger's Sunday 62 and Lee Westwood's final-round 63.

Two-thousand-twelve was off to a very good start for McIlroy. He was not only the world number one—he was a Tiger slayer.

When Obama White House officials extended an invitation to the reigning US Open champion to attend a state dinner honoring British Prime Minister David Cameron, no doubt they were hoping that Caroline Wozniacki would be Rory's "and one." Alas, the WTA Tour in mid-March 2012 was caught between two of its biggest events—Indian Wells in California and the Miami Open—and Caroline couldn't slip away.

So, Rory's "date" turned out to be agent Conor Ridge, who didn't look nearly as good in evening attire. Rory managed at some point to get fitted for a tuxedo from haute designer Alexander Nash in New York. His look featured a polka-dotted tie and a stylishly flared red handkerchief square.

Other expensive tuxes were worn that evening by British actor Damian Lewis, of *Band of Brothers* and *Billions* fame, English business mogul Sir Richard Branson, and American über hunk George Clooney, who at one point in his "starving actor" phase supposedly played to a 12-handicap.

It was the largest state dinner of the eight-year Obama presidency. British band Mumford & Sons provided the entertainment.

The global media speculated that Clooney wasn't the only VIP that night asking McIlroy for tips on their golf game. Both the Commander in Chief and Vice President Biden were spotted chatting in suspiciously intense conversations with Rory.

Rory tweeted the next day: "Unbelievable experience at the White House last night! Big thanks to @BarackObama for the invite! We'll get that golf swing sorted soon!"

Before the Honda tourney started, McIlroy admitted to the press that at Augusta National ten months earlier he had gotten too wrapped up in trying to be something he wasn't—a Tiger clone. Instead of playing his usual game and interacting with the gallery, he tried to emulate the way Tiger created "an aura" of dominance, Rory said.

McIlroy came to this conclusion after he finally made himself look at video of his performance. On Sunday at Augusta, he realized his body language was taut the whole day; even at the beginning of the round, before things went completely south, he was staring at the ground instead of smiling and making eye contact.

At the 2012 Masters, he wanted to exude a different vibe and go back to being himself. It was the first McIlroy epiphany of many to come about how to improve his showing at the Masters. McIlroy had begun what has become his annual Masters ritual: self-reflection followed by self-flogging.

Along with Tiger, the oddsmakers had McIlroy the co-favorite to win the 76th Masters. Rory's "new" mental approach got off to a promising start. He opened with a one-under 71 and followed it with a 69 on Friday. At four-under, he was just one shot out of the lead, which was jointly held by Fred Couples and Jason Dufner.

It all came crashing down on the weekend, when he shot an unsightly 77-76.

He had spent months on the range trying to avoid hitting quick hooks with his driver, the shot that spelled doom during his 2011 Sunday round at both the 10th and 13th tees. He may have overcorrected. In '12, he averted the big hook but was susceptible to the big push.

In mid-round on Saturday, he seemed to lose his go-to drive: the high draw. On the seventh tee, already fighting his swing, he blocked his tee ball dead right into the pine trees, tried unsuccessfully to get back to the fairway, and made an ugly double. He never got back into the tournament, making one slipshod bogey after another. He ended up tied for fortieth with the other co-favorite, Woods. They were fifteen shots behind eventual winner Bubba Watson, who beat Louis Oosthuizen in a memorable playoff.

McIlroy finished forty-first in putting for the week, three-putting six times. Even worse, he finished fiftieth in driving accuracy.

"I've got twelve months [to fix his draw]," McIlroy said. "Obviously you hope you're coming in here to do a lot better. I'll just go to San Francisco and try to get another major at the US Open [at Olympic Lakeside]."

But first, he told the press, he was taking a three-week break. His respite would begin with some time off with Caroline in Denmark.

When he returned, he came back to one of his favorite golfing venues, Quail Hollow, the place where he'd won his first tournament in the United States two years earlier.

McIlroy again played with great verve in Charlotte. His charge up the leaderboard via a Saturday 66 pulled him to within two shots of Webb Simpson's lead.

He ended up falling just short the next day. On the 72nd hole, he had a fifteen-foot putt for birdie that would have won the tournament outright. But it missed on the low side, which meant he went into a three-way playoff with Rickie Fowler and D.A. Points. Fowler won on the first extra hole, canning a five-footer for birdie on Quail Hollow's brutal 18th after a 320-yard drive.

Back in the UK for the last week of May, McIlroy flamed out at the BMW Championship at Wentworth outside London, missing the cut. He conceded that he'd taken his eye off the ball after winning the Honda in March and had enjoyed himself with Caroline at the expense of hitting the range.

Naysayers began pointing out that his frenetic personal life was taking its toll. Between middle-of-the-night flights and corporate obligations, it was tough for Rory to squeeze in practice time. Instead of heading for San Francisco's Olympic Club, site of the 2012 US Open, brimming with confidence as he defended his title, Rory was struggling to keep the ball in play.

Before teeing it up at Olympic, he accepted an invitation from the San Francisco Giants to visit what was then known as AT&T Park to watch batting practice, swap stories with the guys in the locker room, and throw out the first pitch—a daunting challenge for anyone, but especially for someone raised in Europe, where most kids have arms like the Venus de Milo.

RORY LAND

McIlroy's usual Rory Land posse, including dad Gerry, came to the ball yard with him. The Giants went all out, arranging for a local Hibernian club's drum-and-bugle corps, all sporting kilts, to present the colors and play the anthem. A group of young Irish step dancers put on a Riverdance-inspired performance.

The Giants gave Rory a jersey with "McIlroy 12" on the back. Gerry also got a jersey, but his was stitched, "Geraldo," which demonstrates that someone in the Giants' front office had a sense of humor.

All-Star catcher Buster Posey was among the Giant stars to say hello and give the golfer a brief tip on swinging a baseball bat. Giants legend Willie Mays, now sadly gone but then baseball's greatest living player, was in the locker room that evening. Rory, fingering a bat, was introduced to him, although it's not clear the golfer recognized the import of the moment.

One of the Giants asked Rory if he was nervous about throwing out the first pitch. "A little," Rory said. "My object is to keep it in the air as long as possible."

Good thinking. He got a nice ovation as he took the mound wearing his new jersey. Most throw-out-the-first-pitch pitchers assume a position at the base of the mound, looking to avoid humiliation. Not Rory. He went to the top of the bump and toed the rubber. His release will never make San Franciscans forget Juan Marichal, but he achieved his goal: he got the ball all the way to the catcher.

If only the first two rounds at Olympic Lakeside had gone as smoothly as his visit to the ballpark. Rory shot what the *Irish Sun* called a "lackluster" 77 on day one, admitting afterward that his confidence was shot. Olympic played so tough that year that Rory still had a chance to make the cut on Friday but some late-round sloppiness torpedoed his Open defense. A crooked driver was the biggest culprit. His Ulster pal McDowell, the '10 champion down the coast at Pebble Beach, gutted out a two-over score, which fell just one stroke short of winner Webb Simpson.

Irishman Ivan Morris, one of this book's gray eminences, made a perceptive comment on Keogh's *Sun* article that night about Rory's frustrations. "Poor strategy more than poor play" was at the heart of Rory's problems at Olympic, Ivan wrote. "Last year's US Open was not the usual test and Rory got away with freewheeling it. He is young enough to learn—but will he?"

More than a decade later, it's still a legitimate question.

The 2012 Irish Open was held in late June at Royal Portrush, the scene of McIlroy's record-setting round as a sixteen-year-old. If there was a place that could snap him out of his funk, the Dunluce course was it.

Sure enough, between the familiar turf and the adoring County Antrim crowds, McIlroy got a decent chunk of his game back. He ended up shooting 11-under and finishing tied for tenth—his best showing in months.

"I'm definitely close," Rory said after finishing at Portrush. "I definitely feel like I've made a couple of big strides forward since the US Open."

At Royal Lytham & St. Annes in the northwest of England, Rory was again returning to a milieu where he'd enjoyed some success as a teenager. His opening round in the 141st Open Championship, a three-under 67, included six birdies, an encouraging start that soon fizzled.

On Friday, his erratic ball-striking resurfaced in an error-prone 75. Worse, he couldn't correct his wayward shots on Saturday or Sunday, shooting a pair of 73s. Forty-two-year-old Ernie Els, who hadn't won anywhere in the world in more than two years and never led the tournament until his final putt on the 72nd hole, won his second Open championship when Australian Adam Scott collapsed down the stretch.

A reporter at Lytham asked whether Rory could find his game in time for the PGA Championship three weeks hence at Kiawah Island, South Carolina. Rory's answer was philosophical. "I think the thing for me is to stay patient," he said. "If it doesn't happen over the next couple of weeks, no big deal. I've got to keep working away, plugging away, working hard and working on the right things and eventually it will come around."

"Eventually" didn't take very long.

Sidney Lanier, the American poet who served in the Confederate Army during the Civil War, was enthralled by the marshlands along the coasts of the Carolinas and his native Georgia.

"The tide's at full; the marsh with flooded streams/Glimmers, a limpid labyrinth of dreams," Lanier wrote in "Sunrise: A Hymn of the Marshes."

Hard by the Atlantic, Pete Dye's Ocean Course on the extreme eastern end of Kiawah Island took shape amid the marshlands that Lanier spent a lifetime celebrating. Dye's gem is indeed a labyrinth of dreams, and it's left many a golfer, including this one, sadly limpid.

The Ocean Course is Dye's enduring homage to such classic links as Royal Dornoch in the Scottish Highlands and Ballybunion in Ireland. It served as host to 1991's "War by the Shore," the event that transformed the Ryder Cup from a staid gentlemen's exhibition into something that too often resembles a back-alley brawl.

The 2012 PGA was the first time that the Ocean Course had been used for a major championship. By mid-August, Rory had fallen to number three in the world; there was little to suggest in the runup to Kiawah that McIlroy had regained the swagger on display at 1600 Pennsylvania Avenue earlier in the year.

Unlike his performance at the 2011 US Open, McIlroy did not dominate the '12 PGA from the opening drive. His first-round, a five-under 67 in benign conditions, was bogey-free, so Rory not only capitalized on birdie opportunities but managed to avoid big mistakes. It put him in a tie for second, a stroke behind Swede Carl Pettersson.

On Friday, high winds and nasty weather hit Carolina's coastal islands, much as they did in the 2010 Open Championship in the Kingdom of Fife when Rory shot a sky-high 80 the day after his record-tying opening-round 63. He had angered the golf gods by trying to get too much out of his round at St. Andrews.

Caustic American sportswriter Dan Jenkins shook his head while he surveyed the wreckage of Rory's bad-weather round at the Old Course two years earlier. Jenkins was tugging on a cigarette outside the St. Andrews' press center when he said to Brian Keogh: "The kid just didn't know that shooting 75 was a good score."

At Kiawah, the kid got it. This time, Rory recognized that bogeys were inevitable given gale-force winds. His three-over 75—two birdies offset by five bogeys—kept him on the leaderboard, two strokes behind Pettersson, Fijian Vijay Singh, and—lo and behold!—a resurgent Tiger Woods.

At Congressional in '11, Rory had been motivated to show critics that he could bounce back from his humiliation at Augusta two months earlier. At Kiawah in '12, McIlroy wanted to show the world that his romance with Caroline Wozniacki had not dulled his competitive edge. After five consecutive pedestrian performances in the majors, Rory was determined to get back on top of a big-time leaderboard.

Saturday's weather was calmer, but the wind still gusted much of the day. Late in the afternoon, thunderstorms moved in, causing most of the field to finish their third rounds on Sunday morning.

Rory came out red-hot on Saturday, birdieing the first two holes and four of the first eight, all while absorbing one of the weirder moments of his career. On the short par-four third hole,

Rory's three-wood off the tee hit a dead tree in the middle of the fairway, somehow burrowing into a notch in one of its limbs.

It took a few minutes and a TV review before an official established that the ball was indeed stuck in the tree. Rory stayed calm. There was no discernible, you-gotta-be-fuckin'-kiddin'-me fury as Rory reached up and pulled the ball out of the branch.

He took his penalty drop well back of the tree, then hit a beautiful spinning wedge inside ten feet and drained the putt. It has to rank among his most satisfying pars *ever*.

The weather kicked up as Rory was playing number 9, the only bogey he made that day. By the time the siren went off ending play, Rory had surged into a tie for the lead with Vijay Singh at six-under, with Adam Scott a stroke back and Pettersson two behind. With four bogeys on the frontside, Tiger had shot himself off the leaderboard.

Bright and early Sunday, Rory was back at it to complete his third round, again in windy conditions. He scratched out pars on the first three holes, then bogeyed number 13 to fall to five-under. But he birdied the par-four 15th and the par-five 16th to finish off a gritty 67.

At the lunch break, he found himself at seven-under, up three over Pettersson, four over Scott, and five over Singh and Woods.

CBS was airing the PGA, so this time it was the turn of Jim Nance, Nick Faldo, Gary McCord, Ian Baker-Finch, and David Feherty to ooh-and-aah over Rory's final-round ball-striking, which was sublime, at least for the front nine.

Baker-Finch noted at the top of the coverage that were Rory to triumph, he would become the youngest winner of the PGA Championship in history. Jack Nicklaus was twenty-three years and six months old when he won the '63 PGA at the Dallas Athletic Club. McIlroy was twenty-three years and three months old in August of 2012.

Rory began with a solid two-putt par on number 1, then blistered a drive on the par-five second. McCord expressed amazement that Rory only had a five-iron left for his second shot. But Rory pulled it left of the green; it struck a tree almost hole-high, scattering the gallery.

Rory was fortunate; the ball came straight down into some wood chips, well away from the trunk. He played a beautiful little low runner inside six feet and holed the putt.

"Rory made a 'barkie'[2] *and* a birdie!" McCord exclaimed. McIlroy was now eight-under.

At number 3, Rory's three-wood off the tee navigated the far side of the dead tree and settled into the first cut. His pitch smartly rolled inside ten feet. His putt looked like it was going to miss right, but it caught just enough of the hole to nosedive. Nine-under.

Solid pars ensued for the next three holes, highlighted by a delicate long lag putt to three feet that had the CBS guys buzzing again about Rory's touch.

On the par-five seventh, Rory hit another massive drive, followed by a five-iron that skirted the left edge of the green, fifty-five or sixty feet away. It was not an easy lag, Feherty & Co. told viewers. Rory's eagle putt was struck with perfect weight and looked like it had a chance to fall in the left side of the cup. But it stayed just outside the edge. Ten-under.

As he made the turn three-under for the day, Nance pointed out that McIlroy was beginning to distance himself from the field. Ian Poulter had been hot earlier in the round but was fading. Rory's fourth-round playing partner Pettersson was also having trouble gaining traction, as was Scott and every other contender.

Suddenly, Rory was cruising. On the par-four 12th, he hit his second shot inside twelve feet and again snuck the putt in on the high side. Eleven-under.

At this point, CBS spotters were feeding Nance and Faldo information about the biggest winning margins in PGA history, which turned out to be Nicklaus's seven-shot win at the 1980 PGA Championship at Oak Hill.

---

2   "Barkie" is my second favorite form of golfing "junk," behind only "splashie" (i.e., a ball that goes into a water hazard but you still get your par). If you're not playing junk with your golf buddies, you're missing out.

The 21-year-old McIlroy spraying champagne after the Euros' victory in the 2010 Ryder Cup at Celtic Manor in Wales. He played only *meh* in his first Cup but managed to salvage a crucial half-point in his singles match against Stewart Cink. Rory is now a defiant Ryder Cup warrior in the mold of Seve Ballesteros and Ian Poulter.

Rory with Caroline Wozniacki at the Newbury Racecourse west of London. Rory Land pretended the "Wozzilroy" breakup was "mutual and amicable." It was anything but.

Rory's caddie Harry Diamond has been a "Mac Packer" since his teen years. Critics say that Diamond is too deferential, which compounds Rory's tendency to go for low-percentage shots.

NBC/Golf Channel commentator Brad Faxon, a former Tour player, has served as McIlroy's putting coach since 2018. Under Faxon, Rory's putting stroke *looks* better—but the ball still doesn't go in the hole as often as it needs to in big moments.

McIlroy's occasional lack of focus has driven his mentor and Florida neighbor Jack Nicklaus to distraction. Tiger, Rory's boyhood hero, is McIlroy's lead business partner in the Tomorrow Golf League (TGL), a tech-infused indoor golf league that's already been valued at a half-billion dollars.

The gang at Holywood Golf Club celebrating Rory's victory at the '11 US Open. It was close to midnight back home when McIlroy clinched the win. Many of his trophies and much of his memorabilia are still displayed at HGC.

McIlroy was barely 22 when he won the U.S. Open at Congressional. He became the youngest U.S. Open winner since Bobby Jones nine decades earlier.

Gerry and Rosie McIlroy worked multiple jobs literally around the clock to give their only child a chance to chase his dream. Gerry worked as a custodian and bartender; Rosie worked along an assembly line.

Rory abruptly sacked his long-term caddie, Irishman J.P. Fitzgerald, in 2017 despite their success in winning four major championships. After J.P.'s dismissal, they went years without speaking and have still not fully reconciled.

Rory roaring at the '23 Ryder Cup in Rome. The team competition he once dismissed as an "exhibition" has become the nationless McIlroy's Fourth of July, Guy Fawkes Night, and St. Patrick's Day all rolled into one.

McIlroy and Spaniard Sergio Garcia were once so close they served in each other's weddings. Since Garcia jumped to LIV they've been estranged, despite McIlroy's attempt at rapprochement.

Rory's wife, Erica Stoll, a former PGA of America employee, helped save her future husband from the humiliation of missing his tee time at the 2012 Ryder Cup. They're shown here at Marco Simone at the '23 Cup.

Rory, a former resident of Dubai, has dominated golf played in the United Arab Emirates, winning the Race to Dubai six times and capturing four Dubai Desert Classics.

The "Perpetual Lost Boy of Augusta National" chipping out from its famous azalea bushes. Rory has never come down the stretch on Sunday with a chance to win the Masters.

Rory has a love-hate relationship with three-woods. Disgusted with a poor tee shot, he chucked one into the trees that separate Liberty National in Bayonne from the New Jersey Turnpike. The offending club was put on display in the clubhouse.

McIlroy's first-ever Ryder Cup singles match was a draw against American Stewart Cink in 2010 at Celtic Manor in Wales. At first, McIlroy was ambivalent about the Cup; now he's a full-throated warrior.

Photographer Matthew Harris captured this marvelous moment with the three McIlroys after Rory won his fourth Dubai Desert Classic in 2024. When photographers asked the McIlroys to each hold up four fingers to commemorate Rory's milestone, Gerry volunteered that he only had "three-and-a-half" on that hand. His quip caused them to crack up.

The Ryder Cup trophy has come to mean perhaps too much to McIlroy, who says it means more to him than individual accomplishments. He nearly came to blows with innocent bystander Jim "Bones" Mackay after U.S. caddie Joey LaCava obstructed Rory's putting preparation on the 18th tee at the '23 Cup in Italy.

"Golf's ageless Opie Taylor" is beginning to show his age. Even with his hair going gray McIlroy still looks like the Adorable Kid Brother from Central Casting.

The Tricolor meets the Ulster Banner: the tiny island of Ireland has produced four major champions in the last generation: Padraig Harrington of Dublin, Graeme McDowell of Portrush, Rory McIlroy of Holywood, and (not pictured) Darren Clarke of Dungannon.

As a kid, Rory committed Tiger's amateur triumphs to memory. To this day, he can recite minutiae about the young Tiger that wows people, including Tiger. It's been described as a "carnival act."

It's tough to play with a big lead in high winds; Rory's ball-striking began to sour a bit. But he kept on grinding out pars when virtually everyone else was making bogeys. Feherty marveled at the steadiness of his short game. Most of Rory's backside chips rolled out to four or five or six feet. Each time, his putt hit the middle of the cup, occasioning a subtle pump of his right fist when the ball disappeared.

On the par-four 15th, Rory's approach was hoisted so far up that Feherty quipped: "Anything hit that high normally has a movie shown on it."

There wasn't a single blemish on McIlroy's card when he approached the par-five 16th, one of Dye's more fiendish creations: a left-to-right, downhill-then-uphill ogre that has a never-ending sandy area on the left and brings the Atlantic beach into play on the right.[3]

McIlroy mashed his drive so far down the right-center of the 16th fairway that it triggered another round of cackling from Feherty. Rory pulled his long-iron into the sand left of the green, leaving himself a sharply uphill pitch to a green cantering away from him.

Once more, Rory hit a little wedge with exquisite weight and spin. The ball settled inside eight feet or so, leaving him a tricky downhill left-to-righter. Again, it found the middle. More snickering from Feherty; more record-referencing from Nance. Twelve-under.

McIlroy smartly played away from the water on Dye's sadistic 17th, the place where, in '91, Mark Calcavecchia hit the ugliest shank in Ryder Cup history, a three-iron that barely got airborne before plunging into the aqua. It allowed Colin Montgomerie to tie a match that Calcavecchia had dominated all day.

Rory's tee ball found the left rough just past hole-high. With water staring him in the face, he hit a cautious chip that came up seven feet short. His putt once again found the cup. More chortling.

---

[3] Yes, I did birdie number 16 once. Holed a twenty-five-footer. Thanks for asking.

His drive on the finishing hole, a majestic fade down the right-center of the fairway, caused Faldo to wax poetic about a "wee lad" hitting it so far. Rory's short-iron approach spun a foot or so back off the green. It left him a twenty-five-footer to break Nicklaus's thirty-one-year-old record for the biggest margin of victory in a PGA Championship and match McIlroy's winning spread at Congressional fourteen months earlier.

It was an uphiller, with a little left-to-right break. On its second-to-last roll, it went in the left-middle of the cup. Thirteen-under—and the win!

Suddenly, Rory had broken two huge records owned by the Golden Bear, a feat that happens once a blue moon in professional golf.

Gerry had been in Rory's gallery all four days. *Père et fils* enjoyed a heartfelt hug just off the 18th green.

"Their emotional embrace cried relief more than ecstasy," wrote Keogh, who was standing nearby. "While victory in the US Open at Congressional last year announced McIlroy's arrival on the major stage, Sunday's exhibition was the truly watershed moment in the young man's career."

Keogh reminded readers that Gerry had been saying for a decade that "These are Rory's dreams, not his own or those of his wife Rosie." All that may have been true, but how many times did the young Gerry McIlroy stroke a practice putt while saying to himself, "Okay, pal: this one's to beat Nicklaus!" It may have been a Walter Mitty fantasy, but on some level, Gerry was living *his* dream, too.

Rory was asked in the aftermath of Kiawah if he was motivated by criticism in certain quarters. "Yeah, to be honest, it did motivate me. I did want to go out there and prove a few people wrong."

On the day after the championship ended, Faldo told Golf Channel, "It was amazing what Kiawah threw at him during the week and the 75 on Friday was very important. That was a day when quite a few guys shot 80. And he was out there in the worst of it."

J.P. was asked by Karl MacGinty of the *Irish Independent* to name Rory's best shot of the week. He pinpointed a 220-yard four-iron, struck in the middle of Friday's windstorm to a gnarly left-hand pin at number 14. It led to a birdie.

It took a couple of hours for Rory to pose with the Wanamaker Trophy, finish up his media commitments, and thank everyone with the PGA of America. While being escorted from interview to interview in the Ocean Course's Hamptons-style clubhouse on Sunday evening, McIlroy heard a two-year-old boy call out "Rory!"

McIlroy, wrote eyewitness Tim Rosaforte, the now-sadly-deceased *Golf World* correspondent, "stopped dead in his tracks and acknowledged the lad with a sweet, 'Hellooooo.'

"That got the boy's grandfather talking about a scene he witnessed on the course Monday, when a father embarrassed his teenage daughter by yelling out in an autograph line, 'Hey Rory, how about a kiss for my daughter?' The girl cringed but tried to save the moment by saying, 'I'll take a hug.' Hearing that, McIlroy pivoted and went back to give the girl a hug."

Rosaforte was with Rory at his rental beach house Sunday evening as an exhausted McIlroy collapsed into a sofa surrounded by family and friends, many from Ireland and the UK.

Officials were there readying a special shipping crate for the Wanamaker, which weighs twenty-seven hard-to-handle pounds. But first, Rory wanted everyone at the party to have their picture taken with the trophy.

Gerry and Rory confirmed to Rosaforte that their morning had begun with a weigh-in. Months before, Rory had promised his old man that if Gerry could get his weight down to 12 stone, or

168 lbs., by the last day of the PGA, then McIlroy Jr. would buy McIlroy Sr. any automobile he wanted.

At 6:30 that morning, Gerry tipped the scale at a smooth 167.6 lbs., winning the bet—and a Mercedes sedan to be named later. The key to Gerry's weight loss, apparently, was cutting down on alcohol and carbohydrate intake. But that night, flush with victory on two fronts, Gerry couldn't help himself.

Rory didn't party like a rock star; he was too pooped, Rosaforte reported. But it sounds like Gerry did.

Young McIlroy got up early the next morning and flew to Cincinnati to join Caroline, playing in the Western & Southern Open. She lost in the early rounds, prolonging her slump. As her boyfriend was surging, she was struggling.

McIlroy's spectacular late-season binge was just getting started. Three weeks later, he went to Boston for the Deutsche Bank Championship, the second leg of the FedEx Cup. It was there that Caroline's presence caused such a ruckus.

Rory put on another ball-striking show, shooting a Labor Day 67 and holding off a red-hot Louis Oosthuizen by one shot and a hungry Tiger Woods by three.

The match came down to the 72nd hole. Rory had a fifteen-footer that would have sealed victory. But his putt came up a hair short. Oosthuizen had his own putt to send the match into extra holes, but it just slipped past. Rory had won his third tournament on the PGA Tour that season.

Number four came quicky. The next week was the third tournament in the interminable (back then) FedEx Cup playoffs, the BMW championship at Crooked Stick, another Pete Dye design in Carmel, Indiana. Crooked Stick was the place where John

Daly, a last-minute replacement, shocked the world in 1991 by chain-smoking his way to the PGA Championship.

Twenty-one years later, it would be the place where McIlroy survived challenges from a star-studded field, including Tiger, Phil, and Lee Westwood. For the second successive tournament, Rory started the final round a couple shots behind. This time the co-leaders were Mickelson and Vijay Singh. Singh faded early but Mickelson hung tough.

Westwood and Rory were paired together and brought out the best in one another. Lee tied Rory for the lead with a birdie on number 13. But Rory took control of the tournament with birdies on the 14th and 16th.

When Rory's ten-footer rammed into the back of the cup at number 16, Peter Jacobsen on NBC blurted, "Talk about slamming the door shut!"

As Rory walked off the final green having shot another clutch final-round 67, Jacobsen's colleague, anchor Dan Hicks, exclaimed, "This is the guy, *The Man*, in golf right now." He became the first PGA Tour player since Woods in 2009 to win back-to-back.

The Man proved mortal the next week at the Tour Championship at East Lake in Atlanta. His first three rounds, 69-68-68, put him within striking distance. But four early bogeys on Sunday upended his chances of going back-to-back-to-back. Brandt Snedeker ended up dominating East Lake, winning by three shots and earning a $10 million bonus for capturing the overall FedEx Cup.

Rory had to "settle" for a second-place finish and a trifling $3 million check. Had the Tour Championship adopted the staggered structure it did a few years later (where players with the greatest number of points are awarded commensurate strokes under-par), Rory may well have won the 2012 FedEx Cup instead of finishing second.

Solidifying his world number-one ranking and being voted the 2012 PGA Tour Player of the Year were nice consolation prizes. So was watching his girlfriend break out of her slump by winning the Korean Open in late September, her first WTA title of the season.

Now the cherry on the sundae would be to kick some butt in Chicago at the Ryder Cup.

McIlroy kicked butt, alright—his own.

Chapter 16

MEDINAH'S WILD RIDE

The most consequential quarter hour in Rory McIlroy's career did not occur at Congressional or Kiawah or any other golfing venue. It happened on Sunday, September 30, 2012, while he was buckled into the passenger seat of an unmarked police car, hurtling north on Grace Street, west on Illinois Route 64, north up Interstate 355, then west again on Illinois Route 20, desperately trying to get to Medinah Country Club to make his tee time for a crucial Ryder Cup singles match.

As McIlroy climbed into the dark-blue Ford Crown Victoria,[1] he apologized to the cop behind the wheel, who happened to be the deputy chief of the Lombard, Illinois, Police Department.

No problem, the officer said. As he planted his bubble-gum machine on the Crown Vic's roof and jerked the car into "D," he asked if McIlroy suffered from any motion sickness.

"No," came the reply. "I don't care [how fast you go]. Just get there. Get me to that first tee."

Thus ensued a scene straight of *The Blues Brothers*—except there weren't any nuns or Nazis in sight. And instead of Jake and Elwood Blues, it was officer Pat Rollins, now the chief of police in Sugar Grove, Illinois, and Rory McIlroy, then the world's number-one-ranked golfer, who were careening on two wheels through Chicagoland.

---

[1] Yes, there is a certain irony that an Irishman was rescued from a lifetime of humiliation by an automobile named after the 19th century British monarch who sat on her royal derrière while a million of her subjects starved to death during Ireland's potato famines. The Crown Vic came through for Rory. But Vic the Crown didn't come through for his ancestors.

Siren blaring and tires screeching, they exited the parking lot of the Lombard Westin Hotel, gunning toward I-355. Rollins, then a twenty-two-year police veteran trained in part by the FBI, radioed ahead and arranged for cops along the route to Medinah to keep the Route 20 exit ramp and key intersections clear.

Two other police vehicles quickly joined Rollins, running interference. After exiting the interstate, they roared down Route 20, with cars scattering left and right to let them by.

It's nearly nineteen miles from the Lombard Westin to Medinah. In normal traffic, that means a thirty-minute trek and plenty of stopping and starting. But there was nothing "normal" about the traffic around Medinah for the 39th Ryder Cup, especially with the US team poised to regain the Cup after narrowly losing it two years before at Celtic Manor. The American squad went into Sunday singles play at Medinah with a seemingly insurmountable lead, 10-6.

Dan Aykroyd couldn't have scripted the manic scramble's final moments any better, with Rollins following a yellow cop car and an unmarked black SUV as they raced into the clubhouse's semicircular drive. Medinah is one of the most exclusive establishments in greater Chicago. Its members tend to look askance at police cruisers shrieking around their grounds.

Rollins, nevertheless, created one last bit of hubbub. He broke the Crown Vic away from the caravan to rush Rory the last few yards across the asphalt, getting the golfer as close as possible to the men's locker room, not only saving a few precious seconds but enabling McIlroy to avoid the camera crews that were swarming around the parking lot. NBC's Jimmy Roberts and Golf Channel's Steve Sands were among the TV correspondents doing stand-ups with all the *mishigas* happening behind them.

Call up Sands's Medinah parking lot report on YouTube and you'll see a credentialed female PGA of America executive walking back and forth behind him, carrying what appears to be a file folder. That official was none other than the twenty-four-year-old Erica Stoll, the Rochester native destined to become Rory's bride and, as we'll learn, one of the people that day who saved her future husband's bacon.

The NBC/Golf Channel video shows McIlroy in the Crown Vic intently talking on his cellphone, no doubt plotting every logistical move; at that point, he couldn't afford any missteps. By the time Rory swung open the passenger-side door, he had just nine minutes to spare before being forced to forfeit the first hole, and fourteen minutes before he would have been compelled to concede the entire match, according to the rules of the Ryder Cup.

Pat Rollins, later dubbed the "Ryder Cop," had pulled off the near-impossible. By putting the pedal to the metal and ordering cop-car blockers, he'd gotten Europe's top Ryder Cupper to Medinah in a scant sixteen minutes. He must have averaged upwards of 100 miles per hour up I-355 and two-thirds of that down a packed Route 20.

There were a pair of miracles in the southern suburbs of Chicago that day. Of the two, the more spectacular was Pat Rollins's wild ride. Without the officer's quick thinking and lead foot, the Euros' "Miracle at Medinah"—among the most celebrated moments in Ryder Cup history—might never have taken place.

The golfing miracle also wouldn't have happened had Rory's late Saturday afternoon fourball partner, Englishman Ian Poulter, not poured in one clutch putt after another to defeat Zach Johnson and Jason Duffner, giving the Euros a much-needed boost heading into the Sunday singles.

Imagine these lines being spoken by one of the nasal-toned "Chi-CAW-go" cops in the movie *The Fugitive*, because that's *exactly* how Pat Rollins sounds, with his long vowels flattened an extra beat: "Some of my colleagues have said we shouldn't have taken [McIlroy] and the United States might have won the Ryder Cup. But the competition was on the course—not in the traffic around Medinah Country Club."

With broadcast crews dogging him, McIlroy dashed into the locker room, met up with J.P., probably took a quick leak, and splashed some water on his face. He and J.P. then headed out to the putting green, where Rory was greeted by a relieved—and if the Spaniard's facial expression was any indication, incredulous—European Ryder Cup captain, José Maria Olazábal. While hugging McIlroy, Ollie gave him a where-the-hell-have-you-been? look, no doubt reminding Rory that he had all of *quatro maldito minutos!* ("four fuckin' minutes!") to get to the first tee.

The whole time he was on the practice green, McIlroy was chomping on nutrition bars, which may or may not have been the only food he'd consumed all morning; no one at the Westin recalled seeing him inside the hotel restaurant or around its breakfast bar.

McIlroy's entire preparation for a pivotal Ryder Cup singles match in which his team desperately needed every point they could muster, consisted of a handful of putts stroked while getting breathless status reports from Olazábal and Fitzgerald. He also took two irons out of his bag and made a couple of slow-motion practice swings. That was it.

Courtesy of NBC-Golf Channel and Sky Sports, a global television audience watched it all play out in real time. Amid the chaos, the video shows that Rory stayed eerily calm. He may have been churning on the inside, but on the outside, he was all Elwood Blues, cooly shlepping his harmonica case to the next gig as the world around him went batshit crazy.

He was up third in that morning's lineup. Already out on the course were Luke Donald vs. Bubba Watson and Ian Poulter vs. Webb Simpson. Soon enough, there would be muted cheers (from the smaller Euro contingent) and deep groans (from the huge pro-American gallery) coming from all over the course.

With the usual Ryder Cup entourage of coaches, officials, scorekeepers, and hangers-on streaming behind him, McIlroy headed off to exchange a handshake with his American opponent, Keegan Bradley, who had won each of his two doubles matches at Medinah. As the crowd stirred, McIlroy extended both arms to the heavens and waggled his fingers inward in a bring-it-on-motherfuckers! gesture. Many in the bleachers started jeering. Suddenly, the Ryder Cup had taken on the patina of a WWE throwdown.

By then, fans had heard through online and broadcast reports that McIlroy's explanation for his bizarre tardiness was that he'd confused Eastern and Central time. McIlroy said he'd seen a report on television that morning that said he was scheduled to go off at 12:25 p.m., not realizing that meant 12:25 *Eastern time*. In reality, he was slated to tee off at 11:25 a.m. *Central time*.

To tease McIlroy, US fans began chanting "*Cen-tral time zone!*" (clap, clap, clap-clap-clap!), as well as "*What's your tee time?!*"—jeers that didn't stop until the match ended.

"It was funny for the first two holes," McIlroy said later, "and after that I just wanted to shut them up."

As the round progressed, fans also loudly inquired about the severity of Rory's "hangover," as well as bellowing, "*Was she worth it?!*" with more handclaps thrown in for good measure.

Video of the first tee shows McIlroy breezily recounting the time zone confusion to Bradley, who tossed his head back and chuckled in the moments before they were introduced.

At that instant, Olazábal, and his vice captains—Thomas Bjørn of Denmark, Darren Clarke of Northern Ireland, Paul McGinley of the Republic of Ireland, and Miguel Ángel Jiménez of Spain—were most likely not in a chuckling mood. Their weeks of agonizing over team chemistry and *who-should-we-send-out-when-on-Sunday?* had nearly gone up in smoke because a twenty-three-year-old with all the talent in the world couldn't be bothered to get his ass to the course on time.

Even if Rory's tee-off *had been* an hour later, he was still cutting it too close, especially given traffic congestion. Average-guy hackers[2] learn to get to a course an hour ahead to warm up. Professionals, especially in hyper-competitive settings like the Ryder Cup, like to get to a course two hours in advance, so they have plenty of time to relax, hit the range, the putting green, and whatever chipping and pitching facilities are available. At a place like Medinah for an event like the Ryder Cup, those facilities are top-notch.

So, what *was* Rory doing at the Lombard Westin that morning that came damn close to making him the Ryder Cup's all-time goat (not the G-O-A-T, but the old meaning of "goat")? He told the press later that day that he'd slept until 9:00 or so. Then he Facetimed Caroline, who that week was playing the WTA event in Beijing.[3] There's a thirteen-hour time difference between Chicago and Beijing, which means they would have been chatting at roughly 10:30 p.m. Sunday evening, Caroline's time.

They Facetimed for quite a while, McIlroy said, which meant his cellphone was busy. He told the press that he was called several times from a number he did not recognize, so he chose to ignore them—*as well as a ringing hotel room phone!*—to continue his parley (or whatever it may have been) with Caroline.

Meanwhile, back at Medinah, the anxiety level about Rory's absence was at DEFCON 3 and rising. At first, no one in the European camp seemed to notice that Rory was MIA. But as the clock slid toward 10:30, the two PGA of America officials in charge of player liaison and transportation, Maggie Budzar and Erica Stoll—Steve Sands's inadvertent video star—began raising the alarm that McIlroy had not surfaced.

Frantic calls were placed to Rory's cell (he *still* wasn't answering!), his room, and to the front desk of the Westin.

"There was a huge crowd outside the team hotel waiting to video and photograph the players so everyone knew he [McIlroy]

---

2 I've been an average-guy hacker since the Ford administration.
3 Caroline ended up losing in the third round of the 2012 China Open three days later, to German Angelique Kerber, 6-7, 6-2, 4-6.

hadn't come down yet," Budzar told reporters that afternoon, among them Neil McLernan of *The Mirror,* a UK tabloid.

The front desk sent a housekeeper to knock on McIlroy's room door. "A male voice answered not to come in. We figured it was him," Budzar said in McLernan's version of the episode.

A few minutes later, almost exactly at 11:00 Central time, Rory's then-manager and White House state dinner companion, Conor Ridge, finally got through to McIlroy on his cell. Their exchange, according to Rory's own account shared later that day, went like this:

> Conor: "Are you at the golf course yet?"
>
> Rory: "No, I'm not."
>
> Conor: "But you're teeing off in twenty-five minutes."
>
> Rory: "No, I'm not. It's an hour and twenty-five."
>
> Conor: "You're 'taking the mick!'[4] You're at the golf course!"
>
> Rory: "No, I'm not."
>
> Conor: "Well, you had better get here."

McIlroy's post-match remarks included this stunner: "I was just lucky that there happened to be a policeman downstairs who could put the lights on and get me past all the traffic."

Let's give him the benefit of the doubt. Maybe Rory hadn't at that point been fully briefed on the pandemonium he'd caused, but "luck" had nothing to do with the presence in the Westin parking lot of Deputy Chief Rollins, the Ryder Cop, and his souped-up Crown Vic. All credit goes to Budzar and Stoll, who recognized that without extraordinary help, McIlroy was never going to make it to Medinah on time.

---

[4] "Taking the mick!" is disparaging Irish slang, roughly equivalent in this context to, "You're yanking my chain, you dumb Irish asshole!"

Before Ridge got through to McIlroy, Budzar and Stoll had issued an urgent plea to the police. Rollins happened to be on duty when the call came in to get over to the local Westin posthaste.

The rest is history, albeit bizarre history, leavened by two facts: McIlroy not only got to the first tee on time but never trailed in his match against Bradley, buttressing the Euros' dramatic comeback.

McIlroy points to his watch amid the Euro Ryder Cup squad's revelry following the 2012 "Miracle at Medinah."

Second, despite the bedlam going on around them—or perhaps *because* of it—a little spark somehow developed between McIlroy and Erica Stoll. It took the better part of three years and the painful dissolution of McIlroy's relationship with Wozniacki, but that spark led to friendship, which then led to romance, which then led to marriage, a beautiful child, a *very* public divorce filing, followed by a *very* public reconciliation.

RORY LAND

Young Rory McIlroy had led a charmed existence. Only a guy like him could have turned an epic screw-up (forget for a moment about letting down his coaches and teammates, not to mention a worldwide television audience, and think of the resources that several Illinois police departments had squandered to get him to Medinah on time!) into a personal triumph and a "meet-cute" straight out of a corny Hollywood script. Rory not only became a champagne-drenched hero that afternoon, he ended up *getting the girl!*

"I wasn't late for my tee time," he said later with a sly grin. "I was *about to be* late."

Just how big did Rory screw up? Well, the first few hours in a different time zone can throw anyone off. But by the fall of 2012, cellphones were displaying the adjusted time automatically, in big numbers hard to miss. Plus, there's the small matter that Rory had been in the Central time zone for close to a week at that point. Whatever dissonance he may have experienced should have been long gone.

Finally, every member of the squad had been told—*repeatedly*—by the European team staff about their Sunday schedule.

For each side, the Saturday team meeting/dinner on the eve of Ryder Cup Sunday is a combination motivational session and exercise in obsessive-compulsive disorder. After the rah-rah, "C'mon guys, we-can-do-this!" speeches, coaches review in detail who's playing whom the next day, when they need to arrive, and once they finish their matches, the importance of providing moral support to teammates still out on the course, a la the great (and now, sadly, late) Seve Ballesteros, Ollie's pugnacious partner in many a Ryder Cup battle.

The next day's match times are usually posted at the meeting for all to see; a Sunday itinerary is handed out that spells out the next day's transportation, food, and attire details, among other things. Shuttle bus/limos were at the Lombard Westin, ready to whisk the Euros to the course.

If any of this registered with Rory, it was not in evidence the next morning. At that point in his career, the Ryder Cup, despite Ollie's invocations to "Win It for Seve!", was way down his priority list. In his head, it was still an "exhibition." After all, in the last six weeks alone, he had won a major, grabbed two legs of the FedEx Cup, regained his standing as world number one, and been named the PGA Tour's Player of the Year. Compared to all that, the Ryder Cup must have looked like weak tea.

Beyond that, he was lovesick, either pining for his girl halfway around the world or quarreling with her. Or possibly both.

Caddyshack innuendo, which still reverberates a decade later,[5] hints that Rory may have been otherwise occupied that morning and the previous night. But the evidence suggests that he was where he said he was: in his room at the Lombard Westin, solo, Facetiming with Caroline.

It was, nevertheless, infantile behavior. A lot of people were counting on him; he came within a hairsbreadth of letting them all down.

But in grand McIlroy fashion, he fell out of that tree and landed on his feet. More than anything else, his near crackup at Medinah is the thing that made him determined to be a European Ryder Cup warrior, someone in the mold of Ballesteros or Poulter.

It's a testament to Rory's self-belief that he never let Bradley get the best of him. McIlroy's play that week had been almost as erratic as his conduct that morning; he was 2-2 in his four doubles matches and didn't play especially well in any of them. But he shook off those cobwebs and put together solid golf that morning and after-

---

[5] Ask almost any US Tour follower today about Rory's behavior at Medinah and you get a serious smirk and an eye-roll.

noon. It turned out to be the best round, by far, that he played in the '12 Cup.

Not surprisingly, Rory was off a bit at the beginning, driving his opening tee ball into some television cable in the right rough and missing the first three greens—but salvaging par each time. He went one-up when Bradley conceded the fourth hole after a plugged bunker lie led to trouble.

McIlroy chipped in for a birdie on number 6, then made an eight-footer for birdie at number 9 to go two-up. Rory made a spectacular up and down on number 11 from a dicey lie behind a bunker to halve the hole and stay one-up. On the 12th, he bogeyed after a poor chip, prompting a "*USA!! USA!!*" roar from the gallery. Suddenly, he and Bradley were all square.

The match turned on the par-five 14th, when Bradley pushed his second shot behind a tree and couldn't clear a green-side bunker on his third. Keegan managed to save par, which forced Rory to make his four-footer for birdie. It dropped: Rory's nose was again out in front.

On the short par-four 15th, the Euro team's brain trust gathered behind Rory on the tee box. It pains McIlroy to lay up on a drivable par-four, but with a one-up lead and his coaches (plus an entire continent) breathing down his neck, he smartly hit a four-iron down the left-center.

One of his mentors, Vice-Captain Darren Clarke, was puffing a cigar and grinning ear to ear as Captain Olazábal got into Rory's grill and sarcastically "congratulated" him for his judicious tee play. McIlroy responded by taking off his glove and playfully tapping Ollie's nose, which (Earl Weaver-style) was positioned just inches from his own. It was cheeky behavior toward a Ryder Cup legend—and two-time Masters champion!—twice his age, especially coming from a guy who'd come close to screwing the pooch that morning. Yet somehow Rory managed to pull it off without looking overly obnoxious. Everyone on the tee box, Ollie included, had a good laugh.

His (Their?) decision to lay up looked even smarter a few seconds later when Bradley pull-hooked his driver deep into the gallery. Playing first and imparting exquisite spin, Rory zinged his wedge inside three feet of the flagstick, then watched as Keegan feathered his own brilliant wedge over a bunker and inside twelve feet.

But Bradley's putt was stroked wide right; it never had a chance. Rory's birdie tap-in gave him a two-up lead and control of the match.

McIlroy's 2 and 1 victory was never in doubt down the stretch. Most of the gallery, their voices hoarse from taunting Rory, gave him a warm ovation as he and Keegan shook hands on the next-to-last green. Rory was part of the Euros' clean sweep of the first five singles matches, which was precisely what Ollie's charges needed.

Then Rory got to live the dream of every Ryder Cupper, cheering teammates on as the opposition's lead evaporated. The Euros, again led by Poulter, made almost every clutch putt they looked at that afternoon. As is so often the case in Cup play, the American guys kept on coming up empty.

Europe ended up winning eight and tying one of the 12 singles matches, a remarkable feat that ranks up there in Ryder Cup lore with the 1999 US comeback at Brookline, which had been fueled the night before by Captain Ben Crenshaw's "Ah believe in fate" speech, complete with wagging finger. The Euros' win triggered the biggest champagne shower in Chicagoland since the 1985 Bears won the Super Bowl, with Rory among the lead dousers.

"I don't want to think about what sort of abuse I would have got if we had lost by a point and I hadn't got there in time," Rory told the press as the sun set over Medinah. Then he added with a big grin: "But imagine what I would have done if I'd have warmed up!"

Someone in the European camp went out and purchased an enormous alarm clock that was presented to McIlroy as a gag gift amid the party raging outside the clubhouse. Rory hoisted it for everyone to see, laughing the whole time.

He was wearing the Ulster Banner tucked like an ascot under his Ryder Cup quarter-zip.

RORY LAND

Imagine this: What would have happened if Budzar and Stoll hadn't been so conscientious and Deputy Chief Rollins hadn't been so Johnny-on-the-spot? The answer: it would not have been pretty.

McIlroy's reputation would have taken a hit. It would have seriously, perhaps irreparably, hurt his brand. His future wife and her boss saved him from a lifetime of being branded a nitwit—or worse.

In September 1908, a New York Giants baserunner allegedly failed to touch second base on a force play while a teammate scored what would have been the winning run in the bottom of the ninth inning. The gaffe ending up costing the Giants a critical late-season game against the Chicago Cubs. Chicago then went on to win the National League pennant and dominate the World Series against Ty Cobb's Detroit Tigers.

The baserunner's name was Fred Merkle. He was instantly tagged "Bonehead Merkle," an epithet he took to the grave, even though he always maintained that he'd touched second—and the umpires didn't see it.

Would "Pulling a Rory" have entered our language had "Bonehead McIlroy" missed his tee time, as in: "My boss flew in for the big meeting, but I 'Pulled a Rory' and overslept." Or: "Man, I 'McIlroy'd that presentation! I forgot what time it was scheduled!"

This much is certain: today's Rory McIlroy, the guy hell-bent on kicking ass in Ryder Cups, would not abide for one millisecond any slaphappy behavior from a young teammate that might hurt the Euros' chances of beating the Americans.

Chapter 17

THE SWOOSH AND THE SLUMP

Horizon Sports Management's reign over Rory Land lasted about half as long as Anne Boleyn's tenure as Queen of England. Still, Conor Ridge and team had some big moments shilling for Rory.

They went all-out to showcase Rory's new partnership with Nike. On Monday afternoon, January 14, 2013—ahead of the European Tour's Abu Dhabi Golf Championship in the United Arab Emirates—Ridge and Cindy Davis, the president of Nike Golf, threw a party in McIlroy's honor that was described as "lavish" by some and "glitzy" by others.

It began with blaring music, a multi-colored laser show, and a state-of-the-art hologram of Rory swinging a Nike club. It soon segued into a slick video featuring welcome-to-the-family soundbites from such Swoosh stalwarts as Tiger Woods, English football superstar Wayne Rooney, and Roger Federer, the tennis titan whose branding counsel helped lead Rory down the path to Beaverton. The announcement confirmed what *SB Nation* called golf's "worst-kept secret": that Rory was becoming a Nike guy, from top (his hat) to bottom (his golf shoes).

Most significantly, Rory would now be using Nike sticks and a Nike ball for the duration of his contract. "It's the feel of the ball that I find is the most important thing," he said in late '12, "because really, every manufacturer makes great equipment these days."

Well, maybe. Made by Japanese company Bridgestone on the down-low, the Nike tour ball wasn't in the same league as Titleist Pro-V's. Surely, McIlroy knew it.

"Rory is an extraordinary athlete who creates enormous excitement with his on-course performance, while at the same time connecting with fans everywhere," Davis said while sitting on a barstool opposite Rory.

"He is the epitome of a Nike Athlete, and he is joining our team during the most exciting time in Nike Golf's history. We are looking forward to partnering with him to take his remarkable career to the next level."

The epitome of a Nike Athlete—complete with a gratuitous capital "A" in Nike's handout! It was Rory's dream come to life.

Davis led the champagne toasts as Rory, Ridge, and the Horizon team clicked glasses and celebrated the huge deal they'd engineered. The pact's actual number, of course, was probably well below the $200 million-plus package leaked to the press; but whatever it was, it made Rory McIlroy and Conor Ridge very wealthy men.

Then Rory, who assured all parties that he'd been diligently practicing with his new sticks, went out on the Abu Dhabi Golf Club and threw a skunk into the punch bowl. Nothing worked—not the Nike Covert driver, not the Nike wedges, not the Nike Method putter, which soon got the heave-ho, replaced in Rory's bag by his trusty old Scotty Cameron.

The biggest culprit in Rory's back-to-back 75s was the Covert driver, which was supposedly built to spec for him. He couldn't keep it from slicing and hooking into the desert. He missed the cut by a mile in a tournament won by Jamie Donaldson. Tiger didn't qualify for the weekend, either, so it was not exactly the Nike lovefest that Davis envisioned when she climbed on the plane in Portland.

Not to worry, Rory assured the press. It's just a temporary glitch. I'll get it straightened out next time. Then he confirmed plans to take the next four weeks off to spend time with Caroline—a revelation that didn't exactly assuage his critics.

When word hit that McIlroy was signing a big-bucks deal with Nike, forsaking the Titleist clubs and ball that helped him win two majors, it sparked a kerfuffle among golf's pooh-bahs.

NBC's Johnny Miller and CBS/Golf Channel's Nick Faldo led the Greek chorus. The two were quick to point out that an equipment change could hobble Rory's ball-striking.

"I tweeted right from when I heard the news, that this is dangerous," Faldo, never reluctant to express a prickly opinion, reminded viewers on the Golf Channel's *State of the Game* roundtable in February of 2013, with Miller piling on.

Rory blamed his struggles not on new equipment but on rust. He pointed out that he'd had a mid-season swoon the year before and pulled himself out of it. He'd do the same this year. He'd have a chance to turn things around at the Honda Classic at Nicklaus's PGA National, where he'd be on familiar turf as defending champion.

That's when things hit rock bottom.

Despite his early-season scuffling, Rory was still ranked number one in March of '13 when he arrived at his new home in Palm Beach Gardens, five miles away from the Nicklaus-designed PGA National. On the Tuesday night before the Honda Classic, yet another company unveiled McIlroy as its brand ambassador, with pulsating music and a gaudy show that spared no expense.

Bose, the audio equipment-maker, was the latest company to line up in McIlroy's corner, courtesy of Conor Ridge, Colin Morrissey, and Horizon's other dealmakers. Rory was rocking jeans, a casual dress shirt, and pointy shoes as he took center stage at a hotel ballroom to Bose systems-fueled rock music. Bose was proud to introduce him as its first-ever athlete-endorser.

Bose "works hard at their innovations, they aren't conventional, and they're committed to doing things that haven't been done before, just like I am," Rory said.

Sure enough, Rory that week did do something he'd never done before. But it was not exactly the sort of behavior that Bose was seeking from its global brand ambassador.

In the first round at PGA National, he played okay, getting around the course in an even-par 70—his best round of the year so far. The next day, paired with Mark Wilson and Ernie Els, he teed off on the 10th hole to begin round two. One wayward hit after another came off the face of his Covert driver. There was nothing covert about his iron mishits; they were overtly awful. By the time he reached the 18th (his ninth) hole, he was already seven-over and exhibiting the sort of woe-is-me body language that he swore he'd never repeat after his meltdown at the Masters.

The 18th is a par-five over water that invites longer hitters to get on in two. During his win at the '12 Honda, he'd had no trouble getting home with a five-iron in his second and third rounds.

But this time his second shot splashed into the pond, well short of the green. McIlroy, wrote Doug Ferguson of Associated Press, "didn't bother hitting another shot. He shook hands with Ernie Els and Mark Wilson, turned in his scorecard and walked straight to the parking lot."

Three reporters trailed Rory and J.P. as they made their way to Rory's car. Rory was asked in three different ways if he was suffering from any physical malady. Three times he responded "no."

"There's not really much I can say, guys," McIlroy told the reporters. "I'm not in a good place mentally, you know?" *Golfweek* described him as "near tears."

About an hour later, Horizon issued a statement that McIlroy "couldn't concentrate because of a sore wisdom tooth," a fact that Rory had left out of his impromptu press avail. The Horizon missive included an apology from Rory to tournament officials for his sudden withdrawal.

"[The toothache] began bothering me again last night, so I relieved it with Advil," McIlroy was quoted as saying. "It was really bothering me and had begun to affect my playing partners."

Ferguson's account dryly noted that McIlroy "was seen eating a sandwich on the 18th fairway" seconds before stalking off the course. The next day's *New York Daily News* ran a photo of Rory munching a sandwich Dagwood Bumstead would have been proud of. The AP reporter did more digging: McIlroy never mentioned having a sore tooth to Wilson or Els during the round.

Rory, to his credit, sucked it up and issued a blanket apology two days later. In a phone interview with Michael Bamberger of *Sports Illustrated*, he admitted that walking off the course was "not the right thing to do."

"It was a reactive decision," McIlroy told Bamberger. "What I should have done is take my drop, chip it on, try to make a five and play my hardest on the back nine, even if I shot 85. What I did was not good for the tournament, not good for the kids and the fans who were out there watching me."

He reiterated that his sluggish play was not the byproduct of new clubs but the result of a swing that had suddenly gotten "out of sorts."

For the second time in five months, McIlroy had messed up bad. Nike, Bose, and his other corporate sponsors had to be at least a little worried about their representative's maturity level.

SI's other golf-beat guy named "Michael," surname Rosenberg, was at Rory's pre-tournament presser at Doral the next week and filed a remarkable piece that reflected the unique role that Rory and his persona played in the game.

"If you watched Rory McIlroy's press conference here Wednesday, you heard him take full responsibility for quitting at the Honda Classic last week," Rosenberg's article began. "You heard him say he is trying to get his old swing back, and that his painful wisdom tooth is *a* problem but not *the* problem."

"It never ends for McIlroy," Rosenberg continued. "Every day when he wakes up, he is a story. Every night when he goes to sleep, he will wake up to another opinion about him. The hardest question is this: How does he change his life without losing himself?"

Every celebrity has to wrestle with existential questions, but it was particularly tough for McIlroy. In signing with Nike, Rory had put himself between a rock and hard place.

He stayed in that squeeze for weeks. Out of the blue at the WGC Cadillac in Miami, he shot a Sunday 65 and ended up tied for eighth. At Doral, Rory confirmed plans to meet up with Caroline and take the next two weeks off. More grumbling ensued, especially when he finished a distant forty-fifth three weeks later at the Shell Houston Open.

The new ball and sticks still weren't behaving. No doubt a little desperate with the Masters looming in two weeks, Rory made an eleventh-hour decision to play in the Texas Valero Open at TPC San Antonio. He surprised the golf world (and probably himself) by rallying on Sunday to finish second.

His first two rounds at the '13 Masters were heartening: an even-par 72 followed by a two-under 70 that got him past the cutline with room to spare.

His Saturday started with great promise. In brilliant Georgia sunlight, he birdied the third hole to get to three-under for the tournament. Andy Bull of the *Guardian* was in Rory's gallery and wrote that a palpable buzz went through the crowd. It felt like Rory was about to go on a roll.

He didn't. By the time he reached one of his Augusta nemeses, the long par-four 11th, he was just one-under and hemorrhaging.

"For the third year in a row, the 'Big Miss' hit Rory McIlroy at the Masters," Bull wrote, invoking the term that Woods's onetime instructor Hank Haney used to describe Tiger's biggest golfing trepidation.

McIlroy had two big misses on the backside Saturday. The first was a pushed drive at number 11 that went deep into the piney woods right of the fairway. He chipped out but miscalculated the distance the ball would run down the fairway. It ended up dribbling into the pond left of the green.

From there, it was Rory's 2011 misadventure all over again. His fourth shot, a pitch, was scalded over the green. He walked off with a triple, just as he had two years before a quarter mile back up the hill.

At number 15, a par-five, one of his new irons betrayed him; the ball came up short and rolled back into the pond in front of the green. Another poor pitch led to a double. Suddenly, he was six-over and out of the tournament. In two hours, he had gone from the fringes of contention to "Palookaville," as Bull overheard one of the patrons put it.

The next day, Rory rebounded with a 69. But his performances in the Georgia woods were taking on a disconcerting pattern. Big misses were happening too often.

The gloom-and-doom twins of the golf commentariat, Miller and Faldo, turned out to be correct. Rory and his new clubs couldn't put together four good rounds. An opening 67 at Quail Hollow in Charlotte was followed by a 71 and a pair of 73s for a share of tenth place.

The next week, he showed up at TPC Sawgrass with peculiar cuts and scrapes on his face and arms. He'd gotten tangled, he told the press, in a prickly bush while looking for an errant practice round tee ball hit by Rory Lander Mitchell Tweedie. Reporters searched for another explanation but never established one. Those abrasions caused him to miss a practice round.

Band-aided up, he made it to the weekend at The Players, shooting a first-round 66. But he fell back into a familiar pattern, shooting 72, 73, and 70 to fall to eighth. Still, he made the cut, no mean feat for him back then.

At his next stop, the BMW tournament at Wentworth, he shot a 74 and a 75 and didn't sniff the cutline. Back in the States, he shot a 78 in the opening round at Nicklaus's Memorial Tournament and looked like a lost soul. He admitted to Faldo that he was trying everything in an effort to hit the ball straighter; next to nothing was working. He ended up finishing tied for fifty-seventh in Ohio.

At the US Open along the Main Line outside Philadelphia, Rory hung in there for two rounds, shooting a three-over 143 to stay within shouting distance of the leaders at merciless Merion. His play turned ragged on the weekend with a 75 and a 76. He finished in a tie for forty-first in a championship won at one-over by fellow Euro Ryder Cupper Justin Rose.

McIlroy's fortunes did not change when he flew back to Europe for the Irish Open at Carton House Golf Club in County Kildare. He missed the cut on a course where most of the field was going low. Once again, it looked like his confidence had deserted him. Or was it his Nike sticks that had gone AWOL?

Faldo was convinced it was the latter and wasn't shy about expressing that view whenever a microphone was nearby. "Rory very simply messed with a winning formula," Sir Nick growled, with the 142nd Open Championship at Muirfield just days away. A professional golfer only gets a "millisecond of feel" at impact—and Rory had lost it, Faldo claimed.

Nick also alleged that Rory's business commitments and flying all over the planet to be with Caroline were messing with his capacity to focus, hinting that Rory wasn't practicing hard enough.

Faldo's daggers pissed McIlroy off no end. Rory kept firing back ("Nick should know how hard this game is at times!"), but he gave the British knight more ammunition by shooting a sky-high 79-75 at Muirfield and badly missing the cut. Rory's protestations about the blisters he was getting from hitting so many range balls were beginning to fall on deaf ears. He admitted that he was "brain dead" at Muirfield.

"I feel like I'm walking around out there and I'm unconscious," he said, in words that must have caused Maalox Moments for Phil Knight and Cindy Davis in Beaverton.

The staff at Horizon, meanwhile, knew more dyspepsia was coming.

In 2013's last major, the PGA Championship at Oak Hill in Rochester, Rory finally put together four solid rounds. Had his putter behaved, he might have finished better than eighth. Still, he finished three-under on the rugged Donald Ross design, with a first-round 69 and a third-round 67.

His third round must have felt like he was back at the Ocean Course a year earlier. He chip-in for birdie on the 54th hole "left Oak Hill quaking!" CBS's Jim Nance yelled as the gallery erupted. Rory would have needed a spectacular round to catch Jason Dufner on Sunday, but he delivered an even-par 70. Still, a top ten in a major after the slump he'd been through had to help his frame of mind.

A few weeks later, Rory and Caroline got to spend some quiet time together in the Hamptons, courtesy of financier Michael Pascucci and family. Pascucci made his fortune persuading banks and credit unions to partner with him in creating a new financial instrument: the leasing of automobiles. Car-leasing proved popular with both lenders and consumers. It became so profitable that Pascucci sold his company, Oxford Resources, to Barnett Bank in 1997 for some $650 million. Today, his net worth is estimated to be north of a billion.

Pascucci, who caddied as a kid, had always been a golf nut; in mid-career, the Bucknell University alum began investing in golf properties. Among other venues, he acquired the Bear's Club in Palm Beach Garden; his winter home sits close to the Golden Bear's. In 2006, he spent $115 million to buy one of the most exclusive tracts of land in North America: the Long Island bluff overlooking Great Peconic Bay in Southampton.

He hired Jack Nicklaus and Tom Doak to create Sebonack Golf Club, a place worthy of being mentioned in the same breath as designer Charles P. Macdonald's National Golf Links of America to its north, and three-time US Open host Shinnecock Hills Golf Club to its south. Pascucci sought to replicate the ambiance of Augusta National by building nine cottages within an easy stroll of Sebonack's imposing clubhouse. Nicklaus and Doak's course was so well received that by 2013, the USGA had awarded it the US Women's Open.

The financial wizard had gotten to know McIlroy when Rory chose to locate in Palm Beach Gardens and would often practice at the Bear's Club, even before he acquired a home there. Pascucci told Rory about Sebonack's cottages and encouraged him to take some R&R there if his schedule permitted. In late August 2013, Rory took Pascucci up on it.

He and Caroline spent a weekend in one of those cottages, with Mr. and Mrs. Pascucci and their grandchildren playing host. Granddaughter Sophie Barnard was eighteen and about to leave for her freshman year at Georgetown University in Washington, DC. She was one of the better teenaged tennis players on Long Island, with plans to play varsity for the Hoyas. Sophie was also a huge fan of Wozniacki's. When her grandfather said he was hosting Caroline and her boyfriend for dinner that Friday evening, Sophie jumped at the chance to join them.

Rory with the young Cole Barnard in 2013 in the Hamptons on eastern Long Island. Caroline and Rory spent a relaxing weekend at Sebonack Golf Club as the guests of Cole's grandparents, Mr. and Mrs. Michael Pascucci. Photo courtesy of Cole Barnard.

So did her brother Cole, an eighth-grader who already had a decent golf game and loved watching Rory play. His eyes also got big when his grandparents invited him to dinner.

They sat at a big circular table on the clubhouse veranda, Cole remembers, with his grandparents offering good-luck toasts to Caroline for the upcoming US Open at Flushing Meadow and to Sophie for her freshman year at GU. Sophie managed to sit next to Caroline. They had a grand time talking tennis, fashion, and tennis fashion. Sophie's boyfriend at the time, a varsity hockey player at Providence College, was also seated at the table.

Since Sophie was leaving for DC that weekend and needed to finish packing, she didn't ask Caroline for a hitting session the next day. But she's sure that Caroline would have agreed. Cole and his grandfather, meanwhile, talked golf with Rory, who could not have been more engaging, Cole remembered in the spring of '23. The fourteen-year-old screwed up the courage to ask Rory if he could go out on the course with him.

"Sure," Rory replied. They made arrangements to play on Sunday.

Someone, one of his grandparents, Cole thinks, took a picture of Rory and Cole after dinner. Rory is nicely turned out in a royal blue suit with a pocket square. Cole is wearing preppy madras slacks that, a decade later, made him wince. "I don't know what I was thinking with those pants," he laughed. About a 12-handicapper back then, Cole was so excited Saturday night that he could hardly sleep.

Young Barnard wasn't the only Sebonack kid who got to hang with Rory that weekend. Club member Ciaran T. O'Kelly, the Global Head of Equity Trading for Bank of America Securities, and his three sons happened to be on the range when Rory was hitting balls on Saturday. Liam, a first grader and the youngest of the O'Kelly brood, walked up to Rory and asked if he could play with him.

"Sure," said Rory with a big smile.

When he finished his practice session, Rory winked at all three O'Kelly boys and told them to grab their bags and join him on the first tee. Off they went down the first fairway, with dad Ciaran, a native Dubliner and a big McIlroy fan, chuckling at his little guy's *dánacht* (Gaelic for "chutzpah"). The kids had a terrific time as McIlroy patiently helped them with their golf swings. Rory was "very kind and gracious," Ciaran says today.

The McIlroy-O'Kelly friendship didn't end there. In the summer of 2015, the family vacationed in Ireland. Rory arranged for the O'Kelly men to play at Holywood Golf Club. They had a fun afternoon atop Belfast Lough.

Cole Barnard had fun, too, when he went out with Rory that Sunday. Young Barnard recalls that along with his other sister, Lilly, he joined Rory for the backside on the 10th tee. Caddie J.P. Fitzgerald wasn't lugging Rory's bag; he was playing, too, with both bags in a cart. Cole thinks that Rory's then-travel aide, Sean O'Flaherty, was also walking with the group. Sophie's beau, the Providence hockey star, tagged along, too.

Cole remembers that J.P. was a solid player and that he'd never seen anyone play Sebonack the way Rory did that afternoon. You'd never know Rory had been in a slump from his ball-striking that day, Cole recalls. It was a blast, he remembered, talking golf with J.P. and Rory.

Caroline and Sophie had both left the previous day: Wozniacki by limousine for the Open; Barnard by car with her folks to DC.

Friday night's dinner had been so enjoyable that Rory asked if he and his team could join the Pascuccis again Saturday evening. They ended up back on the veranda eating pizza, with Rory, Sean, and J.P. joining Cole, Lilly, their grandparents, and a couple of hangers-on.

Again, everyone marveled at how relaxed and funny Rory was. A decade later, both Barnards recall that Caroline and Rory had been affectionate that weekend. Sophie and Cole weren't surprised five months later to hear that they'd gotten engaged.

The story doesn't end there. Sophie and the Providence hockey player stopped dating during college. A couple of years later, Rory was in Boston to play a tournament. McIlroy and friends went out to dinner at the same seafood restaurant where, by coincidence, the Providence hockey team was dining.

Sophie' ex happened to spot Rory as he was being seated. He proceeded to tell his teammates all about his cool weekend hanging out with McIlroy and getting to see him play Sebonack.

"Bullshit!" his buddies cried. "If you really know McIlroy, prove it! Go over there!"

He sucked it up, walked over to McIlroy's table, and nervously reminded Rory how they'd met. "Absolutely, I remember you!" Rory said, popping up to shake his hand. Rory ended up walking over to the table full of Friar hockey players, greeted everybody, made small talk, and posed for pictures.

In a flash, Sophie's ex went from zero to hero in the eyes of his teammates. It had to have been one of the most satisfying moments of that young man's life.

It had been an idyllic, sun-drenched late August weekend on eastern Long Island. But Wozzilroy and Rory Land were being threatened by storm clouds gathering in multiple directions.

Caroline, prolonging her slump, again failed to advance to the fourth round at Flushing Meadows, losing to Italian qualifier Camila Georgi in straight sets. Naysayers renewed their criticism that her defensive style of play wasn't potent enough to win Grand Slams. Wozniacki's game had slipped badly; Caroline was nowhere near the player she'd been when she and Rory first started dating.

Yes, Rory's golf game was showing signs of coming out of the doldrums, but the fact remained that he still hadn't won anywhere in the world since switching his clubs over to Nike nine months earlier.

He had, however, become an ever-wealthier man. He was now the third-highest off-the-course earner in professional golf, behind only Tiger and Phil. Horizon that spring, moreover, had wired multi-year, multi-million-dollar deals with Omega for McIlroy to represent its luxury timepieces, and with Spanish-based bank Santander to promote its financial services.

Partnering with Omega meant giving up his long-term relationship with another luxury watchmaker, Audemars Piguet. As Horizon was finalizing its deal with Omega, Rory called Audemars's

CEO and explained the situation. He assured him that he would fulfill his appearance obligations for the remainder of his contract.

In words that Chubby Chandler, Conor Ridge, and, twelve months later, Caroline Wozniacki may have found difficult to swallow, Rory told Karen Crouse of the *New York Times* in the spring of 2013: "What we do for a living out here, it's all about relationships. You build relationships from the start of your career, and you want to try to keep certain relationships until the end."

That quote appeared in a Crouse piece dated May 4, 2013 (Rory's twenty-fourth birthday), pegged to the Wells Fargo tourney in Charlotte. Her article, headlined "The Branding of Rory McIlroy," spotlighted the financial success that the Horizon-McIlroy partnership had wrought. It mentioned Rory's long conversation with Federer in Brazil in late 2011. "Federer is a role model," Rory told Crouse. "[He's] someone I can pattern myself after." Crouse's article also stressed McIlroy's desire to narrow his commercial activities. "I don't want a lot of sponsors. I want a few quality ones," Rory told her.

By all appearances, it looked like Horizon had helped Rory achieve that vision. Presumably happy, McIlroy had signed a contract extension with Horizon and Ridge in early 2013.

But Crouse volunteered to me a decade later that something didn't feel right about the Rory-Horizon dynamic. Her editor at the *Times* told her that a source in Ireland was warning that the McIlroy-Ridge relationship had turned sour. She couldn't get anyone around Rory to talk on- or off-the-record about alleged tension.

So, the *Times* went with the story as planned. *Boom!* Two short weeks later at the Memorial, Rory announced that he was seeking to dissolve his relationship with Horizon. It turned out to be an acrimonious split that took eighteen arduous months of lawsuits, countersuits, and public nastiness before being resolved.

Rory's showdown with Horizon played out at the Irish Open in July 2013, five weeks after the rancor first surfaced. It had all the subtlety of a "Tom and Jerry" cartoon. Crouse, who witnessed the cringeworthy goings-on at Maynooth in County Kildare, characterized it as "farce."

On the one side was former Horizon executive Sean O'Flaherty, who had resigned from the firm two months earlier and had now assumed what Crouse called a "nebulous new role" as McIlroy's personal assistant.

On the other side were O'Flaherty's former bosses, Ridge and Morrissey, whose over-the-top behavior was telling the world that they still considered McIlroy *their guy*, an active and ongoing Horizon client. The spurned pair showed up at Rory's press conferences and shadowed him on the course, never more than a few steps removed from defector O'Flaherty.

"It was like watching warring spouses hunker down in an unhappy house so they cannot be charged with abandonment,"[1] Crouse wrote from Maynooth. She may still have been honked that the supposed PR professionals playing cat-and-mouse on the Carton House course had not called her off the branding story a few weeks earlier.

Good lord, what went haywire? After all, in Crouse's article, she quoted Rory as saying, "I think it's a good thing for me that I'm with a smaller company [Horizon]. They are always looking out for what's best for me." For a professional athlete on the cusp of sacking his management firm, it was a baffling statement.

Since all parties have signed nondisclosure agreements, the who-struck-John-first details are not likely to emerge; but it's clear from legal documents that McIlroy believed he had been coerced into signing an "unconscionable and limiting" deal with Horizon at that December 2011 office party. Rory must have come to the conclusion that Ridge's company was making undue compensation

---

1   Even by Crouse's lofty standards, that was fabulous imagery—and it was all done on deadline! Karen's stuff is so good it reminds me of the great A.J. Liebling's dictum: "I'm a better writer than anyone who's faster and a faster writer than anyone who's better." Rory, to his credit, apologized to Crouse when she approached him at the '13 Memorial after the branding article snafu.

in booking his endorsement deals—which amounted to $6.8 million worth, as *Golf Digest* reported in December 2014.

At some point in early '13, McIlroy and O'Flaherty must have become confidants: Rory in all likelihood shared his apprehension that he'd signed (and re-signed) a predatory deal—and Sean, his Horizon liaison, confirmed it. Together with Rory's dad and Dublin businessman Donal Casey, they hatched a plan to separate themselves from Horizon and create their own agency.

But how did it reach that breaking point? Did Rory get "okey-dokey'd" at the holiday party? Did he sign a contract that included a percentage cut for Horizon that was over and above the industry standard of 10–15 percent? It sure looked like it. Did Rory's 2013 frustrations on the course and with his new equipment—plus what was rumored to be his hot-and-cold relationship with Caroline—contribute to the tension with Ridge? Again, that's a good bet.

In truth, McIlroy's deal with Horizon barely lasted a year before it hit serious headwinds. Chubby Chandler and the folks at ISM couldn't be faulted if they enjoyed a little *schadenfreude* over Rory's troubles with the agency that stole him away.

Whatever the circumstances, Rory Land execs and some trusted lawyers (where were they in December of '11?) pulled out a calculator and concluded that by keeping the revenue in-house, they could appreciably increase their margins.

It was the beginning of Rory McIlroy Management Services LTD. But it was hell getting there.

Ridge and Morrissey weren't about to loosen their grip on Rory until they got what they believed was coming to them. A year before, Rory and Horizon had seemed to be on top of the world. He had won five tournaments, including a major, and had captured the money title on both sides of the Atlantic. Huge endorsement deals were in the offing.

Twelve months later, Rory was struggling to put four decent rounds together. And his agency was getting the back of his hand.

RORY LAND

Between Caroline's plummet and the rumble with Horizon, it was a rough stretch for Wozzilroy. On September 16, just a couple of weeks after their getaway in the Hamptons, the tension got ratcheted up when Caroline posted on Twitter a photo of a shirtless Rory snoozing, his head propped against a pillow. His mouth was open and his glasses were perched at an odd angle. Her post read: "Jetlag?@mcilroyrory Lol!!"

When Caroline posted this photo of a jetlagged Rory napping in September of '13. it set off a firestorm in the Irish, UK, and Danish tabloids. The gossip rags were convinced that they were breaking up. Three months later they were engaged.

Caroline's attempt at inducing a lighthearted "lots of laughs" was not well received in certain quarters. Many in the Twittersphere saw it as malicious. Even Wozniacki pal and fellow tennis star Serena Williams tweeted: "Omg Caro u are soooo mean!!!! Love it!!"

Replied Wozniacki: "I know haha!! Can't fall asleep anymore! Always keeping an eye open lol!"

Tabloid media seized on her post as an indication that the couple's relationship had turned rocky. Indeed, the *Irish Independent*, a longtime booster of McIlroy's career, reported that Wozzilroy had gone bust. Citing sources close to McIlroy, Niamh Horan of the *Independent* wrote that the tweet may have pushed Rory "over the edge." Wozniacki was said to be "absolutely devastated" by the reaction to her posting.

The *Independent*, the *New York Post*, and other outlets quoted anonymous sources close to both the "Wozz" and the "Ilroy" saying that the romance was kaput. Caroline fired back a few days later in the Danish tabloid *Ekstra Bladet*.[2]

"I'm so tired of the rumors," Wozniacki complained. "They occur every time Rory and I are apart a few days or do not write on Twitter. There is nothing in it, and from now on I just think that I will keep my private life private."

Hmm. Well, if she and Rory had kept their "private lives private," they wouldn't have gotten themselves into this mess. They had made Wozzilroy everyone's business—and now it was coming back to bite them.

McIlroy had more downtime than he wanted. The guy who had won two lucrative legs of the 2012 FedEx Cup playoffs had to deal with the ignominy of not qualifying for the top thirty for the '13 Tour Championship in Atlanta. Golf writers that autumn reported that Rory was seeing sports psychologists, hoping to regain his confidence and powers of concentration.

"It's a very alien feeling," McIlroy has said after his mistake-strewn 79 at Murfield. "It's something I've never had to deal with before."

---

[2] It means "Extra Newspaper" in Danish, which doesn't sound like a menacing tabloid, does it?

RORY LAND

Rory had accepted an invitation from Adam Scott and others to come Down Under and play in the '13 Emirates Australian Open at Royal Sydney in late November and early December. McIlroy's first round was a solid three-under 69, but he was still seven shots behind his host Scott, who shot a blistering 62.

Rory's second-day 65—he'd stuck his fourth-different Nike driver of the season into his bag that week—put him just two back of Scott, who'd cooled off on day two. Still, Scott was looking to become the sixth golfer ever to win the Australian Triple Crown—the Australian PGA, the Australian Masters, and the Australian Open—in the same year.

It looked like Scott would grab the crown when he shot a 68 to Rory's 70 on Saturday and took a four-shot lead going into the last round. But Scott's long-putter failed him on Sunday and Rory's blade cooperated just enough to let him pull even.

The pivotal moment came on the par-five seventh when, after a massive drive, Rory hit a seven-iron inside ten feet and made eagle. On the 72nd hole, with the score knotted, Rory again blasted his drive down the middle while Scott struggled to get on the green in regulation. McIlroy's short-iron never left the flagstick, coming down twelve feet underneath.

It left him a slick left-to-righter on greens so quick that Rory had compared them to Augusta's. McIlroy finessed the putt up the hill. It fell into the cup on its last roll.

Rory's facial reaction bordered on disbelief. He clearly hadn't expected to win. He let out a big breath of air with both cheeks puffed out, then did his little fist pump move.

For the first time in almost a year, and for the first time as a Nike guy, Rory McIlroy was a winner. "Another great name has found its way onto the Stonehaven Cup," Aussie announcer Ian Baker-Finch intoned.

Over the next twelve months, that name would become even more famous. And more than a little infamous.

Chapter 18

HOYLAKE AND NEW BEGINNINGS

Two thousand fourteen got off to a literal *Bang!* for Wozzilroy. With New Year's fireworks illuminating Sydney Harbour, McIlroy proposed to Wozniacki aboard an exclusive charter boat. As the countdown melted toward zero, Rory placed a diamond-encrusted ring on Caroline's finger, a sparkler almost as spectacular as the rockets exploding against the backdrop of the Opera House. Some outlets reported that Rory spent £100,000 on the ring; others claimed it was north of £150,000.

No matter: a thrilled Caroline spent the next few days posing for pictures to show off her new bauble and the fiancé who gave it to her. Greeted with smiles and applause wherever they went, the couple explored their favorite haunts in New South Wales, trumpeting selfies on social media.

A year earlier, in January 2013, Caroline and Rory had gone on the Sydney Tower Eye Observation Deck Skywalk, a heart-thumping stomp around the highest tourist platform in the Southern Hemisphere. Like so many Wozzilroy moments, it was a staged photo op; the two of them were decked out in official Tower Eye garb, sky-blue onesies that made them look like members of the old punk-rock group Devo.

Rory seemed the more adventurous of the two. At one point, tethered to a safety pole, he began jumping up and down. It delighted the photographers but made his future fiancée feign a heart clutch.

Sky-walking over a cityscape was the perfect metaphor for Wozzilroy. The relationship had always been a high-wire act, teetering on the brink. A big fall was inevitable.

Caroline had hurt her shoulder in late December 2013, just before their betrothal, and was forced to pull out of the WTA tournament in Brisbane. All of a sudden, the couple had some time on their hands Down Under. They enjoyed more sightseeing before Rory had to head off to his next stops—Abu Dhabi for the European Tour's curtain-raiser, and Dubai for its annual Desert Classic.

McIlroy assured readers of the *Irish Sun* in January that his on-course frustrations were in the rearview mirror. He also admitted that naysayers were justified in saying that he had experienced too many off-course distractions in 2013; those diversions had, he conceded, contributed to his disappointing play.

"I was thinking of other things when I really shouldn't have.... But that's the last year I'm ever going to have to go through that. I've learnt from it and am smarter because of it. And it's great that I've gone through it at this stage in my career and not 15 years down the line."

Those brave declarations would ring hollow as McIlroy through the years continued to struggle with maturity and focus.

In their crystal ball projections for the 2014 season, *Sports Illustrated*'s golf-beat writers all pointed to Rory's late-'13 win at the Australian Open as a harbinger. It took a while for McIlroy to get rolling in the new year; once he did, the *SI* guys were proven prophetic—and then some.

The 2014 HSBC Championship was contested at the Abu Dhabi Golf Club. Phil Mickelson accepted a healthy appearance fee to play in the Euro season opener.

Rory and Phil put on a show for fans in the UAE. They traded blows all weekend and finished in a flat-footed tie at 13-under. But Spaniard Pablo Larrazábal shot a final-day 67 and slipped past the two heavyweights by a single stroke.

Later that month, with Caroline in the gallery, Rory shot a scintillating 63 in the opening round of the Desert Classic. He failed to build on his lead, however, shooting 70-69 on Friday and Saturday, and blowing up to a 74 on Sunday.

The highlight of Dubai week occurred when Rory just missed a hole-in-one that would have netted him a smooth £1.8 million. He joked after the round that the big prize "could have paid for my wedding," which elicited guffaws in the press tent. No one laughed harder than Caroline, reported the *Belfast Telegraph*. In Dubai, McIlroy ended up in a tie for ninth at 12-under.

Rory and Caroline managed to squeeze in more time together in mid-winter '14. For once, their schedules meshed. They could use Caro's place in Monaco as a jumping-off point.

In February, Caroline broke out of her slump just enough to make the semifinals of the WTA's Dubai Tennis Championship, a tournament won by Venus Williams. A couple of weeks later, Rory finished in a tie for twenty-fifth at the WGC Cadillac event at Doral. He followed that with a nice showing in Houston, finishing seventh the week preceding the Masters.

His performance at the '14 Masters was also solid, shooting even-par in a tough year for scoring; only seven guys managed to get into red numbers. Bubba Watson won the second of his two Masters championships at eight-under.

McIlroy was done in at Augusta by two double-bogeys in the second round. On the long par-three fourth hole, his five-wood off the tee rocketed thirty yards over the green, nearly tattooing Adam Scott, who was waiting to hit on the fifth tee. At the par-four 10th, Rory hit a solid drive but mangled his approach, finding some nasty bushes and missing an eight-footer that would have saved his bogey.

Those two wild shots cost him the chance to contend. He was beginning to understand, he vowed that week, that the Masters required precision and patience over power. It was not the last time he would claim to have arrived at that revelation.

In the middle of May, Caroline and Rory had a week (almost) to themselves. They spent a couple of days in London, where photographers spotted them canoodling at an outdoor café in Sloane Square and holding hands while window shopping in Belgravia.

Then they flew to Monaco to review plans for their November 2014 wedding. It was to take place at a small chapel in midtown Manhattan, followed by an extravagant reception atop Rockefeller Center. The invitations had just gone out for the fête at the Top of the Rock, a sixty-seventh-floor jewel with breathtaking views of the New York skyline. Former President and Secretary of State Clinton, the Williams sisters, and other sports, business, and political luminaries were among the many VIPs on the two-hundred-person invitation list.

Danish sources back then said that Caroline's mother Anna had been in touch that week to help with preparations. Caroline had already picked out a dress; she and her mom and, presumably, the McIlroys, were working with an expensive wedding planner.

On their last night together, Sunday, May 18, Caroline and Rory went out to dinner at Nobu Monte-Carlo, a five-star Japanese restaurant in the beachside Fairmont Hotel; they sat on the terrace overlooking the Mediterranean. At sunset, Rory snapped a picture of the stunning Côte d'Azur and posted it on Twitter with this message: "Nice view for dinner with @CaroWozniacki at Nobu Monte Carlo," thus reminding his nearly two million followers how much he and Caroline were savoring their engagement.

Less than eighteen hours later, they were broken up—for good. It was all Rory's doing, despite Rory Land's efforts that week to depict the split as "mutual."

Why? What happened on McIlroy's flight the next morning from Nice-Côte d'Azur Airport to London that could have caused their relationship to go *pffft*? Did he suddenly get cold feet? Or, more likely, did his already cold feet get frigid?

Was something said that last night in Monaco or on the drive to the airport that caused McIlroy to get the jitters? If he had doubts, why not ask Caroline to postpone the wedding and keep their relationship intact? Why an irrevocable break mere hours after reminding the world that he and Caroline, together, were loving life?

And why, oh why, lower the boom over his cellphone instead of doing it in person? Surely, he'd had misgivings for a while. Why didn't he confront those feelings instead of letting Caroline and her family send out invitations and continue fretting over the big event?

British journalist Dave Thomas, in a front-page piece in the (London) *Sunday Telegraph* that week, directly addressed McIlroy: "It's not quite as last-minute a decision as Charles dumping Duckface at the altar in *Four Weddings and a Funeral*, but still, Rory, have some consideration. You dropped her while the invitations were in the post. 'Ouch!' doesn't begin to cover that perfect storm of rejection, embarrassment, and abject humiliation."

The same rumor mill that spread innuendo in October 2013 over Caroline's snoozing Rory post soon began buzzing that his relationship with Dublin model Nadia Forde was behind the breakup.

Rory delivered the blow after he arrived in London for the BMW Championship. The fateful call, Caroline later confided, lasted no more than a few minutes. Wozniacki revealed in a fall 2014 television interview with Graham Bensinger, the host of the syndicated program *In Depth*, that at first, she thought Rory was playing a joke. But Caroline soon realized that McIlroy wasn't goofing around; he was deadly serious.

"I was shocked," she told Bensinger.[1] "I thought I'd at least get a face-to-face or something." She wasn't alone: her friends, family, and online followers were also aghast. When one of her closest pals,

---

[1] In a moment that redefined "tacky," Bensinger chose to hit on Caroline in mid-interview.

Serena Williams, heard the news, she reacted with: "No waaaay! I was planning the bachelorette party!"

Before hanging up on May 19, McIlroy should have shared with Caroline his plan to issue a public statement announcing the breakup. But when Rory's communications team (still led by former Horizon executive Sean O'Flaherty, but now under the aegis of Rory, Inc.) quickly put out a release, she was again apparently blindsided.

"There is no right way to end a relationship that has been so important to two people," read the McIlroy statement that caused tremors in the global sports and celebrity world. "The problem is mine. The wedding invitations issued at the weekend made me realize that I wasn't ready for all that marriage entails. I wish Caroline all the happiness she deserves and thank her for the great times we've had."

The language may have been soulless—*Belfast Telegraph* columnist John Lavarty later likened it to the "impersonal, civil-servicey thing a football club says after sacking its manager"—but it served its purpose.

Had McIlroy stuck to that statement and declined to answer press queries, he—and, far more importantly, given the harsh circumstances, his jilted ex-fiancée—might have fared better. But at his Wednesday presser at Wentworth, Rory chose to answer a half-dozen questions about the breakup. At no point did he ask reporters to back off and respect his (or *their*) privacy.

"Yeah, obviously quite a difficult time for Caroline and myself," he volunteered at the top. "And I think the statement really said it all this morning. It was mutual and amicable and we both thought it was the best for us. Time to move on and I think that I've said all that I need to say."

Whoa. There was a lot to unspool there—virtually all of it inaccurate. For starters, the breakup was far from "mutual" or "amicable." Caroline, moreover, was miles removed from agreeing it was the best path forward.

And if it were truly time to move on and let the statement speak for itself, why was McIlroy making it worse—*a lot worse* from the Wozniacki family's point of view—by continuing to talk about it? Caroline later admitted that Rory's refusal to stay mum infuriated her.

Bob Harig, then of ESPN.com, wrote that day: "McIlroy was asked why he felt compelled to announce that he and Wozniacki had broken up. 'Honestly, I don't know,' [McIlroy] said. 'It's one of those things that it was a very public relationship. And I thought it was best that, instead of letting it linger and [spark] rumors, just to have it [out] there as soon as possible.'"

"Honestly, I don't know," is probably not the best way for an adult to explain why they chose to make public a painful private matter.

Given the way things unfolded, it's not unreasonable to infer that Rory Land domos were behind the decision to issue a statement and attempt to spin the breakup Rory's way. Certain members of Rory's camp may have come to believe that Wozzilroy, in all its schedule-busting craziness, was hurting the professional output of their pal and meal ticket.

The same suspicion (probably in spades) can be deduced about Caroline's people. Her slump during their time together had been much worse than Rory's. Those stories in the fall of '13 claiming ill will over snoring Rory came from *someplace*.

But by being disingenuous about what had actually happened, Rory Land was guaranteeing that Caroline's people would seek to straighten the record.

Before the Wednesday press conference ended, Rory was asked if he'd thought about pulling out of the BMW.

"No, I didn't think there was any reason to do that," he said. "I just made a commitment to be here. It's the European Tour's flagship event.... I thought it was my duty to come back and play in this event."

Laughter then filled the room when a reporter blurted, "At least you're at a golf course that you love." It was a sarcastic comment; Rory's struggles at Wentworth were well chronicled.

Rory chuckled as he admitted that Wentworth had given him fits over the years. "I'm trying to go in this week with the mindset of not getting frustrated and just trying to play to my spots and not be frustrated that I might only get to hit driver here two or three times a round."

On balance, Caroline exhibited restraint in her public pronouncements—at least in the immediate aftermath of Rory's bombshell. She did, however, get in a subtle early dig.

"It's a hard time for me right now," she tweeted the day after Rory's press conference remarks. "Thanks for all the sweet messages! Happy I support Liverpool right now because I know I'll never walk alone."[2]

The Liverpool F.C. reference was meant to zing her ex, since he was a rabid Manchester United fan. Over their thirty-four-month relationship, they had issued all manner of posts needling each other about their rival Premier League loyalties.

Given his romantic woes and dismal record around Wentworth, media types didn't give Rory much of a chance that week. Still, he followed his own prescription in round one, shooting a 68 that was highlighted by an eagle on the par-four seventh hole. He ended the day trailing Thomas Bjørn, then the Race to Dubai money leader, by six shots. On Friday, McIlroy didn't make up much ground,

---

[2] Liverpool F.C. fans decades ago adopted the inspirational Rogers and Hammerstein ballad "You'll Never Walk Alone" as their theme song. The old hit from *Carousel* was covered by Liverpool's own Gerry and the Pacemakers in 1963.

shooting a 71 and falling off the first page of the leaderboard. A third-round 69 also failed to put a dent in the Great Dane's lead.

On Sunday morning, Rory was tied for third, but still seven strokes back. Former world number one Luke Donald was in solo second. Donald's career record at the venerable Harry Colt layout was as sharp as Rory's was dull. Luke had won twice at Wentworth and had a string of other impressive finishes.

Rory started the final round with three pars. On the shortish par-five fourth, Rory's twenty-foot eagle bid hung on the lip for what seemed an eternity before finally dropping. A McIlroy birdie at number 7 offset his bogey at number 6. When Donald and Bjørn, playing behind him, both triple-bogeyed number 6, Rory suddenly found himself in contention.

For a long stretch on Sunday, however, it appeared that his old running mate, Shane Lowry, was the favorite to overtake Bjørn and Donald. The young men from County Down and County Offaly were gunning to become the first Irish champion at the Wentworth tourney since Harry Bradshaw in 1958.

McIlroy didn't take control until the final three holes. He made a tough eight-footer to save par at the par-four 16th, then made back-to-back birdies on the two final holes, both par-fives. He got up and down at number 17 from just in front of the green, making a seven-footer that slipped into the high pocket.

At the finisher, he hit a titanic power fade off the tee, followed by a mid-iron that drifted, hole-high, into the right-side bunker. But he deftly blasted out, his ball following the green's right-to-left slope before trickling inside four feet. What proved to be Rory's winning putt clanged into the middle.

He had shot a final-round 66, good enough to win by a single shot over his pal Shane.

"I'm not exactly sure what I am feeling right now," Rory said afterward, admiring the trophy as he ruminated about his first win on European or US soil in eighteen long months. "It has obviously been a week of very mixed emotions. I'm sitting here looking at this trophy, going, 'How the hell did it happen this week?'"

How-the-hell, indeed. On Monday morning, he had been engaged to one of the world's most beguiling women but still mired in a professional slump. By Sunday afternoon, the slump had ended—and so had his romance. Amid all that uproar, Rory had somehow managed to win the European Tour's most prestigious tournament on one of the UK's most demanding courses.

"The real truth of the entire [Wozniacki] business has been twisted out of all recognition under the red-hot glare of the media spotlight they both loved and loathed," wrote Brian Keogh that week. "Or perhaps McIlroy is a far tougher person than we imagined."

When asked by RTE Radio how Rory had managed to overcome all that angst and win at Wentworth, Rory's fellow Irishman and that year's European Ryder Cup captain, Paul McGinley, chuckled, "We will never know. Only Rory can answer that question."

As his astounding summer of 2014 progressed, Rory answered a lot of questions about how he could play so well given his stormy personal life—so many, in fact, that it further enraged Caroline's camp. Indeed, it is one of the curiosities of McIlroy's career that he consistently pulls off fabulous golf while consumed by off-course controversy. Whether it was ending things with Caroline during Wentworth, or the *mishigas* at Medinah, or the car park chaos at Marco Simone, or winning at Quail Hollow on the cusp of filing for divorce, Rory is often at his best when swamped by off-course bedlam.

All that week at Wentworth, he said that the course was his "sanctuary"—a place to push aside his personal problems and concentrate on the thing he loved. That sanctuary got bigger as the season went on, expanding from Virginia Water to Hoylake to Akron to Louisville to Perth and Kinross, Scotland.

The following week, McIlroy delighted fans at Muirfield Village by shooting an opening-round 63 and surging into the lead at the Golden Bear's tournament. But schizoid Rory showed up again. His second-round 78 almost put him out of the tournament, one of those head-scratching McIlroy Moments that has driven Big Jack to distraction. McIlroy rallied to shoot 69-72 on the weekend and finished tied for fifteenth—not a bad showing, but not what he (or his host) expected after his opener.

The 2014 US Open was held for the third time at Donald Ross's masterwork, Pinehurst No. 2, which Ben Crenshaw and his design partner Bill Coore had restored to its primordial roots. Fairways were widened, rough eliminated, and bunkers and sandy areas toughened in ways meant to honor the old Scotsman's vision.

Martin Kaymer ran away from the field by starting with a pair of 65s, then held on to match Rory's winning margin at Congressional three years earlier: eight strokes. The German finished at nine-under, one of the lowest winning scores in US Open history—a statistic that no doubt rankled the suits at the USGA almost as much as Rory's 2011 dismantling of Congressional.

McIlroy only broke 70 once at the '14 US Open—a second-round 68. His play on the weekend was disappointing: a 74 followed by a 73. He had now gone the better part of two years without winning in North America.

His puzzling inability to bring his best golf to the Irish Open continued in mid-June at the Fota Island Resort Club in County Cork. He missed a day of practice when United Airlines managed to misplace his clubs. Once his Nike sticks resurfaced, he played poorly with them, shooting a Thursday 74 on a benign course where almost everyone in the field went low.

His Friday 69—which included six birdies and an eagle offset with six bogeys—wasn't enough to make the weekend. It was doubly painful for Rory, since he had announced that week that the Rory Foundation was taking over for the next four years as the tournament's title sponsor. Rory's financial intervention, many believe, saved the Irish Open from being axed from the European Tour schedule. McIlroy coupled his foundation's support with the sponsorship of the Dubai Duty Free Company, the world's largest airport retailer. Their partnership restored the Irish Open's solvency.

With just a couple of weeks to go before the Open Championship at Royal Liverpool, McIlroy was again searching for consistent play. His uneven scoring continued at the Scottish Open at blustery Royal Aberdeen. His opening 64 was followed by an all-too-familiar 78, occasioning reporters to ascribe it to a "Freaky Friday Complex," referencing a Jamie Lee Curtis movie in which her character undergoes a spooky alteration every Friday.

Rory's third and fourth rounds at Balgownie by the North Sea were less freaky but still frustrating; McIlroy could only get to fourteenth place, nine strokes behind winner Justin Rose. The conqueror of Wentworth wasn't exactly in top form as he headed to the northwest of England and its magnificent links along the estuary of the River Dee.

What *was* in top form was his body. Even some of McIlroy's biggest fans were amazed at Rory's physical transformation. Gone were his adolescent pudginess and squishy physique, replaced by sinew and hard muscle. By July 2014, he was working out twice a day, well on the way toward developing the arms, chest, and legs of a Premier League fullback.

He loved posting pictures of himself working out, with hashtags like #betterneverstops. His followers got used to tweets detailing his grueling routines. By then, thanks in no small measure to Caroline, he'd also cut out junk food.

The crowd at Hoylake, drawn mostly from blue-collar Liverpool and Manchester, tended to be younger, more boisterous, and harder-partying than typical Open fans, as R&A head Peter Dawson pointed out that week. Beer'd up Liverpool F.C., Everton, and Man City devotees put aside their allegiances and rooted hard for the chiseled Man U guy from Northern Ireland.

As they had done three years before at Royal St. George's, Rory and Darren Clarke played an Open Championship practice round together that week. This time, Rory beat his mentor, joking to reporters afterward that maybe it was a good omen.

It was. Displaying the same cunning that enabled him to win big at Congressional and the Ocean Course, Rory dominated the 143rd Open Championship from the first tee shot until the final putt—with the exception of about an hour's worth of play on Saturday. His two-stroke winning margin wasn't as awe-inspiring as his spreads at Congressional or Kiawah, but his performance at Hoylake was every bit as stirring.

Even the day-one presence of a Cheshire pheasant on the sixth green, which pranced around the putting surface as Rory lined up a twelve-footer for birdie, couldn't hurt his mojo. Once the pheasant deigned to depart, he drained the putt. The crowd roared as he grabbed an early lead that was never relinquished.

His surge began with back-to-back 66s that spotlighted every tool in his kit. As Christopher Clarey in the *New York Times* put it, McIlroy's long game was so unerring that he turned Royal Liverpool's par-fives into his "personal playgrounds."

Perennial Open contender Sergio Garcia battled to stay even with Rory all week, but never quite pulled it off. Dustin Johnson was at 136 at the halfway point, four shots behind Rory, but fell back as the weekend progressed.

Rory's roughest opponent turned out to be his old Walker Cup rival, the twenty-five-year-old Rickie Fowler. The Californian, who'd finished second to Martin Kaymer in the US Open the month before, hung tough at Hoylake all four rounds. On Saturday, buoyed by birdies at the par-five 10th and the tough par-four 12th, Fowler moved—briefly—into a tie with Rory.

Having hit a couple of squirrely shots on the front, McIlroy was not scoring as briskly as he had the first two days. His pulled tee ball at the par-three 13th drew a disapproving "Rory, Rory, Rory!" from broadcaster Peter Alliss. Somehow, McIlroy was able to pitch the ball to within six feet, then hole the putt, which turned around his momentum.

J.P., Rory's caddie, later marveled at the calm demeanor his guy showed down the stretch on Saturday. "Usually," AP's Doug Ferguson opined in the R&A's commemorative film of the '14 Open, "you'd expect somebody to collapse…but here you had 'Mr. Rocket Ship' just launch!"

Mr. Rocket Ship's ascent began with holing a twenty-five-footer for birdie on number 14 moments after Fowler had bogeyed up ahead. Rory's stroke restored his two-shot bulge. Within a few minutes, it had grown to three, when Fowler again made bogey.

On the par-five 16th, Rory hit a missile that induced oohs-and-aahs from Alliss. It left Rory with what he later described as "a perfect four-iron." McIlroy proceeded to launch it into the stratosphere; Ferguson called it "vintage Rory." When it finally descended, it was inside twenty-five feet of the flag.

All week, Rory's putting mantra had been "start it over your spot." He said later that as soon as his eagle putt at number 16 hit the spot he had picked out a few feet along its path—the old Dave Stockton dictum—he knew it was good. The gallery exploded, as it would again two holes later when Rory repeated the trick.

Hoylake's closer is a rugged par-five that brings out-of-bounds into play along the right side of the fairway, nearly all the way up to the green, while gorse and other heavy stuff punishes drives pulled left. Again, Mr. Rocket Ship launched a screecher down the middle. He then aimed his second shot at the Ulster Banner flying atop the grandstand, a few feet to the right of the flagstick. His drawn long-iron never left either flag. It landed twenty feet short of the pin and rolled straight at the cup, getting to within eight feet as the crowd thundered. His eagle putt never wavered.

In less than ninety minutes, fueled by two eagles, he'd gone from tied for the tournament lead to six shots ahead!

For all intents and purposes, as Ferguson pointed out, Rory had won the Open Championship on Saturday. As he walked off the 54th green, Rory took off his hat, looked toward the heavens, exhaled, and emitted a huge sigh and smile. He knew if he could keep his head together, he was on the verge of making history.

It's not as if the final round was bereft of suspense. Garcia and Fowler both made runs at Rory, who wobbled at a couple of moments, making back-to-back bogeys at numbers 5 and 6. But he never really looked like he was going to cough up the lead, especially after he got up and down for par from a bunker at number 7. A twelve-foot birdie putt on 9 that snuck into the lower half put Rory back up by three and gave him a comfortable working margin.

Sergio, playing a hole ahead, twice closed to within two strokes—but each time, Rory responded with clutch shots and Garcia fell back. At the par-three 15th, it took Sergio two attempts to extricate himself from a deep greenside bunker, ending his slim chances.

Rickie and Sergio ended up tied for second. It was Fowler's second-consecutive runner-up finish in a major and Garcia's fourth overall.

Moments after tapping in his winning putt on the 72nd green, Rory did his by-now-familiar, waist-high, right-handed fist pump—then took off his Swooshed white cap to acknowledge the cheers, sweeping it from right to left. Even before shaking hands with the officials in his group, he waved his mum onto the green, again using his cap. He had spotted her standing in front of the left-side grandstand, her shoulders heaving.

Rosie has never enjoyed being in the limelight. It took Rory several jabs of the hat—with the crowd egging her on—before she ran onto the green, joining her son for a heartfelt hug. It lasted a while as Rosie's shoulders continued to heave.

Three years earlier, she had given Rory a talking-to in the wake of his struggles at the Masters. Now she was on the outskirts of Liverpool, Belfast's sister city, basking in a moment about which her family had dreamt for years. As the crow flies, it's only 160 miles or so from Lurgan to Liverpool. But at that moment, Rosie McDonald McIlroy was in a different universe.

"This is the first major that my mum has been to that I've won. So mum, this one's for you!" Rory said a few minutes later while cradling the sweetest trophy in sports, the Claret Jug.

McIlroy had seemingly put The Caroline Era—and the three years of angst and clamor that defined it—behind him.

By winning the Open, McIlroy joined Woods and Nicklaus as the only players (at that point) to have won three legs of the career Grand Slam before their twenty-sixth birthdays. The victory also catapulted Mr. Rocket Ship to the top of the 2014 Race to Dubai and lifted him to the second-ranked player in the world.

But the Hoylake storyline that grabbed fans the most was Gerry's Big Wager. His son's win enabled Gerry and three old pals to cash in on the bet they'd made a decade earlier: that Rors would win the Open Championship before turning twenty-six. The long-shot wager generated headlines all over the world and made Gerry McIlroy—already a lionized figure—all the more beloved. Average guys dream of cashing in on a 500-1 flier. Gerry McIlroy, bartender and custodian, had somehow pulled it off!

"If the 'brain dead' episode at Muirfield (in 2013) were the nadir of his career, this was the zenith," Keogh wrote that week. It was "the ultimate dream for a Manchester United fan—a career-defining victory on Liverpool territory."

Indeed, the only off-key moment McIlroy had all week was when he started his Claret Jug acceptance remarks with, "Even as a Man U fan…" Liverpudlians in the crowd lustily booed, causing Rory, Peter Dawson, and the other R&A officials to crack up.

Eyeing the Claret Jug with his name inscribed, McIlroy told the world: "To sit here at twenty-five years of age and win my third major championship and be three-quarters of the way to the career Grand Slam, I never dreamed of being at this point in my career so quickly.... The more I keep looking at this trophy and seeing my name on it, the more it will start sinking in. It feels absolutely incredible."

Almost miraculously, his ex-fiancée Caroline also broke through that Sunday, winning for the first time in 2014 in Istanbul, Turkey. When told the news, Rory grinned; he wished her well, he said.

Rory knew that the pressure on him at the '15 Masters would be immense. A win at Augusta would thrust him into golf's most exclusive club—players who had won all four legs of the professional Grand Slam: Tiger, Jack, Ben Hogan, Gary Player, and Gene Sarazen.

Writers and broadcasters at Hoylake were convinced that golf had entered a new epoch. A reporter asked if Rory had the determination to dominate. "I definitely hope so. I've really found my passion again for golf," he said.

Chapter 19

VALHALLA AND GLENEAGLES

Breaking down Rory's win at Hoylake is relatively simple; sorting out his social life in the summer of '14 is a bit more complicated.

Two days after the Open ended, Belfast photographers snapped images of McIlroy out on a lunch date with twenty-three-year-old model aspirant Sasha Gale, a native of County Antrim, at an eatery along Lisburn Road. A famous athlete out on a mid-day stroll with a wannabe fashion model may have made for mild tabloid fodder, especially in the incestuous world of Northern Ireland, but it wasn't a four-alarm story.

What made it big is what happened next. When pictures of his date with Sasha went viral, Rory placed a contrite phone call to the *other* Irish model he'd been seeing that spring and summer, Dublin's Nadia Forde, who'd apparently been taken aback by the news of Rory's date with Sasha. Somehow, Rory's apologia to Nadia went viral (*Gee, who knew models were looking for publicity?*). Suddenly, the British and Irish press had the story of their dreams: a steamy love triangle—or so it seemed.

Nosy tabloids and social media chatter had linked McIlroy and Forde for months, even before his breakup with Caroline. The *Irish Independent* reported that Nadia and Rory had been seen hanging out together with friends in Dublin pubs and restaurants, allegedly getting cozier as the weeks wore on. Supposed pals of Forde told the papers she wanted friendship, nothing more.

On the Sunday prior to Open Championship week, Forde had flipped her Fiat 500 Abarth sports car in bad weather while driving north from London to visit friends in Manchester. Fortunately, she suffered only minor injuries; still, she was treated for shock for several days at a hospital in Warwickshire. McIlroy reportedly skipped a practice session at Hoylake to visit Forde in the hospital.

A week later, when stories about Rory's luncheon with Sasha began surfacing, Nadia's friends told news outlets she was miffed. "They were getting on great; she thinks [McIlroy] is a really good guy, but then this week it all went a bit pear-shaped," one of Forde's acquaintances told the *Sunday Independent*.

It sparked a media frenzy; paparazzi hounded the two women for weeks. At one point, a gaggle of photographers trailed Forde as she fetched her bag at an airport terminal.

"Nadia feels if they are going to be friends then there has to be respect," that same source told the *Independent*. "Rory apologized to her and seemed upset that he had caused her needless embarrassment."

"[Rory] is like Paul McCartney at the same age," said another chatty source in the saga. "Girls want to spend time with him. It's not that he's the cynical sailor type with a girl [in] every port, he's actually hopelessly romantic." The wannabe Rory Lander couldn't let the reporter go without issuing a stern warning: "Any girl getting ideas of permanence after two or three dates is going to be disappointed."

Wow. That was an awful lot of public melodrama for three young people who claimed to be "just friends." Rory's tabloid life didn't end with the Caroline breakup. In many ways, it got more intense. It even spread across The Pond, where *GOLF Magazine* named him "Playa of the Year."

"Romance," *GOLF's* Josh Sens quipped, "is like golf: Sometimes you just want to play as a single."

The love triangle scuttlebutt soon faded, replaced by conjecture that Sasha and Rory had become an item.

"Rory McIlroy and his new love interest are both back at work—in two very different worlds—after celebrating his Open win together," the *Belfast Telegraph* reported on July 23. Now, a new set of sources were claiming that Rory and Sasha had been seeing one another for more than a month and had, in fact, been together to celebrate Rory's Open win in Hoylake. Those same people were saying that the couple spent three days "partying," sipping adult beverages out of the Claret Jug.

On July 22, McIlroy flew to England to train at an elite fitness academy, while Sasha returned to her regular job as a receptionist at a Volvo dealership in Belfast. Modeling was a side hustle for the former airline hostess who would eventually become a salesperson at the auto shop.

A couple of days later, Rory posted pictures of himself lifting weights, running, and perched in what appeared to be an oxygen tank at the GSK Human Performance Lab outside London. It had become an annual pilgrimage, a chance to test his strength and stamina with fitness professionals eyeing every moment.

As Rory pounded away at the fitness lab, the Sasha story was developing muscles of its own. It was said she and Rory had met at a Belfast party in mid-June. Enterprising research established that her Twitter account had started following Rory on July 1. Described as a "lovely, bubbly girl" who was a "keen bean" for travel, friends said that she and Rory were getting along great, but that modeling and her job in the automobile business—not romance—were her priorities.

In late July, society page writer Frances Burscough filed a sassy piece in the *Belfast Telegraph* about McIlroy's conspicuous dating life. It began, "Blimey, that Rory McIlroy is a fast worker, isn't he? It's only a matter of weeks since he sensationally split from Caroline Wozniacki (just days after their wedding invitations were posted out) and for a while it was clear that he was sticking to his reason, i.e., that he wanted to concentrate on perfecting his golfing game.

"Now, however, after succeeding so spectacularly and clinching his third major title, the Open Championship, he's wasted no time at all in catching up on the dating game, too. Just a few weeks' ago, he was being linked to a young woman called Nadia Forde, a 25-year-old tanned brunette lingerie model and socialite from Dublin.... The pair each denied any romance and by the following day he was out with a different brunette.

"Enter Sasha Gale from Lisburn, another beautiful 20-something brunette and part-time model, who was seen accompanying the golfer to drinks at the Chelsea and lunch at The Albany."

Burscough's piece ended: "Look, as far as we know, he's just a hugely successful world-famous multi-millionaire who can doubtless have his pick and choice of a vast colony of pretty girls the world over. Fair play to him, he's done a lot to get this far and he deserves to have some fun now."

Rory's fair and fun play would continue, unabated, through that summer and into the fall. His interactions with the vast colony would continue to fuel the rumor mill.

McIlroy finished his marketing gigs in London and flew to Akron to prepare for the 16th World Golf Championship-Bridgestone Invitational, the third WGC event held that year. Overhauled in 1960 by Robert Trent Jones Sr., a designer famous (some would say "infamous") for brawny golf courses, Firestone has long been considered one of the beastliest parkland tracks in the United States.

McIlroy's bravura performance in the 2014 WGC-Bridgestone added to his legend. CBS's broadcast crew members were unabashed admirers of Rory's swing and didn't restrain themselves when it came to gushing over his ball-striking. As the weekend progressed, they kept spotlighting how he was hitting the ball into Firestone precincts rarely visited even by the longest of sluggers. On more than one occasion, Rory drove the ball past the crosswalks where fans were trudging across the fairway. On Saturday, it looked like one woman did the hokey-pokey as Rory's tee ball bounded past her.

Rory picked up where he left off at Hoylake, shooting a 69 and a 64 the first two rounds. Remarkably, though, he trailed Sergio Garcia by four shots. Sergio had tied the course record on Friday with a career-best 61, a scary-good score at Firestone.

In Saturday's third round, Rory shot a 66 after he birdied the final two holes for the second successive day, eliciting hoots from Jim Nance and Nick Faldo, who'd stayed on the air well into the evening after a thunderstorm disrupted play. Yet McIlroy only shaved one shot off Garcia's lead.

To overtake Sergio, who was playing some of the best golf of his life, Rory would need a strong start on Sunday afternoon. He came out firing, birdieing the first three holes, then knocking a long-iron inside seven feet on the par-three fifth—and rolled that putt in, too. It only took him an hour to surpass Sergio, who'd finally come back to earth.

It was around the turn, after McIlroy had grabbed a two-stroke lead, that the CBS choir started singing worshipful hymns. As Rory launched his drive at number 9, Nance blurted: "Seriously, David: who drives it better than that?!" Feherty, who was standing next to Rory and Sergio on the tee box, was emoting, "Just towering, high, majestic!" As it fell to earth, Faldo jumped in with, "In the middle of the diamond, again!" It finally stopped 345 yards down the fairway.

On number 14 tee, it was Baker-Finch's turn to be gob-smacked as he reviewed the replay of Rory's drive. "It's just amazing, a full coil back and a complete uncoil through! It's absolutely perfect!" That one went 330 yards.

On the final hole, hitting into the wind, Rory again gave his tee ball the full treatment. "He just 'wellied' it!" Faldo enthused, invoking British slang that apparently pays tribute to the Duke of Wellington, vanquisher of Napoleon.

As Rory's body language on number 18 was coaxing the ball left, Nance observed that it must be heading right. But after a couple of hops it glanced off the first cut of rough and kicked back left. Perfect, again. But this time, his "wellie" job only went 328 yards!

Rory's second consecutive 66 again relegated Sergio to runner-up. It wasn't just McIlroy's driving exhibition that week, which McGinley on Sky Sports called the best he'd ever seen. It was McIlroy's clutch putting that made the difference. Rory holed four tough putts on the backside—an eight-footer for birdie on the 11th regained the lead from Sergio, and three putts inside six feet on the 13th, 14th, and 15th clinched the tournament when Garcia made a bad bogey at the par-three 16th.

Suddenly, Rory was the world's number-one golfer again, the first time he'd recaptured the position since the week after he stalked off PGA National in 2013, claiming a toothache.

"I'm just really pleased to get my first World Golf Championship so soon after winning the Open," Rory said to the press. "Hopefully I'll go to Valhalla [the PGA Championship] in good form and try to get three in a row."

Keogh wasn't the only correspondent to note that Rory had a glint in his eye at Firestone, a "steely look of determination" that meant trouble for his opponents. At least in the summer of 2014, Rory possessed what writer John Updike famously saw in baseball slugger Ted Williams: "He radiated, from afar, the hard blue glow of high purpose."

Rory's hard glow got bluer the following week in the Bluegrass State. In Norse mythology, Valhalla was the mythical place where Viking warriors slain in battle were admitted into the afterlife. Norsemen believed that Valhalla offered their martyred brethren decadent feasts and pleasures of the flesh for perpetuity.

Not all golf architecture mavens considered the twenty-five-year-old Nicklaus design to be divinely inspired. When Valhalla first surfaced as a major championship venue, Brad Klein wrote in *Sports Illustrated* that it "seems to have been conjured from thin air and plopped into prime time. Purportedly stern enough to stand up to the world's best players, Valhalla has never been tested by so much as a Kentucky State Amateur. It is a course without a past. All it seems to have is a brilliant future."

Valhalla's celebrity was attributable to the fact that, back then, the PGA of America owned a big chunk of it and stood to double up on profits.

Given the big names involved down the stretch—McIlroy, Mickelson, Fowler, and Stenson, the 96th PGA Championship made no small amount of revenue for CBS and the PGA of America. Plus, because of rain delays, it bumped into primetime TV: Sunday's final round didn't finish until well past eight o'clock Eastern Daylight Time, with Rory's clinching putt going down in virtual darkness.

In some ways, it's a shame that Mickelson and McIlroy didn't go mano a mano on Sunday. It's true that Mickelson only ended up a stroke back and led for a while in mid-round when Rory faltered with a couple of early bogeys. But Rory was playing in the final group; Mickelson and Rickie Fowler were a group ahead of McIlroy and his playing partner, Bernd Wiesberger, an Austrian journeyman enjoying the golfing moment of his life.

Not only was Rory's shot-making and putting other-worldly, so was his course management. And not just on Sunday but throughout the week. It helped him pull off the first three-in-a-row winning streak on the PGA Tour since Tiger in his salad days.

Having regained the number one spot, McIlroy comported himself like the best player in the world—at least through the first fifty-eight holes. On Thursday, he overcame an early double-bogey to shoot 66.

On Friday, juiced by an eagle on the par-five seventh, McIlroy shot the first of two consecutive 67s to grab the tournament lead.

He was again driving the ball prodigious distances, with the CBS gang breathlessly reporting the yardages like archaeologists hollering "Eureka!" over relics unearthed inside a dig.

More importantly, Rory was keeping the ball in front of him and, it appeared, not taking undue risks. For the first three days, birdies seemed to flow effortlessly off his putter blade. He ended the third round one shot ahead of Fowler and four up on Mickelson.

But that wasn't the case early Sunday afternoon. Two early bogeys, including Rory's old bugaboo, a pulled putt from six feet at number 6, suddenly put Fowler in the lead, with Mickelson, who was on a heater with four birdies on the frontside, now surging near the top, too. Henrik Stenson blitzed the outward nine with one more birdie than Mickelson and also briefly passed McIlroy.

A lengthy thunderstorm delay didn't make things any easier.

McIlroy's three foes were so hot that, by the turn, Rory had fallen three shots in arrears; it looked like his winning streak had come to an end. But on the 10th hole, an uphill par-five, Rory hit one of the most celebrated shots of his career: a thinned, 283-yard three-wood that moved left-to-right, landing in front of the green and thrumming two-thirds of the way through the putting surface. It finally settled almost exactly hole-high, inside eight feet of the cup.

CBS had a blimp shot replay of McIlroy's shot. From that perspective, viewers could not tell how low and hot the ball had been struck. All that fans could see at home was the ball skimming up the hill and, seemingly on command, stopping in the shadow of the flagstick.

But in real time, Faldo correctly deduced that Rory had "necked it"; with the ball still shrieking up the fairway, Sir Nick gave it his full doom-awaits prophecy. By the time the ball had struck the apron, however, Faldo was whistling a different tune. He and Nance immediately recognized that the ball was going to "get close, *very* close!" as Nance put it.

Rory's eagle putt tumbled into the middle. Suddenly, he was only one shot back. First Stenson, then Fowler, ran into bogey trouble on number 14. Mickelson did the same at 16.

McIlroy responded to the opening like a champ. At number 13, a short dogleg-right par-four guarded by a rocky gorge, his long-iron tee ball was nicely positioned down the right side of the fairway. His wedge spun to within eight feet. His birdie putt never left the center of the cup.

Rory's driver continued to stay warm but one backside putt after another grazed the lip, refusing to drop. With darkness beginning to envelop the course, he won the tournament on the 17th hole, a longish uphill par-four. He hit one of his few poor drives of the week, a push that found the right-side fairway bunker. But his short-iron out of the sand had that crisp *fffzzz* sound. Rory knew right away that he'd hit it on the button. He raced out of the bunker to get a better look. It came down soft, sticking inside twelve feet.

The putt was a left-to-righter, slightly downhill. For a moment, it looked like it might not have enough *oomph*. But it trickled into the cup.

By now, it had become seriously dark. With a two-shot lead, McIlroy faced the specter of having to return on Monday morning to finish the par-five 72nd hole. Rory asked officials if he and Bernd could be allowed to tee off before Fowler and Mickelson cleared the fairway. Rickie magnanimously agreed—a suggestion that was perhaps *too* magnanimous for Mickelson's taste, if his grimace and pained body language were any indication. Lefty, two shots back, chafed after officials signaled to Rory and Berndt to tee off.

Curiously, Rory chose to hit driver instead of a safer three-wood; much like number 17, he pushed his tee ball to the right. But this time, instead of a sand trap, a huge pond protected the right side of the fairway.

On TV, McIlroy's ball disappeared down the slope toward the hazard, causing hearts to palpitate from Dingle to Derry, where it was past one o'clock in the morning. But Rory was lucky; his ball stopped a yard short of the red line. Had conditions been dryer, Nance and Faldo quickly pointed out, Rory's ball may have slithered into the drink.

McIlroy had a wide-open shot to play it safe and put his ball into the middle of the fairway of the par-five. Naturally, he bit off too much and hit the ball into a greenside bunker, adding another layer of drama.

A minute early, from just off the edge of the green, Mickelson's chip had nearly clipped the hole for an eagle; Rickie's long putt missed, too. Even with Lefty making birdie, Rory had a cushion.

He blasted out of the bunker to twenty-five feet or so from the pin, then hit a perfect lag through the twilight gloom inside a foot. McIlroy trailed by three shots at the turn but had come home in a blistering 32.

This time, Rory's victory gesture—the quiet, repeated right-hand fist pump—was augmented by a big roundhouse right thrust downward. It all happened in near-pitch darkness, with television lights and bright photo flashes lending a spooky feel to the proceedings.

His win enabled Rory to become the first player since Pádraig Harrington in 2008 to win consecutive majors.

"To win my second major this year and my fourth at the age of twenty-five, I can't describe the feeling right now, it's been incredible," McIlroy told the press. He also chortled while discussing his eagle at number 10.

"The ball flight was probably around thirty feet lower than I intended. And the line of the shot was probably around fifteen yards left of where I intended. It was lucky, it really was. You need a little bit of luck in major championships to win," he said.

Keogh called Rory's performance at Valhalla "a display of guts and steel that was a joy to behold for everyone bar his victims."

Rory understood that Valhalla was a lot different than his wins at Congressional, Kiawah, and Hoylake. "To win it in this fashion and this style, it means a lot. It means that I know that I can do it. I know that I can come from behind. I know that I can mix it up with the best players in the world down the stretch in a major and come out on top."

Ryder Cup captain McGinley, three weeks away from leading the Euros against the Americans at Gleneagles, saluted McIlroy's "single mindedness" as the biggest differentiator in his summer-of-'14 dominance.

"You don't see it when you speak to him one-on-one," McGinley told Keogh. "But when you watch him play on TV, you see the focus, you see his eyes, you see how he hones in on a shot that he knows is important and that he can pull it off…Rory should bottle it because it's the secret."

Talk to any veteran correspondent and they'll tell you as they clinked glasses that night filled with Kentucky bourbon that they were convinced Rory would end up with double-digit majors—maybe even take a run at Tiger's then-fourteen or Jack's eighteen. Hell, Nicklaus himself predicted that Rory would end up with more than a dozen.

How Rory wishes he could have bottled the hard blue glow he emitted that summer and fall of 2014. Whatever it may have been, he's never quite gotten it back.

After hoisting the Wanamaker Trophy, it took McIlroy a couple hours' worth of interviews and photo ops before he and his posse were able to go wheels-up at what is now called Louisville Muhammad Ali International Airport. It was pushing midnight; they were headed to the "city that never sleeps" for a little R&R.

Once his private jet got airborne, Rory took a celebratory selfie. He was sitting in the foreground center, with members of his inner circle arrayed behind him, a couple with beers in hand. It had been a long day. No doubt everyone was knackered. But they were all grinning ear-to-ear.

"Flying high with the team after my 4th major victory!!!" McIlroy tweeted. "NYC here we come!! Thanks for all the support and well wishes."

The traveling Mac Pack consisted of Gerry McIlroy, Michael Bannon, J.P. Fitzgerald, Sean O'Flaherty, Harry Diamond, Ricky McCormick, and Mitchell Tweedie: respectively, Rory's dad, coach, caddie, tour manager, future caddie and best man, and two old buds and business partners. It was the all-Irish "entourage," Keogh wrote that week, "that's been with him through thick and thin."

The roller-coaster ride of the last three months alone would have tested the mettle of any organization. Eighty-three days separated Rory's breakup with Caroline from his triumphant trophy ceremony in Louisville. In between, he had won four mammoth tournaments, including two majors, and become the face of golf, unquestionably its best player, the "next Tiger."

Shepherding McIlroy from place to place, generating new revenue streams, choosing smart things to do with his time and money, and helping build his philanthropic foundation were now bigger and more ambitious tasks. Winning back-to-back majors had catapulted Rory into a different realm. More than ever, Rory Land could pick and choose the corporate brands, events, and appearances that, combined, would project the larger brand of Rory McIlroy.

"They are the people that I confide in and the people that I can tell everything to, and it's great to have a solid bunch of people like that around you that you can rely on," McIlroy said that summer. "Obviously there's a lot of people around me who keep me on an even keel. My mum and dad are obviously the two biggest influences on my life and I've got a great bunch of friends from home and I've got a great team around me."

The managing director of Rory, Inc., from its outset in September 2013, once McIlroy terminated his Horizon relationship, was veteran Dublin businessman Donal Casey, an actuary by trade. Casey had worked his way up to CEO of Irish Life Corporate Business and, eventually, co-managing director of Aon Hewitt Ireland. He was consulting for Horizon, helping to cement some of its big deals for McIlroy, when Rory—with Casey and O'Flaherty's assistance—cashiered Conor Ridge and company.

Casey stayed a decade as Rory, Inc.'s top exec, taking the company to record levels of revenue growth and profitability. One perceptive observer of Rory Land that I interviewed called Casey a "very sharp business strategist" who was the clear "brains of Rory's operation."

Donal Casey resigned, without much explanation, in August 2023. He was replaced by Sean O'Flaherty, who'd come a long way from the guy Horizon assigned as Rory's touring aide in 2011.

Rory, Inc.'s, original directors were Rory, McIlroy Sr., Casey, and longtime Irish businessman and McIlroy family friend Barry Funston (who was later switched to director of the Rory Foundation). In 2017, O'Flaherty was elevated to director.

Once Casey left six years later, two other Irish businessmen and McIlroy intimates were added to the board: Peter Crowley and Neill Hughes, the co-founders of FL Partners, a Dublin-based investment boutique. FL Partners had been a McIlroy sponsor since he turned pro in 2007.

It's instructive that Rory has chosen not to reach beyond the all-white-male Dublin-Belfast axis to populate his board of directors. Given his cross-sports, cross-border, cross-gender appeal, it would stand to reason that he'd want his board to be more diverse and reflect knowledge of other business sectors, cultures, and markets.

But to date, Rory has elected to keep his board insular, all-Irish and all inner-circle.

Rory Land hit NYC hard for twenty-four hours. Then they (or at least Rory) flew to the UK.

Manchester United, Rory's Premier League favorite, wanted to honor Rory at halftime of a match at Old Trafford, hallowed home of the Red Devils. Rory took in Man U's 2-1 "friendly" win over Valencia, partied that night with a few of the Man U guys, then flew back to New York to do a photo shoot with Tiger.

Globetrotting Rory must have been pooped, but he chose to play in the '14 FedEx Cup playoffs. The first leg of the playoffs that year, the Barclays, was held the following week across the Hudson River in northern New Jersey, at the Ridgewood Country Club, a 1929 A.W. Tillinghast gem.

It was the summer of the ALS Ice Bucket Challenge, where celebrities and ordinary folks kept nominating people online to contribute toward finding a cure for Lou Gehrig's disease by having a bucket of ice dumped on their heads.

Rory, apparently an admirer of the TV show *Suits*, nominated actress Meghan Markle. The ingenue, whom he'd never met, agreed on two conditions. The first was that Rory personally do the ice pouring; the second was that she would have a chance on camera to make an appeal for enhanced ALS research funding.

Ms. Markle happened to be in NYC on Wednesday of Barclay's week, visiting a friend in Manhattan. A photo opportunity, not an alien concept to the publicity-conscious Markle, was arranged on the rooftop of the friend's midtown apartment.

A cooler full of ice and a step stool were procured for the big moment. Up climbed Rory and down went the ice over the squealing Ms. Markle's head, neck, and peasant blouse. What emerged was not dissimilar to a wet T-shirt contest, not an entirely unpleasant image for male fans of her TV series. Years later, *Suits* enjoyed a second life after Markle married into the British royal family; it became a big hit on Netflix.

Presumably once she toweled off and changed, Meghan and Rory went out for drinks at the Fitzpatrick Manhattan Hotel at Fifty-Seventh and Lexington, where McIlroy was staying for the week. There they bumped into owner John Fitzpatrick, a fifty-four-year-old Dubliner whose family has long owned and managed exclusive hotel properties on both sides of the Atlantic. As chair of the Irish-American Fund, Fitzpatrick was an outspoken advocate of reconciliation between Northern Ireland and the Republic. An intimate of Bill and Hillary Clinton, he was a big player in New York's political, philanthropic, and social scenes.

Fitzpatrick invited the couple to join him and some twenty friends for dinner at Cipriani's Downtown, a four-star Italian restaurant in Soho known for its voluminous wine list. It made for a fun—and long—evening. The next morning was round one at Ridgewood, thirty miles west. Royal family historian Tom Bower, author of *Revenge: Meghan, Harry and the War Between the Windsors*, writes that Rory showed up in Bergen County "worse for wear after a hectic night."

McIlroy played like a guy nursing a hangover, shooting a three-over 74 on a day when most of the field, including eventual winner Hunter Mahan, went low. "[Rory's] performance suffered," Bower drolly observed. Citing sources close to Markle, Bower claims that Rory saw Meghan again on Thursday evening. "I wasn't quite on my game," Rory conceded later. "I was enjoying myself."

On Friday, the party boy snapped out of his funk to shoot a 65 and get back into the tournament, sort of.

Ms. Markle in that period had a serious boyfriend in Toronto (where *Suits* was filmed), a celebrity chef named Cory Vitiello. Chef Vitiello was said to be less than enthralled with his girlfriend's budding friendship with McIlroy, especially after Markle waxed lyrical about Rory on her blog.

"Ah yes," she wrote. "Rory McIlroy. THE Rory McIlroy. Whispered (and shouted) to be the foremost golfer in the world, loved by Tiger, respected by Palmer, and dumper of frigid water on to my lone head for the ALS Ice Bucket Challenge. *That* Rory McIlroy.

"He is a force who has the propensity to actually work hard and play hard—relishing intense practices to substantiate his title, embracing nights of sipping Opus One (his bold and impressive choice of wine),[1] and indulging in group dinners at Cipriani—for the balance, of course.

"And yet, beyond his work/play ethic, the most endearing quality of this man is his character—as real and honest as they come, appreciating a simple smile, never shunning a fan photo, enjoying a plate of pasta with veal ragù, and expressing a love for his parents that is rarely seen in men his age. Or at any age, to be honest. He is not just the real deal…he is real. And perhaps that is what makes him even more cherished."

Whoa! Bower claims that Vitiello twice confronted Markle, asking her if she'd had an assignation with her "cherished" friend. Both times she answered "no."

Bower also wrote that Markle was "keen" to exploit her relationship with Rory. "She encouraged the media to publish photographs of McIlroy and herself. As she would later admit, she 'occasionally set up a paparazzi photo or let info slip out to the press.'"

Two months later, Markle was able to arrange a speaking opportunity for herself at the One Young World conference in Dublin, a favorite Fitzpatrick philanthropy to which she had lent her support. On Friday evening, October 17, Rory joined her for dinner at the "swanky" (in Bower's words) Fade Street Social Restaurant in Dublin's Temple Bar District. Irish society page columnist Alexandra Ryan reported that the couple looked "smitten," with Meghan allegedly gazing intently at Rory through the course of the evening. Bower cites Fitzpatrick in suggesting that it wasn't the only time Markle and McIlroy saw one another in Dublin that week.

In contrast with his social life, McIlroy's other late summer 2014 FedEx Cup performances were humdrum. At TPC-Boston, Rory disappointed the Irish-Americans in attendance by finishing tied for fifth, four strokes back of winner Chris Kirk. At Cherry Hills

---

1   Today, Opus One sells for $400-plus a bottle.

in Denver—sacred golfing ground since it was the site of Arnold Palmer's only US Open victory—McIlroy had not one but two weekend four-putts on the par-three 12th hole, finishing tied for eighth, behind winner Billy Horschel.

The next week's PGA Tour season-ender was the first one in more than two decades that did not include Phil Mickelson or Tiger Woods. Commentators wondered aloud if this would be the week that Rory would put a firm stamp on his quest to become *the* successor to Tiger and Phil.

For a while, McIlroy followed the script. After an opening 69, his Friday 65 stifled Freaky Friday talk. His Saturday 67 put him in Sunday's final group with his old Walker Cup antagonist Horschel.

Rory was no doubt looking for a reprise of his final singles-match dusting of Billy at County Down in '07. But their last-round duel in Atlanta looked more like the team matches in Newcastle, when Billy got the better of him.

A double-bogey at number 5 put Rory behind the eight ball. A dubious decision to go for a low-percentage shot at number 9 gave critics of Rory's course management plenty of ammunition. After he hit a wild hook off the tee, TV microphones picked up J.P. urging Rory to play it safe from a tough lie next to an out-of-bound fence.

"Nah," Rory jabbed back. "I'm just going to have a go and see where it ends up."

It ended up okay—Rory was able to salvage a bogey—but it would cause renewed head-scratching from golf's graybeards about McIlroy's impetuosity. How could such a gifted player riding the hottest streak of his career continually engage in self-destructive behavior?

A decade later, they're still asking the same question, as McIlroy so often sideswipes promising rounds with low-percentage shots.

A late flurry of three birdies enabled Rory to tie Jim Furyk for second in Atlanta. Still, he finished three shots short of Horschel, who enjoyed one of the greatest moments in his professional career. McIlroy ended up finishing third in the FedEx chase, winning a cool couple of million on top of his $8 million-plus on-course earnings that year.

From the Euros' perspective, the 2014 Ryder Cup lacked the histrionics of the '12 affair at Medinah. Rory didn't "oversleep" or leave Paul McGinley, his captain, wondering where the hell he was.

Almost all the soap-opera recriminations at Gleneagles came from the American side, where Phil Mickelson, in the wake of yet another flat performance by the US squad, led an uprising against captain Tom Watson. Lobbing verbal grenades at the American with the fourth-most major championships in history gave Lefty something to dwell on besides the FBI investigation of his gambling jones, which had gone public in the weeks leading up to the Cup. Euro fans endlessly razzed Mickelson about his reckless habits.

About the only suspense for the Euros pre-match was a minor disturbance between Graeme McDowell and Rory. It wasn't personal animus so much as G-Mac's belief that Wee Mac hit the ball so damn far off the tee that, at times, it made him a tough partner.

McDowell argued that it was rough being Rory's junior partner. "You know, he's standing there beating it 350 yards down the middle, and I put my tee in the ground thinking there's not really a lot of point in me hitting this tee shot and find myself throwing myself at it, and literally, it didn't help my game much at Medinah." Still, G-Mac said he wanted to be Rory's partner, having gotten used to the asymmetry in McIlroy's game.

McIlroy's takedown of Rickie Fowler in the Sunday singles match was so thorough—Rory won four of the first five holes outright, leaving Rickie looking bewildered—that it's easy to conclude McIlroy was at his Hoylake best in Scotland. In truth, Rory's play on the decade-old, Nicklaus-designed PGA Centenary Course was only so-so in the team matches.

McGinley, reading the tea leaves, kept the Macs separated, sending out Rory and Sergio Garcia in the anchor morning fourballs match. The two erstwhile teen-dreams came off the 18th green spitting mad when Keegan Bradley, partnered with Gamblin' Phil, made clutch back-to-back shots on the final two holes to win, one-up. Watson's men led—temporarily, it turned out—2½-1½.

The Spanish-Irish duo only clicked marginally better in the afternoon foursome match, when they halved their match against Jimmy Walker and Rickie Fowler. The Euros won the other three matches Friday afternoon to seize a 5-3 edge overall—a lead they never handed back.

Saturday morning, Rory again achieved a half in his fourball duel, this time partnered in the anchor position with Medinah hero Ian Poulter against Walker and Fowler. The Americans were able to win two matches outright on Saturday morning, to draw within a single point, 6½-5½. They got no closer.

Rory finally won a match on Saturday, when he and Sergio combined to drub Jim Furyk and Hunter Mahan, 3 and 2. Overall, the Euros stomped the Americans in the afternoon foursomes, fueled by the Ryder Cup-record *ten straight birdies* from the Justin Rose-Henrik Stenson partnership. The Euros took a 10-6 lead into the Sunday singles—exactly the score by which they trailed two years earlier, when Deputy Chief Pat Rollins pulled off the Real Miracle at Medinah.

Sunday's singles matches were anticlimactic, since the Americans never really threatened to overtake the Euros. Rory's manhandling of Fowler in Sunday's third match presaged a beatdown, with Martin Kaymer and Jamie Donaldson also thrashing their US opponents. In sum, the Euros won five Sunday singles matches, halved two others, and won the Cup going away, 16½-11½.

It all led, inexorably, to Mickelson's post-match pouting in the press center, where he blamed the poor US showing on Captain Watson—with the eight-time major winner sitting a few feet away. The Americans had now lost three Ryder Cups in a row and six of the last seven. The Euros seemed to have the secret sauce. And one of its key ingredients was Wee Mac, the cocksure lad from County Down, now once again the best player in the world.

Chapter 20

COURTROOMS AND COURTING

Two thousand fourteen was McIlroy's third Ryder Cup. He hadn't exactly kicked ass in any of them, but he'd had his moments and been part of three winning teams. At Gleneagles, he avoided self-inflicted controversy.

Still, he again managed to stir attention in the global tabloids. An unexpected addition to his entourage that week stimulated media interest when she began posting photographs of herself with Rosie and Gerry McIlroy and other Rory Landers.

"Golf is my girlfriend at the moment," McIlroy had assured the press before the event started, perhaps disappointing a certain Volvo dealership employee across the Irish Sea. But before long, online chatter was suggesting that he was dating his third brunette fashion model of the season, a South African actress, corporate brand ambassadress, and TV spokesperson of Indian descent named Shashi Naidoo.

When reached by reporters, Ms. Naidoo, a thirty-three-year-old divorcée, denied being in a romantic relationship with McIlroy "or any golfer, for that matter," which made for a curious denial. Although she had never previously evinced much interest in the Ryder Cup, the South African claimed she was in Scotland to lend her support to the European squad—not for a dalliance with Rory.

Still, while at Gleneagles, she seemed to spend a lot of time in the company of Rory Landers. She posted pictures of herself driving Rosie around in a golf cart and enjoying light moments with Gerry, Sean O'Flaherty, and the rest of the Mac Pack. It's also telling that she removed those postings from her social media after a few days. They had served their purpose.

It's not known if Rory called Nadia or Sasha to give them a heads-up that the tattle pages would again be tattling. It appears that none of these relationships survived beyond the late summer and fall of '14.

Only one thing is certain: for a guy supposedly tired of living life in the glare of the klieg lights and gossip rags, it was peculiar behavior. You needed a scorecard to keep track of it all.

You also needed a scorecard to keep track of McIlroy's legal maneuverings that fall and winter. His eighteen-month odyssey to extricate himself from his contractual commitment to Horizon Sports Management was—finally—reaching a head. The Irish media couldn't get enough of the sensational charges and counter charges that each side was hurling against the other. Dublin's white-shoe legal community couldn't get enough of it, either; the fight was costing Horizon and Rory, Inc., a fortune in barrister fees.

Since Horizon had declined McIlroy's settlement offer—said to have started around £5 million and upped to £10 million by the turn of the year—the trial in Ireland's high court at the hoary Four Courts building in Dublin was set to begin in February 2015. It was already considered among the costliest legal actions in Irish corporate history. If the trial were to last six to eight weeks, as experts claimed, attorney costs would go through the roof, in the neighborhood of €100,000 *per day*, the *Irish Times* reported. No wonder the Four Courts' nickname was the "Four Goldmines"!

The issues and legal precedents animating the proceedings were far from clear-cut, which is why they kept a battery of lawyers and litigation consultants pounding away for a year and a half.

Had the twenty-two-year-old Rory McIlroy in December of '11 really been coerced into signing an agreement he didn't understand? Had Horizon been deliberately disingenuous in identifying the size of the fees they would pocket in negotiating deals on McIlroy's behalf?

Rory shows up at the February 2015 trial proceedings in Dublin where he was seeking to cashier his second management firm.

Had Rory Landers colluded to impugn Horizon's integrity and undermine its capacity to conduct business? Four onetime Horizon employees and consultants had jumped ship to Rory, Inc., including its managing director, Donal Casey, who as a Horizon consultant had helped wire the Nike and Omega deals, among others. Casey had also helped iron out an amicable settlement with sunglass and apparel maker Oakley when the longtime Rory sponsor sued, claiming that its "right of first refusal" had been violated by the Nike deal.

Ridge's people were demanding to know what other potentially proprietary information was now being shared with Rory and Gerry McIlroy. There were thousands of documents that the litigants were forced to disclose, some of which became public, incensing one side or the other.

An early 2013 email (written fifteen months *before* the Caroline breakup), sent by Conor Ridge to his Horizon deputy Colin Morrissey, revealed that Wozniacki (the note referred to her, a bit disdainfully, as "Woz") may have been behind Rory's opposition toward making a contribution to UNICEF. It was Caroline's belief, the email said, that donations to large nongovernmental organizations like UNICEF often went wasted; she apparently preferred to give money to smaller and leaner philanthropies.

Moreover, Ridge wrote that Woz wanted to combine her charity-giving with Rory's to generate a bigger impact. Before Rory broke things off, it appears that she envisioned a joint Caro-Rors foundation and was agitated that Horizon had insinuated itself in what she viewed as private decision-making.

Whatever the reason, Rory was peeved that Horizon made a $166,000 contribution to UNICEF in his foundation's name without clearing it with him. It wasn't the money, his people said in court documents; it was the principle.

As the weeks wore on, the sniping became more personal and vindictive. Horizon's side asserted that technophile O'Flaherty, their former employee, had spearheaded an effort to destroy incriminating Rory Land emails and text messages. Allegedly at O'Flaherty's direction, McIlroy and his people had wiped laptops clean and at one point reverted their cellphones to "factory settings"—all in an effort to throw a wrench into the discovery phase, Horizon claimed.

The cellphone, et al., issue became less potent in late '14 when the judge issued a ruling in favor of Rory and his lieutenants: McIlroy's people did *not* have to hand over their devices.

This procedural "win" failed to whet Rory's appetite for legal combat. He clearly wanted to avoid a drawn-out trial. His attorneys informed Rory that he would have to take the witness stand, most likely for multiple days—perhaps as long as two weeks!

The Horizon side knew that Rory was loath to testify. They also knew that in the wake of the Caroline breakup, he did not want to subject himself to further brand-chafing scrutiny. Finally, they knew that Rory didn't want to discuss certain items—with all their pocketbook repercussions—under oath.

Horizon knew his £10 million offer was malleable. The closer they got to Rory testifying, the greater the chance he'd up the ante.

Rory attended several hours of the first day of (largely administrative) proceedings, sitting on a back bench while wearing thick glasses, perhaps to make himself look older and more studious.

Sure enough, on February 3, 2015, day two of the trial, both sides asked the judge to grant them more time to broker a settlement. The two parties were up most of that night and into the next morning. As street sweepers moved through Dublin's City Centre, an agreement was finally hammered out.

A terse joint statement was issued on February 4. All it said was that the matter "had been settled to the satisfaction of both parties, who wished each other well for the future." It also stipulated that the litigants would be making no further comment. A nondisclosure provision swore all parties to secrecy and to avoid demeaning one another. A decade later, that confidentiality pact has stayed intact.

Little has surfaced about the settlement, beyond suggestions that it cost McIlroy roughly $20 million in a payout to his former agency. It also cost him at least $5 million, possibly double that, in legal fees.

Ouch. It was a hell of a price to pay, but McIlroy now had full control over his own business operations—and the autonomy to pursue commercial and investment opportunities as he saw fit. He was his own agency now; there'd be no more hefty fees going out the door. Rory had also learned a painful lesson about the consequences of signing a contract that hadn't been fully vetted.

His 2011 Horizon deal would be the last agreement he ever initialed at a holiday party.

McIlroy continued to play superb golf on both circuits through the fall and winter of 2014–'15. He kept on finishing at or near the top.

At the Omega Dubai Desert Classic in January, Rory blitzed the field to win his second gigantic coffee-pot. A 66-64-66 start ensured that McIlroy's final round would be a casual stroll through the Al Badayer desert. A Sunday two-under 70 gave him a three-shot win over Swede Alex Noren. It ultimately set up what became his third Race to Dubai trophy eleven months later.

The 2015 Masters was something of a mixed bag for McIlroy. He shot four rounds under par, but never put a scare into the twenty-one-year-old Jordan Spieth, who built an insurmountable lead thrashing Augusta National the way Rory had thrashed the Majlis Course in Dubai three months earlier. McIlroy's weekend 68-66 at Augusta pulled him into a tie for fourth.

Still, he was never really in contention. Indeed, through 2024 and sixteen career appearances at the Masters, McIlroy has never come down the stretch on a Sunday afternoon with a realistic chance to win.

The WGC World Match Play that spring was held at Harding Park, a treasured public course not far from the Golden Gate in San Francisco. Rory, the number-one seed, advanced past his first three opponents, then drubbed Japan's Hideki Matsuyama, 6 and 5. Things got tighter in the quarters, when he had to bounce back from an early deficit to get past Brit Paul Casey on the 22nd hole.

In the semifinals, it looked like Jim Furyk had McIlroy's number as Rory's driver went balky late in the round. Furyk had a one-up lead on the par-four 16th when Rory pushed another wayward tee ball. But he managed to slip his wedge from heavy rough onto the green hole-high, matching Furyk's birdie. On the long par-three 17th, Rory's iron was expertly drawn inside six feet of the cup, while Furyk's ran to the right fringe.

When Rory's birdie putt dropped and Furyk's missed, the match was suddenly all square heading into the par-five 18th. Another pushed drive by McIlroy appeared to give Furyk the advantage. But Rory's long-iron out of thick rough found the left-front of the green, forty-five feet or so away from the cup. Furyk, meanwhile, hooked his fairway wood into the rough short of the green. Furyk's third-shot wedge ran well past the flag.

Rory stunned onlookers by holing his eagle putt, which crashed into the hole. His dramatic one-up victory over Furyk put him in the finals that afternoon against Gary Woodland, which Rory won going away, 4 and 2.

It was his second WGC victory in eight months, solidifying his position as the planet's top-ranked golfer. The win in San Francisco was not unlike his victory at Valhalla. When he needed to kick things up a notch, he did. He was perched atop the golfing world—and it seemed almost effortless.

He was still radiating that hard blue glow.

―――――

Oddsmakers liked his chances at the 115th US Open, which was held in the most improbable of places, an eight-year-old course built on a rehabilitated garbage dump off Puget Sound. The USGA was insistent on holding its national championship in the long-ignored Pacific Northwest. It also wanted to reward municipal decision-makers for their foresight in reclaiming an old waste site and making it a world-class—well, at least a *future* world-class—public golfing venue.

Chambers Bay, alas, was almost universally panned. The Robert Trent Jones Jr. layout wasn't ready for a Washington state am, let alone a US Open. Players deplored the combination fescue/poa annua greens, which were compared to horror shows, sand pits, and in one unforgettable metaphor, to the tops of cruciferous vegetables. Dave Sheinin of the *Washington Post* called the faux links of Chambers Bay a "moonscape monstrosity."

Still, the patchy course produced a memorable finish when Dustin Johnson managed to three-putt the 72nd hole from just outside twelve feet, handing a second consecutive major to Jordan Spieth, whose flatstick was so hot back then that he could hole putts on any surface, including cauliflower heads.

Rory's assessment wasn't as barbed as some of his colleagues, but he did allow that it would be okay if the USGA didn't come back to Chambers Bay for another couple of decades. McIlroy played only *meh* the first three days. On Sunday morning, he was eight shots back.

In the middle of his final round, however, he got smoking hot, a la Johnny Miller at Oakmont in 1973. McIlroy birdied holes 7, 8, 10, 12, and 13. Suddenly, he was two-under and on the verge of throwing a scare into the leaders. But his Big Mo petered out when he bogeyed 15 and 17.

Despite the late miscues, he was delighted with his ball-striking for the week. It was his putting that let him down, he said. He ended up tied for ninth.

His game was nicely coming around as the 144th Open Championship loomed in mid-July. Per usual, he went home to Northern Ireland early that month, planning to play a couple of links courses with his old man to get ready for St. Andrews—the place where five years earlier he'd been battered by a second-round 80 in high winds.

On Saturday, July 4, less than two weeks before the start of the Open, McIlroy got together with his buds for a soccer "kickabout"—something they'd done a hundred times since they were kids. This time, they decided to take the A2 a few miles north to play in Bangor.

A few minutes into the action, running unmolested, McIlroy's left cleat apparently got caught in the turf. He twisted his ankle so severely that he tore his left anterior talofibular ligament. It wasn't a tweak or a sprain; it was a rupture.

Within a couple of days, McIlroy made it official: he was out of the Open. He posted a picture of himself standing on crutches, sporting a big boot and a rueful smile. It was a shame: McIlroy became the first reigning Open champion not to defend his crown since Ben Hogan in 1954, when it wasn't easy for an American to travel to the UK.

A few crabby commentators lit into McIlroy for unnecessarily exposing himself to injury. But most were reasonable, pointing out that a golfer, even one in his mid-twenties, can get hurt climbing out of the shower or riding in a car. Accidents happen. Dustin Johnson missed a Masters because he slipped on stairs in his stocking feet.

Rory's biggest priority was to get himself ready for the next major, the PGA Championship, which took place the following month at Whistling Straits in Wisconsin. Somehow, Rory healed quickly enough to compete. He played okay, finishing in the top twenty at nine-under, eleven shots back of Australian Jason Day, who played out of his mind in beating the red-hot Spieth.

Spieth in 2015 came within a handful of shots of becoming the first golfer since Bobby Jones in 1930 to win the Grand Slam—the "impregnable quadrilateral," as Golden Age sportswriter George Trevor coined it—in the same calendar year. For Jones, an amateur, the Big Four were the British and US Amateurs and the US Open and Open Championship in Britain. For Spieth, it was the professional quartet identified in 1954 by writers Herbert Warren Wind and Dan Jenkins: the Masters, the US Open, the

Open Championship, and the PGA Championship. In '15, Spieth came almost as close to winning the Grand Slam as Jack Nicklaus had in 1972.

———

With his ankle now fully healed, McIlroy hoped to return to the game's pinnacle in 2016. He didn't quite get there, at least not in the majors. But he ended up with three great trophies and a much fatter pocketbook.

Chapter 21

ERICA AND ASHFORD CASTLE

McIlroy's social carousel finally began to slow down in late 2014. At some point that fall, his friendship with Erica Stoll, the then-twenty-six-year-old PGA of America executive who'd rescued him from ignominy at Medinah two years before, blossomed into romance.

They'd become pals after the '12 Ryder Cup, presumably exchanging texts and emails and perhaps seeing one another at PGA Championships and the '14 Ryder Cup at Gleneagles. Erica may have become something of a confidante after McIlroy's relationship with Wozniacki fell apart. Ms. Stoll back then was renting a West Palm Beach condo not far from McIlroy's home.

If Rory wanted to keep his post-Caro dating life private, he'd done a lousy job up to that point. The Irish and UK gossip sheets were all over his encounters with the famous and the wannabe famous.

It all makes his relationship with Stoll more intriguing. No one seemed to know that Rory and Erica had begun seeing one another. It wasn't until well into the new year that they let friends in on their secret. For this romance, there'd be no cutesy photo ops or tipping off the paparazzi. Rory was playing this one close to the vest.

He was lucky that Erica was still available and apparently willing to look past his tabloid entanglements. Not much is known about her background; she has always preferred to keep a low profile.

Erica grew up in Irondequoit, New York, an upscale bedroom community of fifty thousand northeast of Rochester along the shore of Lake Ontario. At least one branch of the Stoll family is apparently old Rochester; a building bearing their name sits in center-city.

She was an all-conference tennis player for the Eagles of Irondequoit High. After enrolling in the Rochester Institute of Technology's school of business, she earned a marketing degree in 2008. Soon after graduating, she was offered a job with the PGA of America.

"The way PGA employees present themselves is so admirable and professional," she later told the *Rochester Democrat and Chronicle*. "That's the kind of job I want, and it's doing something I love."

Stoll served the PGA of America in several capacities, from office manager to the coordinator of championship volunteer operations. By the 2012 Ryder Cup at Medinah, her fourth year with the organization, she was working as deputy director of player liaison and transportation, which is how she and her boss came to save Rory on that crazy Sunday morning.

The couple spent New Year's Eve that winter in a €5,000-per-night suite at Ashford Castle, a medieval fortress on the border between Counties Mayo and Galway in the West of Ireland. Once owned by the Guinness family, it's been transformed into a five-star resort. The couple so enjoyed the castle that they spent New Year's Eve the following year there, too.

In April 2015, six months or so into their dating relationship and a week after the Jordan Spieth Masters, Erica and Rory visited Rochester. It may have been the first time that Rory had met Erica's mom and dad. The couple was spotted dining out at the restaurant 2 Vine (now REDD) in Rochester's East End and joining Erica's friends at the Magpie Irish Pub.

A few weeks later, they visited Rory's hometown while he was playing in (and hosting) the 2015 Irish Open at Royal County Down. That week, they were photographed in public for what could have been the first time, holding hands while walking through a crowd of people at the famed Newcastle links. They were trailed by Rory's bodyguard, the "Ginger Ninja," the beefy gentleman with the red hair and Nike regalia who's been a fixture walking a step behind Rory for many years. Nine years later, he was the guy helping Shane Lowry restrain Rory during the Bones Mackay ruckus at Marco Simone.

During that same stretch in 2015, Rory sat down with the *Times of London*. For the first time, he acknowledged that he and Erica had grown close.

"I am very happy in my love life," McIlroy told the *Times*. "We haven't really been putting it out there. She is from America, which is why I like to spend time in Palm Beach.... The past six or seven months have been really nice."

Despite Rory's ankle injury that forced him to miss the Open at St. Andrews in July and put him on the shelf for a month afterward, their romance continued apace. During their courtship, McIlroy discussed with the *Irish Independent* his girlfriend's desire to stay out of the limelight.

"She is a very low-key person, not the kind to broadcast stuff, but that side of my life is really good just now," Rory said. "We are excited, our parents are excited, so it is a really happy time."

In early 2017, in a sit-down with the *Independent's* Paul Kimmage, McIlroy shed some light on the early days of their relationship. "The thing I love about it is that we were friends before anything romantic happened," he explained. "I found it refreshing being with someone who was living a normal life rather than, 'Oh! My jet is 30 minutes late!' I could speak to her about anything."

By saluting Erica's "normal life," McIlroy was, quite consciously, providing a wry commentary on his "abnormal" and chaotic life with Caroline. But the tipoff that Erica was providing him something that Caroline couldn't—or wouldn't—came in his next remark: "I love that she knows everything about me, and there was no judgment there…I thought at the time [2011-2014] that being with someone that was in a similar position to you was the obvious answer. But it isn't, because you can never get away from it. You can never detach yourself and try to come back to the real world."

His clincher was: "I don't feel Erica wants to change me in any way. I can be myself around her: there's no bullshit, no acting, no show."

Rory's insights with Kimmage were not made off-the-cuff. McIlroy and Kimmage have an agreement: during the holidays, schedule permitting, Rory meets with the journalist to review the past year and look ahead to the next. In 2017, Rory knew Kimmage would ask about Erica; he had plenty of time to think through his responses—and maybe kick them around with Rory Land advisors.

It's safe to deduce from Rory's comments that there was plenty of playacting, showmanship, and other phony "bullshit" that went down with Caroline. And that he somehow felt he couldn't be himself around her.

Kimmage's interview is the closest Rory has ever come to admitting that there was considerable artifice at the heart of Wozzilroy. The question Rory has never answered—perhaps because he still hasn't figured it out himself—is why it took him so long to do something about it.

Despite all the hoopla surrounding McIlroy and Stoll's wedding, they managed to keep its details quiet until the very end.

"[He's] a huge celebrity in Ireland, but Erica very much keeps herself to herself and she's not into being out there at all and I think that's the way they wanted to keep the wedding, so fair play to them," Rory's old buddy Shane Lowry told the *Independent*.

McIlroy confided in friends that he wanted to propose to Erica during a long-planned trip to Paris in late 2015, but the terrorist attacks in November that year gave him pause.

"We had planned to go to Paris since May," he told the *Independent* a few months later. "[If] we didn't like the mood of the place, didn't feel comfortable, we would go somewhere else," he said. Once they arrived and checked into their Paris hotel, McIlroy felt comfortable enough to proceed as planned.

On the evening of December 3, 2015, Rory posted a picture of the Eiffel Tower illuminated by spotlights, which the Irish and UK media interpreted to mean that he'd popped the question—and that she'd said "yes." Soon enough, Rory Land confirmed it.

Remarkably, for the second time in less than two years, McIlroy was engaged. Seventeen months would elapse, however, before he and Erica said "I do."

It was an expensive exchange of vows, since it was consummated at their favorite place, Ashford Castle, which these days charges a €25,000 fee for a wedding ceremony *with just two guests*. Do the arithmetic for a reception with a rumored 160-plus guests. Tabloids estimated that the Stoll-McIlroy soiree cost, all told, something on the order of €1 million, since just renting the joint ran them at least €250,000.

The security expenses alone were fearsome. Ashford Castle's staff was famed for its discretion, but the place went into overdrive to accommodate Rory's nuptials. In addition to roving perimeter patrols, three layers of security personnel ringed the castle and its sprawling grounds. Locals said it was reminiscent of the security carried out for President Ronald Reagan's visit in 1984.

Guests and hundreds of wedding staffers received special color-coded bracelets that had to be displayed to gain access to different parts of the estate. Rory Land retained the services of rock group U2's security chief, who personally inspected all perimeter posts. Any nosy photographer or celebrity gawker was to be abruptly escorted off the premises.

For four sumptuous days, guests were treated to exquisite wine and the haute cuisine of the resort's celebrated French chef, Philippe Farineau. Folks could try falconry or go clay-pigeon shooting, the

Daily Mail reported, while family members were treated to a private boat tour of the monastic ruins on Inchagoill Island.

Rory had hoped, he joked with reporters, to walk down the aisle wearing a green jacket as a new Masters champion. But he again fell short at Augusta in '17. The champion that year was none other than Sergio Garcia, who a few days after the ceremony in Butler Cabin served as one of Rory's groomsmen, along with Rory Landers from the Holywood-Belfast-Dublin business spheres. Harry Diamond, of course, served as Rory's best man.

Other guests included the pride of County Westmeath, One Direction hunk Niall Horan; *Fifty Shades of Gray* heartthrob Jamie Dornan; Gwyneth Paltrow's ex, Coldplay frontman Chris Martin; and Rory's fellow Irish Ryder Cuppers Padraig Harrington, Paul McGinley, and Shane Lowry.

The Irish and UK media couldn't get enough of the big bash. A couple of outlets reported—erroneously, it turned out—that Martin and Coldplay would be entertaining at the reception. So, guests "only" got to enjoy Ed Sheeran and Stevie Wonder. Sheeran had to be helicoptered in for his brief performance: he was in the middle of a lengthy concert tour.

Two different pop magazines supposedly offered the couple a castle-load of money to cover and "shoot" the wedding, but Rory and Erica, to their credit, turned them down. By all accounts, everyone inside the moat had a fabulous time.

The *Daily Mail* also reported that the couple took a ten-day honeymoon to the Caribbean that included a stop at the luxurious Sandy Lane Hotel in Barbados. The five-star resort boasts three courses. It's not known if Rory coaxed his bride onto the links; supposedly, she doesn't enjoy playing golf but can't get enough tennis.

The couple's desire to keep their private lives private—the obverse of Wozzilroy—has also driven their marriage, at least until discord surfaced in the spring of 2024. Erica's Instagram account has been kept carefully guarded.

They chose to settle in Palm Beach Gardens in Rory's home, the spread with a tennis court and swimming pool that he purchased from Ernie and Liezl Els. As of fall 2024, they were building a manse—the preliminary work alone supposedly cost $10 million—in Virginia Water, England, near the Wentworth course and its superb indoor golf training facility, with plans to move there semi-permanently.

Erica happens to share a birthday with Arnold Palmer. When Palmer learned of the coincidence during Erica and Rory's courtship, he joked that they should hold a combined birthday celebration someday. He passed away in 2016 before the party could be arranged.

On September 10, 2019, Rory posted this message: "September 10th…a special day for 2 very important people in my life. My wife Erica and Arnold Palmer share a birthday today. They never got to have the joint party they talked about having a few years ago. Arnold would have been 90 today and Erica is, well…much, much younger! They have both taught me so much and made me a better man. I cherished every moment I got to spend with Arnold and I cherish the life I get to spend with Erica. Happy Birthday guys!!"

A year later, amid the global coronavirus pandemic, their child, a daughter named Poppy Kennedy McIlroy, was born at the Jupiter Medical Center. Erica and Rory managed to keep their impending parenthood a secret, not confirming the news until she was into her final few weeks.

"We're about to be parents very soon, so we're obviously super excited," McIlroy said during a post-round interview. "Yeah, we've been sharing the news with friends and family, obviously, but I didn't think it was something that I really particularly needed to share out here. It's a private matter, but we're really excited and can't wait for her to get here."

When the blessed event occurred, McIlroy announced the news on Instagram. He included a black-and-white photo of new-born Poppy squeezing her father's pinky finger, writing, "She is the absolute love of our lives. Mother and baby are doing great. Massive thank you to all the staff at Jupiter Medical Center and Dr. Sasha Melendy for their amazing care ♥♥."

Young Poppy has enlivened a couple of Masters Par-3 tournaments, skipping around the lush course with Wendy and Shane Lowry's two little ones, all sporting adorable caddie outfits.

After Rory won the 2023 Scottish Open, Erica and thirty-four-month-old Poppy were standing next to the 18th green at the Renaissance Club in East Lothian, ready to congratulate him. As he approached, Erica urged Poppy, "Say, 'Well done, Da-da!'" Which Poppy did.

An instant later, though, Poppy spotted Tommy Fleetwood, Rory's great pal and playing partner that day. She squealed, squirming out of her mother's arms to greet her Uncle Tommy. As Poppy ran away, Erica said to Rory, "She wants to give Tommy a hug." Rory laughed and said, "We all need a hug!"

The highlight of Rory's 2016 campaign was—finally!—ending his drought in the Irish Open. He had missed the cut at the three previous Irish Opens, including the '15 affair at Royal County Down. What made his early exit at Newcastle doubly painful was that Erica was with him that week, making her public debut as Rory's paramour, plus it was his first year serving as tournament host.

In '16, McIlroy was determined to make amends. The K-Club, Arnold Palmer's leafy design outside Dublin that features the River Liffey meandering through its grounds, was the site of that year's national championship; a decade earlier, it had hosted the Ryder Cup. With all the rain that spring, Palmer's gem was a mélange of pastel greens, packed with exuberant fans pulling for McIlroy.

Rory didn't disappoint, shooting 67-70-70 in tough conditions and taking a three-shot lead at the 54-hole mark. But his Sunday play was spotty for much of the round. Scotsman Russell Knox caught and passed him on the back nine. Fortunately for Rory, though, his hero Arnie had built par-fives on numbers 16 and 18. The long holes played into Rory's strength: if he could keep big drives in play, both holes were reachable.

One of the Irishmen clamoring for Rory to rally was Conor Ruane, a Dublin barrister and golf buff who knows every inch of the K-Club and most of Ireland's other acclaimed layouts. Seven years later, over lunch at Boxty in Dublin's Temple Bar District, Conor could bring back McIlroy's two fairway woods at the closing par-fives as if they'd happened the day before. Of the two vaunted shots, the one at 16 was the more remarkable, he said.

At that point McIlroy was trailing, although a Knox three-putt would soon put the Highlander's lead in jeopardy. In spitting rain and a hurting right-to-left breeze, with water and a ton of sand guarding a precariously narrow 16th green, McIlroy had to crush a three-wood to get his ball onto the putting surface. He was taking a big risk: there was no margin for error.

Rory hit a towering fade that bucked the wind and disappeared into the haze. Fans sucked in their breath as the ball reappeared over the water hazard. Finally, there was an explosion of noise as Rory's shot landed a few yards beyond the water and bounded to within thirty-five feet of the cup. A smart two-putt birdie put Rory back in command.

Ruane says that Rory's three-wood was the most exhilarating golf shot he's ever witnessed. Had it fallen short, McIlroy would have, once again, broken a lot of Irish hearts. Instead, it led to victory in an Irish Open that captivated the whole country and provided the European Tour with one of its best moments of the year.

Rory's five-wood second at number 18, which nearly went into the hole for an albatross, gets more video love these days. But Ruane believes the three-wood at 16 was the more daunting shot, given the stakes and the severity of the penalty.

McIlroy admitted that walking up the 72nd hole, at long last a winner in his home island's championship, was among the most emotional moments of his career. "I don't normally cry over victories but I was trying to hold back the tears on the 18th green, just looking up and seeing all my friends and family and the support I have had this week," he said as he eyed the magnificent Waterford crystal trophy.

Irish golf commentators were convinced that hitching his foundation to the event had given Rory extra incentive. McIlroy further endeared himself by donating his €666,660 winner's prize to the Rory Foundation. When combined with the other charitable funds that were generated through television revenue, box office, and merchandise sales, the 2016 Irish Open Sponsored by the Rory Foundation had raised more than €1 million during the week, with the bulk of the money going toward children's charities throughout the island.

It was a stunning personal triumph for the now-twenty-seven-year-old McIlroy, a lovely way to spotlight his philanthropy and celebrate his betrothal to Erica with family and friends. Try as he might, he's never been able to replicate that moment in Ireland.

The US Open at Oakmont and the PGA Championship at Baltusrol, on the other hand, offered McIlroy nothing but frustration. An opening round 77 outside Pittsburgh and a first-round 74 in central Jersey both presaged missed cuts.

He played better at the Open Championship at Troon that summer, finishing in a tie for fifth, but never came close to scaring winner Henrik Stensen or his dogged pursuer, Phil Mickelson. A third-round 73 sealed McIlroy's fate.

Still, Rory was able to snare two other trophies in September that year. He again delighted a huge contingent of Irish-American fans at the Deutsche Bank Championship at TPC-Boston, the second round of the FedEx Cup playoffs. His opening round 71 was followed by three scorchers that got hotter each day: 67-66-65.

Englishman Paul Casey began the tournament with three 66s and had a six-stroke lead over Rory after three rounds. But McIlroy, playing a couple of groups ahead, blitzed the frontside with a 31; his scorecard included five circles and no squares. By the end, Casey needed to sink a fifty-foot eagle putt on the 72nd hole to force a playoff. It missed. McIlroy had won his second crown in Boston.

When McIlroy gets on a roll, as he did in the final round of the 2016 Tour Championship at East Lake in Atlanta—when his driver booms, and his iron shots zing at flagsticks, and his putts rattle into the cup—he doesn't walk down a fairway so much as *bounce*. When everything is going his way, McIlroy's gait takes on a buoyant snap, his Irish smile crackles, and his shoulders pop back and forth.

It's more than a bit cocky, but as Nicklaus himself has pointed out, it's not a swagger or a strut. There's a little-kid quality to it that makes it endearing. Now that McIlroy has gotten into his mid-thirties, the Rory Bounce is not quite as lively as it used to be, but it's still there, at least on occasion.

Sometimes, when he's feeling especially frisky, Rory will toss in a couple of wide-arcing hand claps, a la LeBron James sending chalk flying as he pounds his mitts together at the beginning of a game.

When McIlroy holed out a spectacular uphill wedge from 137 yards on Sunday for an eagle at East Lake's number 16 to suddenly vault into contention, he ran through his entire repertoire for J.P. Fitzgerald and a delirious gallery. Rory gave his caddie the same kind of playful shove that Elaine used to give Jerry on *Seinfeld*, flexed his shoulder blades, repeatedly bashed his hands together, and hopped his way toward the green, all with the crowd roaring.

"I've never seen him this excited!" marveled NBC's Johnny Miller, "Not even during his four majors!"

Rory still had to birdie the par-five final hole to force a three-way playoff with Kevin Chappell and Ryan Moore. McIlroy put his second shot into the greenside bunker right of the hole, then finessed a sand shot to within a foot or two to finish off a lustrous 64.

On the first hole of sudden death, back at number 18, McIlroy hit one of his signature six-irons, a soaring fade from 211 yards that dropped like a wedge and ran six feet right of the cup, setting up what would have been the winning putt for eagle. But Rory's effort carried too much speed and spun out, right to left, leaving him doubled-over.

Moore made his birdie putt; Chappell missed his, so Ryan and Rory advanced to the second playoff hole. Two more playoff holes ensued, with McIlroy missing another chance to close out Moore.

Finally, back at his beatified 16th for the fourth playoff hole, Rory's fourteen-footer for birdie crashed into the bottom for a two-trophy win: the Tour Championship *and* the FedEx Cup. With the combined prize money, that putt was worth some $12 million—just under a million bucks per foot!

McIlroy's performance in Atlanta that year was so supreme that it almost "salved his wounds," as one Irish journalist put it, about not winning a major that season. Those wounds would soon begin to fester.

It's not fair, but McIlroy has had to grapple with irksome (and potentially dangerous) questions about his national and religious identity since he was a kid. Not unlike African-American parents pleading with their teenaged sons to refrain from making quick hand movements around cops, Gerry and Rosie warned young Rory not to comment on the sectarian issues that roiled Northern Ireland in their childhoods—especially his great uncle's assassination. Saying nothing (or at least saying as little as possible) was always preferable to saying something—and running the risk of reprisal.

The *Irish Sun*'s Brian Keogh had interviewed the seventeen-year-old McIlroy and his mum and dad at their home on Belfast Road in December 2006. Rory's meteoric rise was big news all over Ireland and the UK.

It was a sprightly interview. Back then, Rosie and Gerry made for good copy; they've since become wary of the press and almost always decline interviews. They've also urged family and friends in Holywood to stay tight-lipped. It's not easy to get folks to chat about the town's most celebrated family—even after a couple of pints at Ned's or the Dirty Duck. Trust me: I've tried.

But things were different in the old days. For a couple of hours, they went back and forth in the McIlroy's living room, sharing amusing stories—including Gerry and his buddies making their wild Open wager—and sketching out Rory's plans to turn pro that fall after the Walker Cup.

Brian thanked them, gathered his notes, packed up his tape recorder, and began heading back to Dublin on the A2 when it hit him that he'd forgotten to ask a key question. He turned around, drove back into town, and asked the attendant at a service station if it was okay to park his car there for a few minutes. Keogh jogged over to the McIlroy's home, steno pad in hand.

He knocked on the front door and was pleased to discover that Rory was still home. It was just the two of them chatting in the doorway.

"There's a question I forgot to ask," Keogh said. "Do you consider yourself more Irish or more British?"

It had not been Keogh's intent to ask the youngster such a barbed question without his parents present, but that's what happened.

Rory hesitated before answering. "I would identify myself as British," he eventually said, perhaps trying to recall talking points his parents (or advisors) had taught him. "I'm from Northern Ireland so I'm a British citizen and I've got a British passport. I'm Northern Irish but I can have an Irish passport if I want…I didn't have any experience of all the Troubles. Holywood is a quiet area and nothing really goes on."

For a teenager, McIlroy showed poise. His language might have been a bit choppy—but what kid's argot wouldn't be? He could have skirted Keogh's query—but that's a lot to ask of a youngster. Had his parents been there, they might have cleared their throats, shaken their heads, and told the reporter to get on to the next question.

As the years rolled by and similar queries were put to McIlroy, he gave a fuller exposition—but the sentiments were essentially the same: "Proud to be British. Proud to be Irish. From birth a British citizen. Carry a British passport. Grateful for all the help from the Golfing Union of Ireland and support from people throughout the island, including the Republic. My generation has moved past The Troubles. Next question."

The less said, the better. Until the spring of 2024, he never really volunteered any observations about The Troubles or drew analogies to them.

With the restoration of golf as a Summer Olympic sport slated for the 2016 Rio de Janeiro Games, Rory couldn't "next question" whether he would play for Ireland or Britain. Like it or not, if he wanted to compete for a medal, he would have to decide, one way or the other, which colors he would wear. McIlroy had made it more difficult for himself by telling the (London) *Daily Telegraph* in 2009, while still a tender twenty, that if he ever had a chance to compete in the Olympics, it would probably be for Britain.

In the mid-2010s, he tried to sidestep the question whenever it came up. Many observers concluded that his reluctance meant he would represent Britain in Rio and hadn't figured out how to break the news to Irish fans. That view turned out to be wrong—but the soap opera lasted a couple of years before Rory decided to *represent* the Tricolor without fully *embracing* the Tricolor.

It turned out that fears over the Zika virus's long-term impact on male virility caused McIlroy and many other athletes to skip the Rio Games. By then, Rory was so fed up with the unremitting queries about his national allegiance that he claimed playing in the Olympics "wasn't worth the hassle." When the International Olympic Committee decided to reinstate golf, "all of a sudden it put me in a position where I had to question who I am," he complained to the *Irish Sunday Independent* in late summer 2016.

"Who am I? Where am I from? Where do my loyalties lie? Who am I going to play for? Who do I not want to [anger] the most?" McIlroy seethed. "I started to resent it. And I do. I resent the Olympic Games because of the position it put me in. That's my feelings toward it. And whether that's right or wrong, that's how I feel."

A columnist later asked McIlroy why he'd gotten so pissed. Rory didn't mince words.

"Well, I'd had nothing [for months] but questions about the Olympics—'the Olympics, the Olympics, the Olympics!'—and it was just one question too far," he snarled. "I'd said what I needed to say. I'd got myself out of [going to Rio], and it comes up again. And I could feel it. I could just feel myself go, *'Boom!'* And I thought, 'I'm going to let them have it.'" And he did.

When Justin Rose won the gold in Rio, McIlroy texted the Englishman a congratulatory note. Justin texted back, asking Rory if he felt he'd missed out by not going to Brazil.

The *Sunday Independent* quoted Rory as saying, "I said, 'Justin, if I had been on the podium [listening] to the Irish national anthem as that flag went up, or the British national anthem as that flag went up, I would have felt uncomfortable either way.'"

Then in one of those ineffable McIlroy Moments where he takes on the world, he ranted, "I don't know the words to either anthem. I don't feel a connection to either flag. I don't want it to be about flags."

Hmm. So, the Olympics shouldn't be about flags, eh? That's a novel concept to which the International Olympic Committee and, like, several billion people worldwide might take exception. And one of them is now Rory McIlroy.

As columnist David Walsh wrote in May 2024 in the *Sunday Irish Times*, "Even [McIlroy] winces [today] if reminded of what he said about golf's return to the Olympics in 2016. 'I will watch the

Olympics but not golf. Probably events like track and field, swimming, diving, the stuff that matters."

Ouch!

Five years later, in consummate McIlroy style, he was singing a different song about "the stuff that matters." In fact, McIlroy was so enthused about playing in the Tokyo Games that UK journalist James Corrigan was moved to compare the thirty-two-year-old's infatuation with the Olympic spirit to St. Paul's conversion on the road to Damascus.

"I've been proven wrong this week—and I'm happy to say that," McIlroy told the press with a big smile. He loved the whole experience, admitted that he felt a rush of pride when an Irish rowing team won gold, and expressed disappointment that he wouldn't be able to see an equestrian competition—long, apparently, a McIlroy family favorite.

"When your sport is in the Olympics, you're all part of something that's a bit bigger than yourself and your sport, that's a great thing," crowed the guy who five years earlier couldn't say enough nasty things about the Games.

A Rory won a medal that week—but, alas, it was the wrong one.

Rory Sabbatini, a short-tempered South African whose salad days in professional golf were behind him, wasn't picked for his homeland's squad. But Sabbatini's second wife happened to hail from Slovakia, a country with a paucity of world-class golfers and—even better from Sabbatini's point of view—porous Olympic eligibility rules. The native of Durban was—*presto!*—a member of the Slovakian Olympic team.

When he caught fire with a final round (and course record) 61 at Tokyo's Kasumigaseki Country Club East Course, Sabbatini found himself—improbably—receiving the silver medal. Sabbatini almost grabbed the top prize: American Xander Schauffele eked past him by just one stroke.

McIlroy wore the official Irish Olympics green polo, which featured St. Patrick's shamrock perched atop the Olympic rings. But, unlike his teammate Shane Lowry, in Tokyo Rory chose not to wear the white cap with the shamrock's green trim.

"Why?" he was asked. "My head is so small that I have to get Nike to make me custom hats, so whenever I'm in a team event and the hats aren't custom, they're all too big," he answered.

But a source close to the Irish Olympic committee suggested that Rory, a Nike partisan, didn't want to be seen wearing a cap made by Adidas, even if the three-stripes logo wasn't visible.

Swooshless and hatless, Rory and six others—local favorite Hideki Matsuyama, American Collin Morikawa, Briton Paul Casey, Chilean Mito Pereira, Columbian Sebastian Munoz, and Chinese Taipei's C.T. Pan—finished three shots back of Schauffele and two behind Sabbatini. A manic seven-man playoff ensued, spread out in two groups.

Matsuyama and Casey both bogeyed the first playoff hole, which left a fivesome, all of whom teed off together on the second playoff hole. Morikawa stuffed his iron into tap-in range. Pereira's birdie putt horseshoed out.

McIlroy's downhiller from twelve feet or so took an abrupt right turn and grazed the lip, staying out. *Golf Digest* speculated that Morikawa's ball mark may have caused Rory's putt to take its detour.

Whatever, Rory missed the chance to continue competing for a bronze medal, which ended up going to Pan when the Taiwanese player holed a clutch birdie putt to force a two-man playoff hole. Morikawa, whose father's family was of Japanese descent, shocked onlookers by bunkering his approach on the next hole, playoff hole number 3, opening the door for Pan.

Schauffele was joined on the medal stand by two of the darker dark horses in the field. The Californian dedicated his gold medal to his father, a West German decathlete whose career was tragically cut short by injuries suffered in a car crash. McIlroy happened to bump into Xander's dad as he left the playoff green. The two exchanged a warm hug.

"I have never tried so hard in my life to finish third," McIlroy told the press. As he showed in Paris in '24, his conversion is now complete: he's as rah-rah about the Olympic experience as anyone. In Paris, he even wore the Irish team lid.

The 2016 Ryder Cup will be forever remembered for three things: the crackerjack mano-a-mano duel on Sunday between Patrick Reed and Rory McIlroy; the fact that the United States finally broke through with a victory after losing three consecutive Cups; and Rickie Fowler's hangdog expression when photographers asked the American golfers to kiss their better halves—and Rickie didn't have one to kiss. Fowler produced a crestfallen look that Jack Benny would have admired.

Hazeltine Golf Club, a muscular 1962 design by Robert Trent Jones Sr., was the host of the '16 Cup, where the US squad was determined to redeem itself after three straight embarrassing performances. A Ryder Cup task force, commissioned after the Gleneagles debacle two years earlier, had given US players greater input and influence. Davis Love III, a more approachable figure than his predecessor, Tom Watson, was chosen as captain. Love's counterpart was Rory's friend and mentor, Ulsterman Darren Clarke.

The American squad flipped the script at Hazeltine, delivering big putts in the clutch and taking a 9½-6½ lead into Sunday singles. The American star at Hazeltine and, for that matter, Gleneagles, was a surprise: prickly Patrick Reed, who'd drawn more attention for his transgressions on and off the course than for actually winning tournaments. Reed went 2-1-1 Friday and Saturday at Hazeltine following a 3-0-1 performance in Scotland. Never shy about self-promotion, Reed anointed himself "Captain America" and was thrilled when Love put him in the lead-off slot Sunday morning against McIlroy, who'd gone an impressive 3-1 during the team matches.

With so much at stake, the crowd was huge along the rope lines of the first tee Sunday morning: at least two dozen deep plus a packed grandstand, remembered Jeff Ritter of *Sports Illustrated*, who ducked under the ropes himself to see Rory vs. Reed. Ritter started counting the number of credentialed reporters hanging around the first tee and stopped at a hundred.

The media guys witnessed what Ritter, seven years later, called, "The greatest Ryder Cup singles match I've seen. I suspect it's also the best singles match anyone alive has ever seen. I don't know how you top it."

Reed was eager to prove his chops against McIlroy, who was just days removed from winning two big FedEx Cup events, including the season-ending Tour Championship. Now in his fourth Ryder Cup, Rory wasn't subtle in responding to the surprisingly combative Minnesota crowds; he did more than his share of gallery taunting.

But all that was mild compared to what went down with Reed. Rory danced a little jig on the first tee when a festively dressed quintet of Euro fans sang one of their weird odes to the Ryder Cup. He came out swinging, saving par on the first hole and birdieing the second to take a one-up lead.

Tension between the two ratcheted up on the drivable par-four fifth. Rory had the honors and put his tee ball on the front fringe. Reed then smashed his drive over Rory's ball and sank the eagle putt. The match was even.

A hole later, McIlroy jarred a longish birdie putt and let out a primal scream. Reed canned his own putt and proceeded to give McIlroy an exaggerated Dikembe Mutombo wag of his right index finger; the crowd went crazy. There was more of the same at number 7, where Rory made his third successive birdie without winning a hole.

But it was at the par-three number 8 when things went berserk. By then it had gotten so heated that Ritter scribbled in his notebook: "REED/RORY PUNCH EACH OTHER IN FACE?"

The American put his iron over the top of the flag to twenty-two feet or so. Rory pulled his tee ball some sixty feet left. Somehow, Rory's bomb exploded into the cup. McIlroy proceeded to strut across the green doing the "I-can't-hear-you!" tug on the back of his right ear, taunting the crowd, which booed at the top of its lungs.

Reed then holed his putt on top of Rory's yet again and promptly went into a Chuck Berry duckwalk, complete with a wagging finger waved directly at McIlroy. Now the crowd was going rock-concert apeshit.

"It was the loudest noise, before or since, I've ever experienced on a golf course," Ritter recalled.

Things got so nuts that Rory must have sensed it getting out of control. Grinning and shaking his head, McIlroy waited at the edge of the green for Reed. The two exchanged fist bumps and slaps of the back.

"It was cool," Ritter wrote. "A sign of mutual respect, and acknowledgment for just how absurdly great they'd played that stretch of holes."

"Absurdly great" is right. Rory had made four birdies on the spin and still didn't have a winning hole to show for it!

The back nine was less combustible but still contained plenty of drama. Reed went two-up at number 16 but then hit a sloppy pitch at 17 and allowed Rory to pilfer the hole.

Both hit stellar drives on 18, followed by equally stout approaches: Reed hit his short-iron seven feet past the hole; Rory's spun back to five or six feet.

McIlroy never got the chance to putt. Reed banged the winner into the middle. Another duckwalk ensued. Reed had won one of the most hotly contested singles matches in Ryder Cup history, putting a whammy on McIlroy that he again administered two years later at Augusta.

The Americans drubbed the Euros, 17-11, to reclaim the Cup. It would not be the last time that a crazy-ass Ryder Cup singles match got away from Rory.

Chapter 22

FRUSTRATIONS DEEPEN

The year 2017 proved to be frustrating for McIlroy. He had a half-dozen top-five finishes around the world but didn't win any of them—the first time since 2013 that he didn't win in either Europe or the US.

The previous October, he had finished eight strokes back of winner Hideki Matsuyama at the WGC-HSBC Championship in China. Two months later, he lost to Brit Graeme Storm in a playoff at the South African Open, then finished tied for fourth at Bay Hill, tied for fifth at the WGC-Bridgestone, and solo second to Irishman Paul Dunne at the British Masters at Close House.

His performance in the majors was lackluster: a tie for seventh at the Masters with only one round under 70; a missed cut at a big-thumpers' US Open track (Erin Hills in Wisconsin) that seemed made-to-order for him; a tie for 22nd at the PGA Championship on one of his favorite layouts, Quail Hollow in Charlotte; and the aforementioned tie for fourth at the Jordan Spieth-dominated Open Championship at Birkdale.

By late in the season, McIlroy had grown so disconsolate that he felt he had to fire J.P. Fitzgerald to see if a new bagman might provide a jolt to his game. It didn't. The only close encounter McIlroy had was the second-place finish against a weaker field at the British Masters in early fall '17.

The next year, 2018, will forever go down in McIlroy lore as his ill-fated attempt to smack-talk Patrick Reed at the Masters.

RORY LAND

Rory went into the Masters a heavier favorite than normal. He had come from behind three weeks earlier to capture an unexpected victory at Bay Hill. His putting had gotten so catawampus that he'd turned to guru Brad Faxon in mid-March. Faxon's counsel seemed to pay immediate dividends. He smoothed out Rory's stroke, got him to be more athletic, to relax and "feel" more over the ball, and to focus on an intermediate spot to negotiate the apex of the putt—a variation of the old Dave Stockton axiom.

At one of the tougher layouts on the PGA Tour, McIlroy shot 67-64 over the weekend to storm past Bryson DeChambeau and Justin Rose. On Sunday, when he chipped in at the par-four 15th to assume command, he gave Harry Diamond the full shoulder-shimmy-bounce into a high-five.

A lot of astute golf watchers believe that Bay Hill is the best precursor to Augusta, so the hype surrounding Rory in Georgia was intense. He played solidly the first two rounds at the Masters, shooting a three-under 69 followed by a Friday 71.

On Saturday, Rory shot a sublime 65. It included a lovely wedge from well back at the short par-four third, a chip-in for eagle at the par-five eighth, a spectacular par save from the azalea bushes left of the 13th green, and a seventeen-foot no-doubter at the finishing hole.

The birdie at the 18th got Rory into the final group on Sunday with his Ryder Cup archrival. Rory and Reed hadn't yet become avowed adversaries; that would only happen after Reed defected to LIV.

Had McIlroy skipped the Augusta press center that evening, he would have been better off. Instead, he chose to question whether Reed might stumble the next day since he had Georgia roots and had never really been in the pressure cooker of a major championship.

It was out of character for McIlroy to go that route. To put it charitably, he hadn't correctly sized up his quarry. Golfers egotistical enough to refer to themselves as "Captain America" are the sort of guys who *revel* in trash talk.

McIlroy did not cover himself with glory the next day. The first tee box was rough on both players. Reed pulled his drive left into the trees. Rory blocked his drive so badly right that he thought about hitting a provisional.

But Rory got lucky; not only was his ball found, but he had a decent lane through the woods. He was able to shoehorn a shot into the greenside bunker, blast out to seven feet or so, and sink the par putt. When Reed missed his par attempt, Rory picked up a stroke and was only trailing by two.

A few minutes later, he was poised to tie for the lead. A titanic 370-yard drive around the corner at the par-five second set up a seven-iron second. He almost pulled an "Oosthuizen" or a "Sarazen," holing his shot for a Masters albatross. Instead, it settled a scant four feet past the cup.

But McIlroy caused gasps in the gallery when his eagle putt failed to touch the cup. He got his birdie, but his shoulders slumped as he walked off the green.

His old gremlin, hole number 3, came back to bite him. It was the same old story: a short pitch that went awry and a lengthy par putt that refused to drop.

It set the tone for the rest of his round, which featured missed opportunities, errant chips, and slipshod bogeys. He ended up shooting a two-over 74 and finishing in a tie for fifth. It was Rickie Fowler and Jordan Spieth who mounted Sunday charges. McIlroy hit only eight greens and missed six putts inside seven feet. Brad Faxon's new protégé had been a confident putter for three days, but on Sunday his Augusta Jab resurfaced. He finished dead last in the field that day in strokes gained putting.

Reed won with a modest one-under 71. Had Rory shot 68—the number often cited as Tiger's "par" at Augusta in Woods's prime—he would have forced a playoff. Instead, it was more heartache for Rory and more grist for Rory's critics. His 74 was the only over-par score of any player in the last few groups.

"I played probably some of the best golf I've ever played here, it just wasn't meant to be," McIlroy told reporters. "Of course, it's frustrating and it's hard to take any positives from it right now but at least I put myself in a position, that's all I've wanted to do."

One interested observer of McIlroy's game had some pointed suggestions about what Rory needed to do better at Augusta. Sports psychologist Dr. Gio Valiante, a mental performance coach, counts 2013 US Open champion Justin Rose, 1997 PGA champion Davis Love III, and nine-time PGA Tour winner Matt Kuchar among his many golf clients.

Valiante didn't hold back while being interviewed on Golf Channel the morning after the '18 Masters. "Augusta National can punish if you play too aggressively," Valiante observed. "So, until [McIlroy] starts to play more maturely—until Rory learns how to play more patient and tactical golf—I don't see him winning at Augusta. [McIlroy] has to learn to play the way that Jack Nicklaus did at the height of his career… *managing* his game."

It was a tough indictment of a guy who at that point had played in ten Masters. But Valiante isn't alone in questioning McIlroy's mental approach and course management at Augusta or his apparent inability to learn lessons from year to year.

"I only have one criticism of Rory," Jack Nicklaus said six years later on Golf Channel's *Live from the Masters*. "You have to concentrate 100 percent of the time [at a place like Augusta]. For some reason, Rory always has a little bit of a lapse somewhere around the tournament. He'll find a double-bogey or triple-bogey that sneaks in there. I don't know how he does it or why, but it happens."

When coupled with the Bear's 2023 Faldo podcast comments about Rory not recognizing the danger lurking in certain shots at Augusta, it makes for a lethal combination: periodic lapses in concentration coupled with a tendency to take unnecessary risks.

Whether it was a lack of concentration or too many reckless swings, McIlroy's opening-round 80 at the 2018 US Open at Shinnecock Hills on eastern Long Island added up to a missed cut, exacerbating his big-moment woes. So did a 50th-place finish in the PGA Championship at Bellerive in St. Louis that summer.

But in July at Carnoustie—the Scottish links course hard by the North Sea, where the eighteen-year-old Rory had made his Open Championship debut—McIlroy played inspired golf on a brutally tough course, losing to Francesco Molinari by just two shots.

Molinari was playing superb golf that summer, so crazy-good with his irons that Golf Channel anchor Rich Lerner had started calling him the "Italian Hogan." In his first—and only—appearance in an Open Championship, Ben Hogan had triumphed at Carnoustie a mere sixty-five years earlier. Hogan was dubbed the "Wee Ice Mon" by Scottish admirers whose grandkids and great-grandkids were now heaping similar praise onto Molinari.

Rory started with a pair of two-under 69s at Carnoustie, which got him onto the bottom rung of the leaderboard. He stayed there with a Saturday 70, leaving him behind Molinari and Justin Rose, who shot 65 and 64, respectively. Tiger Woods also climbed into contention on moving day, shooting a 66 that delighted the galleries.

Birdies are always hard to come by at Carnoustie and were particularly stingy that Sunday afternoon in blustery conditions. Trailing by two on the backside, McIlroy made his move on the shortish par-five 14th, putting a middle iron into the center of the green, about fifty-five feet from the cup.

Rory yelped when his bomb slammed into the back of the hole, tying him for the lead. He gave the moment a big hammer-down thrust with his right arm, coupled with a little jig. It looked like he had Big Mo; maybe one more birdie coming in would do the job.

But it didn't happen. There's no harder stretch of closing holes in the UK than Carnoustie's. Rory hit a perfect three-wood off the tee on 18, which was playing dead downwind that day. He left himself a partial wedge, which he came off of, pushing it right and short of hole-high, some twenty feet away from the cup. His birdie effort borrowed too much on the right side.

A few minutes later, Molinari's wedge at 18 hit inside five feet. A clinching birdie followed. The Italian Hogan had replicated the feat of his nickname-sake.

It was a narrow miss for McIlroy, but still a miss—his second experience that year losing to Molinari. Francesco had beaten him by the same two-stroke margin at the BMW Championship at Wentworth in late May, shooting a 68 to Rory's 70 on Sunday.

The August-September swing that season also proved frustrating. His first three rounds at the WGC-Bridgestone at Firestone in Akron were in the 60s, but a Sunday 73 plunged him into a tie for sixth. At the FedEx Cup playoffs, he finished tied 12th at Boston, then shot a sparkling 62-69-63-68 at the Donald Ross-designed Aronimink Golf Club outside Philadelphia,[1] but finished two shots back of winner Keegan Bradley, who beat Justin Rose in a playoff.

At the season-ending Tour Championship at East Lake in Atlanta, Rory got a chance to showcase his athletic skills in the final round—but not in a way he would have preferred. He was paired in the final group with his boyhood hero Tiger; weirdly, it was the first time that Rory and Tiger had played together in a PGA Tour event in the last group on Sunday—and it's likely to be the *only* time.

Woods, who had started the season outside the world's top thousand players and was still recuperating from his fourth back

---

[1] I personally witnessed Rory shooting a 28 during his second nine at Wednesday's pro-am at Aronimink that year. Crazy good.

surgery, was angling to win his first event in five long years. Tiger had, remarkably, finished second to Brooks Koepka at the PGA at Bellerive the previous month.

When Woods shot 65 on Saturday and took a three-shot lead over Rory, it guaranteed that he would be followed by a huge and raucous throng as he sought his eightieth career win on the PGA Tour and first since the 2013 WGC-Bridgestone.

Rory, probably trying too hard, came out skittish, his putter again uncooperative. Tiger, meanwhile, fired up the gallery by birdieing the first hole and taking a four-shot bulge over McIlroy.

A double-bogey on number 7 sealed Rory's fate, bumping him off the leaderboard. By the time they reached 18, Tiger was holding an insurmountable lead over Billy Horschel and Justin Rose; Rory was, literally, an also-ran.

Officials at East Lake decided to give the Tour Championship an Open Championship feel by allowing fans onto the fairway and apron as the final group approached the 18th green. Suddenly, Rory was about to be engulfed by a sea of humanity. It looked as if he would get trampled as fans jockeyed to get close to Tiger.

McIlroy gave Tiger a quick wave and bolted at a full sprint toward the green, with Harry and the bag trailing him. Security jumped in to protect Tiger and his caddie, Joey LaCava. Everyone survived the onslaught.

Tiger's victory at East Lake was a ratings bonanza, injecting a ton of excitement into the Tour and raising the hope that Woods could return to his exalted perch. Seven months later, 150 miles southeast of Atlanta, he did.

The 2018 Ryder Cup was held in an unlikely venue, Le Golf National in Guyancourt outside Paris. McIlroy and Justin Rose, commentator Paul McGinley feared, were still suffering from the "hangovers" administered by Woods a few days before. Captain

Thomas Bjørn had his work cut out for him getting his two stars past the bad mojo they had experienced in Atlanta.

The American squad, which hadn't won on European soil for a quarter-century, was determined to come out firing. They did, taking a 3-1 lead on Friday morning in the team fourballs.

McIlroy's improbable partner for the Friday morning session was Thorbjørn Olesen, Bjørn's fellow Dane and, when clicking, one of the better putters on the European Tour. Rory didn't hit it well, Olesen didn't putt it well, and the two were swamped, 4 and 2, by Dustin Johnson and Rickie Fowler.

The afternoon foursomes, however, were dominated by the Euros. Partnered with his old Medinah buddy, Ian Poulter, Rory turned it around, beating Bubba Watson and Webb Simpson, 4 and 2. Poulter-McIlroy was part of a four-match sweep that afternoon. The Euros grabbed the lead and never looked back.

On Saturday, it was more of the same. This time paired with Sergio Garcia in the morning fourballs, McIlroy hit some clutch shots down the stretch in beating Brooks Koepka and Tony Finau, 2 and 1. The Euros had now doubled up the American team score, 8-4.

The Saturday afternoon foursomes saw the two squads split their four matches, with Rory and Poulter getting hammered, 4 and 3, by Jordan Spieth and Justin Thomas. Still, the Euros had a 10-6 lead.

Out in Sunday's opening match were Jupiter, Florida, pals McIlroy and Thomas. They didn't put on quite as spectacular a show as Rory and Patrick Reed had two years earlier at Hazeltine, but there were still plenty of pyrotechnics.

The first hole was a harbinger. Both players had birdie putts: Thomas from twenty feet, Rory from inside ten. J.T. poured his putt into the back of the cup; Rory missed his on the low side. But

Rory came back to win the next two holes and take a one-up lead that quickly became two.

A couple of rimmed-out McIlroy putts allowed Thomas to get back to all square. J.T. looked for sure like he'd thrown away the 12th hole, but he jarred his second chip to tie the hole. A bad Thomas three-putt gifted McIlroy the par-four 13th.

A bizarre moment occurred on the par-five 14th, when J.T. missed an eagle putt, leaving it close to four feet out of the hole. Rory, who had some five feet left for his own birdie after a pushed mid-iron from 224 yards, inexplicably conceded the putt of a guy who had just shanked a four-footer *on the previous hole!* Rory then missed his own putt—a turn of events that might have caused Captain Bjørn to *skalle* (Danish for "plotz") had the overall match been closer. It was another head-scratching McIlroy Moment in the heat of battle.

The match came down to the 18th hole, when J.T. laced a perfect tee ball and watched McIlroy shove his drive into a plugged lie in a fairway bunker. Rory gave the shot an enormous *whack* but wasn't able to clear the lip. When his desperate third shot toppled into the greenside pond, the match was over.

For the second consecutive Cup, Rory had lost a wild singles duel. But this time, the Euros tattooed the Americans, with Francesco Molinari and Tommy Fleetwood emerging as heroes. The Italian Hogan, two months removed from his conquest of Carnoustie, went 5-0 at the '18 Cup. It's a mark that, five years later, Rory came within two monster Patrick Cantlay putts of matching,

---

A few days after the Cup ended, Rory was at the Dunluce Course at Royal Portrush to play a quick practice round in anticipation of the Open returning to Northern Ireland the following year for the first time in almost seven decades. He also did a photo shoot with kids to commemorate the Open Championship's new letter sculpture, which was making the rounds to generate interest in the '19 tournament.

"The Open returning to Portrush is massive for Northern Ireland," McIlroy said. "I never thought I would have the opportunity to play in a major championship at home and I'm really looking forward to it." Close to 200,000 spectators were expected to see the event in person, not to mention 600 million households around the world.

The year 2019 would prove to be—simultaneously—one of the most satisfying and one of the most exasperating in McIlroy's career.

Chapter 23

HUMILIATION AND REDEMPTION

The first hole at the Dunluce Course is not particularly imposing. It's a medium-length, straightaway, uphill par-four whose tee box sits well above the level of the fairway, making for great grandstand viewing. The element that makes number 1 intimidating are the white out-of-bound stakes that line both sides of the fairway.

To purists, those markers violate the spirit of links golf, which is not supposed to be constrained by artificial OB. In 2005, when sixteen-year-old Rory was rampaging his way to a record-shattering 61, it's doubtful that he gave Portrush's white markers a second thought. The teenaged McIlroy stood on that elevated tee, grabbed a driver or three-wood depending on wind conditions, and just ripped a corker down the middle.

But it's one thing to be a kid competing in the North of Ireland Amateur; it's another to be a thirty-year-old professional with the weight of your homeland on your shoulders. In the runup to the Open Championship, McIlroy repeated to anyone who would listen that he was treating it as "just another tournament." But it wasn't "just another" anything, of course.

"Sport has an unbelievable ability to bring people together," McIlroy said at his Wednesday presser. "We all know that this country sometimes needs that…people are coming here to enjoy it and have a good time and sort of forget everything else that sort of goes on."

That statement was Rory at his best: kind-hearted, insightful, deferential to history and sociology, and self-effacing about his role in it all. It also illustrates the depth of the burden he was carrying—not just for himself but for his beleaguered homeland. For McIlroy, it proved too much: it was Ryder Cup-style pressure, but ratcheted up to "11."

Fellow Northern Irishman Darren Clarke, the 2011 Open champion, was given the honor of hitting the first shot in '19. The County Tyrone native had every intention, he said later, of hitting a three-iron on the first tee. But Clarke's knees were knocking so badly that he knew he had to go with a bigger-headed club. He chose driver, made a decent pass, and was relieved to see it heading down the middle.

Clarke got the gallery roaring when he knocked in his birdie putt at number 1, then made two other early birdies to grab the first-round lead for a chunk of Thursday morning.

Many of the folks who watched Darren tee off stuck around to witness McIlroy's opener. They gave the County Downer a thunderous ovation as he bounded onto the box.

"No, a McIlroy win wouldn't have bestowed nationwide peace," mused English journalist David Cannon. "Yet, the Irish are a prideful people, and their hopes were fastened, welcomed or not, to the 30-year-old's back."

A hurting wind was gusting right-to-left. Rory stuck with the gameplan he had doubtless developed with Harry Diamond and Michael Bannon, two Ulstermen who knew every inch of the old Harry Colt layout.

McIlroy pulled out a two-iron, took a quick glance—maybe *too* quick—down the fairway, and moved over the shot. With the benefit of hindsight, it's easy to summon the moment on YouTube and skewer McIlroy for his club choice, or for not picking the correct target, or for improperly gauging the wind. He was nervous, probably as jacked as he's ever been on a golf course, and he may have gone through his routine too abruptly.

Whatever the cause, he pulled the shot. Badly. Within a second or two, microphones picked up McIlroy muttering "Sit!" He continued muttering "Sit!"—six times in all—until the ball finally conked a spectator, coming to rest in gnarly gorse outside the white stakes. He hit a provisional, which also went left into the nasty stuff. But his second tee ball, unlike the first, was in-bounds.

His next shot, his fourth, was another pull. It failed to scare the left edge of the green, plunging into what looked like impermeable cabbage. On-course announcer Andrew Coltart, a Scotsman, found McIlroy's ball. It had gone so deep into the gunk it was unplayable.

Rory took a penalty drop, punched the ball onto the green to about ten feet—and missed his putt for a triple. It wasn't close.

The kid who dreamed of playing an Open Championship in his homeland, the beloved local favorite, the prodigy who stunned the world by shooting a 61 on that very course before he started shaving, had begun the tournament with a quadruple-bogey eight. He was four-over ten minutes into his round.

His quad was not the most humiliating moment of McIlroy's day. That came five hours later at number 16, when having fought back with two birdies and just one additional bogey, he angrily jabbed at a bogey putt less than a foot long—and to his horror, watched it rim out.

McIlroy played the last three in five-over, tripling 18, and came trudging home with an unfathomable 79.

Rory was living a nightmare. It was the backside of his '11 Masters, all over again. Except this time, it was unfolding an hour's drive from what he called "home-home," with half of Holywood in his gallery.

"I don't think it was [nervousness]," he said in response to a question about the first tee. "It was a bit of a tentative golf swing with a hard wind off the right, and the ball just got going left on me."

If he wanted to play the weekend, he had no choice but to shoot lights out the next day. He and several thousand of his closest friends gave it their best shot.

Rory birdied five of the first twelve holes on Friday, sending the gallery, which got bigger as the afternoon wore on, into a frenzy. At the par-three 13th, a poor tee ball led to a bogey. But Rory sent more waves of excitement surging through the crowd by birdieing 14 and holing a tough twelve-footer on 16, the infamous "Calamity," the par-three that he also birdied in his epic '05 round.

To make the cut, however, McIlroy needed to birdie one of the last two holes. He hit his tee ball at number 17 into the fescue but got his approach into makeable range. His birdie bid missed.

On the long par-four 18th, which the R&A had turned into a huge amphitheater, Rory pulled his 195-yard approach left—the dreaded McIlroy Miss. The ball skipped hard; it ended up skittering into the swale left of the green. His chip didn't come close.

In the press center afterward, Rory tried to hold it together. But he was choking back tears. Surely, he felt like he had let everyone down. He was asked to describe his emotions.

"There's a lot of them," McIlroy said, clearing his throat. "As much as I came here at the start of the week saying I wanted to do it for me, you know, by the end of the round there today I was doing it just as much for them as I was for me."

The whole experience had been an "eye-opener" for him, he said. His Friday 65 tied the course record for the renovated Portrush—but it still wasn't good enough.

Why do golfers playing big tournaments at their "home clubs" have such trouble? It's happened to Mickelson at Torrey Pines in his native San Diego and to Englishman Tommy Fleetwood when the Open is played at Royal Birkdale in his hometown of Southport. Even Southern California's Tiger Woods has never won at Riviera, the L.A. course on which he made his Tour debut as a high schooler.

"The problem is that when you focus on results, you are actually less likely to get those results," sports psychologist Dr. Jim Taylor has written in *Psychology Today*. "If you are focusing on results, you're not focusing on the process, namely, what you need to do to perform your best to get those results. This 'result focus' can cause you to get really nervous before competitions, which makes it nearly impossible for you to perform your best."

Counsel like that is easy to transmit—but much harder to absorb, especially for a golfer experiencing high levels of stress in front of rabid hometown fans.

"You have to perform as if you have nothing to lose," Taylor wrote. "You perform your best when you let go of expectations, pressure, and fear of failure…when you turn off your mind and just let your body do what it knows how to do."

Controlling his mind in big moments remains perhaps Rory's biggest hurdle. His mind was no doubt racing five years later on those short putts on the 70th and 72nd greens at Pinehurst No. 2.

A month later, at a presser before the 2024 Open Championship in Scotland, Rory admitted that his brain was preoccupied by what Bryson DeChambeau was doing at Pinehurst and not sufficiently focused on his own "process."

Rory has gotten off to some horrendous starts in major championships. A close second to his 2019 nightmare at Portrush would be his 2017 first round at Royal Birkdale.

By the sixth hole on Thursday at the '17 Open Championship, he was already five-over—and tumbling into the Irish Sea. On their way to the seventh tee, his caddie J.P Fitzgerald turned to Rory and snapped: "You're Rory Fucking McIlroy!! What the fuck are you doing?"

Or words to that effect.

J.P.'s little tirade gave Rory the ass-kick he needed. He recovered that day to shoot a 71. After a 68 and 69 in rounds two and three, he climbed into contention and ended up finishing fourth, behind only Jordan Spieth (winning his third career major), American Matt Kuchar, and China's Haotong Li.

In the press center Thursday evening at Birkdale, McIlroy gave full credit to Fitzgerald for his turnaround. "[J.P.] has had to [get tough with me] a few times, and he's never afraid to do that," McIlroy said. "I feel today it helped a lot more than at other times because I needed something. It wasn't that I couldn't look within myself. I was trying to look within myself. But J.P. kept me positive out there, so that was very much appreciated."

It was unusually effusive praise, warming hearts in caddyshacks all over the world. Loopers don't often receive that kind of press-tent love from their bosses.

J.P. would have been within his rights to tongue-lash Rory one more time at Birkdale. During a par-three tee box jam-up in Saturday's round—just as McIlroy was stringing together birdies and beginning to challenge the leaders—he chose to goof around rather than stay focused.

Broadcaster Ken Brown, a funnyman analyst with a Scottish brogue, was doing a stand-up with his crew a few yards from the tee box. A couple of waiting players and caddies began throwing pebbles at Brown to distract him. Rory jumped in, waiting for Ken to turn toward his camera before tossing pebbles with a malicious grin.

Just a little harmless mid-round fun? Maybe. But how often does a golfer get on an Open Championship leaderboard? There are only so many chances in a career. It was going to take every bit of concentration McIlroy could muster to overtake Spieth, who was holing everything from everywhere that weekend. Rory couldn't afford to let anything deflect his focus.

If J.P. tried to discourage Rory from his pebble-tossing, there's no video or documentary evidence. But given how Rory praised him at Birkdale, imagine the shock less than two weeks later when McIlroy suddenly announced that he was dismissing J.P.

Pro golfers split from their caddies all the time for all sorts of reasons—some understandable, some not. That same summer,

Phil Mickelson and Bones Mackay had gone their separate ways after a twenty-five-year partnership. Once the smoke cleared, the Mickelson-Mackay split made sense: Gamblin' Phil had stiffed his caddie out of hundreds of thousands of dollars in back pay and bonuses. Bones was forced to go public and brandish a lawsuit before Mickelson belatedly made him whole.

But coming so soon after Rory had saluted J.P., the news caused headshaking throughout the golf world. Like it had in confirming McIlroy's breakup with Wozniacki three years earlier, Rory Land did its best to spin J.P.'s discharge as amicable. At his presser before the '17 WGC-Bridgestone in Akron, McIlroy said he was reluctant to use terms like "fire" or "sack" to describe what happened with J.P.

"It was partly to do with him and mostly to do with me," McIlroy said. "I wasn't playing the best and was frustrated at myself and taking it out on him. And whether that was [related] to a club I'd hit or wanted to hit…it was not good."

The timing was especially peculiar, given the upcoming venues on the Tour schedule that summer: Firestone, where Rory won in the middle of his '14 hot streak; and Quail Hollow in Charlotte, where McIlroy had won the Wells Fargo tournament twice (and has since added third and fourth wins). Fitzgerald had been on Rory's bag for all but ten of his worldwide wins at that point, as well as all four of his major championships.

During his interview, McIlroy called J.P. a close personal friend and said he would remain one. He then used a phrase that, in retrospect, sounded like it had been workshopped by Rory Land: "Sometimes to preserve a personal relationship you have to sacrifice a professional one."

Rory's sentiment sounded tender, even noble. But just as with the messaging Rory Land developed around the "toothache" and later the Caroline breakup, it wasn't truthful.

J.P., no doubt as part of his severance package, stayed mum in the months following his banishment. But in October 2019, Fitzgerald admitted to the *Daily Mail* that he had not spoken with McIlroy since he'd been handed his walking papers more than two years before. So much for the need to "preserve a personal relationship."

Just as he'd done with Caroline, Rory had, out of the blue, severed contact with someone who had been dear to him. Two Irish journalists I interviewed said their sources confirm that the McIlroy-Fitzgerald split was rancorous—that J.P. never understood why he was forced out.

When I asked Chubby Chandler for his views on J.P.'s sacking, Rory's former agent—the guy who helped bring Fitzgerald into McIlroy's fold—got agitated and abruptly ended our interview. For public consumption, J.P. says he harbors no grudge. Privately, people say, it's a different matter.

Fitzgerald took two years off from caddying (which suggests a healthy severance), then briefly worked for the mercurial Matthew Wolff, a young American believed back then to have a big upside. After a couple of tournaments, the partnership fizzled when J.P. questioned Matthew's tee box decision-making. Wolff shouldn't have been so hasty. His game has gone south; he's struggled since going to LIV. He could have used a wise head like J.P.'s.

Fitzgerald did enjoy success caddying for Frenchman Victor Perez, who won the 2019 Dunhill Links and a lot of prize money with J.P. But that relationship also ended.

One factor that may have contributed to J.P.'s demise was the easy friendship that developed between Jordan Spieth and caddie Michael Greller. Greller was a Seattle math teacher who looped on weekends to earn extra cash. He happened to draw Spieth's bag when Jordan played in Seattle. The two clicked and became buds. The even-keeled Greller seemed to have a calming influence on the excitable Spieth.

Rory no doubt aspired to emulate that dynamic by choosing his old pal (and recent best man) Harry Diamond to take J.P.'s place. McIlroy sought someone he enjoyed being around. But he also may have wanted someone who wouldn't challenge him too much—the way J.P. did, at least on occasion.

There was a lot going on in McIlroy's world in 2017, some good, some bad. Early in the year, just ahead of the South African Open, he cracked a rib, probably the result of auditioning too many golf clubs; by then, Nike had folded its club-manufacturing business and Rory was free to choose a successor. The injury plagued him through the spring.

In April, he endured another disappointing Masters performance, only breaking 70 once. Later that same month, he got married. In May, he officially switched to TaylorMade. In June, he played miserably with those new sticks at the US Open at Erin Hills, missing the cut.

When Spieth (with Greller on his bag) again thrashed him at Birkdale in July, it may have been the final straw. McIlroy had to make a change for change's sake. J.P. got caught in the squeeze.

Chapter 24

THE MENTAL AND MONEY GAME

Rory McIlroy is almost never pictured wearing glasses. But when he is, it's clear that he's got a fairly serious astigmatism, which might explain, in part, why even with corrective contact lenses, he seems to have trouble reading greens. His glasses aren't Coke-bottle jobs, but they're not skinny, either. His specs give him something of a nerdy look, which is probably why he avoids wearing them.

But the reading habit those glasses presumably helped engender is one of the qualities that separates McIlroy from most professional athletes. Reading is not a recently acquired habit. Journalist Lorne Rubenstein remembers bumping into the young McIlroy in hotel lobbies and clubhouses with his head buried in a book.

Rory has turned members of the media corps into his own ersatz book club. At press conferences, he enjoys going back and forth with reporters on the latest literary releases, especially self-help tracts.

What does it say about Rory that he's got such an appetite for self-reflection? Dr. Patricia Peters Martin, a clinical psychologist (and my Georgetown classmate), told me it suggests that McIlroy is searching for a larger purpose, something that helps him accept the inevitable frustrations that come on the course. Rory himself has said that he wants to strengthen his capacity to focus on the next shot without obsessing about it, which is no easy trick. It's an emotional and intellectual tightrope; like a lot of other golfers, he needs help in balancing it all.

Sports psychologist and bestselling author Bob Rotella, who preaches that "golf is not a game of perfect," has been a frequent McIlroy counselor for the last decade, perhaps longer. Rory has become so dependent on the Charlottesville-based therapist that in 2023 he flew Rotella to Augusta during Masters week to help him deal with the stress of trying to complete the career Grand Slam.

Over the years, McIlroy has admitted that he's a "miserable prick" in the days leading up to Augusta and warns everyone around him to give him space. Having Rotella there might help ease his angst, he must have thought. Unfortunately for Rory, he missed the cut, which made for a painful Friday departure and an awkward goodbye to his counselor.

We can't know what Rotella shares with Rory, of course, but most likely it's imparting techniques to relax his mind, sharpen his powers of concentration, and not let errant shots rattle him. Rotella's counsel generally revolves around three must-dos: play with confidence, rely on a repeatable routine, and try to have fun. Rotella is famous for telling his clients amusing and illustrative stories that reinforce those themes.

Dr. Gio Valiante, author of *Fearless Golf* and a frequent guest on podcasts and Golf Channel programs, told me that Rory appears these days to lack the mental freedom to play with the controlled fury required to win a major. Once a golfer becomes a "brand," Valiante argues, too often their on-course instinct is to protect that brand by playing cautious or tentative golf—instead of the free and flowing golf that made them great in the first place.

Rory's game, especially his putting, has fallen into that trap, Valiante believes. He also thinks that McIlroy has developed what he calls a "domain-specific" mental block about playing the Masters.

For a professional to be humiliated on a golf course, as McIlroy was at the 2011 Masters and again at the 2024 US Open at Pinehurst, inflicts grief and guilt, especially on someone as sensitive as McIlroy, Valiante argues. McIlroy is a "wonderful person," caring and compassionate, Valiante says. But to begin winning majors again, he has to understand the "psychological shift" that occurred within him a decade ago.

"Golf is what I do but it's not who I am," Rory has said many times in various ways over the years. Another McIlroy mantra is that friends and family members will continue to love him even if he misses a cut or blows a Sunday lead, which reflects wisdom gained from Rotella and other counselors.

Every professional golfer has a coterie of buddies and hangers-on from way back. But in Rory's case, those people have been attached to him since his days as an early-teen phenom. He was viewed as their ticket out of North County Down, their gateway to a life of money and glamour. When he loses a big one, he may feel like, somehow, he's let down those people.

But it's the specter of disappointing his mum and dad that may bedevil McIlroy the most. Almost every golfer owes much to their family. But for only-child Rory, the sense of debt he feels to the working-class parents who upended their own lives *for him* cuts especially deep. Early in his career, when he came up short in a major, he admitted that he felt he had somehow cheated Rosie and Gerry. His hangup was utterly unfounded, of course. Rosie and Gerry didn't feel that way at all; win or lose, they were proud of their son.

Still, it's doubtful that Rory has completely conquered his guilty conscience, despite all the books and counseling sessions. When combined with his oft-stated desire to avoid being consumed by golf, it makes for a combustible mix: pangs of guilt on the one hand; faux detachment on the other.

Toss in his disquieting habit of losing focus at key moments, plus a nervous putter and a propensity for attempting low-percentage shots, and it all adds up to the McIlroy Whammy: a "domain-specific" mental and emotional block that now appears to extend beyond the Masters.

Dr. Martin and other counselors will tell you that they often encourage intellectually curious patients—and McIlroy certainly fits that bill—to read materials aimed at boosting their self-esteem. Rory has expressed admiration for any number of self-help books over the years, beginning with *The Greatest Salesman in the World* by Christian spiritualist Og Mandino, which has been around for half a century.

Greatest Salesman is an allegorical tale about making the most of the journey toward self-belief. To learn and succeed as a "salesman," Mandino counsels that you have to form positive habits to build a positive foundation.

Mandino identifies a series of yes-you-can! beliefs to help you become the best version of yourself. A typical admonition is: "Persist Until You Succeed!"

Sure, it is pabulum, but it still gets taken to heart because it speaks to people's desire to make themselves more confident and assertive. If a message like "Replace Your Bad Habits with Good Habits!" helped McIlroy become more disciplined—or at least *try* to—then Mandino's guidance was worthwhile.

A recent McIlroy must-read, psychologist's Adam Grant's *Hidden Potential* (2023), preaches that strength of character is more important than native intelligence. Grant explores how anyone can unlock their potential through stick-to-it-iveness.

"The true measure of your potential is not the height of the peak you've reached, but how far you've climbed to get there," Grant advises. Augusta, St. Andrews, LACC, Pinehurst—they're all valleys out of which Rory has had to do some yeoman climbing.

Another Rory favorite, American marketeer Ryan Holiday's *The Obstacle is the Way*, also champions perseverance. Hang tough, Holiday advises, regardless of what gets thrown at you. It is too bad Holiday didn't know the life story of Rory's paternal grandparents, because it's every bit as compelling as the examples cited in his 2014 book.

Obstacles aren't obstacles, Holiday argues, they're opportunities. Confront your challenges, turning them into chances to grow as a person and business executive. Don't waste time complaining about events outside your control. Don't give in to anger or cynicism. Be stoical at all times.

Platitudes? Of course, but you can understand why they'd appeal to a guy who whacks around a ball for a living and admits that, from time to time, doubt creeps into his head. Holiday's emphasis on stoicism, moreover, may have prompted McIlroy to read Marcus Aurelius's *Meditations* before the Sunday singles round in Rome at the 2023 Ryder Cup.

There are only a few things we can control in life—and a lot of things we can't, opined the early-AD Roman emperor. By remaining calm and tight-lipped, we can make smarter choices.

The previous night, McIlroy had been anything but stoical in his set-to with Bones at Marco Simone, not far from Aurelius's old stomping grounds. That morning, having absorbed *Meditations'* messages, Rory was cool as a cucumber in dispatching Sam Burns to help Team Europe win back the Cup.

The Romans never crossed into ancient Caledonia in their first-century-AD invasion of Britannia. But as part of his admonition to remain stoical, Aurelius might have approved an old Scottish aphorism: "You never regret what you don't say."

Rory might want to scribble that one down and tuck it in his wallet for quick reference.

By far the most interesting of McIlroy's self-reflection bibles is Susan Cain's *Quiet: The Power of Introverts in a World That Can't Stop Talking*, a 2012 bestseller. Cain's premise is that society tends to undervalue introverts, the quiet but resilient people (like herself) who make business, families, and a lot of other things tick. Introverts may not necessarily be the folks you want to party with, Cain writes, but they're the people you want to hire. And perhaps marry.

Why would a guy so comfortable in the limelight, so ebullient and outward-looking, want to study life lessons offered by the bookish and the inner-directed? Well, for a lot of reasons.

Introverts are generally risk-averse; extroverts tend to be risk-takers, Cain maintains. If there were ever a golfing risk-taker, it's Rory McIlroy, the heir to Arnold Palmer. Well, at least to the Arnold Palmer that ricochets around McIlroy's imagination, the mythic Cherry Hills swashbuckler invented by journalists-extraordinaire Bob Drum and Dan Jenkins—and perhaps taken too much to heart by The King himself. Palmer didn't drive every par-four in Denver that day in 1960: Drum and Jenkins just made it seem like he did.

Is it because—just maybe—Rory isn't quite the balls-to-the-walls buccaneer that he seems to be while plundering a course? Is it because a part of McIlroy longs to be a quieter guy ruminating over life's quieter moments? Maybe, from the beginning, the only child has forced himself to be more of an extrovert than he really is. That's certainly the take of Lorne Rubenstein, who has been observing Rory since Carnoustie in '07.

Is there, perhaps, a bit more Rosie in him than we appreciate? After he blitzed Xander Schauffele at Quail Hollow in '24, he wished Rosie a Happy Mother's Day, called her the glue that had always held together their family, and volunteered that he wished he were more like her.

Still, two weeks earlier, it was the extroverted Gerry in him that impelled him to climb that stage in New Orleans and belt out "Don't Stop Believin'!"

Dr. Martin is quick to say it's impossible to reach meaningful conclusions about someone in analyzing them from afar. But her suspicion is that Rory's interest in "going quiet" reflects a desire for more solitude—in sum, his oft-repeated desire to lead a more "normal" existence. That's not an easy proposition given his commercial persona, which demands that he be "up" and accessible to the public almost every minute.

Remember: this is a guy who's now gone ten years without winning a major, which means that armchair psychologists, including columnists, network analysts, Golf Channel panelists, and a nosy biographer, have a field day discussing his perceived "weaknesses"—one of which is that he thinks too damned much!

The cottage industry that has sprung up around appraising Rory's psyche is more than a bit bizarre. A ton of laymen—like me—arrive at conclusions to which we have no business arriving.

For what it's worth, my theory is that a big part of McIlroy regrets quitting Sullivan Upper early and skipping college, where he would have had the chance to challenge himself, mull existential thoughts, and contemplate the meaning of life and golf, a la Michael Murphy in *Golf in the Kingdom*.

It's not hard to imagine the eighteen-year-old McIlroy reveling in the freshman philosophy class reviled by everyone else. Instead of joining the bookstore stampede to grab CliffsNotes for Philo 101, McIlroy might have tried reading Plato, Hegel, and Kant in the raw.

McIlroy has an aesthetic side, which is why a couple of his juvenile paintings still hang in the hallways at St. Patrick's and Sullivan Upper. He no doubt would have enjoyed taking art appreciation courses in college and doing more painting himself.

There's also a bit of a poet inside Rory, as there is in so many Irish men and women. Surely, he was exposed to Yeats, Joyce, Heaney, and all the rest at Sullivan Upper. But he would have gotten a lot out of college literature courses.

In my view, much of Rory's decision to step into the void on LIV was motivated by his desire to prove to peers, the press, and—above all—himself that without a college education, he still had the moxie to analyze a problem, develop a solution, and provide dogged leadership.

What he didn't know, of course, was that the PGA Tour's senior management team was feeding him inaccurate data about the Tour's financial stability and—behind the scenes—was torpedoing his efforts.

As of fall 2024, Rory McIlroy had earned the better part of $100 million plying his trade as a professional golfer, some two-thirds of it on the PGA Tour. But that haul pales in comparison to what he's pocketed as a "brand ambassador," the euphemism corporations use to describe VIPs who shill for their products and services. Between 2017 and 2024, press accounts estimate that McIlroy brought in some $250–$300 million from his corporate partnerships with TaylorMade, GolfPass, Optum, Workday, Nike, Omega, and others. Previous McIlroy partnerships netted much more.

The job of brand ambassador involves more than appearing in TV, print, and online ads. It also means showing up at events with the company's executives, big shareholders, vendors, suppliers, and customers. Ambassadors are often tapped to help a company roll out new product lines or generate press interest in a particular service. McIlroy's partners also make good use of him online, especially since he's conversant in social media.

Rory is a sought-after ambassador because he's good at it. Marketing division heads want to tap McIlroy's natural charisma and winning way with people. He always finishes at the top of lists of most-influential and most-admired golfers, remarkable for a non-American. He is also considered one of the most telegenic athletes in any sport.

A lot of brand ambassadors phone in their obligations—but not McIlroy. Not unlike the care he puts into signing his autograph, he takes pride in giving his level best to corporate partners; he recognizes that his interaction with his sponsors and their constituents make up a big part of his own brand. His partnerships get a lot of love on Rory's website.

Rory's relationship with innovative health services company Optum is something of a template for the celebrity diplomat. His personal adherence to fitness and nutrition makes McIlroy an effective Optum spokesperson, says Allen Hermeling, the company's Senior Vice President for Sponsorships and Growth.

Optum and McIlroy "share a mission," Hermeling noted when we talked. The company is devoted to helping people live healthier lives, which has been Rory's mantra for the past fifteen years. Rory has also been devoted to strengthening mental health services, another Optum priority.

McIlroy is helping Optum "de-stigmatize" mental illness, says Hermeling. One of Optum's big outreach initiatives for young people is called Active Minds. Rory has endorsed the program through personal and virtual appearances in Florida, North Carolina, and other places.

"The way Rory interacts with kids is beautiful to watch," says Hermeling, who worked for five years in the Chicago Cubs' marketing and branding operations. "The reverence the kids hold him in is awesome to see in person."

If there's one word that describes Rory's dealings with Optum's audiences it's "authentic," he adds. Since McIlroy is so personally committed to physical and emotional health, people, including reporters, listen to what he has to say.

Rory went above and beyond the call of duty for Optum during the COVID pandemic, participating in Zoom conferences with healthcare professionals and doing virtual reach-outs to kids enrolled in Active Minds.

Hermeling also says it's been "amazing" to get to know Gerry McIlroy. "You can see where Rory gets his strengths." Rory's father doesn't have "an ounce of pretense—and neither does Rory," he says.

At Quail Hollow in 2019, Rory helped spotlight an effort to deliver six hundred meals to kids in need through Optum's partnership with the Boys and Girls Clubs of greater Charlotte. During the pandemic, Rory also worked with Optum to thank nurses and healthcare workers for their around-the-clock service. When the company identified a group of frontline providers who were crazy about golf, Rory surprised them with a video chat, which they loved.

Optum has used Rory in a TV ad known as "All Aspects." The commercial highlights how McIlroy's success on the course begins with his commitment to health care and fitness. We see Rory working out in the gym and juggling balls in the early-morning haze. "I have the kind of support system that keeps me at the top of my game," Rory intones. "Optum believes everyone should."

McIlroy's corporate relationships have deep roots. His partnership with Nike goes back more than a decade and has survived the company's decision, less than five years into Rory's deal, to eliminate its golf equipment business. McIlroy has chosen to re-up with Nike apparel because he's devoted to the company's ethos—plus they pay him extremely well.

Rory no longer appears in slick and funny Nike ads with Tiger since Woods ended his relationship with the retailer. But over the years Nike spent millions reminding viewers that Rory idolized Tiger as a kid. One long bio piece went so far as to hire actors to play Gerry and Rory in the old days, watching Tiger on TV and using his heroics as inspiration for young Rory to practice even harder.

Nike also used the adult Rory and Tiger to spoof the Larry Bird-Michael Jordan "H-O-R-S-E" ad, by showing off the golfers' prowess on the driving range. We see Tiger and Rory compete to hit balls into all kinds of strange places, including some unsuspecting guy's kitchen, a private office, and a wedding reception. It ends with a wide-eyed Rory holding up a glass of water with a golf ball in it and quizzing Woods, "How did you do that?" Tiger responds, "You'll learn, kid."

All these ads and others enhanced McIlroy's mystique. But one that might have hurt Rory because it was *too* hagiographic was a 2015 Omega commercial set in what appears to be Dubai. We see Rory hitting balls in slow motion against the backdrop of ultramodern skyscrapers while The Script's self-reverential "Hall of Fame" pulsates in the background.

The ad was so grating that *Golf Digest* begged McIlroy and Omega to take it off the air. Even McIlroy admitted that it was over the top and volunteered that he wasn't crazy about the use of the song. Psychologist Valiante believes that the Omega ad may have dented McIlroy's mindset by prematurely crowning him king.

Valiante maintains that the best professional athletes exist in a psychological spectrum defined by "Mastery" at one end and "Ego" at the other. At their best, the likes of Tom Brady, Michael Jordan, and Tiger Woods are able to divorce themselves from big-moment pressure and play with a free and easy abandon, aka "Mastery."

Other athletes, and this would certainly be true of McIlroy post-2014, tend to get caught up in the "Ego" of the moment. Instead of playing loose, they tend to become uptight, too concerned about what that moment might mean for them and their careers. An "Ego" golfer gets "steer-y" coming down the stretch of a major, Valiante argues.

Rather than releasing his putter head toward the target in clutch moments, McIlroy too often becomes tentative, which usually results in a miss to the right. Or he grips the putter too tightly and pulls his left arm left, as he did on the 16th hole on Sunday at Pinehurst No. 2.

Is the Omega ad to blame for McIlroy's prolonged slump in the majors? Of course not. But allowing such a fawning ad to air around the world was another unforced error on Rory Land's part.

McIlroy has become in recent years a balls-out entrepreneur, looking to push golf's envelope onto different platforms and into a variety of lifestyles. In early 2019, he partnered with Golf Channel and its parent company, NBC Sports Next, to create a new offering called GolfPass.

It was designed to be a one-stop-shopping platform for golf geeks, using new technologies and digital media to enable golfers to make tee times, buy apparel and equipment, gain access to streaming videos, expert training commentary, and inside chatter about the world of golf.

With an assist from the COVID pandemic, which triggered a big—if temporary—uptick in golf participation, GolfPass has more than met expectations. By early '24, GolfPass had streamed nearly 100 million minutes of video, from tutorials featuring famous instructors and players to reruns of the Golf Channel's greatest hits: *Feherty* and *Big Break*, among them. It also offers programs like *Ask Rory*, an interactive show where Rory and cohost Martin Hall field questions about golf from celebrities and ordinary folks, and *The Conor Moore Show*, which spotlights the Irish comedian's surprisingly entertaining impersonations of big-name golfers. McIlroy is Moore's biggest fan and booster.

NBC's offspring Peacock, as well as Samsung and Roku, are among the many streaming platforms that now offer GolfPass. Nearly 2.5 million golf course ratings from ordinary folks have been generated through GolfPass, which has cultivated partnerships with online booking platforms TeeOff and GolfNow.

McIlroy was also an early investor in Puttery, an upscale restaurant franchise that flips miniature golf on its head. Instead of (*forgive me, Putt-Putt*) a tacky outdoor course with windmills and clowns' noses, Puttery brings mini-golf inside, surrounding it with fun obstacles and a pleasant and "immersive" dining experience.

One of Puttery's flagship outlets is in Charlotte, McIlroy's home away from home, because of his four-times-a-winner success at Quail Hollow. The chain has also expanded to Washington, DC, Philadelphia, Miami, and Houston, with others in the offing.

Restaurant-goers are notoriously fickle, so it's hard to know if Puttery will make it over the long haul. But early returns have been positive.

McIlroy's most ambitious golf-related investment is TGL, the tech-infused indoor golf experience that he's helping to underwrite in partnership with Tiger Woods, the Tour, and veteran sports executive Mike McCarley. TGL's debut was delayed a year to early 2025 when the roof of its south Florida bubble collapsed during a power outage.

TGL will spotlight a half-dozen "teams" of four PGA Tour players each competing in virtual course matches. The idea is that on Monday and Tuesday evenings in the winter and early spring, two-hour matches will be televised on one of the ESPN family of channels. Players will swing against the backdrop of a big screen that will simulate a fairway or a green, projecting their shots via "arc" graphics and other tools. TGL will even have a playoff at the end of the season, with a pair of semifinals leading to a championship matchup.

Tiger and Rory helped persuade a lot of big names to invest in TGL, among them tennis legend Serena Williams, Formula One superstar Lewis Hamilton, MLB standouts Mike Trout and Shohei Ohtani, and a raft of NBA and NFL players.

The TGL arena, known as the SoFi Center, is located on the campus of Palm Beach State College, just a few miles from Tiger's and Rory's Florida homes. TGL's parent company, TMRW (Tomorrow) Sports, is eyeing expansion into other arenas.

It's hard to know as of this writing if TGL will attract enough eyeballs over the long haul to be a success. But it's already been awarded a kick-ass number from the financial markets. A June '24 Series A funding round gave TMWR Sports a half-billion-dollar valuation—a neat trick for an outfit that hadn't yet staged an event!

Will people tune into its debut, especially since Tiger and Rory are involved? Sure. But will they continue to click the remote to watch faux golf? That's a different proposition. TGL may not, however, be dependent on big viewing numbers. It's counting on gambling platforms to embrace the concept—and for people who enjoy wagering on golf and golfers to plug in on a regular basis.

McIlroy has been a car buff since he was a kid. Like so many Europeans—and now, thanks to Netflix's *Drive to Survive*, Americans, too—Rory has been a Formula One guy for a long time. In 2024, he announced an investment in the Otro Capital Group, a consortium of elite athletes (Patrick Mahomes and Travis Kelce, among them) and bucks-up businesspeople, which has committed €200 million to the BWT Alpine F1 Team.

The Otro/Alpine deal has given Rory a chance to go behind the scenes at F1 races. He enjoys donning earphones so he can tune into driver-pit crew chatter. He also enjoys hanging out with F1's golf-mad drivers and crew guys.

McIlroy has also expressed interest in acquiring a piece of his beloved Man U franchise, but to date has not been able to make that happen. It's also clear that Rory would like to expand his sports-related portfolio and have it become an integral part of Rory, Inc., as it moves into its second decade.

The world of professional sports has produced only a handful of billionaire athletes. Don't bet against McIlroy getting there.

Chapter 25

BEYOND THE PANDEMIC

Among the least significant things devastated by the global COVID pandemic was Rory McIlroy's golf game. Even with the Portrush heartbreak and pissing off a chunk of Ireland by pulling out of the Irish Open at Lahinch, McIlroy's 2019 had been impressive: four wins in three separate countries, nineteen top-ten finishes in twenty-five starts worldwide, a strokes-gained metric that will someday wow visitors to the World Golf Hall of Fame, and the season-end topper: being voted by his colleagues the PGA Tour Player of the Year.

All of that came on the heels of a scruffy patch in '18 and early '19 where McIlroy struggled to close the deal. Nine times in that stretch, Rory played in the last group but failed to bring home a trophy. The "Rory-can't-close" meme began showing up with a vengeance online and in the golfing media.

All of which evaporated when, in mid-March '19, he finally got over his Pete Dye mental block and won at TPC Sawgrass, beating Jim Furyk by a single stroke. Rory's final-round 70 at Ponte Vedra included an early double and a sloppy bogey on number 14 that induced a strong rebuke ("That [putt] was pathetic!") from Paul Azinger in the NBC booth.

But a few minutes later, McIlroy redeemed himself with a deft shot from the right-side fairway bunker on the par-four 15th, knocking his approach to within fifteen feet. His downhill slider found the middle of the cup for an unlikely sandy-birdie.

When Rory followed that with another birdie at the par-five 16th, hitting his nine-iron (!) second to within twenty feet, and made routine pars at the daunting 17th and 18th holes, he had slayed the Dye monster that had intimidated him for more than a decade.

Alas, it did not presage a win at the Masters. The 2019 Masters was, of course, the Return of Tiger, which Rory viewed from afar. Only a final round 68 got McIlroy to five-under and a tie for 21st.

At the PGA Championship at Bethpage, Rory struggled for three rounds to recapture the magic that had allowed him to finish tied for 10th as a twenty-year-old at the 2009 US Open at The Black. His Thursday round was prototypical Rory: he led the field in strokes gained off the tee but was near the bottom in strokes gained putting and chipping. His Friday round was so sluggish that he needed a backside 31 just to make the cut.

Brooks Koepka again ran away with the PGA. Still, another good Sunday allowed Rory to backdoor his way into a tie for ninth—the ninth time in eleven starts that season that he'd finished in the top ten.

He won a national open that spring—just not the one that counts as a major. McIlroy's play on Sunday at the 2019 Canadian Open at the Hamilton Golf and Country Club bordered on genius. As Joel Beall in *Golf Digest* put it, "Rory McIlroy is blessed with a curse. He can make golf, an impossible game, look impossibly easy. It is a marvel, the catalyst for his immense popularity."

Tied for the lead at 13-under, Rory, already immensely popular with Ontario galleries, was smart enough that day to cloak himself in Canadian red. His day began with a scorching drive and a short pitch that rattled the flagstick before rimming out. His drive at number 2 also set up an easy pitch that settled within four feet. It was more of the same at the reachable par-five third: his thirty-five-footer for eagle came up just short. Ditto at the short par-four fifth, where his three-wood off the tee settled on the fringe, some thirty feet short of the flag.

After five holes, he was four-under for the day, 17-under for the tournament, and cruising. Six more birdies—including one set up by a gorgeous iron at the par-three hockey-rink hole that delighted his partisans—put him on a 59 watch. A bogey at 16 stalled his momentum, but he came right back with an eagle at the par-five 17th, which caused Peter Kostis of CBS to revive the breaking-60 talk. Alas, a bogey at the final hole pushed him to 61.

The crowd went even crazier when Rory the Showman pulled out a Toronto Raptors jersey from his golf bag and hoisted it for everyone to see. The Raptors that week defeated the two-time defending champion Golden State Warriors to win their first-ever NBA crown.

He was red-hot going into the next week's US Open at Pebble Beach, which had overwhelmed him nine years earlier. He played alright at Pebble but never quite climbed into contention. A Sunday double-bogey at the tough par-four second eliminated any chance for last-day heroics. He ended up tied for ninth at five-under, eight strokes back of winner Gary Woodland, whose 13-under is one of only a handful of times in US Open history that the champion has bettered 10-under.

The week following the 2019 Open Championship at Portrush, at the FedEx-St. Jude's Invitational in Memphis, McIlroy bounced back by wowing the crowd with a Saturday 62, one of three rounds he shot under 70 that week. A Sunday 71 produced a tie for fourth in the tournament won by Koepka.

A week later it was more of the same at the Northern Trust at Liberty National in Bayonne, New Jersey, the first leg of the 2019 FedEx Cup Playoffs. Three rounds in the 60s got Rory into a tie for sixth, four shots behind Patrick Reed.

Medinah Country Club, the site of McIlroy's 2012 Ryder Cup hijinks, was set up so benignly by the Tour that Rory's 11-under was good only for a tie for 19th. Justin Thomas won the second leg of the FedEx Cup with an almost unseemly 25-under.

McIlroy gained a measure of revenge against Koepka, Reed, Thomas, and everyone else by dominating the Tour Championship that year at East Lake. His tee game was so superb that NBC's Dan Hicks said he staged a "driving clinic" all week. Even his three-woods off the tee were going scary-ass distances.

Rory's Sunday 66 put away Xander Schauffele by four shots and Koepka by five. The match turned on the par-four seventh hole when Koepka, who had grabbed the lead, hit a couple of sloppy shots and made a double. McIlroy patiently waited on the green while Brooks slapped it around, then drained his twelve-footer for birdie, giving the moment a little fist pump. It was a three-shot swing. Suddenly, McIlroy was tied for the lead.

Down the stretch, Rory kept on stuffing wedges inside fifteen feet and converting putts. At number 18, he laced yet another gorgeous drive on the par-five, deliberately put his long-iron into the greenside bunker, blasted out to five feet, and holed the birdie putt. Although his Sunday score in Ontario was five shots lower, McIlroy's Sunday performance two months later in Atlanta was every bit as crisp.

When McIlroy is at his best, as Rubenstein has written, there's a "freedom" and a "fluidity" to his swing that separate him from every other pro on the planet.

That free-flowing swing was again on display eight weeks later at the WGC-HSBC Championship in Shanghai. McIlroy once more defeated Schauffele, this time in a head-to-head playoff after both finished at 19-under in regulation. McIlroy won with a long-iron second into the par-five 18th that nearly caused analyst Frank Nobilo to do a cartwheel. It was a scorching high fade that got to within twenty-five feet, setting up a tap-in birdie and the win when Schauffle's birdie bid missed.

It was McIlroy's fourth win of the year, on two continents in three separate countries. Weirdly, it would be his last for a long time.

As he left the Sheeshan International Golf Club in early November 2019, McIlroy had no way of knowing that a deadly virus was then being spread at an outdoor market five hundred miles west in Wuhan. The SARS-CoV-2 virus would end up killing seven million people worldwide, a million of them in the United States.

In mid-March the following year, amid massive COVID-caused closures throughout North America, McIlroy led the Tour's push to cancel the Players Championship after a single round. Rory cited his mother as an example of why society needed to be vigilant in containing COVID; Rosie was an asthma sufferer. It made her susceptible to catching easily spread viruses, her son explained. Of all the celebrities who spoke up that week, it was McIlroy's resoluteness that stood out the most.

After his Shanghai victory, the third WGC win of McIlroy's career, McIlroy played well at Torrey Pines to finish tied for third. Only a second-round 73 kept him from competing with winner Marc Leishman, the Aussie. Two weeks later, another Aussie, Adam Scott, won at Riviera in Tiger's Genesis International. McIlroy again shot only one round north of 70, a Sunday 73, but it was enough to shove him down the leaderboard into a tie for fifth.

The next week brought an almost identical finish at the WGC-Mexico Championship at the Club de Golf Chapultepec outside Mexico City. Four solid rounds in the 60s produced a solo fifth-place finish, four shots behind Reed. Another fifth-place finish occurred a couple weeks later at Bay Hill. Brutal Friday through Sunday conditions led to an even-par finishing score, four back of winner Tyrrell Hatton.

All in all, McIlroy had gotten off to a solid start in 2020 before COVID made it all come crashing down. Once spectator-less play resumed in mid-June, McIlroy had trouble finding his game. Without enthusiastic fan support, McIlroy was a lost soul. His only top-ten finishes the rest of the year were a tie for eighth at one of his favorite haunts, East Lake, for the season-ending Tour Championship won by Dustin Johnson; another tie for eighth in September at the delayed US Open at Winged Foot, where Bryson DeChambeau dominated the field; and a tie for fifth at DJ's bizarre win at the pre-Thanksgiving Masters.

McIlroy examined DeChambeau's performance at the renowned Tillinghast design in Westchester County and concluded—incorrectly—that Bryson's length off the tee was responsible for his big win. It wasn't. Even casual fans (like me) recognized that DeChambeau owed his victory to brilliant chipping and lag-putting. All that weekend, Bryson kept getting up and down from one dicey spot after another.

Statistically, Rory's driving was right there with DeChambeau. Still, Rory decided he needed to "chase distance" off the tee; if a Rory Lander challenged their boss's view, we never heard about it.

McIlroy spent the rest of 2020 and early '21 trying to increase the already-turbo-charged speed with which he hit his driver. Predictably, his quicker tempo not only soured his driving, but the rest of his game, too.

In March of '21, he sheepishly admitted that he'd gone too far after he played poorly at the Players, missing the cut. He scrapped his be-like-Bryson project. But it was another example of McIlroy acting impetuously—in defiance of golfing analytics, no less—and being abetted by a quiescent Rory Land.

In April, he missed the cut at the Masters again, shooting a dismal 76-74 in a tournament won by Hideki Matsuyama and his caddie Shota Hayafuji, whose reverent bow to Augusta National after replacing the flagstick at the 18th hole encapsulated what the Masters means to fans the world over.

Rory, being Rory, bounced back to win his next tournament—the Wells Fargo Championship at Quail Hollow, the third time he'd won on the demanding track.

The press instantly made Rory a big favorite going into the PGA Championship the following week at Pete Dye's Ocean Course at Kiawah, the place where McIlroy had decimated the field nine years earlier. He never looked comfortable at Kiawah and didn't come close to breaking 70. It was the Phil Mickelson victory march that year; Gamblin' Lefty became the oldest major championship winner in history.

At the US Open at Torrey Pines, where Jon Rahm kept sinking tough left-to-right putts in the clutch, McIlroy played okay, but only managed one round under 70 in knotting for seventh at one-under, five back of Rahm's winning score.

That July, at the Collin Morikawa-dominated Open Championship at Royal St. George's, McIlroy led the field in birdies but made so many mistakes that he finished tied for 46th!

The highlight of his 2021 FedEx Cup Playoffs run was a fourth at the BMW Championship at Caves Valley outside Baltimore. But the week before, at Liberty National in northern Jersey, McIlroy made headlines by chucking his three-wood in the general direction of the New Jersey Turnpike, landing it in a tree. His spoon had committed an unpardonable sin: it had ballooned a ball into the right rough that only traveled 215 yards on a par-four 480-yards long.

In McIlroy's defense, it wasn't the club's first crime. It had, at least in Rory's eyes, been a serial reprobate all summer. "Sometimes," Joel Beall of *Golf Digest* empathized that week, "a club needs to die." The ejected three-wood summed up McIlroy's week: he finished tied for 43rd.

Like 2019, 2022 would prove to be a bounce-back year for McIlroy. It started with an out-of-the-blue win in October of '21 in the Nevada desert at the CJ Cup at The Summit outside Las Vegas. He shot four rounds in the 60s, including a 62 on Saturday, and on Sunday held off Rickie Fowler and a red-hot Collin Morikawa.

McIlroy seized control on the par-five 14th with a forty-foot putt for eagle from just off the green. The putt never wavered as it stormed up the hill. Commentator Trevor Immelman marveled all week at McIlroy's firm and fluid stoke.

In early January, McIlroy finished third at the Dubai Desert Classic, just a shot out of the two-way playoff between winner Victor Hovland, a then-twenty-four-year-old from Norway already ranked in the world's top five, and runner-up Richard Bland, a European Tour journeyman on the cusp of joining LIV.

The spring and summer of '22 marked the high-water point of Rory's outspoken opposition to the Saudi-backed tour. Commentators as far-ranging as Barry Svrluga and John Feinstein of the *Washington Post*, Martin Samuel of the *Daily Mail*, Brandel Chamblee of Golf Channel, Eamon Lynch of *USA Today/Golfweek* and Golf Channel, and scores of others were lauding McIlroy for his flinty and conscientious leadership. At that point, he was viewed as a white knight; the issues surrounding the breakaway league soon got much murkier—and so did his image.

Under most circumstances, a professional golfer starting ten strokes back on a Sunday morning, who goes out and cards a thrilling 64, barreling up the leaderboard and muscling his way into a solo second, would be saluted for his guile and cunning. But since the golfer was Rory McIlroy, and the venue was the Masters, that round of eight-under engendered almost as much eye-rolling and pooh-poohing as outright praise.

"It was classic Rory," the naysayers' argument went. "Sure, he shot 64, but that's only because he was completely out of contention and playing without any pressure. Had he gotten within a couple of shots, he would have tightened up."

There was an element of truth to that view. McIlroy *was* way behind at the start of the final round and had little chance to scare the eventual winner, Scottie Scheffler, then showing off his awe-inspiring skills for the first time on a major stage. The way Scottie was playing, no one was going to put much of a dent into his lead.

Nevertheless, that shouldn't detract from Rory's artistry that Sunday afternoon. His birdies included a monster putt from off the green at number 7, a chip-in down the hill on the treacherous 10th green, and a spectacular hole-out from deep into the right-side bunker on 18 that had the crowd roaring—especially a minute later when Collin Morikawa followed suit.

McIlroy played the par-five 13th that afternoon like a virtuoso, slinging a perfect three-wood around the corner, feathering an eight-iron over the flagstick and backing it up inside six feet, and coaxing in a left-to-right eagle putt.

His 64 was just one off the Masters record, jointly held by Nick Price and Greg Norman. In truth, Rory could have been a couple of shots lower. He failed to birdie both the par-five second and the par-five 15th. The old McIlroy glitch, the late-round pulled tee ball, hobbled him down the stretch. The hooked drive at 15 was especially painful; it cost him a chance to go for the green in two.

Still, as he and Morikawa exchanged a hug on the 72nd green, Rory must have felt like his Masters jinx had finally been quashed. He had licked the course on a Sunday—something he'd never done before. His weekend putting and wedge game held up, albeit while out of contention.

"I don't think I've ever walked away from this tournament as happy as I am today," McIlroy told the press as Scottie was completing his victory march. "It gives me confidence going forward not only into the next Masters next year but to the rest of the season, as well."

For the "rest of the season," McIlroy did appear to be buoyed by his Sunday heroics at Augusta. But the next year, back amid the azaleas and the Georgia pines? Ask Bob Rotella how that one turned out.

McIlroy continued to play solid golf as the spring of 2022 turned to summer, just not well enough to get over the hump in a major. In May at the PGA Championship at Southern Hills, he shot a flawless 65 on Thursday and was five shots back of leader Will Zalatoris at the start of play Saturday.

His third round went south at the par-three sixth when his tee ball found the water hazard. His double-bogey there begat bogeys at numbers 7 and 8. A birdie at the short par-four ninth only temporarily staunched the bleeding.

At number 11, a 168-yard par-three, he chunk-pulled his tee ball into a deep swale, failed to scrape it onto the green on his first attempt, then pulled off the *pièce de résistance*, managing to three-putt from ten feet for a humiliating triple.

At that point, he was languishing at two-over, fully ten shots behind leader Mito Pereira. But three backside birdies at least got him back to red figures.

On the 18th, though, his popped-up second shot plunked onto the green sixty feet right on the pin. His first putt motored nearly twelve feet past; his second failed to find the cup. McIlroy stormed off the course, skipped the press tent, and went directly to the range.

He must have found something. He came out smoking on Sunday, birdieing numbers 2, 3, 4, and 5 to surge up the leaderboard. But another poor tee shot on the par-three sixth, his second of the weekend, choked his momentum.

Scowls and muttered curses followed as McIlroy struggled to hit his irons close. For the last two-thirds of the round, he wasn't able to can a putt longer than four feet until the final hole. When his eleven-footer to save par dropped, a sardonic smile creased Rory's face. Still, despite his uneven play, he finished only three shots out of the playoff, where Justin Thomas beat Will Zalatoris for J.T.'s second career win in a major.

McIlroy was still searching for solutions in early June at the Memorial, where he finished in a tie for 18th, with only a single round in the 60s. All that changed the following week when he defended the Canadian Open crown that he'd won pre-COVID in

'19. The 2022 edition was contested at tony St. George's Golf and Country Club in Toronto.

Crowd favorite McIlroy torched St. George's the way he'd lit up the Hamilton Golf and Country Club three years earlier. Over the weekend, he shot a blistering 127—a 65 and a 62—to outlast J.T. and Tony Finau.

In Toronto, he drew raves from the retiring Faldo for his wedge control, the way he was flighting the ball down while hitting one splendid finesse shot after another. He also drew raves from a crowd that chanted his name all weekend.

As McIlroy made his sixth birdie of the round at number 9, CBS's Jim Nance informed viewers that Rory had done something he'd never done before on the front nine of a PGA Tour event: he'd shot a 29. McIlroy had no intention of stopping there. He came within a few yards of driving the short par-four 10th. His delicate chip in thick rough rolled to the front edge of the cup and hung there, a millimeter from dropping for eagle.

Rory was just getting started. His second-shot short-irons to each of the next two holes danced around the cup, the gallery egging him on as he tapped in for two more birdies. Once again in Ontario, there were murmurings about McIlroy breaking 60.

The Ulsterman gave Thomas and Finau hope on the 70th hole by making a bogey that had Sir Nick fulminating one last time about McIlroy. But Rory responded with spectacular shots at the two closing holes.

His pitch on the 71st from light rough never left the flagstick as it came to rest three-and-a-half feet short. His sawed-off wedge on the 72nd nimbly halted ten feet behind the flagstick, then tantalized the huge throng by slowly spinning back toward the hole, as if on a yo-yo string.

To finish things off, Rory nudged a right-to-left four-footer that slipped into the right-hand pocket, enabling him to win by two.

It was Rory's twenty-first career victory on the PGA Tour, which put him one up in the lifetime sweepstakes over Greg Norman. Rory didn't hold back in letting the world know the disdain with which he held the LIV ringleader. Like the polished politico that he had become, McIlroy never mentioned his rival or his organization by name.

"I had extra motivation [given] what's going on across the pond," he said. "The guy that's spearheading that tour has 20 wins on the PGA Tour and I was tied with him and I wanted to get one ahead of him. And I did. So that was really cool for me—just a little sense of pride on that one." That sense of pride included making ten Sunday birdies.

For the second time in three years, McIlroy had captured the Canadian Open the week before the US Open. Winning on the Tour is tough enough. Winning two events in succession, with the second one being a major, is brutal.

The 122nd US Open was held on one of golf's most fabled courses, The Country Club in Brookline, Massachusetts. Brookline is where 109 years earlier, a twenty-year-old club caddie named Frances Ouimet, whose immigrant family lived across the street, had shocked the world by defeating Englishman Harry Vardon and Scotsman James Braid to win the 1913 US Open. Many believe that Ouimet's Miracle was the moment that cemented America's place in the golfing universe.

There was no beating Englishman Matthew Fitzpatrick that week, who had won the 2013 US Amateur at Brookline as an eighteen-year-old. Fitzpatrick putted those fiendish William S. Flynn greens like he'd sculpted them. His pair of weekend 68s was enough to hold off Will Zalatoris, who reprised his Southern Hills' brilliance, and Scottie Scheffler, both of whom finished a stroke back, five-under to Matthew's six-.

As for Rory, his showing at Brookline was eerily reminiscent of his play at the PGA a month earlier: three solid outings marred by a mediocre Saturday that dug too big a hole. McIlroy hung tough on Sunday, never more than three or four shots out of the lead, but never quite getting over the hump—as the *Global Golf Post*'s Scott Michaux pointed out.

A Rory birdie at Brookline would almost instantly be followed by a bogey, Michaux noted. "McIlroy couldn't muster the charge he needed to put pressure" on Fitzpatrick and the other contenders, he wrote.

Rory drained three early birdie putts: a 25-footer on number 1, a 22-footer on 4, and a 17-footer at the par-3 sixth. "But each time he took a step up he took a subsequent step back, with bogeys at no. 3, no. 5 and no. 7," Michaux wrote.

Golfers can't repeat the same mistake day after day at a major and expect to win, Michaux pointed out. "The signature third hole, which snakes through fescue-shrouded puddingstone outcroppings, proved McIlroy's undoing," he wrote. "The 499-yard par-four played sixth hardest on the week in a stroke average of 4.29, but McIlroy averaged a full bogey, making double, bogey, and bogey on it the last three days.

"When [McIlroy] walked off with another [bogey] there on Sunday after short-siding himself in the rough left of the green, the four strokes he'd yielded to par on that hole stood between himself and the outright lead at the moment," he observed.

In Michaux's mind, McIlroy's "most egregious mistake" came at the short par-four fifth, which he stubbornly kept trying to drive all week despite substandard results. On Sunday, he again attempted to muscle his three-wood onto the green, but yanked it well left. His pitch from nasty rough barely made the putting surface; his long lag chugged fifteen feet past. His second putt never had a prayer. Suddenly, he was back to one-under and effectively out of the tournament.

It was the archetypal McIlroy bogey, the sort of WTF gaffe that has long driven Jack Nicklaus and Nick Faldo to distraction. Why not scrape a five-iron off the tee onto the short grass and hit a dead-hand wedge, you know, all but *guaranteeing* your par, which is always a good score at a US Open? Why try to "John Daly" your way onto a tiny target surrounded by rotten fescue?

"I have to stay patient at this point because if I just keep putting myself in position, sooner or later it's going to be my day and I'm going to get one," McIlroy philosophized in Brookline.

The next "one," though, brought nothing but heartache.

The 150th edition of the Open Championship was played where it should have been: on the Old Course at St. Andrews, the ancient town that has nurtured the game for most of a millennium. By July 2022, the debate over LIV had reached a new decibel level; there was intense speculation during Open week that the upstart Saudi league would soon be luring away other stars.

Rumors swirled at St. Andrews that one of those big names would be Cameron Smith, the easy-going Aussie with the wispy mustache and unkempt mullet whose golfing strengths were the mirror opposite of McIlroy's. Smith has an inconsistent long game, especially off the tee, but is a genius at chipping and putting.

The highlight of Rory's third round was his eagle hole-out from a greenside bunker on the short par-four 10th, known as "Bobby Jones" after the Open champion beloved by the people of St. Andrews. McIlroy, who'd driven the ball brilliantly all week, had belted his tee shot at number 10 into the right-side pot bunker fronting the green.

Rory, then a shot back of Hovland, was fortunate that the ball didn't bury underneath the lip. He had plenty of room to work his wedge. Scottie Scheffler and Dustin Johnson were in the group ahead, waiting to hit on the nearby number 11 tee box.

When Rory's corkscrewed wedge bolted up the green, dribbled slightly to the right, and plummeted into the hole, it set off one of the loudest roars ever heard between the firths of Forth and Tay. The folks surrounding Scheffler and Johnson screamed so hard that the two golfers scrunched their heads and shoulders, as if a bomb had gone off behind them.

Still standing in the bunker, McIlroy threw one of his roundhouse rights when the ball disappeared. He popped out of the trap, gave Harry a quick half-hug, and with his left fist clenched high, jogged onto the green to retrieve his ball. DJ and Scottie shook their heads in amazement as the crowd continued to buzz.

Virtually everyone cheering must have had the same thought: McIlroy's hole-out was an omen! Surely, the 150th Open champion was destined to be the adored guy from across the sea!

If only McIlroy's hole-out had occurred on Sunday. But it didn't.

Smith on Sunday made almost everything he looked at, birdieing five straight holes beginning with number 10. After Rory missed a six-footer for birdie at number 3, it seemed to portend one miss after another. It's true that McIlroy didn't make a bogey that Sunday. But he only made two birdies, both of them two-putts, one at the par-five fifth, the other when he drove the green at the short 10th. Eighteen holes, thirty-six putts: not nearly good enough.

The Aussie pretty much waltzed to victory; only Cameron Young was able to stay within a shot. Rory's hopes faded at "Long," the daunting par-five 14th, when his second shot, dubiously struck with his driving iron (how many driving irons has McIlroy hit in his career from a fairway?) shot through the green and left him with an awkward third that he couldn't get close enough to the hole.

His par at 14 felt like a bogey. It also must have felt like, yet again, a major championship trophy was slipping from his grasp. He hit good drives on the next three holes but, each time, came up empty on the green. Observed Scott Michaux: "McIlroy frittered away reasonable birdie opportunities all day when scoring chances were in abundance."

On the short par-four 18th, a green he'd driven many times in practice rounds and previous competitions, he flared his tee ball into the breeze and came up well short of the Valley of Sin. His twenty-seven-yard eagle pitch, which he needed to hole to tie Smith, was struck too firmly; it ran eighteen feet past the cup. His comebacker, now meaningless, had no chance.

McIlroy put on a brave face in the Open media center. "Disappointed, obviously," he said. "I felt like I didn't do much wrong today, but I didn't do much right either. It's just one of those days where I played a really controlled round of golf. I did what I felt like I needed to apart from capitalizing on the easier holes."

Had his putter blade flowed, the outcome might have been different. But as Dr. Valiante has pointed out, Rory's final-day putting stroke amid his majors' drought has often gotten tentative. It certainly was Sunday at St. Andrews in '22.

In year one of *Full Swing*, Netflix presented McIlroy as a beleaguered steward of the Tour: pissed about its cave-in on LIV, to be sure, but still a conscientious leader, a guy with the best interests of the Tour and its members at heart. The inaugural year of the series was bookended by poignant images of McIlroy.

Episode one began with a photo of toddler Rory (wearing an Irish knit sweater in his freckled adorableness) and his dad that was taken at Holywood Golf Club, circa 1992. It's meant to tug on viewers' heartstrings, not unlike an image of Andy and Opie Taylor sitting on their front porch swing in Mayberry.

Year one's final episode ends with McIlroy having won—for a third time—the FedEx Cup's Tour Championship at East Lake. Rory walks into the men's locker room after having just finished his media interviews. He's a bit self-conscious, aware that the Netflix camera crew is awaiting his arrival. McIlroy is solo: no doubt by design, there's no member of the Rory Land retinue with him.

East Lake's locker room attendant is shown gesturing toward a small bar, asking the newly crowned champ if he'd like something to drink. McIlroy surveys his choices, then points toward his favorite. "I'll have whatever red [wine] that is," he says, grinning.

Rory takes his glass, then plunks down on a bench, pooped but triumphant. "Look: Rory has won!" the Netflix producers want us to believe. "He's beaten back the bad guys—and he's professional golf's big winner!"

If only that had been true.

Despite the PGA Tour's best promotional efforts, the culmination of the 2022 FedEx Cup playoffs was *not* the world championship of golf. That had occurred five weeks earlier at St. Andrews. And it had been won by a player—Cameron Smith—who was on the cusp of jumping to that *other league*, leading an exodus that seemed to get bigger by the week. Soon enough, Jon Rahm and Tyrrell Hatton would join the jumpers.

Still, Rory put on a riveting show in Atlanta. Paired with his Old Course foe Smith, he was given a starting mark of four-under, six shots back of FedEx Cup points-leader-by-a-mile, the nerveless Scottie Scheffler.

McIlroy's tournament had begun on Thursday morning with a wild hook off the tee in the middle of a rain squall that dissipated as quickly as it had developed. By the time he walked off the first green, he had been whacked with a triple. By the time he walked off the second green, having made a slaphappy bogey, he was trailing Scheffler by ten strokes—and Scheffler hadn't even teed off!

His entire tournament pivoted on one of his favorite holes in America—East Lake's uphill sixth, a par-five that bends dramatically to the right. Over the years, McIlroy has hit some Olympian blasts off of number 6's tee, but his first-round drive in 2022 wasn't one of them. It was a fat-ass push: he was lucky it didn't land in the bunker that guards the right elbow of the fairway. He had a sidehill stance in the cabbage but was able to advance the ball 150 yards or so; it stayed in the right rough, however.

McIlroy played his third shot back in his stance and punched a wedge onto the front of the green. The ball moved a couple of feet to the right, danced around the cup for an instant, then fell in its right side. He had made the unlikeliest—and luckiest—of eagles. In one swoop, he had erased two-thirds of his opening triple.

By the time his first round had ended, he had played the final fourteen holes in seven-under. No one was talking about him contending for the lead at that point, but at least his 67 hadn't put him too far back. He was now trailing Scheffler by eight shots.

Another 67 on Friday meant he was in arrears nine shots to Scheffler, who fashioned a second-day 66 to go with his opening 65. It seemed all but impossible for Rory to catch the Texan, who was beginning to exhibit the caliber of golf that has made him far and away the world's dominant player of the early '20s.

On Saturday, McIlroy got off to sizzling start in Hotlanta, birdieing numbers 2 and 3 with brilliant iron shots. Again, the par-five sixth proved crucial. This time, his monstrous fade found the short grass on the right edge of the fairway.

He didn't seem to love his four-iron second shot, moving sharply to his left as the ball hung in the air. But it found the right edge of the green, hitting so softly that it came to rest just three feet past the cup. It was a fabulous shot that caused analyst Andy North to reprise his guttural approbation from Rory's run at Congressional in 2011. Rory converted his second eagle of the week at number 6—this one more conventionally.

McIlroy was still trailing Scheffler by six. But North and his colleagues were beginning to make noises about Rory mounting a charge. Those noises grew louder as McIlroy continued to churn out birdies. By nightfall, Rory had shot a 63, but remarkably, still trailed Scheffler by the same amount—six shots!—as his pre-tournament deficit.

Paired in Sunday's final twosome, Scheffler and McIlroy both made careless bogeys on the first hole. Scottie never really found his rhythm that afternoon, a complete aberration. Rory, though, continued his stirring play. He caught up to Scottie with birdies on numbers 3, 5, 6, 7, and 12.

A McIlroy bogey on number 14, however, put Scheffler back on top by a shot. After a big drive on 14 tee, Rory came up and out of a wedge, hitting a flare that landed in nasty rough on the hole's short side. His lob-wedge third barely made the fringe. NBC's Azinger, of course, called it a "tragic" error and suggested that Rory may have shot himself out of the tournament.

It didn't take Rory long to overcome his "tragedy." On the next hole—the long, par-three 15th over water that intimidated Bobby Jones as a kid (Once asked how he played the hole, Jones answered, "With an old ball")—Rory's middle-iron found the middle of the green, some thirty-five feet from the cup.

He stroked a bold putt, his putter head extending through impact like the young Nicklaus; it broke about a foot left-to-right. It smacked into the back of the cup and dived straight to the bottom. It was the sort of final-round banger-inner that Rory had desperately needed at St. Andrews but didn't get. When Scheffler failed to follow suit and also couldn't birdie the par-five 18th, Rory eased to the trophy presentation.

With the threat from LIV on everyone's mind, PGA Tour Commissioner Monahan was on hand to toss bouquets at Rory before handing him the big-bowled silver cup. McIlroy returned the favor by thanking Monahan for his leadership and telling the crowd that the PGA Tour provided the best golf played anywhere in the world—and how proud he was to be part of it. The crowd hollered its approval.

Then McIlroy went to the media center, reiterated his messages, and headed off for his solo encounter with the locker room attendant, the Netflix crew, and his glass of pinot noir. Or maybe it was cab sav.

"This is McIlroy's dilemma," wrote Rory's occasional tennis partner Dylan Dethier in *GOLF Magazine* that week.

"It's often unclear whether [McIlroy is] golf's hero or tragic hero; he's endlessly talented, hard-working, swashbuckling and he wins nearly every prize with ease, but those that he wants the most—namely the major championships—continue to elude him," Dethier wrote.

Along with CBS's Amanda Balionis, Dethier became one of *Full Swing*'s narrators, the insiders who explained the nuances of the Tour's structure and folkways. Dethier's piece also questioned the hullabaloo that the Tour had built up over the years with the FedEx Cup and its season-ending Tour Championship. Yes, McIlroy had now won three of them, which is impressive, but what did it mean exactly?

"There is also some dark irony to McIlroy's victory," Dethier wrote. "He has championed the PGA Tour as the top circuit because of its tradition and legacy, but the FedEx Cup doesn't have a particularly meaningful history. In fact, critiques of the FedEx Cup overlap with critiques of LIV: it's contrived, it's a money grab, it's hollow, the rules change all the time and so on. And because McIlroy has decried LIV as a short-term cash-grab, there's some irony to him winning the Tour Championship's $18 million prize, the single richest in the world."

"But weaponizing those critiques is mostly missing the point," Dethier concluded. "McIlroy's win was significant not because of his monetary gain but because of his emotional investment."

Dethier picked up on the theme that Karen Crouse, Michael Bamberger, and others established when McIlroy was still rocking baggy pants. It's his emotion—that volatile thing he wears on his sleeve—that defines him. Both ends of the Rory-ian spectrum were on display in the 2021 and '23 Ryder Cups.

At Whistling Straits, McIlroy and the Euros got waxed (19-9) by a US team bent on revenge. McIlroy set the tone for the Euros, playing poorly with Ian Poulter (they were drubbed 5 and 3 by Patrick Cantlay and Xander Schauffele) and then again with pal Shane (they were spanked 4 and 3 by Tony Finau and Harris English). Rory found himself benched for the Saturday morning match. Saturday afternoon didn't get a lot better; he again lost 4 and 3, this time paired with Poulter against Dustin Johnson and Collin Morikawa.

In the lead-off position in Sunday singles, he beat Xander Schauffele, 3 and 2—but it was too little, too late.

Once the Yanks clinched, Rory was interviewed on Sky Sports. He twice broke down and had to halt the interview to compose himself. A few minutes later on NBC, he again blubbered, apologizing for letting down his teammates.

"I have never really cried or got emotional over what I've done as an individual," he said on camera, blinking back tears. "I couldn't give a shit. But this team, and what it feels like to be a part of, to see Sergio break records, to see Jon Rahm come into his own this week, to see one of my best friends, Shane Lowry, make his Ryder Cup debut...all that, it's phenomenal and I'm so happy to be a part of it."

I couldn't give a shit about individual accomplishments? *Whoa.*

This from the guy who used to diss the Ryder Cup and barely got his ass to the course on time for a pivotal singles match? It's impossible to imagine Hogan or Nicklaus or Woods getting teared up over a Ryder Cup loss. Or being that indifferent toward big-time personal achievements.

At Marco Simone, his emotion nearly boiled over when Cantlay's caddie, Joey LaCava, chose to tromp around the 18th green in celebrating the bomb that his guy had drained to—shockingly—seize the lead against Matthew Fitzpatrick and McIlroy after Cantlay and Wyndham Clark had trailed the entire match. As Joey wandered back and forth, taunting the European fans who had—in fairness—been taunting him all day, LaCava didn't seem to understand that he was disrupting Rory's concentration in lining up a putt that would have tied the Americans.

Lowry wasn't the only member of the Euro squad screeching at LaCava to cut the crap. Thomas Bjørn and Fred Couples, LaCava's pal and former boss, were having their own "argy-bargy," as Rory later put it, on another section of the green. F-bombs were being hurled in every direction, with the pissed-off gallery adding to the ruckus. It was fortunate that no blood was spilled. Rory's putt wasn't close. Still, the Euros had a formidable 10½-5½ lead going into the Sunday singles.

Rory had reportedly calmed down as the European squad reassembled in its team room. But Shane, the son of the Gaelic football legend, stormed into the room spitting nails. Lowry stood on a chair and started hollering about not letting the f-ing Americans push them around.

McIlroy got incensed all over again. He bolted out of the room, apparently looking for an American to yell at. Bones Mackay, who'd had nothing to do with what had transpired on the 18th green and hadn't been in an argy-bargy with anyone, happened to be standing just outside the carpark drive.

With Shane and McIlroy's "Ginger Ninja" bodyguard in hot pursuit, Rory confronted Bones and unloaded on him about how much he resented LaCava's behavior. Shane arrived within a few seconds and immediately began multitasking: pulling Rory away from Bones while tongue-lashing Mackay at the same time.

Poor Erica was caught in the middle of the *mishigas*. Low-key personalities generally don't like to be seen on global television ensnared in a shouting match. It couldn't have helped whatever tension was developing in their marriage. At least part of the reason her husband was angry is that he wanted to pull a "Francesco": to go a perfect 5-0 in a Ryder Cup the way Molinari had in '18. Cantlay's long-distance makes on the 17th and 18th greens denied him the chance; LaCava's oblivious march had poured salt into his wound.

That night and the next morning, Rory consulted Marcus Aurelius's musings on stoicism, which helped restore his emotional bearings, he said afterward. In Sunday singles, Rory stomped Sam Burns, 3 and 1, in the fourth match to help Europe to a 16½-9½ drubbing of the Americans. Rory never gave Burns, a streaky player and a scary good putter, a chance to get into the match.

RORY LAND

Slurping champagne at Marco Simone was the highlight of Rory's late 2023–'24 campaign. Sure, he won a fourth Dubai Desert Classic and got to hold that hilarious "I've-only-got-three-and-a-half-on-this-hand" photo op with his dad and mom. He also had the fun of winning the two-man team tourney in New Orleans with Shane, having Lowry pick him up like a sack of potatoes after the CBS interview ended, and getting to karaoke Journey onstage.

Then there was beating Schauffele at Quail Hollow after he trailed badly early on Sunday, blasting in for eagle from the sand trap short of the 15th green, his second eagle of the round. Schauffele, of course, had the last laugh, winning the PGA at Valhalla the next week, and then the month after Rory's late-Sunday breakdown at Pinehurst, winning the Open Championship at Troon.

Rory had no trouble dusting Xander in a "minor." But he couldn't summon the chutzpah to beat him in a major—which has been the story of McIlroy's career since 2014.

Finale

"THE FURTHER SHORE"

During his press conference before the May 2024 Wells Fargo Championship—a tournament he'd go on to win in spectacular fashion—Rory McIlroy explained one more time his belief that, for the good of the game, the PGA and DP World tours needed to resolve their differences with LIV Golf and its Saudi PIF benefactors. At that point, McIlroy had been embroiled in the LIV debate for three years. The "shitshow," as he characterized it, had worn him down.

Between the LIV drama, his long drought in major championships, and the commotion in his personal life (which, within days, would become public), golf's Opie Taylor wasn't ageless anymore. The old McIlroy mop top, not so mop-py these days, was flecked with gray.

In Charlotte, Rory chose to pursue a different tack about LIV. He invoked an analogy he'd never used. Indeed, he broached the one issue he was taught as a kid to avoid at all costs: the ugly religious strife that has long roiled his homeland and family.

McIlroy predicated his comments on the urgency of reaching an accord before golf suffered further—and perhaps fatal—damage. The game should look to the Northern Ireland peace talks for inspiration. To end golf's schism, he argued, both sides would need to make concessions. It was the willingness to reach a "reasoned, principled compromise," as US mediator George Mitchell put it, which was the basis of the 1998 pact that ended the worst of The Troubles.

"Neither side [in Northern Ireland] was happy," Rory said in Charlotte. "Catholics weren't happy, Protestants weren't happy, but it brought peace. And then you just sort of learn to live with whatever has been negotiated, right?"

Right. The moment was, again, McIlroy at his finest: thoughtful, conciliatory, cognizant of history. It even came with two uses of his favorite verbal tic. "Sort of" is Rory's go-to conversational crutch, that slight bit of shading that frees him to make bold assertions.

It was hell getting there, but McIlroy ended up in the right place on LIV. The idealist within him (my psychologist friends will groan, but for simplicity's sake, let's call it "Gerry") had given way to the pragmatist (aka "Rosie").

Continuing to trash or ignore LIV would only lead to further dislocation, McIlroy had reluctantly concluded. The Saudis had bottomless resources and the wherewithal to spend them. The longer the established tours refused to budge, the greater the likelihood that the Saudis would outspend and outmaneuver them, further crippling the game.

After all, as LIV partisans love to point out, all the Saudis have to do to get more money is suck it out of the desert. No matter how successful PGA Tour Enterprises (the US Tour's relatively new for-profit entity) might prove to be, it will never spark enough revenue to compete with oil derricks as far as the eye can see.

By mid-2024, the sports-washing Saudis had already wangled into the highest echelons of professional soccer, tennis, boxing, auto racing, and other pursuits. In women's tennis, PIF's circular logo has become a familiar part of the TV backdrop. A Saudi presence in men's professional golf was inevitable. Better to work with them and try to channel their investment to advance the game's global growth, McIlroy reckoned, than keep shoving them away and invite greater chaos.

Even the Golf Channel's Brandel Chamblee, an outspoken LIV detractor, had come around to McIlroy's position. Through all the ups and downs of the LIV saga, Rory McIlroy, in his mortal way, had sought to stay on the right side of history.

Sooner or later, the tours will have to compromise, McIlroy said in Charlotte. Let's make it sooner—and use the Good Friday Agreement deliberations as a template. So, the Ulsterman-raised Catholic, who'd spent the better part of two decades rebuffing queries about The Troubles, volunteered a reference to his homeland's anguish *without being prodded by a reporter*. Given McIlroy's apprehension about being seen with the Irish Republic's Tricolor just two weeks before in New Orleans, it was a remarkable moment.

In 2015, writer Charles Seifert was hectored by a Rory Lander to delete any mention of the family's involvement in The Troubles from his *New York Times Magazine* profile. The McIlroy intimate finally backed down when Seifert pointed out that there had been multiple references to Joseph McIlroy's murder in the *Times* alone, plus stories in a dozen other outlets on both sides of the ocean.

McIlroy's acknowledgement in Charlotte was long overdue; let's hope it signals a breakthrough. Rory, often bullheaded, is rarely shy about letting peers, the press, and the public know where he stands, not just on the divisive issues confronting professional golf, but on culture, film, literature, food, wine, and just about everything else.

Since, as we've learned, he often changes his opinions, and tends to be every bit as chesty about his *new* conviction as he was about his *old*, his attitude rankles people. That was certainly true of his views toward LIV, where his flip-arounds confused a lot of Tour members. Xander Schauffele said as much during the '24 Olympics when he dismissed McIlroy's latest LIV commentary by saying, "He kind of bounces around with his opinion, you know."

Rory's judgment in handling his peers' frustrations over LIV often left something to be desired. At a meeting during the Canadian Open in June 2023, in the middle of Commissioner Monahan's presentation attempting to justify the rationale behind the framework agreement with PIF, McIlroy got into a verbal tussle with Tour member Grayson Murray, an American.

Murray, citing the concerns of rank-and-file guys, challenged Monahan's integrity and skewered the Tour's proposed new structure, which favored elite players. Rory, for reasons that aren't entirely clear, given the way the commissioner had hung him out to dry, came to Monahan's defense, snapping: "Just play better, Grayson." Murray wasn't the only one in the room who found McIlroy's remark condescending.

Murray didn't hesitate. "Fuck off!" he barked at McIlroy. Rory later apologized and claimed that tensions in the room cooled. Still, sources say that bad feelings persisted.

A year later, the moment became poignant when Murray, who'd struggled with depression and substance abuse, committed suicide. He was distraught; his fiancée had broken off their engagement.

"At the end of the day golf is golf and, yeah, we play it for a living, but it pales in comparison to the things that actually matter in life," Rory said a few days after the tragedy.

"I've had to realize that at times and I'm still sort of working my way through that in terms of not making golf the be-all and end-all for me," he said. Athletes, McIlroy reminded reporters, are just as vulnerable as everyone else to emotional distress.

For all those years, the all-too-human McIlroy refused to discuss the cataclysm that had devastated his homeland. McIlroy wasn't alone. For many people in the North of Ireland, The Troubles were too real and too recent.

But *Derry Girls*, Kenneth Branagh's film *Belfast*, the book and Hulu series *Say Nothing*, and the work being done by organizations such as the Senator George J. Mitchell Institute for Global Peace, Security and Justice at Queens University Belfast, have begun to change all that. People now recognize that, much like systemic racism in the United States, the only way of truly getting past The

Troubles is to study their root causes and vow never again to let them fester.

Ulsterman David Feherty, who knew Rosie and Gerry McIlroy before their son was born, said years ago about his homeland's tumult: "Hatred, you're not born with. It's a learned behavior. It's ingrained to the extent that it's really only education that can get us past it."

Amen.

Rory Land would do well to contribute to that education, inside and outside Northern Ireland. Strengthening mental health services, especially for young people, has long been one of Rory's heartfelt priorities.

Forgive my presumption, Rory Land, but you should work with groups expressly devoted to helping people cope with Troubles-related PTSD. Instead of recoiling from The Troubles, Rory should embrace the effort to enlighten people about Ulster's sad legacy—and, as McIlroy started to do in Charlotte, draw parallels that go beyond professional golf.

Rory himself may suffer from a condition that shares certain symptoms with PTSD. When a golfer suffers a tough loss in a big tournament, argues Dr. Valiante, the pain causes their adrenal glands to work overtime, which sends shockwaves toward their heart and hotwires their psyche.

Once that scar tissue has taken root, it's tough for the brain to set it aside, Dr. Valiante pointed out to me in the wake of Rory's late-Sunday struggles at Pinehurst. Would McIlroy have been better off hitting that putt on the 70th green right away instead of marking it, backing away, and letting the pressure build within his nervous system?

Maybe. We'll never know, will we?

No matter how many "regular" events Rory McIlroy wins, it will never be enough to mute his critics. As of fall 2024, the thirty-five-year-old McIlroy had won forty-two times worldwide, twenty-six of them on the US Tour. In this day and age, where fields are so strong and deep no matter where tournaments are played, it's an extraordinary record.

And still…it's not enough. The only victories that matter to certain golf grandees are major championships. In their view, McIlroy's career wins in majors—stuck at four for a decade now—betray a character flaw.

McIlroy is the victim of his own preternatural success. By winning multiple majors so quickly—and doing it with such style and panache—he created expectations that became exceedingly difficult for him to fulfill.

New York Post columnist Mark Cannizzaro is just one of many insiders who told me they were convinced after McIlroy's come-from-behind victory at Valhalla in the 2014 PGA Championship that Rory was destined to get to double-digit wins in the majors, maybe even threaten Big Jack's eighteen.

But it didn't happen. Why?

If you ask experts that question, invariably they'll chuckle, shrug their shoulders, and offer up some variation of: "Because golf is hard."

There's a reason that players as accomplished as Sergio Garcia, Fred Couples, Davis Love III, David Duval, Justin Leonard, Tom Kite, and the late Tom Weiskopf won only one major. There's a reason that players as talented as Rickie Fowler haven't won *any*. Most mortals lack the drive, the swagger, and the obsessive powers of concentration required to win multiple majors.

In 2014, when McIlroy went on that phenomenal run that included winning big ones at Hoylake and Valhalla, Paul McGinley was among the many awed by the fierceness that Rory projected that July and August.

McIlroy rarely radiates that glow anymore. As Irish golf savants Seamus McEnery and Ivan Morris told me as I started this project, Rory doesn't intimidate opponents the way Jack, or Ben, or Tiger did in their primes.

Jaime Diaz is correct: the quality that makes Rory an engaging human being (see *Favorite, Every Mom's*) may be his undoing. It *is* hard to be normal and great.

Chat with a psychologist, and they'll tell you that we—his fans—can't have it both ways. We can't salute Rory for being gregarious, kind-hearted, and wonderful with kids—someone with a good heart and a good soul—then in the next breath slam him for not being hard-assed enough.

Tiger's mother used to tell her son that, inside the ropes, it was okay to hate his opponents. His career-military dad raised Tiger to take no prisoners, to get his rivals down and stomp them.

Rosie and Gerry may have been blue-collar tough, but it would never have crossed their minds to implant such belligerence in their only child. Quite the contrary: talk to any of Rory's amateur opponents and they'll tell you how fun and welcoming Gerry and Rosie were in the old days. Hell, today even *Tiger* talks about how much he loves being around Rory's parents!

Remember what Rory did immediately after coming from behind to beat Scottie Scheffler at the 2022 Tour Championship? He made a beeline to Scottie's parents sitting next to the 18th green, hugged them, and told them how much he admired their son. Scottie's dad returned the favor, telling Rory how much the Scheffler family admired *him*.

In the fall of 1960, when the great Ted Williams refused to come out of the Red Sox dugout to acknowledge the cheers after hitting a home run in his last-ever at-bat at Fenway Park, writer John Updike was sitting in the stands. He scribbled on his scorecard a phrase that later appeared in his celebrated *New Yorker* essay bidding adieu to The Kid: "Gods don't answer their letters."

What we love—well, what *I* love—about Rory McIlroy is that he answers his letters…and then some. Next time you're at a tournament, watch one of his RMPIMs with kids. It'll make your heart skip a beat. He's also marvelous, as McEnery points out, at adhering to actor Jack Lemmon's maxim: he "sends the elevator back down" to lift promising young people. When Rory ended the 2024 season by winning the DP World Tour's final tourney at Jumeirah—and with it, his sixth Race to Dubai crown—he gave his protégé Tom McKibbin, Holywood's own, a big hug. Tom, a beneficiary of the McIlroy-endowed practice facilities at HGC, had just earned his first-ever PGA Tour card. Rory was thrilled for the kid.

Will McIlroy win another major, perhaps a couple more? Maybe, but only if he aces the Trevino Test ("No soft bogeys!") and the Nicklaus Test ("Concentrate harder and play the percentages!"). It also wouldn't hurt to improve his lag putting in the clutch, aka the Tiger Test.

But above all, he's got to ace the (Seamus) Heaney Test. He needs to believe in his heart of hearts that a further shore really is reachable from here.

Well, how about winning the Masters and joining that elite group of immortals who have won all four legs of the career Grand Slam? That's a tougher task. There's a reason Augusta has been McIlroy's Great White Whale. He struggles on those wicked-fast greens and, year-to-year, tends to repeat the same dubious shots.

Let's see a quick show of hands. *Who else is tired of Rory pulling his approach into the pond next to the 11th green at Augusta?*

Unanimous, eh? That's what I thought.

During the '23 holidays, Rory and Shane Lowry sat down with Paul Kimmage of the *Irish Independent*. In mid-interview, Shane suddenly challenged the other guys to name the colors of all thirty-two of Ireland's county-based Gaelic football squads. Shane and Paul immediately went into a rapid-fire exchange, racing through team colors like schoolkids at recess.

But Rory couldn't compete. He sheepishly admitted that he could only name County Down's red-and-black and a couple of others. All things being equal, it wouldn't be a bad idea for the sports nut who grew up nationless to take to heart more of Ireland's county colors. Or to embrace the three Irish colors that matter the most: green, white, and orange.

Rory would also do well to prick the bubble that envelops and—in my view—hobbles Rory Land. The don't-challenge-the-boss mentality that persists on the course also permeates Rory Land decision-making, especially on the communications front. Rory needs to shake things up—and abide by the counsel of the professionals he hires.

Sure, the Mac Pack has provided great companionship, helping to make him (and themselves, not incidentally) a bunch of money. But Rory has also gone zero for his last forty majors and messed up (again!) down the stretch at the '24 Olympics. Something isn't clicking at big moments. It's past time for him to try something different.

His 2024 "change"—a one-day trip to Vegas and über-instructor Butch Harmon for a lesson in wedge play—appeared to pay dividends at Quail Hollow and Pinehurst. Then, weirdly, in the high winds at Troon, he seemed to forget Butch's flight-them-down instructions and started ballooning his short-irons. Another mishit wedge on the 69th hole at Le Club Nationale cost him an Olympic medal.

Rory has taken on an awful lot over the past few years. I worry that it's overwhelmed his nervous system—and I'm not alone. I've heard that concern expressed by scores of correspondents, Tour followers, and fans. He's still overexposed and overextended; as long as he stays that way, we'll continue to overanalyze him. He's that human and that likeable.

Since age nine, he's been the Great Hope of a divided and still-troubled land. That's too much pressure for anyone to bear, especially someone, like McIlroy, trying to lead, in his own imperfect way, a Ted Lasso Life.

To start winning majors again, Rory McIlroy doesn't need to study self-help manuals or agonize over his "hidden potential" or contemplate the insights of some ancient Roman potentate. He just needs to remember the first two lines of that fabulous song from *Welcome to Wrexham*: not to forget where he comes from or what he's made of.

Rory is the child and grandchild of people who survived societal anarchy. They, in turn, are descended from people who survived famines and economic ruin and the heartbreak of loved ones fleeing their homeland.

McIlroy needs to remember that his grit has grit. Instead of jumping from one motivational tract to the next, believing that this mantra or that adage will somehow turn around his big-moment fortunes, he ought to keep pictures of his grandparents—Eva and Jimmy, Bridie and Danny—in his wallet.

Marcus Aurelius has nothing on Jimmy McIlroy. Commanding Roman legionnaires in battle? Is that any tougher than inhaling toxic fumes and being hoisted way up, day after day, year after year, to paint massive cranes so you can give your kids, and their kids, yet unborn, a better life?

The final whistle just sounded. Shite, but these past couple of years have been an up-and-down experience for Rory and Rory Land—a "real epic," as the Gaelic football-crazed Irish are wont to say. And he's still a pup! What other epic stuff awaits?

So, what's our ultimate takeaway? Maybe that Rory Daniel McIlroy needs to rediscover himself: his roots, his family, the things in his life, as he put it after Grayson Murray's tragic death, that truly matter. Jimmy's grandkid ought to think about spending more time in Holywood and less time hanging out with Hollywood A-listers and their ilk. More Guinness at Ned's; less Opus One at fancy restaurants.

It would also help Rory's mojo if he could putt like he did as a twelve-year-old playing for Sullivan Upper in the Ulster Schools Cup against those rich kids five years his senior from the Royal Belfast Academical Institution.

Not to worry: Rory won't forget to sing when he wins a major. His old pal Shane Lowry will be close by as McIlroy lifts the big trophy. Let's hope the tune they choose is a bit more stirring than "Don't Stop Believin'!"

Sources

PRIMARY

McIlroy/McDonald/Holywood/ North County Down History

Jennifer Martin, PhD, Principal, Artema Research and Writing Services, Ulster University-trained genealogist, Belfast, Northern Ireland

Collections Team at the Linen Hall Library, Belfast, Northern Ireland

Reference Desk, Holywood Library, Holywood, Northern Ireland

Robin Masefield, head of Holywood History Group, County Down, Northern Ireland

Karen and Trevor Murray, Holywood Golf Club members, Holywood, Northern Ireland

Chris O'Neill, Principal, St. Patrick's Primary School, Holywood, Northern Ireland

Academics/Experts on The Troubles/ Irish Economic and Labour History

Former US Senator George J. Mitchell, Special Envoy/Mediator, Northern Ireland Peace Talks (1996-1998)

Professor Richard English, Director, Senator George J. Mitchell Institute for Global Peace, Security and Justice, Queens University Belfast

Francis Higgins, author, Troubles historian, and tour guide, Titanic Quarter/Belfast shipyards

Michael Maguire, Honorary Professor, Senator George J. Mitchell Institute for Global Peace, Security and Justice, Queens University Belfast, and former Ombudsman, Police Service of Northern Ireland

Professor Emmet O'Connor, author and Irish Labour History Specialist, Ulster University Derry-Londonderry

Professor Robert Savage, author and Irish Studies Specialist, Boston College

Chris Thornton, producer, BBC-Northern Ireland; co-author, *Lost Lives*; and former Belfast newspaper reporter

Irish/UK Golf Journalists and Commentators

Tony Dear, free-lance correspondent, Bellingham, Washington, and former reporter, the *Guardian* and other outlets

Dermot Gilleece, retired golf columnist, *Irish Sunday Independent*, and former golf correspondent/columnist, *Irish Times*

Gareth Hanna, sports correspondent, *Belfast Telegraph*

John Hopkins, correspondent/columnist, *Global Golf Post*, and former *Times of London* correspondent/columnist

Anna Jackson, anchor and correspondent, Golf Channel

Brian Keogh, manager, *Independent News and Media*; coordinator, Irish Golf Desk archives; and former columnist/correspondent for the *Irish Sun*

Adam McKendry, sports correspondent, *Belfast Telegraph*

Irish Golf, Literary, and Culture Mavens

Stephen Crowe, former Rory competitor in amateur golf, and construction executive, Belfast, Northern Ireland

Peter Hanna, former golf professional, Lurgan Golf Club, Lurgan, County Armagh, Northern Ireland

Seamus McEnery, County Clare, Republic of Ireland, devotee of Irish golf and Lahinch Golf Club

Ivan Morris, County Limerick, Republic of Ireland, devotee of Irish golf and Lahinch Golf Club, and noted equestrian

Conor Ruane, County Dublin, Republic of Ireland, barrister and devotee of Irish golf

The wait staff at the Dirty Duck Alehouse, Holywood, Northern Ireland

The wait staff at The Maypole Bar, aka "Ned's," Holywood, Northern Ireland

Golf Legends

Mike Davis, former CEO, United States Golf Association, golf course design consultant

Eddie McCormack, Irish amateur champion, dairy farmer and agribusiness executive

Paul McGinley, former European Ryder Cup captain, Sky Sports/Golf Channel commentator

Jim McLean, famed golf instructor, *Golf Digest* contributor

Andy North, ESPN analyst and two-time US Open champion

Neil Oxman, Tom Watson's former caddie, and political strategist

Pat Ruddy, founder and designer, European Club, Ardanairy, Brittas Bay, County Wicklow, Republic of Ireland

Tom Watson, eight-time major champion and golf course designer

US Golf Journalists and Commentators

Ryan Ballangee, founder, *Golf News Net*, former correspondent for several outlets

Michael Bamberger, member, *Fire Pit Collective*; former *Sports Illustrated* and *GOLF Magazine* correspondent; and book author

Mark Cannizzaro, correspondent/columnist, *New York Post*

Michael Collins, correspondent, ESPN, and former PGA Tour caddie

Karen Crouse, freelance writer, book author, and former correspondent, *New York Times*

Tom Coyne, golf author and raconteur

Jaime Diaz, commentator, Golf Channel; correspondent, *Golf Digest*; and book author

Bill Fields, founder, *The Albatross*; former correspondent for several outlets; and book author

Ron Green Jr., correspondent, *Global Golf Post*

Damon Hack, anchor, Golf Channel, and former correspondent, *New York Times* and *Sports Illustrated*

Rex Hoggard, correspondent, Golf Channel

Scott Michaux, correspondent, *Global Golf Post*

Ian O'Connor, columnist/correspondent, *New York Post*; former ESPN correspondent; and book author

Jason Sobel, ESPN correspondent; reporter, The Action Network

Geoff Shackelford, golf design consultant and founder, *The Quadrilateral*

Clinical/Performance Psychologists

Patricia Peters Martin, PhD, Longmeadow, Massachusetts

Gio Valiante, PhD, Rollins College, Winter Park, Florida

Golf Historians and Gurus

Brad Klein, golf historian and author, Donald Ross scholar, former architecture editor, *Golfweek*

Mark Frost, novelist, screenwriter/producer, and author, *The Match*

Lorne Rubenstein, author, Tiger Woods book collaborator; creator, *Score Golf*

McIlroy Business Partners

Alan Hermeling, Senior Vice President of Sponsorships and Growth, UnitedHealth Group (Optum)

Michael Pascucci, financier and developer, Apogee Golf Club, and his grandchildren, Sophie and Cole Barnard

SECONDARY

Books

Aurelius, Marcus, *Meditations*, Dover Publications, New York, 1997

Boswell, Thomas, *Strokes of Genius*, Penguin Group, New York, 1987

Bowers, Tom, *Revenge: Meghan, Harry, and the War Between the Windsors*, Atria, London, 2024

Cahill, Thomas, *How the Irish Saved Civilization*, Doubleday, New York, 1995

Cain, Susan, *Quiet: The Power of Introverts in a World That Can't Stop Talking*, Crown, New York, 2012

Coffey, Thomas M., *Agony at Easter: The 1916 Irish Uprising*, the MacMillan Company, New York, 1969

Connery, Donald S., *The Irish*, Simon & Schuster, New York, 1970

Coogan, Timothy Patrick, *Ireland Since the Rising*, Frederick A. Praeger, London, 1966

Coogan, Timothy Patrick, *The Troubles: Ireland's Ordeal and the Search for Peace*, St. Martin's Griffin, London, 2002

Costercalde, Claude, *Sullivan Upper School*, Booklink, Holywood, County Down, Northern Ireland, 2009

Coyne, Tom, *A Course Called Ireland*, Penguin Group, New York, 2009

Coyne, Tom, *A Course Called Scotland*, Simon & Schuster Paperbacks, New York, 2018

Darwin, Bernard, *The Golf Courses of the British Isles*, Storey Communications, Hong Kong, 1988

Doyle, Justin, *Rory's Glory*, G2 Rights Ltd., Kent, UK, 2014

Doyle, Justin, *Rory: His Story So Far*, G2 Rights Ltd, Kent, UK, 2012

Dyer, Geoff, *The Last Days of Roger Federer and Other Endings*, Fabar, Straus and Giroux, New York, 2022

Feinstein, John, *Feherty: The Remarkably Funny and Tragic Journey of Golf's David Feherty*, Hachette Book Group, New York, 2023

Feinstein, John, *The Majors: In Pursuit of Golf's Holy Grail*, Little Brown and Company, New York, 1999

Finegan, James W., *Emerald Fairways & Foam-Flecked Seas: A Golfer's Pilgrimage to the Courses of Ireland*, Simon & Schuster, New York, 1996

Finegan, James W., *Blasted Heaths & Blessed Greens: A Golfer's Pilgrimage to the Courses of Scotland*, Simon & Schuster, New York, 1996

Frost, Mark, *The Greatest Game Ever Played*, Hyperion Books, New York, 2002

Grant, Adam, *Hidden Potential*, Penguin Random House, New York, 2023

Heaney, Seamus, *The Cure at Troy*, Farrar, Straus, and Giroux, New York, 1991

Higgins, Francis J., *Tall Tales & Short Stories: The Men of the Belfast Shipyard*, Brown's Square Publications, Belfast, 2022

Holiday, Ryan, *The Obstacle is The Way*, Portfolio, New York, 2014

Johnston, Kevin, *In the Shadow of Giants: A Social History of the Belfast Shipyards*, Gill & MacMillen, LTD, London, 2008

Joyce, James, *A Portrait of the Artist as a Young Man*, B. W. Huebsch, New York, 1916

Keefe, Patrick Radden, *Say Nothing: A True Story of Murder and Memory in Northern Ireland*, Anchor Books, New York, 2012

Logothetis, Paul, *Rory McIlroy: Golf Champion*, SportZone, Minneapolis, 2013

Mandino, Og, *The Greatest Salesman in the World*, Bantam Books, 1968

Murphy, Michael J., *Golf in the Kingdom*, Penguin Books, New York, 1971

O'Connor, Emmet, *A Labour History of Ireland, 1824-2000*, University College Dublin Press, Dublin, 2011

Ruddy, Pat, *Fifty Years in a Bunker*, Ruddy Golf Library, County Wicklow, Ireland, 2007

Ruddy, Pat, *Holes in My Head*, Ruddy Golf Library, County Wicklow, Ireland, 2019

Shipnuck, Alan, *LIV and Let Die: The Inside Story of the War Between the PGA Tour and LIV Golf*, Avid Reader Press, New York, 2023

Thornton, Chris, et al., *Lost Lives: The Stories of the Men, Women and Children who Died as a Result of the Northern Ireland Troubles*, Mainstream Publishing, Edinburgh, 1999 (at Linen Hall Library, Belfast, Northern Ireland)

Tuohy, Frank, *Yeats: An Illustrated Biography*, New Amsterdam, New York, 1976

Wind, Herbert Warren, *Following Through*, Ticknor & Fields, New York, 1985

Wind, Herbert Warren, *America's Gift to Golf: Herbert Warren Wind on the Masters* (edited by Martin Davis), The American Golfer, 2011

Worrall, Frank, *Rory McIlroy: The Biography*, John Blake Publishing Ltd., London, 2013

Irish/UK Newspapers

Belfast Telegraph
Irish Central (online site)
Irish Independent
Irish Examiner
Irish News
Irish Sun
Irish Times
Irish Golf Desk Archives (maintained by Brian Keogh)
Daily Mail
Daily Telegraph
The Guardian
The (London) *Mirror*
Times of London

US Newspapers/Sites

The Athletic
Augusta Chronicle
Deseret News
Florida Times-Union
New York Daily News

New York Post
New York Times
Salt Lake City Tribune
Washington Post
Wall Street Journal
USA Today
Yahoo! News

Periodicals/Newsletters

The Albatross, written by Bill Fields
GOLF Magazine
Golf Digest
Golfweek
Golf Monthly
Global Golf Post
Irish Golfer Magazine
Money
The National
Psychology Today
Score Golf, Lorne Rubenstein, contributor
Sports Illustrated
The Quadrilateral, written by Geoff Shackelford

Key Newspaper/Periodical Pieces

Bamberger, Michael, "The Player of the Year, Rory McIlroy," *GOLF Magazine*, December 2014

Bamberger, Michael, "Hair Apparent," *Sports Illustrated*, April 7, 2009

Bell, Stephanie, "*The Modest, Shy (and Very Proud) Mum*," *Belfast Telegraph*, July 21, 2014

Cannizzaro, Mark, "McIlroy Charted Course from His Club in Northern Ireland to Atop the Golf World," *New York Post*, July 11, 2011

Clarke, John, "For Rory McIlroy, It All Started at Royal Portrush," *New York Times*, July 16, 2019

Cobain, Ian, "Life During Wartime, How West Belfast Became the Frontline of The Troubles," *The Guardian*, November 3, 2020

Corrigan, James, "Ex- Holly Provides McIlroy Shoulder to Cry On," *Daily Telegraph*, April 11, 2011

Crouse, Karen, "The Branding of Rory McIlroy," *New York Times*, May 4, 2013

Crouse, Karen, "McIlroy and Wozniacki Striving with Some Success, for Ordinary," *New York Times*, March 23, 2013

Culpepper, Chuck, "McIlroy's Lengthy Dry Spell Leaves His Hometown Hoping," *Washington Post*, July 18, 2024

Diaz, Jaime, "A Little Advice for a Young Golfer, Hush!" *Golf World*, March 14, 2011

Diaz, Jaime, "Rory Gets the Arnie," *Golf Digest*, February 2024

Kimmage, Paul, "Ryder Cup Rock Bottom, Open Heartbreak," (two-part series) *Irish Independent*, November 27, 2022

McGuire, Bernie, "Rory McIlroy's Holy Grail," *Irish Golfer Magazine*, 2011

Moriarty, Jim, "Nothing This Kid Does Surprises Me," *Golf World*, June 27, 2011

McGrory, Brian, *Boston Globe*, "An Officer and a Gentleman (and a Police Dog)," as reported in *Golf Digest*, September 2011

Miller, Brody, "Rory McIlroy's Next Step? It Might Be Just Being Like Everyone Else," *The Athletic*, June 14, 2023

O'Connor, Ian, "Rory McIlroy, Two Irelands, and a Complicated Open Homecoming," ESPN.com, July 15, 2019

O'Dowd, Eamon, "Rory McIlroy's Tragic Relative," *Irish Central*, August 14, 2014

Priest, Evin and Smith Aaron, "The Art of Being Rory McIlroy," *Golf Digest*, September 2020

Rubenstein, Lorne, "McIlroy in Full Flight is Golf's Biggest Delight," *Score Golf*, August 31, 2022

Samuel, Martin, "Rory McIlroy's Outspoken and Principled Stance," *Daily Mail*, July 7, 2022

Samson, Curt, "Life in the Big Pool," *Golf World*, April 8, 2013

Seibert, Charles, "Rory McIlroy Has the Best Swing in Golf," *New York Times Magazine*, March 31, 2015

Sens, Josh, "Planet Holywood," *GOLF Magazine*, December 2011

Sirak, Ron, "Unassuming and UnTigerlike," *Golf World*, June 27, 2011

Shipnuck, Alan, "Inside Rory's Big Deal," *Sports Illustrated*, February 4, 2013

Slater, Georgia, "Golfer Rory McIlroy Says He Hasn't Played with President Trump Out of Choice," People.com, May 15, 2020

Stanage, Niall, "Northern Ireland's McIlroy Transcends Boundaries," *New York Times*, July 10, 2011

Thomas, Dave, "How Not to Do a Rory McIlroy," (London) *Sunday Telegraph*, May 25, 2014

Tuttle, Brad, "Could 25-Year-Old Rory McIlroy Be Golf's Long-Awaited Savior?" *Money*, July 23, 2014

Updike, John, "Hub Fans Bid Kid Adieu," *New Yorker*, October 22, 1960

Podcasts

GOLF's Subpar, hosted by Colt Knost and Drew Stoltz
Sir Nick's Roundtable, hosted by Nick Faldo
Trapdraw/No Laying Up, hosted by TC and Randy

Acknowledgments

In January 2023, when I started this project, I had no idea that men's professional golf would end up being consumed by an ugly civil war—and that my subject, Northern Irish superstar Rory McIlroy, would be caught in its crossfire. Nor did I know that Rory's personal life would become almost as tumultuous as his professional one.

To put it mildly, 2023–2024 proved to be an up-and-down experience for McIlroy and what I came to call Rory Land: hence the book's title. McIlroy took his (completely) unauthorized biographer for a roller coaster ride as crazy as anything at Portrush's amusement park. For that, I say "Thanks, Rors."

At the top of my thank-you list is Lorne Rubenstein, the dean of Canadian golf correspondents and a member of his country's Golf Hall of Fame. Lorne, a fabulous writer, is a fellow Herbert Warren Wind buff and an admirer of Rory's swing and golfing panache.

Lorne put me in touch with his friend Ivan Morris, an Irish raconteur and golf nut, who in turn introduced me to *his* friend, Seamus McEnery, *another* Irish raconteur and golf nut, who in turn introduced me to *his* friend Conor Ruane, *another*...well, you know the rest. Seamus and Ivan are in their seventies and routinely shoot their age or better, sometimes at sainted Lahinch! Conor is a fine player, too. Now I know what it's like to be around Irish wit and whimsy all the time. It's a lot of fun.

So was dealing with Dr. Jennifer Martin, the genealogist with three degrees from Ulster University who did incredible work in unearthing the McIlroy and McDonald family heritages. If you've got an Irish ancestry that you want to unlock, track down Jenny at Artesma Research and Writing. She's brilliant.

"Brilliant" also describes the work Irish golf correspondent Brian Keogh has done over the years in maintaining the archives of the Irish Golf Desk. Need dope on the '16 Irish Open or the '05 Irish Close or just about anything else in the world of golf? Check out Brian's archives: it's user-friendly and all-free. When you get there, you'll have the added bonus of reading Brian's stuff, which is always sharp and often funny and poignant.

Speaking of poignant, the Hanna men—golf club professional Peter and his son, Gareth, a reporter with the *Belfast Telegraph*—gave me their two-generation perspective on their (and Rosie McDonald McIlroy's) troubled but resilient hometown, Lurgan. It was much appreciated. So was my lunch in Holywood with Adam McKendry of the *Belfast Telegraph*, who walked me through the folkways of "The Twelfth." The ever-patient folks on the Collections Team at Linen Hall Library in Belfast were also terrific to work with.

Big thanks, too, to John Hopkins, the esteemed British journalist. John covered scores of events in the old days with the likes of Herb Wind, Bob Drum, Dan Jenkins, and the great Irish journalist Dermot Gilleece, who also generously gave me his time and insights. Oh, to have been a fly on the wall in those old press tents and pubs!

To the wait staff and regulars at Ned's and the Dirty Duck Alehouse in Holywood, thanks for a great week and hope to see you again. Ditto St. Patrick's Primary principal Chris O'Neill, who tipped me off about the Guinness at Ned's. And great thanks to Stephen Crowe, my Hoylake interview subject who, by chance, turned out to be Rory's playing partner during his record-setting round at Portrush in '05.

I learned much over beer with American journalist Adam Schupak in three countries and two continents. I also enjoyed getting to know Bill Fields, *Albatross* creator and NBC Golf "spotter" extraordinaire, who invited me to join the NBC/Golf Channel crew at a restaurant in Liverpool the night before the '23 Open Championship. Everyone around the bar got to predict a winner. Bill picked Collin Morikawa. I picked Shane Lowry. They both missed the cut. Did anyone pick the eventual winner, Brian Harman? Of course not.

Also great thanks to Jaime Diaz, Damon Hack, Anna Jackson, Rex Hoggard, and the other Golf Channel principals who were extremely kind to this novice golf writer. American journalist Ian O'Connor's 2019 piece about the McIlroy family's tragic involvement with The Troubles helped stir my interest in the topic. Ian's article cited the James Joyce quote that I use in the book. In a different piece, Ian called Rory a "lost boy" at the Masters. I added capitalization, the adjective "Perpetual," and a reference to Pinehurst No. 2. Huge thanks to Ian.

In the Primary Sources section, I created a grab-bag category called "Golf Legends." It was an honor to tap the expertise of Tom Watson and Andy North, who could not have been more engaging. Tom, the son of a B-24 navigator based in New Guinea, even expressed interest in reading my books on WWII, which was almost as cool as watching the fifty-nine-year-old Watson come within a hairsbreadth of winning the Open Championship at Turnberry back in '09.

Neil Oxman was caddying for Tom that amazing Sunday along the Irish Sea. He's convinced that if Watson's approach to the 72nd green had hit a foot or two shorter it would have held the green and Tom would have won. Damn. Neil was a hugely helpful resource. So was Mike Davis, former USGA CEO, as well as the Pascucci/Barnard families of Eastern Long Island and South Florida.

So, too, were golf journalists Ryan Ballangee, Mark Cannizzaro, Bob Harig, Michael Collins, Jason Sobel, and Scott Michaux, among many others.

Huge thanks, also, to the ever-patient and kind Gretchen Young and Madeline Sturgeon at Regalo Press.

And finally, I owe the biggest debt to Elizabeth and our growing family: Ally, Connor, Trevor, Shane, Andrew, Katie, and Abby. They let T-Pops go to Ireland and the UK for two weeks, solo.